MARRIAGE

BIBLICAL GUIDANCE FOR YOUR
CRUCIAL CONVERSATIONS

MARRIAGE

ITS FOUNDATION,
THEOLOGY, AND
MISSION IN A
CHANGING WORLD

EDITORS

CURT HAMNER, JOHN TRENT,
REBEKAH J. BYRD, ERIC L. JOHNSON,
AND ERIK THOENNES

MOODY PUBLISHERS
CHICAGO

Scripture quotations marked ESV are from the ESV® Bible (The Holy Bible, English Standard Version®), copyright © 2001 by Crossway, a publishing ministry of Good News Publishers. Used by permission. All rights reserved.

Scripture quotations marked (NIV) are taken from the Holy Bible, New International Version®, NIV®. Copyright © 1973, 1978, 1984, 2011 by Biblica, Inc.™ Used by permission of Zondervan. All rights reserved worldwide. www.zondervan.com. The "NIV" and "New International Version" are trademarks registered in the United States Patent and Trademark Office by Biblica, Inc.™

Scripture quotations marked NASB are taken from the New American Standard Bible® (NASB), Copyright © 1960, 1962, 1963, 1968, 1971, 1972, 1973,1975, 1977, 1995 by The Lockman Foundation. Used by permission. www.Lockman.org.

Scripture quotations marked (NLT) are taken from the Holy Bible, New Living Translation, copyright © 1996, 2004, 2015 by Tyndale House Foundation. Used by permission of Tyndale House Publishers, Inc., Carol Stream, Illinois 60188. All rights reserved.

Scripture quotations marked NET are taken from the NET Bible® copyright ©1996–2016 by Biblical Studies Press, L. L. C. All rights reserved.

Chapter 1, "The Trinity, the Incarnation, and the Meaning of Marriage and Sex" has been taken from *The Incarnation of God: The Mystery of the Gospel as the Foundation of Evangelical Theology* by John C. Clark and Marcus Peter Johnson, © 2015, pages 209ff. Used by permission of Crossway, a publishing ministry of Good News Publishers, Wheaton, IL 60187. www.crossway.org.

Edited by Pamela Joy Pugh
Cover and interior design: Erik M. Peterson
Cover illustration of birds copyright © 2018 by vectorkat/Shutterstock (32079766). All rights reserved.

Library of Congress Cataloging-in-Publication Data

Names: Hamner, Curt, editor.
Title: Marriage : its foundation, theology, and mission in a changing
   world / Curt Hamner, John Trent, Rebekah J. Byrd, Eric L. Johnson, and
   Erik Thoennes, editors.
Description: Chicago : Moody Publishers, 2018. | Includes bibliographical
   references and index.
Identifiers: LCCN 2018016844 (print) | LCCN 2018033316 (ebook) | ISBN
   9780802494825 () | ISBN 9780802413833
Subjects: LCSH: Marriage--Religious aspects--Christianity. |
   Marriage--Biblical teaching.
Classification: LCC BT706 (ebook) | LCC BT706 .M35 2018 (print) | DDC
   234/.165--dc23
LC record available at https://lccn.loc.gov/2018016844

All websites and phone numbers listed herein are accurate at the time of publication but may change in the future or cease to exist. The listing of website references and resources does not imply publisher endorsement of the site's entire contents.

We hope you enjoy this book from Moody Publishers. Our goal is to provide high-quality, thought-provoking books and products that connect truth to your real needs and challenges. For more information on other books and products written and produced from a biblical perspective, go to www.moodypublishers.com or write to:

Moody Publishers
820 N. LaSalle Boulevard
Chicago, IL 60610

1 3 5 7 9 10 8 6 4 2

Printed in the United States of America

With the hope of setting forth the glory of Christian marriage
as it was from the beginning,
the editors dedicate this book to the generations to come,
our children, and our children's children and their generations,
"for a time we cannot see."

CONTENTS

CONTRIBUTORS

EDITORS

Curt Hamner Cofounder (along with his wife, Rhonda) and President, Between Two Trees. BA, Biola University; MA, Dallas Theological Seminary

John Trent Gary D. Chapman Chair of Marriage and Family Ministry and Therapy, Moody Theological Seminary. President and Founder of the Center for Strong Families; BA, Texas Christian University; ThM, Dallas Theological Seminary; PhD, North Central Texas Federation of Colleges and Universities

Rebekah J. Byrd BA, Moody Bible Institute; Certificate in Spiritual Direction, North Park Seminary; MA, Wheaton Graduate School

Eric L. Johnson Senior Research Professor of Pastoral Care, Southern Baptist Theological Seminary. BTh, Toronto Baptist Seminary; MA, Calvin College; PhD/MA, Michigan State University

Erik Thoennes Professor and Chair of Theology, Talbot School of Theology/Biola University. Pastor, Grace Evangelical Free Church of La Mirada. BA, Central Connecticut State University; MA, MA, Wheaton College Graduate School; PhD, Trinity Evangelical Divinity School

---

Gregg R. Allison Professor of Christian Theology at Southern Baptist Theological Seminary. BS, Northern Illinois University; MDiv, Trinity Evangelical Divinity School; PhD, Trinity Evangelical Divinity School

Craig Blomberg Professor of New Testament at Denver Seminary. BA, Augustana College; MA, Trinity Evangelical Divinity School; PhD, University of Aberdeen

Darrell Bock Executive Director of Cultural Engagement and Senior Research Professor of New Testament Studies, Dallas Theological Seminary. BA, University of Texas; ThM, Dallas Theological Seminary; PhD, University of Aberdeen

Chris Brooks Senior Pastor, Evangel Ministries. Radio Host, *Equipped with Chris Brooks*. BA, Michigan State University; MA, Biola University

L. Eugene Burrus Counselor, Hope Counseling Center. BA, University of Mobile; MDiv, Southeastern Baptist Theological Seminary; PhD (candidate), Southern Baptist Theological Seminary

John C. Clark Associate Professor of Theology, Moody Bible Institute. BA, Spring Arbor University; ThM, Dallas Theological Seminary; PhD, University of Toronto

James F. Coakley Professor of Old Testament, Moody Bible Institute. BA, Calvary Bible College; MDiv/ThM, Grace Theological Seminary; DMin, Covenant Theological Seminary

Ron L. Deal President of Smart Stepfamilies and Director of FamilyLife Blended. BA/BS, Oklahoma Christian University; MMFT, Abilene Christian University

Darryl DelHousaye President of Phoenix Seminary. MDiv, Talbot Theological Seminary; DMin, Western Seminary

Deborah Gorton Program Director and Associate Professor, Moody Theological Seminary. BA, Arizona State University; MA, Fuller Theological Seminary; PhD, Fuller Theological Seminary

Chuck Hannaford Clinical psychologist. President and founder, HeartLife Professional Soul Care. BS/MS East Texas State University; PhD, University of North Texas

William A. Heth Professor of Biblical Studies, Taylor University. BA, University of Michigan; ThM, Dallas Theological Seminary; ThD, Dallas Theological Seminary

Timothy R. Jennings President, Come and Reason Ministries. BS, University of Tennessee; MD, University of Tennessee College of Medicine

Marcus Peter Johnson Associate Professor of Theology, Moody Bible Institute. BA, Moody Bible Institute; MA, Trinity Evangelical Divinity School; PhD, Trinity College, University of Toronto

Beth Felker Jones Professor of Theology, Wheaton Graduate School. BA, DePauw University; MTS, Duke Divinity School; PhD, Duke University

Jason E. Kanz Clinical Neuropsychologist, Marshfield Clinic. BA, Northwestern College; MS, Mankato State University; PhD, University of Iowa

Crawford W. Loritts Jr. Senior Pastor, Fellowship Bible Church. BS, Cairn University; Doctor of Divinity, Moody Theological Seminary

Mike Mason Author. BA, University of Manitoba; MA, University of Manitoba

Brett McCracken Senior Editor, The Gospel Coalition. BA, Wheaton College; MA, UCLA

Sean McDowell Assistant Professor, Biola University. BA, Biola University; MA, Talbot School of Theology; PhD, Southern Baptist Theological Seminary

John McGee Senior Director of Marriage Ministry and Resources, Watermark Community Church. BA, Oklahoma Baptist University; ThM, Dallas Theological Seminary

Jarred Pingleton Vice President of Professional Development, American Association of Christian Counselors. BS, Evangel University; MA, University of Missouri-Kansas City; MA/PsyD, Rosemead School of Psychology at Biola University

Jonathan T. Pennington Associate Professor of New Testament Interpretation, Southern Baptist Theological Seminary. BA, Northern Illinois University; MDiv, Trinity Evangelical Divinity School; PhD, University of St. Andrews

Andrew J. Schmutzer Professor of Bible, Moody Bible Institute. BA, Moody Bible Institute; ThM, Dallas Theological Seminary; PhD, Trinity Evangelical Divinity School

M. Ashley Schmutzer Owner, Hope Counseling Services. Adjunct Professor, Moody Bible Institute. BA, Criswell Bible College; MA, Wheaton Graduate School

Juli Slattery President and Cofounder, Authentic Intimacy. BA, Wheaton College; MA, Biola University; MS/PhD, Florida Institute of Technology

Greg Smalley Vice President of Marriage and Family Formation, Focus on the Family. BS, Grand Canyon University; MA Denver Seminary; MA/ PsyD, Biola University, Rosemead School of Psychology

James Spencer Vice President of Moody Center Online. BS, University of Illinois at Chicago; MDiv, Moody Theological Seminary; MA, Wheaton Graduate School; PhD, Trinity Evangelical Divinity School

Amy E. Spiegel Author. BA, Taylor University

James S. Spiegel Professor of Philosophy and Religion, Taylor University. BS, Belhaven College; MA, University of Southern Mississippi; PhD, Michigan State University

Donna Thoennes Adjunct Professor, Biola University. BS Central Connecticut State University; MA, Wheaton Graduate School; PhD Trinity Evangelical Divinity School

Tony Wheeler Vice President at the Center for Strong Families. Director and Professor of MA in Family Ministries, Barclay College. BA, Barclay College; MSFT, Friends University; PhD, Kansas State University

David Woodall Professor of New Testament and Greek, Moody Theological Seminary. BA, Cedarville College; MDiv, Grand Rapids Theological Seminary; ThD, Grand Rapids Theological Seminary; PhD, Trinity Evangelical Divinity School

Mark S. Young President of Denver Seminary. BA, Marshall University; ThM Dallas Theological Seminary; PhD, Trinity Evangelical Divinity School

Priscilla R. Young BA, Bryan College

SECTION 1

FOUNDATION

THE IMPORTANCE OF BEGINNING THE CONVERSATION

by Curt Hamner and John Trent

Every book has a story behind it. Ours started with a conversation between two close friends. As we, Curt and John and our wives, sat around a rough-hewn table in beautiful Forest Falls, California, our discussion revolved around what we had both seen in numerous churches, seminaries, and with Christian couples across our country and beyond . . . something deeply concerning.

Anywhere you look, culture and the courts have changed the role of marriage in society, even changing the very definition of what comprises a marriage. The church of the twenty-first century has tried to carefully navigate this changing landscape of contemporary marriage. But in doing so, it has often chosen to stand back—either confused on what to say or not wanting to sound divisive or demeaning of others, particularly in light of the incredible anger and venom launched at any who dare say anything positive about marriage in its traditional form.

Yet at the same time, this fear of being unkind or out of step with society has resulted in too many shepherds underfeeding their flock! Clear teaching and preaching on marriage from God's Word has often been set aside or neglected altogether. Uncertain of what to say and wary of controversy, pastors, teachers, and lay leaders have begun to say little or nothing about marriage's foundation, theology, beauty, and purpose. As a result, as one of our authors, Sean McDowell, will share later, it isn't that a high view of marriage, based on God's Word and the reality of His love, hasn't been "made but found wanting —the case simply hasn't been made."

Marriage was designed to be a bright, bold expression of God Himself—His love, commitment, and redemption. God's design for marriage with its beauty and reflection of His love cannot be changed or thwarted, no matter what any court or the court of public opinion has decreed. Marriage more than matters! It isn't going away, any more than God's church is going away. Marriage is and remains one of the most powerful pictures of God's love and the gospel.

Yet when we try to fully examine the institution of marriage, or even raise the idea of a theology of marriage today—that is, what we believe marriage is or should be—many Christian couples and even scholars, clergy, and counselors will respond, "We don't actually have a theology of marriage."

The truth is, we all do have a theology of marriage. But too often it is formed by our experience, the latest trend, a 5-4 high court verdict, or an editorial page. There exists then, in the church and among Christian families today, a great need for marriage, as it's given to us in God's Word, to be unleashed. *From the beginning, marriage, in its beauty and reality was never meant to hold a defensive position!* We need not defend marriage, but learn again to elevate marriage to its original glory and beauty.

What we both felt that afternoon in California was the desperate need for a foundational work on marriage that wasn't just an encyclopedia that catalogues theological ideas and stays on a shelf. Rather, this project should be a tool that could spark and actually launch deep, important conversations between theologians and practitioners. We want to encourage pastors and counselors to engage in the discussion of our day and help lay couples and small group leaders who are serious about marriage know what topics and Scriptures to share and focus on. Above all, this work should lift up God's intention and design.

A TOOL TO RAISE UP MARRIAGE

People may point to divorce rates, outside-of-wedlock births, or increasing cohabitation statistics as ironclad reasons why marriage is outdated or irrelevant. Yet think about what happened on May 19, 2018. Many millions of people around the globe tuned in to watch the royal wedding of Prince Harry and Meghan Markle. In St. George's Chapel, six hundred guests along with the multitude of viewers worldwide—many getting up in the middle of the night to watch the event live—heard from several ministers and readers how marriage is a gift of God, how God is its Creator and Sustainer. They heard of Jesus' role in bringing love into the center of a couple's home and world. And they listened to how, from the Song of Songs, the love God brings a husband and wife is a flame that "many waters cannot quench" and how "If a man were to give all he owned for love, it would be utterly despised." And even if that man is a prince, "all he owns" is quite substantial—yet still inadequate.

Say what you will, but what was spoken on a beautiful day in a breathtakingly beautiful setting during that service were strong words of God's role in creating and sustaining marriage. *And it was a picture that lifted up millions of people's view of marriage.*

Absolutely, what drew people to watch was celebrity, royalty, wealth, and position—and the desire to be that person in the carriage and castle. Yet people still long for the kind of love they saw in a husband who whispered to his bride (that we know thanks to professional lip readers hired for the event) "You look amazing" and "I am so lucky." And people with no spiritual understanding or interest still heard and wished for the high words spoken in a ceremony to be true in their own everyday lives and marriages. Even in the reality of our brokenness, where so many marriages fall short, there is a mystery and wonder to marriage that brings even royals to their knees.

What we spoke about that day in California was our committing to doing everything we could to help the church quit playing defense: to work to put marriage, in all its beauty, on display before a world that longs for genuine love and purpose. True, not every wedding event displays acres of flowers, fifty-foot long veils, and hundreds of thousands of well-wishers. But what should remain is the church's affirmation of God's place, purpose, and creative design for marriage.

For this to happen, we felt strongly that it would require people across many of the silos we have in the church to begin talking together—to break down the silos and, in our terminology, to begin and sustain a continuing conversation on marriage. With all the challenges and failures linked to marriage, we have God's amazing and uplifting picture of marriage we can discuss.

There is so much to share about biblical, life- and heart-changing marriage. The conversation begins with the book you hold, which falls into four sections. First, the foundation that undergirds marriage and illuminates the institution's depth and beauty: including reflections of God's nature, His commitment to us, language in Scripture, the choice to marry or not. Next, we move into key descriptive aspects of marriage: embodiment, unity and distinction, gender, sexuality. We then go to challenges: dealing with shame, marriages that fall short of the ideal, the difficult topics of divorce and remarriage. Finally, we discuss the mission of marriage, including its place in the body of Christ, its affirmation from natural law, the legacy to future generations. Marriage, even under attack, may be one of the greatest tools for evangelism available to the church today.

It's important for us to say upfront that much of what you'll find here, particularly in the core theology chapters, is not light reading . . . though engaging, challenging, important, discussable. But this work isn't meant to provide a sprint through a theology of marriage but rather, a deeper dive than many have ever taken before into just why marriage is so important and wonderful as God's creation.

Accompanying the chapters, you'll find one or more continuing insight that highlights or applies to that chapter's content, adding to the conversation based on God's Word and applied wisdom. These articles will serve to bolster the "talking together" of different disciplines that launches with this book.

As weighty and important as the topics and writers that are found here are, this is not meant to be the final word on marriage. Our goal is to put before the church the highest view of marriage we can, based squarely on God's Word. But it's also to launch the conversations we need to have on marriage's wonder, purpose, and mission that need to be discussed and promoted in our day. As is the case with any collaborative project—and certainly with one on such an important and broad topic—each of the editors brings a different perspective. While we all don't necessarily see eye-to-eye on everything, we each believe that the collaborative process is worth it, and that it has resulted in an important contribution to our understanding of marriage from a broad evangelical perspective.

There is so much to say and so many experts, both theologically and in ministry and counseling who would have contributed, who we simply did not have space to include to be a part of this book. Our commitment is to provide a place for the conversation to continue. Readers will be able to weigh in at www.continuingconversations.com, a place where each of these chapters and the key topics represented will keep the discussion going. Consider: it isn't hard to be relevant if being biblical doesn't matter and it's not hard to be biblical if being relevant doesn't matter. To be both biblical and relevant about marriage is the goal of this project. We invite you to the website to be part of the conversation because marriage more than matters!

As you read about the story and language of marriage, may you find inspiration to see more clearly God's love for His people and more ways to love others like Jesus, beginning with your own marriage and family, and spilling down to your own children, grandchildren, and over a world that indeed needs marriage.

THE TRINITY, THE INCARNATION, AND THE MEANING OF MARRIAGE AND SEX

by John C. Clark and Marcus Peter Johnson

They covered their nakedness. With eyes opened to their broken humanity, the terrible and tragic reality of their sin, the very first thing our primal parents did was cover their naked bodies. The dawn of sin had shed its first dark light on the sexuality of the perpetrators; from this awful new beginning, it exposed a deep rupture in what is so precious to God: male and female he created them. So the first grand cover-up began. In a feeble effort to cover up their sin and shame, to protect themselves not only from themselves but also from God, Adam and Eve attempted to fashion their own rescue—by hiding. Yet nothing sufficed. The fig leaves proved futile, as did the trees of the garden. They were acutely aware of their nakedness, but only God knew what it meant. So he sought them out in that condition, ripe as they were with the potential for sexual distortion and violence, initiating what only an incarnate God could at length complete. He exchanged their coverings with coverings of his own making and eventually exchanged their nakedness—with his own.

The second grand cover-up began many years later, east of Eden, and continues today. It too was preceded by a shame-soaked nakedness. But this time the nakedness belonged to God, hanging on a Roman gibbet, exposed to public ridicule, awash in blood, sweat, and spit. God was doing the unthinkable, plumbing the depths of our sin—all the way down. He took to himself our fallen nakedness, our sin-compromised sexuality, sanctifying and justifying our sexual perversion in his death and resurrection. He reconstituted our humanity, re-creating us as the image of God: male and female he *re-created* them.

But even though God became naked for us, we seem to prefer him covered up. As if to insist that our sexuality was not a prime casualty of the fall, and therefore not in need of salvation, we cover up our Savior. Too ashamed and too "modest" to allow God to suffer our sexual sin and shame, we clothe Jesus on the cross. In the first cover-up, God graciously clothed us; in the second, sadly, we return the favor. The irony ought to be revealing. Right at the point where we need God to both judge and redeem our unholy nakedness, we insist that he be clothed.

A crucified but clothed Jesus speaks volumes about the church's understanding of marriage and sex. If we have only a clothed Christ, how are we to understand and interpret our nakedness? If *the* Word of God did not subject himself to our nakedness and shame, can he still function as the subject of our words about God at this most crucial of points? When the church is theologically deaf and blind to the implications of God's self-giving in Christ regarding our sinful sexuality, our broken maleness and femaleness, the clothed Christ may be a powerful explanatory symbol. In clothing and therefore cloaking Christ, we are bound to turn elsewhere for what ought to be a specifically theological undertaking. So the church's attempts to speak to marriage and sex, and their multitudinous distortions, have too often been merely political, moral, ethical, social, or psychological—but rarely christological, Trinitarian, ecclesial, and sacramental. If the church fails to regard her deepest theological beliefs as pertaining to marriage and sex, then marriage and sex are bound to be understood in relatively trivial ways, and treated accordingly. Do we really believe that the deepest and most intimate human relations can be properly understood and addressed when detached from God's self-disclosure and self-bestowal? If not, then let us be forthright about it, for marriage and sex are fundamentally theological issues, and unless we wish to relegate our thinking about them to the relative obscurities of moral sentiments and political platitudes, we desperately need to know and say what they have to do with God himself.

We hear often enough about what God hates and thus opposes. From pulpit and paper, from book and blog, we hear variously that God hates divorce, adultery, premarital sex, homoeroticism, and many other sexual and relational sins. What we get far less often are theologically rich accounts as to *why* God hates and opposes distortions of marriage and sex. Do they break God's command, or even more to the point, do they break his image and break his heart? Apart from a christological and Trinitarian account of the beauty, wonder, and mystery of gender and sex, we fear that the church's teaching will be reduced to moral bromides—even if superficially adorned with biblical proof texts. Primarily, what we hope to offer in this chapter is a description of how marriage and sex are *internally and directly*, rather than externally and peripherally, related to the gospel of God's self-giving in Christ through the Spirit, why marriage and sex are thus so very precious and holy, and why that description necessitates a triune and incarnate God.

DIVINE INDWELLING: PERSONS IN INTIMATE UNION

Marriage and sex are not self-explanatory. They are beautiful and sacred mysteries that point beyond themselves to the mystery of our three-person God and to his redemptive self-giving in the incarnation. Theology is meant to found, form, and fund the church's deepest convictions and experiences, giving holy expression to the meaning of our lives, sanctifying our thought and speech against the inevitable depreciation and trivialization that occurs whenever we divorce the grandest human realities from their divine origin. Marriage and sex surely qualify as issues needing theological interpretation, not only because they exist at the center of our human experience, but also because they were given to us by God as echoes in the created world of who God is and how God loves us. Again, a failure to think theologically where we need it most—that is, at the point of our deepest, most intimate relations—is especially dangerous for the church. Such a failure forces the church to look elsewhere to explain what marriage and sex mean. Just as we cannot grasp the meaning of God's love for us apart from understanding that God is the very love by which he loves us, we cannot grasp the meaning of our deepest personal intimacies apart from the intimacy that God *is*. The meaning of these relations, basic and foundational to every human existence, can neither be grounded in nor exhausted by creaturely investigation. "Indeed," writes Michael Reeves, "in the triune God is the love behind all love, the life behind all life, the music behind all music, the beauty behind all beauty and the joy behind all joy."[1]

The love, life, harmony, beauty, and joy we were created to experience are echoes of a reality that transcends and interprets them. That reality is the love-creating, life-giving, harmonious, beautiful, and joyful personal communion shared by the Father, Son, and Spirit. The importance of the theological term *perichōrēsis* [referring to the triune relationship of the three members of the godhead] comes to the fore. [This term has] vast significance for the church's articulation of the inner life of God in faithfulness to the witness of Jesus Christ, who opens to us the mystery of God's eternal three-person existence. This term gives sacred expression to the interrelations among the persons of the holy Trinity, asserting no less than that God has eternally been, and will eternally be, a mutually indwelling and interpenetrating communion of persons who exist in self-giving, life-giving love. Indwelling and interpenetrating personal love is *who God is*. God the Father is who he is only in union with God the Son; God the Son is who he is only in union with his Father; and the Father and Son are who they are only in the communion of God the Spirit. The term *perichōrēsis* is important in relation to salvation, directing us to the fact that God does who he is, which is to say that in redeeming us, God the Spirit joins us to God the incarnate Son so that we may share in the life and love of God his Father. The eternal life we receive in salvation is the life shared by the Father with the Son in the Spirit. God loves us and gives us life through the love and life that he is. Without their grounding in the reality of God, life and love become mere abstractions that end up forfeiting their significance—literally, their purpose as *signs*.

The reality of the perichoretic communion that exists among the persons of the Trinity alerts us to a provocative insight that ought to give us pause: the personal and sexual intimacy that Adam and Eve experienced as they became one flesh was not the first indwelling or penetration to occur among persons. It was, of course, the first of all human sexual unions, but the first indwelling or penetration among persons belongs to the eternal union between Father, Son, and Spirit. God is who he is by virtue of the indwelling intimacy shared by the divine persons; apart from it, God would not be his triune self. This most sublime of all realities is reflected in our human existence, for we are who we are by virtue of the indwelling intimacy shared by human persons, apart from which we would not be ourselves.[2] The existence of every descendant of Adam and Eve depends upon a prior union of persons—necessarily male and female—who share indwelling intimacy. The fact that a human has being is predicated upon the existence of two others joined as one. Thus, any given human being requires two others in such a way that human existence is necessarily and fundamentally tripersonal.

Although it would be difficult to find a more obvious way in which our triune God images himself in us, we would be remiss not to mention another, perhaps less obvious, way: every human literally dwells inside another as he or she moves from that crucial point of conception to birth—another way in which humanity is defined by interpersonal indwelling.

These echoes of God's interpersonal life in our own existence might be written off as merely coincidental or forced analogies if not for the striking correspondence between our original birth and our new birth, the original creation and the new creation. In the redemption and re-creation of the world, God the Son was sent by his Father in the power of the Spirit to be birthed into our humanity. He was made one flesh with us that we might be made one flesh with him by the Spirit, and so experience new birth and eternal life in his. Our original existence and our new existence are both constituted by interpersonal indwelling. When God deigned to image himself in our humanity, both in the original creation and in the new creation (Jesus Christ), he did so in a way that is essential to who he is. A truly Christian anthropology, in other words, must be founded on christological and Trinitarian grounds:

> What is needed today is a better understanding of the person not just as an individual but as someone who finds his or her true being in communion with God and with others, the counterpart of a trinitarian doctrine of God. . . . God is love and has his true being in communion, in the mutual indwelling of Father, Son, and Holy Spirit—*perichoresis*, the patristic word. This is the God who has created us male and female in his image to find our true humanity in perichoretic unity with him and one another, and who renews us in his image in Christ.[3]

MALE AND FEMALE HE CREATED THEM: THE IMAGO DEI

What we have thus far referred to as echoes or reflections of God's tripersonal unity in human existence have their scriptural origination in the first chapter of Genesis. Here we see that God spoke something about his human creatures that should leave us speechless. Among all that the Father created through and for his Son by the Spirit, God did something utterly unique with his human creatures—he created us in his image: "Then God said, 'Let us make man in our image, after our likeness.' . . . So God created man in his own image, in the image of God he created him; male and female he created them" (Gen. 1:26–27 ESV). The church and her theologians have wrestled with this text for two millennia, attempting to give interpretive expression to the fearful and wonderful blessing pronounced here by God. What exactly does it mean that humankind is the imago Dei? What is it about humans that constitutes us as God's likeness? The history of the church's interpretation on this point is far too vast to recount in the space of this chapter.[4] Suffice it to say that two strands of interpretation have been characteristic. One interprets humanity as the image of God with relation to our rational, moral, or volitional faculties—often called the substantive theory of the image. The other interprets the image in relation to the ensuing mandate for humanity to "rule over" or superintend the creation (Gen. 1:26, 28)—often called the functional theory.

Such theories are indeed helpful in attempting to delineate what marks humankind as distinctive among God's creatures, as part of an extended accounting for the ways in which we image God. However, they cannot account for something basic to a proper understanding of that image. Specifically, neither theory, as commonly or popularly understood, requires for its application that humankind be what God says we are: both male and female. A male does not require a female, nor does a female require a male, in order to moralize, exercise reason and will, or exercise dominion over the earth. Such things might be done reasonably well by a single human being. But a solitary male or female most certainly cannot image God in a way that is most basic to who he is: depicting his personal, relational, and life-giving intimacy.

Recall our text: "Then God said, 'Let us make man in our image, after our likeness.' . . . So God created man in his own image, in the image of God he created him; male and female he created them."[5]

The plurality in God's address has been a source of consternation among many modern Christian commentators, who, under the tutelage of the currently dominant mode of historical-grammatical interpretation, tend to hold the doctrine of the Trinity in hermeneutical abeyance in their exegesis of Genesis. The "us" and "our" of God's self-reference thus become problematic: Who is God talking to? This question necessarily arises for those who insist on delaying the theological, canonical, and Christian implications of the text in search of an interpretation that is strictly suitable to the original author and audience.[6]

We believe, however, that it is incumbent upon modern Christians to recognize the Trinitarian implications of this text, as the church has done for the vast majority of her two-thousand-year existence. "Indeed," writes Martin Luther, "it is the great consensus of the church that the mystery of the Trinity is set forth here."[7] Stopping short of a christological, and thus Trinitarian, interpretation of the creation account bypasses Christ's self-disclosure as the very Word of God by whom all things, including humans, were created (John

For every work or act of creation is threefold, an earthly trinity to match the heavenly.

First, not in time, but merely in order of enumeration there is the Creative idea, passionless, timeless, beholding the whole work complete at once, the end in the beginning: and this is the image of the Father. Second, there is the Creative Energy or Activity begotten of that idea, working in time from the beginning to the end, with sweat and passion, being incarnate in the bonds of matter: and this is the image of the Word. Third, there is the Creative Power, the meaning of the work and its response in the lively soul: and this is the image of the indwelling Spirit.

And these three are one, each equally in itself the whole work, whereof none can exist without other: and this is the image of the Trinity.[8]
—Dorothy Sayers

1:3; Col.1:15–17), the One in whom alone the imago Dei can be properly interpreted.

The Nicene-Constantinopolitan Creed (381), to which all orthodox Christians subscribe, has us confess belief in Jesus Christ as the One "by whom all things were made," and in the Holy Spirit as "the Lord and Giver of life," so that the church may joyfully affirm that God the Father created humankind through and for God the Son by God the Spirit. What is most basic to God's inner life is wonderfully and fearfully reflected in his human creatures, who, as male and female, and *specifically* as male and female, image the interpersonal intimacy inherent to God's inner being. Thus, the phrase "male and female he created them" functions to give specificity to the phrase "in the image of God he created [them]." Our existence as male and female is not something that God "tacks on" to the solitary human already in his image. On the contrary, our existence as male and female is *intrinsic* to that image.[9] This is not to say that being male and female *exhausts* what we may say about the imago Dei, but that the distinction-in-communion that characterizes humankind as male and female is absolutely basic to the *imago Dei*. As Colin Gunton writes, God "replicates" his communal being in our humanity:

If, first, to be created in the image of God is to be made male and female, what is implied is that in this most central of all human relatedness is to be found a finite echo of the relatedness of Father, Son, and Holy Spirit. To be God, according to the doctrine of the Trinity, is to be persons in relation: to be God only as a communion of being. It is that which is replicated, at the finite level, by the polarity of the male and female: to be in the image of God is to be called to a relatedness-in-otherness that echoes the eternal relatedness-in-otherness of Father, Son and Spirit.[10]

Male cannot properly echo or image God by himself, nor can female by herself. Adam, apart from Eve, could not fulfill what it means for man to be the *imago Dei*—alone, he would have been a distorted, "not good" image: "The LORD God said, 'It is not good that the man should be alone. I will make a helper fit for him'" (Gen. 2:18). That God pronounced negatively upon his creation at the point of Adam's solitude is telling: "It is the only negative assessment in the creation narrative," observes Henri Blocher, "and it is emphatically negative."[11] Something was not right, and it apparently could not be remedied with another male or a beast, either of which might have provided Adam superior strength in tending the garden.[12] Would it not be better to say that it was impossible for Adam to be the blessed imago Dei by himself, precisely because he could not be male and female—persons in communion?[13] That would certainly qualify as "not good," for it would mean that creation was bereft of God's image. "In isolation man would not have been good," writes Karl Barth. "That is, he would not have been created good . . . we might say that it would not be good because solitary man would not be man created in the image of God, who Himself is not solitary."[14] The solitary man can only and ever reflect a unitarian God.

Enter Eve. Into Adam's isolation, and out of Adam's flesh and bones, the image-fulfilling Eve was created. What a glorious event this must have been for Adam, and for his Creator! Adam sang for joy as he was joined by the one who was "bone of my bones and flesh of my flesh" (Gen. 2:23), exulting in the fulfillment of humanity, the completion of the image of God: "in the image of God he created him; male and female he created them."[15] Once Eve was present, humanity was able to reflect the personal and relational intimacy that God is. Eve's presence meant that humanity could experience life-giving interpersonal penetration and indwelling, a finite and temporal echo of God's triune, perichoretic life.

So from the time of the first male and female, every human being, every image of God, has had something extraordinary in common: each of us owes our existence to both a divine and human union of persons. We are created by, and image, God, who, as a union of persons, is one God. We are also created by, and image, our parents, who, as a union of persons, are one flesh. Personal union is the ground of all human *being*.

For the church, the sacred beauty of marriage and sex is to be maintained as a "*theo*-logical" reality whether or not it can be maintained on the level of the world's abstract ethical or political whims. The church delights in the holy love and intimacy of male and female because the church exists as a sign of the holy love and intimacy that brought humankind into existence. This is why the church must proclaim that the differentiation between, and the union of, male and female is utterly holy and beautiful. Indeed, it is precisely the distinction of our persons that allows for the beauty and holiness of the union—as it is with God. Human persons are defined by both the distinction and the union—as it is with the Trinitarian persons. Humans are distinctly male or female, but neither can exist except for the life-giving union between male and female.[16]

To celebrate and delight in the holy marriage and sexual union of others is by no means to denigrate the status of the imago Dei in males and females who are themselves not married. Far from it. Every human life is living proof of having shared most intimately in the union between male and female—our existence completely depends upon it. Each of us exists as the living bond between the male and female from whom we came. We are persons, in other words, who necessarily derive our personhood from others. We are not, and cannot be, who we are except by virtue of the one-flesh union of male and female. Contrary to the modern *zeitgeist*, humans are not self-defined. It is for this reason that the church should view with proper suspicion unqualified talk of the "single" person, for in reality, there is no such person. Each of us, whether or not we are joined in holy marital union, is constituted by interpersonal communion.[17] Our lives are not only shaped by way of sexual procreation, but also by the ways in which our nonsexual relational intimacies profoundly affect who we are and how we know ourselves. We share together, and never as isolated individuals, the mystery and wonder of our existence as male and female persons.[18]

The fall of humankind into sin, however, introduced a rupture in the image. East of Eden, male and female are not how they are supposed to be, created as they were to delight in their distinction and rejoice in their union. In fear and shame they cover themselves and hide, a feeble attempt at self-justification. The tragedy of the fall, and the corruption and condemnation that followed, manifests itself in the lives of broken images in manifold ways, but perhaps never so clearly as in our broken and distorted intimacies. The differentiation between, and the union of, male and female are utterly sacred, for they echo God's holy existence. Tragically, then, trespasses against the holy distinction, and violations of the holy union, typify the story of humanity east of Eden. Fractured images muffle and mute the holy echo in myriad ways, joining what should be divided and dividing what should be united. Cornelius Plantinga envisions the fall as entailing both the confusion and disruption of God's creation:

> According to Scripture, God's original design included patterns of distinction and union and distinction-within-union that would give creation strength and beauty. . . . Against this background of original separating and binding, we must see the fall as anti-creation, the blurring of distinctions and the rupturing of bonds, and the one as the result of the other.[19]

From this tragic "anti-creation," male and female are by no means exempt. The unraveling of creation leads to confusions and disruptions that seek to rob males and females of their God-given strength and beauty. These perversions are pervasive among God's fallen images, and are exacerbated in our attempts at sexual self-definition and self-justification, when we take pleasure in what God does not. What God has joined together, we are prone to separate, and what God has separated, we are prone to join. In either case, the image becomes rather dim. We desperately need to be re-created; we need reimaging.

THE TRUE IMAGE OF GOD: JESUS CHRIST WITH HIS BRIDE

While interpreting the meaning of the *imago Dei* in humanity must employ careful consideration of Genesis 1 and 2, it must not terminate there; the issue is a canonical one. The incarnate Son of God is the true imago Dei, the fully authentic human person, the fulfillment and destiny of God's creaturely images. In other words, Jesus Christ ultimately defines for us what it means to be the image of God. When we speak of Christ as the true and perfect image of God, we must avoid the temptation to collapse that image into his deity, as if it were his divine nature, per se, that constitutes him as that image. That would hardly be good news for human beings. The significance of Jesus being the quintessential image of God lies not in his existence as the eternal Son—for whom the ascription "image" would border on blasphemy—but in the fact that the eternal Son has become human.[20] Prior to the incarnation, the Son did not "image" God. The *imago Dei* is a predicate of created humanity, not humanity's Creator. God the Son is the true and full image of God precisely because, without ever ceasing to be fully God, he became truly and fully human. The enfleshing of God provides us with the "theo-logic" of the *imago Dei*.

It was into the confusion and disruption of the anti-creation that this most inexplicable reality transpired. God the Son was born into our flesh. He was born into the world that had been created by him and for him, taking on the humanity he had created. The descriptions of him in Scripture are tantalizing. He is, after all, the "image of the invisible God, the firstborn of all creation" (Col. 1:15). He is the "exact imprint of [God's] nature" and the "firstborn among many brothers" (Heb. 1:3; Rom. 8:29). And he is all of this as the second and last Adam (1 Cor. 15:45, 47). In Christ, God is not only re-creating the world and reconciling it to himself, he is also reimaging the world in himself. Jesus Christ is the quintessential image of God, the new Adam through whom creation has begun again. He is the new creation, in whom we are re-created and reborn into the image of God we were originally created to be. In order to enact this astounding act of re-creation, rebirth, and reimaging, the last Adam came to share fully in the humanity of the first. But as with the first Adam, so with the last: to truly image God, he needs his bride. It is not good for him to be alone.

If Jesus Christ is indeed the last Adam, the true fulfillment of the image of God in our humanity, we should expect that he would fulfill what was said of humankind in the beginning: "So God created man in his own image, in the image of God he created him; male and female he created them." If, as we have argued, "male and female" is descriptive of, and basic to, the imago Dei, we should expect that Jesus would satisfy that description. In a most beautiful and transcendent way, this is exactly what he does. He refuses to be who he is as the quintessential image of God without us. Indeed, the purpose of the incarnation is that Christ may have for himself an eternal bride, his holy church. In his act of unparalleled condescension and self-giving, God the Son became incarnate, joining himself to us, so that through his birth and baptism, through his faithful and obedient life, and through his death, burial, resurrection, and ascension, we might belong to him as his beloved. By the Spirit, he births us anew, baptizing us into his death and resurrection, justifying and sanctifying us, so that we may be one flesh and one body with him forever. In the beginning, Adam and Eve were united together as one flesh, the profound mystery of God's creative purpose begun. In the new beginning, Christ and his bride are united together as one flesh, the profound mystery of God's creative purpose fulfilled:

> For no one ever hated his own flesh, but nourishes and cherishes it, just as Christ does the church, because we are members of his body. "Therefore a man shall leave his father and mother and hold fast to his wife, and the two shall become one flesh." This mystery is profound, and I am saying that it refers to Christ and the church. (Eph. 5:29–32)

Right at the beginning of creation, God implicated the male and female in a mystery, that of the two becoming one. It was a beautiful and blessed mystery, no doubt full of rejoicing and wonder as the two came to experience each other, and thus life, as God intended it. And yet, as Paul tells us, this profound mystery was not self-defining, for it was a mystery that ultimately anticipated another. When God created humankind male and female in his image and joined them together as one flesh, he involved humanity in a mystery-sign, the fulfillment and reality of which awaited his incarnation. "The two shall become one flesh" is a mystery at the center of both creation and redemption, and Jesus Christ is the meaning of that mystery, because he is that mystery in himself. By assuming our flesh into union with himself—healing, sanctifying, and justifying our broken humanity in his life, death, resurrection, and ascension—we become one body and one flesh with him through Spirit-wrought faith. Thus, the mystery of creation is fulfilled in the mystery of redemption: the last Adam with and in his bride, and his bride with and in him.

Jesus Christ is the true image of God. However, he is not that image, any more than the first Adam was, as a solitary, independent being. Just as Adam would have been incomplete without Eve, Jesus would be incomplete without his bride. To echo the astounding pronouncement of Scripture, the church is none other than Christ's body, "the fullness of him who fills all in all" (Eph. 1:23). The promise that the church is the "fullness of Christ" is so extravagant as to sound blasphemous. Is not Jesus Christ complete in and of himself? Is it really true, in Calvin's words, that Christ "reckons himself in some measure imperfect" until he is joined to his bride?[21] What sounds at first like blasphemy is, in light of the incarnation, the astounding promise that Jesus will not be who he is without us. In the extravagance of his self-giving love, he has taken our humanity into union with himself so that, through his one act of atonement, we might be joined to him forever as his body and bride through the Spirit. In other words, the bridegroom "fills himself" with his bride; he becomes one flesh with his church in order to redeem, reconstitute, and re-create us as the *imago Dei*. In creation, Eve is the fullness of Adam, and together they are the image of God. In re-creation, the church is the fullness of Christ, and together they are the fulfillment of that image. In the incarnation of the Son of God, in the mystery of Jesus Christ, creation and salvation converge.

When God the Son became incarnate, he gave to marriage, and to the physical intimacy inherent to it, a meaning it could never have had on its own. This is true not merely because he upheld marriage as divinely ordained, but more importantly *because he fulfilled in himself the reality for which marriage is a sign.* The marital intimacy of the first human pair was a sign imbedded in their bodies of an intimacy to come, a marriage through which Christ would reconcile and reunite sinners to God. The union between Adam and Eve was, we might say, the *proto-protoevangelium*—the very first glimpse of the gospel recorded in Scripture, Genesis 3:15 notwithstanding. "The two shall become one flesh" (Eph. 5:31; cf. Gen. 2:24) *refers to* the saving union between Christ and the church (Eph. 5:32).[22] When God joined together the first male and female, he etched into creation a foretaste of a holy union to come, against which the gates of hell could never prevail.

This sacred marriage between Christ and the church possesses cosmic redemptive significance, for it is a blessed union that runs into eternity. God began creation with a marriage, he redeemed a fallen creation through a marriage, and he will finally consummate his unfathomable love for us in an everlasting marriage (Rev. 19:6 –9). No one has expressed this as beautifully as Jonathan Edwards:

> The end of the creation of God was to provide a spouse for his Son Jesus Christ that might enjoy him and on whom he might pour forth his love. And the end of all things in providence are to make way for the exceeding expressions of Christ's close and intimate union with, and high and glorious enjoyment of, him and to bring this to pass. And therefore the last thing and the issue of all things is the marriage of the Lamb. . . . The wedding feast is eternal; and the love and joys, the songs, entertainments and glories of the wedding never will be ended. It will be an everlasting wedding day.[23]

All sorts of people are fond of repeating the Christian statement that "God is love." But they seem not to notice that the words "God is love" have no real meaning unless God contains at least two Persons. Love is something that one person has for another person. If God was a single person, then before the world was made, he was not love.[24]
—C. S. Lewis

In Jesus Christ, the marital union between male and female has been forever sanctified. Fulfilling that original creative sign in a truly majestic and transcendent way, he came to dwell with and in his bride, sharing with us who he is as the true image of God, giving new and eternal life to our flesh from his own. Regardless of how secular culture defines it, marriage, for the church, must be defined by the gospel of Jesus Christ. Marital intimacy is divinely intended to mirror the saving intimacy between God and humanity in the person of Jesus Christ. Further, because the church is one with Christ, even as he is one with his Father through the Spirit, marriage is a sacred manifestation, on a creaturely level, of the intimacy between the triune persons of God. Accordingly, the one-flesh union between male and female necessarily transcends typically abstract moral, ethical, political, and social definition. Rather, marriage is to be understood primarily in light of God's self-revelation in Christ, and so given christological and Trinitarian definition by the church. In so doing, we will delight and take courage in confessing that marriage is a sacred and beautiful sign given to us to reflect God's ineffable love. In the union between Christ and the church, God has accomplished his redemptive and re-creative purposes, making us his beloved sons and daughters forever. In Jesus Christ, we find that God will stop at nothing to bring us into the life and love that he is. Indeed, he is willing to become what he was not—incarnate—and literally spend himself in suffering, misery, humiliation, and death to secure us as the objects of his eternal affection. As the recipient of God's love, Christ's bride comes to share in the triune family of God, forever enjoying the love that defines all love, the life that defines all life, and the personal intimacy that defines all personal intimacy. Let us heed Edwards again:

Christ has brought it to pass, that those who the Father has given to him should be brought into the household of God, that he and his Father and they should be as it were one society, one family; that his people should be in a sort admitted into that society of the three persons in the Godhead. In this family or household God [is] the Father, Jesus Christ is his own naturally and eternally begotten Son. The saints, they also are children in the family; the church is the daughter of God, being the spouse of his Son. They all have communion in the same Spirit, the Holy Ghost.[25]

MISIMAGING GOD AND OURSELVES

When God created Adam and Eve, joining them in marital union, he established within our humanity a sacred sign of his love. The self-giving, life-giving personal intimacy and indwelling that exists in the union between male and female was intended to mirror what God is like. It was, furthermore, an anticipation of the gospel, the exceedingly good news that the incarnate Savior would become one flesh with his bride, the church, re-creating our humanity in his self-giving, life-giving "at-one-ment." The union between male and female is thus given sacred definition in Scripture; it is to be interpreted in relation to the holy marriage first established by God at creation and quintessentially fulfilled in redemption.

Between these two great marriages, however, stands a great divorce. By the rupture introduced into creation through sin, the image of God suffered distortion and division; we became alienated from God, and therefore alienated from ourselves and from one another. The image of God was broken *in* us, and therefore broken *between* us. Broken images by definition badly reflect God, and we do so in seemingly innumerable ways, but none more serious than the ways we distort God and therefore ourselves in our fallen intimacies and longings. The ravages of sin were bound to penetrate deeply into what makes us human: "in the image of God he created him; male and female he created them." And so they have. We were created by God to mirror his self-giving, self-denying, humanizing, procreative, unconditional, and indissoluble love. Yet east of Eden, sadly, human love is all too characteristically selfish and self-gratifying, dehumanizing and objectifying, life-thwarting, conditional, and soluble. Sin has turned us inside out, as it were, leaving us curved in on ourselves. Disoriented by our self-orientation, we have become perversely proficient in unholy marital and sexual self-definition. Given the holy gravity of human sexuality, the effects on our closest personal intimacies have been devastatingly weighty. After all, distortions and confusions of marriage and sex strike deep at what makes us human, distorting and confusing not only who we were made to be, but also how God images himself.[26] For the holy bride of Jesus Christ, the implications are more severe still, for when we implicitly or explicitly condone or participate in unholy marital and sexual expressions, we obscure the very gospel we are privileged to share.

Because the stakes are so high, the distortions of which we speak demand theological assessment. This is to be distinguished from arrogant and self-protective finger-pointing, which might suggest that each of us, in various ways, was or is not subject to, or a purveyor of, the maladies we seek to assess. It is also to be distinguished from an assessment born of joyless negativity rather than deep appreciation and joyful wonder at the holiness of marriage and sex. But we must assess them theologically, for if our theology has nothing to say to us here, it ultimately has little to say at all. In what follows, we will briefly highlight several of the most important and far-reaching symptoms of our marital and sexual sickness, acutely aware that there is far more that could be said, and perhaps said far better. The intended goal, for the authors and readers alike, is the liberation and joy that comes from repentance in Christ Jesus, the embodied Lord of our sexual identity.

PUTTING ASUNDER WHAT GOD HAS JOINED TOGETHER

Marital union is a sign given to humanity that lends shape and substance to human love, for it images the indivisible, immutable love that God is. Divorce is thus also a sign, a countersign, that disfigures and disintegrates human love, implying as it does that God's love is divisible and unstable. As that countersign, divorce signals a rupture in the most essential of human relations, the union between male and female. It is a sign embedded in the anti-creation, and it constitutes an attempt to do the impossible: put asunder what God has joined.[27] In the new creation—the humanity of Jesus Christ— God has issued a resounding "No!" to this false sign, establishing, once again through marriage, an unbreakable sign of his indissoluble love. When Christ united himself in one flesh with his bride, he secured that union forever in himself, anchoring it in the eternal love of his Father through the Spirit. Because of his indefatigable and everlasting faithfulness, the church lives in the comfort and security that there is absolutely nothing that can divorce us from his love (Rom. 8:35–39). Christian marriage has the sacred privilege of sharing in this sign of the new creation, the gospel, in which God overcomes our infidelities and divisions.

Understanding and rejoicing in the union between Christ and his church, we must ask ourselves very difficult questions, questions intended to lead us to the healing that can come only from our repentance in him. T. F. Torrance gives voice to these questions: "If Christian marriage is meant to reflect that union, how can the Church tolerate divorce? What would divorce mean but that Christ can and may cut off his Church, that he holds on to us only so far as we prove faithful? Where then would we fickle and faithless sinners be? . . . This must make us ask whether the current attitude to divorce in the Church is not evidence of something very wrong, in fact evidence of a serious weakness in its grasp of the Gospel."[28]

As difficult as such questions might be, can we ask any less if the mystery of marriage has indeed been fulfilled and reconstituted in Christ—that is, without ripping marriage from its proper context and moorings in the gospel? In so asking, we must not tread haphazardly and insensitively over the complexities that wither or break marriages under the pain of abuse or infidelity. Christ is, and will remain, an utterly faithful Savior despite our unfaithfulness. But we must ask these questions, just as surely as we must answer them, in the kind of humble and trusting repentance that shows that we have not grown cold toward our Bridegroom and his gospel.

JOINING TOGETHER WHAT GOD HAS PUT ASUNDER

It was not good for Adam to be alone. He needed Eve so that together they could be the *imago Dei*, and he needed Eve so that together they could fore-shadow the life-giving union between Christ and his bride. But just as it was not good for Adam to be alone, neither was it good for Adam to be joined to another Adam, for two reasons. First, the image of God in humanity requires the male and the female: "in the image of God he created him; male and female he created them." Just as surely as solitary Adam could not image God, neither could Adam multiplied by two. Male and female are personal distinctions within our common humanity that define humanity, whereas Father, Son, and Spirit are personal distinctions within the one God that define God; where God is concerned, union requires distinctions among persons. Second, two Adams, or a hundred more for that matter, could not fulfill the mandate that immediately followed their creation: "And God blessed them. And God said to them, 'Be fruitful and multiply and fill the earth'" (Gen. 1:28).

Fruitfulness and multiplication require that humanity be the image of God: a life-giving, fruit-bearing union of distinguishable persons. How very much like God this is! The unity of the Father and Son in the Spirit is the life behind every life, the reason for the existence of everything and everyone (John 1:1–4; Col. 1:16; Heb. 1:2). Where God is concerned, the creation of life requires distinctions among persons.

If the fall is anti-creation, and necessarily includes distortion of the image of God in humanity, we might expect exactly what we find east of Eden: divisions and confusions among male and female—a dividing of what God has joined, as we have seen, but also a confusing of what God has distinguished. As lamentable as it surely is, we should not be altogether surprised when we read in Scripture that fallen images, who have "exchanged the truth about God for a lie," are given to sexual confusion: "For their women exchanged natural relations for those that are contrary to nature; and the men likewise gave up natural relations with women and were consumed with passion for one another" (Rom. 1:25–27). The fact that this passage occurs in the context of Paul's teaching on idolatry is telling. The sexual manifestation of self-worship is the anomaly of same-gender sex—the attempt to unite ourselves with ourselves. If idolatry means that we are curved in on ourselves doxologically, it means that we may also be curved in on ourselves sexually. Holy worship and holy sexuality both require someone who is "Other" than us. Blocher writes:

> Immediately we can understand why the Apostle Paul makes a close connection between idolatry and homosexuality (Rom. 1:22–27). This sexual perversion as a rejection of the other corresponds to idolatry in its relationship to God, the rejection of the Other; it is a divinization of the same, the creature.[29]

God sets himself against sexual idolatry, homosexuality, for ontological reasons, not political or moral reasons. As the Life of the world, he is implacably opposed to all creaturely forms of self-worship, sexual and otherwise, because idols are incapable of giving life. Confused worship, like confused sexuality, signals the death of humanity.

VIRTUAL SEX

The one-flesh union that God forged between his male and female image is the gift of personalization; the two come to experience their humanity in a uniquely intimate way in the joining of their persons. This is a gift that redounds to every human being, for each of us is a product of, and defined by, just such a union. Divorce and homoeroticism are two ways in which this gift is obscured, one an unholy separation of persons, the other an unholy confusion. Pornography is a third. Constituted by its objectification and thus dehumanizing of the other, pornography is the absurd attempt to make the gift of sexual union what it cannot be: impersonal. It is a case of sexual unreality, a voyeuristic endeavor to steal the pleasure of sexual intimacy from that which defines it. Pornography is an invitation to the contradiction of sexual autonomy.[30] Counterfeits are sham substitutes, and pornography is no exception. It substitutes the holy images of God for impersonal images on a screen; self-giving love for self-involved lust; life-giving communion for life-sapping masturbation; and the beauty and fulfillment of personal union for the shame and regret of personal preoccupation.

Pornography promises sexual gratification, a promise impossible for it to deliver seeing that it is everything holy sexual union is not. It stands in stark contrast to holy intimacy precisely because it contradicts who God is, and who he is for us in Christ. God is, by definition, a communion of living persons who dwell with and in one another in self-giving, life-creating love—a love that always exists for the benefit of the other. By contrast, pornography is a stimulant to idolatrous intimacy, a self-preoccupied love devoid of the possibility of life, which seeks to exploit rather than give, deriving pleasure at another's expense. The contrast is exacerbated when we consider the way in which God is for us in Jesus Christ. By becoming incarnate and suffering the abasement of our fallen humanity from cradle to grave, God the Son brings us, by the Spirit, to share in the living communion of life and love he has with his Father. In so doing, he re-creates, reimages, and authenticates our humanity in his own. Pornography is salvation's polar and evil opposite. It is dehumanizing through and through, seeking selfish pleasure in the objectification and abasement of others. Whereas in salvation Jesus Christ personalizes us by joining us to himself, in pornography we depersonalize others whom we keep at a distance. Because pornography so thoroughly distorts the nature of sexual love, the results of such self-indulgence are devastating. Pornography, far from being a merely private affair, in fact functions as a demonically effective stimulant to every other sexual sin; it is a perverse gateway to a myriad of sexual adulterations and abuses, and wreaks havoc on holy marriages.

God blessed and sanctified birth when he created the first male and female in his image: "Be fruitful and multiply and fill the earth." This fruitful multiplying was intended as a reflection of God's own life-giving interpersonal love. God resanctified birth forever in Jesus Christ when he was conceived in the womb of Mary by the Spirit, a conception through which our lifeless humanity would be given new birth in his. Conception and birth, no less than marriage and sex, are given their meaning in Christ. The life that proceeded from the union of Adam and his bride was a sign of the new and eternal life that would proceed from the last Adam and his bride—life and new life, procreation and re-creation, birth and rebirth. The life that comes forth from the union of male and female has a double reflection, mirroring both the procreative union of the persons of the Trinity and the procreative union of Christ and his church. The male and female union is pregnant with life, echoing who God is in his personal relations and what God does in the gospel of our salvation. In describing why human birth is so very precious to God, we must go even a trembling step further: the new birth we receive in Christ Jesus comes about because in the incarnation, God himself experiences conception and birth! The sanctification of birth has taken place in the incarnation of God.

The meaning of sexual union is thus tied inextricably to new life.[31] Herein the ignominy of abortion becomes apparent: it means that the male and female have said "No!" to the meaning of their union at the point where God has issued a resounding "Yes!" Abortion is a total misconstrual and manipulation of the meaning of sexual intimacy.[32] As such, debating about the inception of life, as important as that is, misses the larger and looming theological point: "Why do we kill approximately 4,000 unborn babies every day in the United Sates alone?" asks Christopher West. "Because we are misusing and abusing God's great gift of sex. Make no mistake: in the final analysis, the abortion debate is not about when life begins. It is about the meaning of sex."[33] If fruit-bearing is a gift inherent to the blessing of sexual union, then the question of whether such life actually exists is nonsensical.

Common to all sexual and marital distortions—divorce, homoeroticism, pornography, and more—is the obscuring, refusal, or termination of life, possible or actual. In abortion, the "No!" to life is issued in such a way as to beget violent and bloody repercussions, leaving personal and relational devastation in its wake for all involved.[34] Like all murder, abortion is an assault on God because it is an assault on his image. It takes place, as does all hatred for God, in the shadow of Golgotha, where our contempt was exposed to its depths: nothing would satisfy our rebellion save the bloody termination—shall we say abortion?—of God's true image, his one and only begotten Son. God experiences birth, but he also experiences its violent end.

In this violent end, the incarnate God suffers his own judgment on our sinful distortions, distortions that run deep into our being—all the way down to our naked bodies and the deepest personal intimacies that require them. In the midst of our marital and sexual sin, in our nakedness and shame, in the throes of the relational devastations we wreak upon ourselves and one another, God does the unthinkable. In Jesus Christ, God hangs battered, bruised, and bloody on a cross, naked and ashamed, the supreme demonstration that his love knows no bounds. There is no condition of ours, however humiliating and shameful, that God will not suffer to bring us forgiveness, healing, and peace. When we are included in Jesus Christ, we are put to death in his death, the death of our fallen humanity, the death of our broken marital and sexual self-definitions. And just as the Father raised the corpse of his Son from the dead by the Spirit, so we are raised in his resurrection, liberated from death and brokenness to share in his holy life.

The crucified, resurrected body of Jesus Christ is the judgment and salvation of our broken bodies. Jesus is the Lord over our twisted marital and sexual falsifications, but always as our merciful Savior. He alone is atonement and healing for our divided, confused, objectified, and aborted relations. The nakedness, humiliation, shame, torture, death, and burial that God in Christ suffers has as its end the glorious union between the resurrected Christ and his church. The everlasting, indissoluble, humanizing, and life-giving communion he establishes with his bride is the beginning of the re-creation of humanity in his image. In Christ, the church is re-established and re-oriented as male and female in the image of God, given freedom in repentance and forgiveness to experience marital and sexual holiness. In the mystery of Christ and his church, one flesh forevermore, marriage and sex become holy signs redeemed and fulfilled. Male and female God has created us, Christ and bride he has re-created us. We would do well to put this to prayer:

> Lord Jesus Christ, as you freely give yourself to your bride the Church, grant that the mystery of the union of man and woman in marriage may reveal to the world the self-giving love which you have for your Church; and to you with the Father and the Holy Spirit be glory and honor, now and forever. Amen.[35]

CHAPTER 2

THE REVELATION OF GOD'S COMMITMENT

by Erik Thoennes

Commitment and intimacy work together. It is within the framework of commitment that security, vulnerability, and freedom flourish; it is unwavering lifetime commitment that creates a context in which relational intimacy and passion thrive.

Has the value of commitment eroded in American culture? If so, what happened? The sexual revolution of the 1960s is one contributing factor. By the late 1970s, Americans had learned to see the world through the lens of radical individualism and freedom of choice. The most rewarding life, according to this mindset, is described as one untethered from stable commitments that would limit individual freedom of expression.

Unbridled individual freedom may seem ideal or desirable, but in actuality it leads to alienation in personal relationships and fragmentation in society.

A move away from long-term commitment has invaded almost every area of life in our current society. The average employee tenure is only 4.2 years and the average person has 12–15 job changes in their career.[1] Meaningful local church involvement is in decline,[2] and a lower percentage of people are getting married than ever, while sex is becoming less and less sacred.[3] It is no wonder then that marriage itself is suffering and that divorce is tragically common.

The correlation between commitment and intimacy is confirmed throughout the Bible, in both human relationships as well as in our relationship to God. Social scientists also tell us that there is a clear connection between commitment and relational bonding and attachment.[4] (Attachment will be covered more fully in chapter 11.) Mutual trust, grounded in a lifetime commitment, gives birth to true joy and the ability to give oneself to another without reservation.

TRUST IN MARRIAGE BEGINS WITH TRUST IN GOD'S PROMISES

Our ability to trust the one to whom we are married begins with our ability to trust the One who invented marriage. Our willingness to be naked and unashamed before our spouse begins with our willingness to be naked and unashamed before our Creator. Every married person is a frail and fallen individual; even those who, as believers, are new creations in Christ grapple with the old nature. The only way to be sure we will not waver in our commitment is to cast ourselves into the strong enabling arms of God, whose promises are always kept.

God's promises began in the garden with Adam and Eve, when He told them He would solve the horrific problem—loss of fellowship with a holy God—their failure to obey in the garden caused, and He set His plan in motion to redeem what had been tragically lost. And even when mankind's wickedness was such that "the LORD regretted that he had made man on the earth" (Gen. 6:6 ESV),[5] God promised Noah that He would continue His saving work through saving him and his family (Gen. 9:9–16).

Later, God told Abraham that He would bless him and make him a great nation that would be a blessing to all the nations of the earth (Gen. 12:2–3); and He kept His promise and provided a son for Abraham even in his old age (Gen. 13:2–4; 17:1–7). Fourteen generations after Abraham, David was assured that his own descendants would bring about the Messiah and that even his sin would not keep God from staying true to His covenant (1 Sam. 7:1–17).

As we know, this Messiah did come, and in Christ we have the fulfillment of all God's gracious commitments. "For all the promises of God find their Yes in him. That is why it is through him that we utter our Amen to God for his glory" (2 Cor. 1:20). It is because God is supremely faithful that we can rest in His gracious provision to enable us to keep the vows we make in His presence when we say "I do." Because He gave us His Son, we should never doubt that He will enable us to remain faithful, even in the toughest of marriages. "He who did not spare his own Son but gave him up for us all, how will he not also with him graciously give us all things?" (Rom. 8:32).

REAL LOVE INVOLVES DAILY SACRIFICE

A mature person knows that true love is not defined by mere sentimentality or fleeting passions. Real love often involves real sacrifice. Jesus' love for His bride, the church, cost Him His life, and true followers of Christ are willing to sacrifice daily for those they love. Going even further, Jesus said that there is no greater love than love that is willing to die for another (John 15:13).

Although few reading this book will be called to literally die for their spouse, we are called to die to self in countless ways so that the love in our marriages points to the love that Christ has for His church. When we live in Him, we learn to love like Him.

The daily self-sacrifice in marriage is not so dramatic as, for example, that of a soldier or firefighter who may be called on to lay down his life for another, but it is no less heroic. Our culture desperately needs to see examples of Christlike love in Christian marriages. No calling is greater for the married Christian than to be faithful and die to self for the good of his or her spouse.

This discipleship is lived daily and is centered on trust in Christ, determination to be like Him, and following in His steps wherever He leads. Without discipline and obedience, true discipleship does not exist, and neither does Christian love.

As long as I can remember, I've avoided using the term "fall in love." Even when I was young, it seemed to me that using a verb like "fall" to describe entering into something so profound as a loving relationship trivialized what love really is, especially when referring to love in marriage. If you think about it, most of the terms we use to describe being in love tend to devalue the serious volitional commitment involved in a loving relationship. We say that we are "lovesick," or "head over heels," or "crazy about" the one we love. We even go so far as to compare being in love to being intoxicated or smitten.[6]

Describing love in these terms implies that when we are in love, forces outside our control have overtaken us. The natural response to this inclination is, as we've mentioned, a lack of willingness to make serious commitments. One example of this is that cohabitation continues to increase worldwide and continues to undermine stability in marriage, parenting, and society.[7] Another is that couples are marrying later than any other time in human history,[8] and even the traditional marriage vow of "forsaking all others" may be replaced by something less final as often happens today.

Keeping one's options open is more prevalent than ever. A radical validation of one's immediate subjective experience as determinative of right and wrong has made personal preference, comfort, and convenience the great idols of our day. Ideals such as fidelity, commitment, and exclusive devotion, even in marriage, seem passé and oppressive. In addition to these troubling trends, the overly sentimental, romanticized conceptions of love and marriage portrayed in romantic comedies and love songs lead many to have unrealistic expectations that invariably end in bitter disappointment when the reality of daily difficulties and challenges comes. Thankfully, we need not be limited to these false views of love, because God has, in His Word, given us His perspective on what actually comprises love and marriage.

THE TRIANGULAR LOVE OF GOD

Contrary to the commitment-phobic and shallow ideas about love and marriage, the Bible offers a profoundly challenging and meaningful alternative. At the heart of the biblical idea of love is a controlled determination to faithfully and selflessly devote oneself to another, and to relentlessly seek his or her good. The ultimate model for this kind of love is God Himself, who calls Himself the Husband of His people and who loves His bride with extravagant, wise, compassionate, holy love. This kind of love becomes the foundation of all true love. This does not mean true love lacks passion or relational intimacy but that these are anchored by an enduring covenant commitment.

Psychologist Robert Sternberg's triangular theory of love is helpful at this point. While at Yale University, Sternberg studied interpersonal relationships and determined that "consummate love" requires three components: intimacy, passion, and commitment.[9] Sternberg says that "The amount of love one experiences depends on the absolute strength of these three components, and the type of love one experiences depends on their strengths relative to each other."[10] Intimacy is the feeling of closeness or attachment. Passion consists of feelings of enthusiasm or excitement and often involves a strong physical and emotional dynamic. Commitment is a conscious decision to remain devoted to someone. Intimacy without passion or commitment is only fleeting. Passion without intimacy or commitment is merely infatuation. Commitment without intimacy or passion is "empty love."

When we consider the full picture of God's love in the Bible, it becomes clear that His is a consummate love with perfect intimacy, passion, and commitment.

Intimacy

God's love creates interpersonal *intimacy* with those He loves. This intimacy has been experienced for all eternity among the persons of the Trinity. Jesus gives a couple of stunning glimpses of their intimacy in His High Priestly Prayer: "And now, Father, glorify me in your own presence with the glory that I had with you before the world existed" (John 17:5) and "Father, I desire that they also, whom you have given me, may be with me where I am, to see my glory that you have given me because you loved me before the foundation of the world" (John 17:24). Within the relations among Father, Son, and Spirit, there has always existed perfect mutual love and glorification.

Through union with Christ by faith in Him, believers are invited into fellowship with Father, Son, and Spirit. "I made known to them your name, and I will continue to make it known, that the love with which you have loved me may be in them, and I in them" (John 17:26). The benefits of being found in the Son are astounding. By the indwelling presence of Christ through the Spirit, and because we are now co-heirs with the Son, we are now "partakers of the divine nature" (2 Peter 1:4) and welcomed into intimate fellowship with the Father, Son, and Spirit. Because the Father delights in the Son, He now fully delights in those who are identified with him.

Passion

God's love is *passionate* in that it flows from the depths of His emotional life. The complexity and depth of our emotions is one of the main ways we see a beautiful manifestation of the image of God in human beings, the pinnacle of His creation. Repeatedly throughout the Bible, we see God as perfectly holy and also as expressing a full range of emotions from grief (Eph. 4:30), to joy (Zeph. 3:17), to intense anger (Ex. 4:14), to love (Eph. 2:4). When God speaks of His inability to abandon His rebellious people, He says it is because of His passionate love for them. Describing His pursuing, forgiving love God says, "My heart recoils within me; my compassion grows warm and tender" (Hos. 11:8b). God undoubtedly feels deep passion for His covenant people.

Commitment

In addition to passion and intimacy, God's love is anchored in His unwavering covenant commitment. His love is fully trustworthy because, out of His sovereign freedom, God has chosen to wed Himself to a people whom He loves with a never-changing devotion. God's covenant commitment to His people is grounded in His deep covenant love and faithfulness (*hesed*), which is to be mirrored in human marriage. When there is unwavering exclusive devotion in marriage, it creates security, safety, and a lifelong perspective to nurture profound intimacy. This reality calls for the strengthening of exclusivity and lifelong fidelity in marriage as mandatory for understanding marriage from a biblical perspective.

To understand the lifelong exclusive commitment that biblical marriage demands, we must first understand that human marriage is not an end in itself. It is intended to point beyond itself to the faithful love of God and to the kind of relationship He has with His people. Marriage is intended to display the glory of God's undying commitment to His people. This is why God hates infidelity, divorce, and even idolatry of any kind. When we understand God's jealousy for the faithfulness of His people to be devoted wholeheartedly to Him, we will grow in our devotion to Him and to the one we've committed to in marriage.

THE RIGHTEOUS JEALOUSY OF GOD[11]

It is right and good for us that God is a jealous God. When we understand that God's jealous love has intimacy, passion, and commitment, we will be able to rest in that love because we know how committed God is to maintain it. We will also have the understanding necessary in our marriages to love the way He does. Like God, we too should value faithfulness and abhor infidelity.

Repeatedly, throughout the Bible, God reminds His people that He is a jealous God.[12] His jealousy is for His own honor, as well as for the faithfulness of those with whom He has established a covenant relationship. Any violation of the exclusive favor in this relationship is met with God's strong emotional response of jealousy, which results in wrathful and—important to include—restorative action.

The jealousy of God is vital to the essence of His moral character, the impetus for worship and confidence on the part of His people, and a ground for fear on the part of His enemies. Godly jealousy is always a relational emotion in which the one who is jealous desires exclusive favor in the relationship.[13]

At its core, jealousy is an emotion based in perceived infidelity to covenant exclusivity. This desire to remain exclusively favored in covenant relationship grows out of the recognition of the righteousness of fidelity. It is also based in the passion for the pleasure fidelity produces. Faithfulness then is never merely a cold commitment, but it is driven by a desire to find the joy, passion, and satisfaction that faithfulness produces.

We also see from biblical accounts that humans demonstrate godly jealousy in relationship to other persons and on behalf of God.[14] Human jealousy is seldom uncontaminated with sin, can be unwarranted,[15] and can be taken to ungodly extremes.[16] Nevertheless, there is an important place in the Bible for human jealousy that is righteous and godly.

Description of godly jealousy

The concept of jealousy is present in Scripture in some instances without using the word. However, the Greek and Hebrew words that may be translated "jealousy," are nevertheless vital to a proper understanding of the biblical teaching on this concept. Most biblical reference sources provide good general definitions of jealousy and acknowledge the possibility of a positive sense for it.[17] The Hebrew and Greek words *qināh* and *zēlos*, which may be translated "jealousy," have similar, yet a broad range of meanings. In addition to "jealousy," other possible translations are "zeal," "envy," "ardor," or "emulation."

Jealousy expresses the unique character of the covenant relationship between Yahweh and His people. Because of the negative connotations associated with the word "jealousy," it is vital to work with an accurate definition of the English word in its biblical context.

We'll define jealousy as the ardent desire to maintain exclusive devotion within a relationship in the face of a challenge to that exclusive devotion. Necessary requirements for jealousy to be present are: a lover, a beloved, a rival, infidelity expressed in some way by the beloved, and an emotional response to that infidelity.

GOD'S JEALOUSY FOR THE FAITHFULNESS OF HIS PEOPLE

The first commandment

God's ardent interest in His own glory and honor is a part of His eternal nature. The primary way God is glorified in all of creation is through the faithfulness of His people with whom He has established a covenant relationship. When His people are unfaithful, He reacts—as a righteous expression of His holiness—with jealousy.

God's demand of exclusive faithfulness is most clearly seen in passages like Exodus 20:3–5:

You shall have no other gods before me. You shall not make for yourself a carved image, or any likeness of anything that is in heaven above, or that is in the earth beneath, or that is in the water under the earth. You shall not bow down to them or serve them, *for I the LORD your God am a jealous God*, visiting the iniquity of the fathers on the children to the third and the fourth generation of those who hate me. (emphasis added)

The Ten Commandments are of primary importance because of the theological grounding they provide for the faith and life of Israel. The first commandment establishes the exclusivity of God as the object of His people's worship. "Every form of substitution, neglect, or contempt, both public and private for the worship of God is rejected in this commandment."[18] Yahweh desires to be the ultimate object of the affection of His people. While God's jealousy incites Him to wrath and is ultimately about the preservation of His glory, divine jealousy is a loving concept. "He himself wants to be the object of the worship and service of the Israelites, and he wants to make himself an image (cf. e.g., the image of the Lord as Israel's Husband in the prophets, e.g., Jer. 2:2; Hos. 1–3)."[19] In this way God's jealousy "coincides with his love."[20]

Marriage as a metaphor

The marriage metaphor that describes God's relationship with His people in Scripture is central to understanding God's jealous love. This marriage imagery at the heart of the covenant is the reason biblical writers see idolatry of any kind as spiritual adultery, so the sexual imagery that accompanies this metaphor intensifies the jealous denunciation of spiritual adultery. The harlotry of God's people is graphically portrayed in the Bible.

That God compares His relationship with His people to a marriage should engender a great appreciation for how completely He has entered into time, space, and human relationship. When we consider that God is entirely self-sufficient and independent, it is staggering that He has, nevertheless, chosen to enter into an intimate relationship with His people to the point that He is moved to intense, jealous love when they spurn Him. We can understand why Augustine would in wonder ask God how this could be so. "What am I to you, that you should command me to love you and, if I do not, you should be angry with me and threaten great miseries?"[21]

The marriage metaphor used to describe the covenant and the sexual imagery used to describe infidelity, provide the foundation for the sacredness of marriage and sex. In addition to invoking an appreciation for the depth of

God's love for His people, it should also instill a deep reverence and respect for human marriage and sexual relations. Because these gifts from God illustrate the spiritual relationship God has with His people, they should not be trivialized or perverted in any way.

Reaffirmation after unfaithfulness

After His people rebel and worship a golden calf at Mount Sinai—and despite their infidelity—God reaffirms His faithfulness to His covenant. The core aspect of this obedience is once again expressed in the violent rejection of idolatry:

> Take care, lest you made a covenant with the inhabitants of the land to which you go, lest it become a snare in your midst. You shall tear down their altars and break their pillars and cut down their Asherim. (Ex. 34:12–13)

In reestablishing the covenant, Yahweh grounds it once again in uncompromising devotion to Him. The reason given for this reiteration of the first and second commandments is the same as in chapter 20—divine jealousy. "For you shall worship no other god, for the LORD, whose name is Jealous, is a jealous God" (Ex. 34:14). This justification for God's exclusive demand expands on the jealousy found in the first and second commandments of Exodus 20 by deepening God's self-description. Not only is He jealous, but His jealousy is such a significant part of His character that His "name is Jealous." For God to say that His name is Jealous makes jealousy a central and primary characteristic of His being and actions.[22]

Infidelity as a metaphor

Another important biblical emphasis in the Bible to add to our understanding of God's jealousy is how He uses metaphors of sexual infidelity. God compares Israel's disobedience to the first and second commandments to an unfaithful, sexually promiscuous wife. He says that they must destroy the altars, sacred pillars, and Asherim or else they "might make a covenant with the inhabitants of the land and they would play the harlot with their gods" (Ex. 34:15 NASB).

This concern for covenant fidelity extends to future generations as well: "and you might take some of his daughters for your sons, and his daughters might play the harlot with their gods and cause your sons also to play the harlot with their gods (v. 16 NASB).[23] The marriage and sexual imagery used

51

here is a central emphasis within the divine jealousy theme.[24] As said earlier, idolatry within the covenant context is the equivalent of spiritual adultery. Like any good husband who truly loves his wife, God expects absolute fidelity and reacts with anger in its absence. But divine jealousy is also a source of assurance and faith for those in devoted covenant relationship with Him. John Piper writes,

> It is a horrifying thing to use your God-given life to commit adultery against the Almighty. Since God is infinitely jealous for the honor of his name, anything and anybody who threatens the good of his faithful wife will be opposed with divine omnipotence. God's jealousy is a great threat to those who play the harlot and sell their heart to the world and make a cuckold out of God. But his jealousy is a great comfort to those who keep their covenant vows and become strangers and exiles in the world.[25]

Yahweh has the right to exclusive favor simply because He is God, and He specifically demands it from those with whom He has established His covenant relationship. This covenantal relationship with His people is as a marriage, and any violation of it is cause for a jealous reaction.

His pursuit of the beloved

While God's jealousy is foundational for His wrath and indignation, it also motivates His relentless pursuit of His loved ones when they go astray. "It is our confidence that the divine Lover will win His bride."[26]

God's jealousy is the very real response He has to the infidelity of His people and the primary motive for His wrath and harsh judgment. But it is also the emotion and motive behind His inability to allow His wayward loved one to stray from His side forever. His jealousy is the catalyst for the process that ensures the restored relationship with His people and the great blessings they receive as a result of that restoration. There is a profound relationship between jealousy and love. Because of His great love for His beloved, Yahweh will bring judgment on her from her lovers; His angry jealousy will be satisfied and He will restore her and bless her. His jealous love will ensure that she fulfills her covenant role.

The depth of His love for His people will not allow for ambivalence when they are unfaithful. Because the marriage metaphor is at the foundation of God's covenant, jealousy is the natural and expected response of the spurned husband. Therefore, "instead of treating *qin'â* (jealousy) cynically, one should hear in the word the legitimate, nay amazing, passion of God for one whom he loves."[27]

The jealous love of God ensures the fulfillment of the covenant promises and restoration of His people. It is this same jealous love of a husband that Isaiah speaks of that will bring the return from exile.

> For *your Maker is your husband.* . . . In overflowing anger for a moment I hid my face from you, but with everlasting love I will have compassion on you," says the LORD your Redeemer" . . . "For the mountains may depart and the hills be removed, but steadfast love shall not depart from you, and *my covenant of peace shall not be removed,*" says the LORD, who has compassion on you. (Isa. 54:5, 8, 10 NASB, emphasis added)

It is this same love that Jeremiah speaks of as God promises his covenant faithfulness.

> "Behold, the days are coming," declares the LORD, "when I will make a new covenant with the house of Israel and the house of Judah, not like the covenant that I made with their fathers on the day when I took them by the hand to bring them out of the land of Egypt, my covenant that they broke, *though I was their husband,*" declares the LORD. (Jer. 31:31–32)

And in this same love Hosea bases his assurance that the people of God will remain His people.

> "*I will betroth you to me forever.* I will betroth you to me in righteousness and in justice, in steadfast love and in mercy. I will betroth you to me in faithfulness. And you shall know the LORD." (Hos. 2:19–20, emphasis added)

The other side of God's jealous love is His compassionate undying commitment to His covenant promises. Israel was to remember that, "the intensity of his wrath at threats to this relationship is directly proportional to the depth of his love."[28] While Israel may have dreaded the anger of God's jealousy, the prophets always reminded her that this same jealousy ensured that her rebellious heart would not triumph. The sovereign jealous love of her faithful divine husband would.

A powerful example of godly jealousy from the New Testament comes from Paul's ministry to the church at Corinth.

> I wish you would bear with me in a little foolishness. Do bear with me! *For I feel a divine jealousy for you,* since I betrothed you to one husband, *to present you as a pure virgin* to Christ. But I am afraid that as the serpent deceived Eve by his cunning, your thoughts will be led astray from a sincere and *pure devotion to Christ.* For if someone comes and proclaims another Jesus than the one we proclaimed, or if you receive a different spirit from the one you received, or if you accept a different gospel from the one you accepted, you put up with it readily enough. (2 Cor. 11:1–4, emphasis added)

Paul recognized that the Corinthians were flirting with a different gospel and a different spirit than the true one. Their devotion and loyalty to the true Christ was in peril. Their failure to spurn the false teachers in Corinth was adding up to idolatry. Paul knew that to follow after another gospel was to be unfaithful to the one to whom they had been betrothed.

Paul's goal in his boasting, and in his ministry among the believers as a whole, was to bring about a "sincere and pure devotion to Christ" (v. 3). Paul uses this imagery of devotion and chastity to speak of the "wholeness and purity which is toward Christ" that he jealously wanted for his flock in Corinth.[29] Prompting Paul's jealousy for Corinthian fidelity was his fear, based on disturbing evidence (v. 4), that their minds and affections might be corrupted so that they would lose their single-minded faithfulness to Christ.[30]

This jealousy Paul experienced was grounded in the marriage metaphor used to describe God's relationship with His people. The theme of God as a husband to His people is prevalent in the Old Testament, as we've seen (esp. Isa. 54:5–6, 62:5; Jer. 3:1; Ezek. 16:8; Hos. 2:19–20), and that image intensifies and is more clearly defined in the New Testament, as the church is called the bride of Christ (Eph. 5:23–32; Rev.19:7–9, 21:2, 9).

The marriage process of Paul's day involved the betrothal, which established the commitment, and the nuptial, which consummated the marriage.[31] The betrothal made the marriage legally binding even though the wife remained a virgin until the nuptial. Often a year would separate the two ceremonies, and the betrothal could only be broken by death or divorce. If fidelity to the marriage was broken for any other reason, it was considered adultery, and deserving the capital punishment of an adulterer (Lev. 20:10). The sober responsibility of preserving the bride's chastity fell on the shoulders of her father (Gen. 29:23; Deut. 22:13–21).[32] Paul's use of the marriage metaphor shows "the closeness of intimacy and inviolability of the union of the Christian with his Saviour."[33] It also strongly emphasizes the lordship of Christ over the church.[34]

Paul saw himself as a responsible father in the lives of the Corinthian believers. Because his ministry was responsible for their conversions, "Paul sees himself as the agent of God through whom his converts were betrothed to Christ."[35] "I betrothed you to one husband, to present you as a pure virgin to Christ" (2 Cor. 11:2b).

That Paul's jealousy arose from the feelings of a responsible and loving father gives us a beautiful example of intense jealousy, combined with a tender pastoral concern. His pastoral concern tempered and informed his angry indignation and jealousy. In addition to his ability for hard rebuke, the Corinthians knew he also had deep love for his people: "Apart from other things, there is the daily pressure on me of my anxiety for all the churches" (2 Cor. 11:28). Paul's boasting did not come from pride or spite, but from fatherly concern for the good of his children. "Paul's God-filled heart yearns to protect them and keep them for the ultimate human experience, viz. union with Christ alone."[36]

Paul desired to be able to "present" the Corinthian believers to Christ without their devotion lacking in any way. The betrothal obviously refers to the conversion of the Corinthians, and their nuptial as the return of Christ. Paul guards the church of Corinth with affectionate jealousy—not self-regarding but divine—lest anything should rob her of her chastity between betrothal and the day of presentation.[37]

Paul is aware that the intervening time between betrothal of conversion and the nuptial of the second coming of Christ presents perilous challenges to fidelity. He wants the Corinthians to remain chaste for Christ until the wedding day of His return. But for now, the temptations continue and costly decisions must be made by those who claim the betrothal, for the jealous love of God calls the bride to keep herself chaste for her coming bridegroom.[38]

The betrothal of conversion brings about an exclusive relationship between God and His people. She, the church, has only one husband and Paul emphasized this exclusivity of the church's relationship with Christ with the "one husband" imagery of verse 2. Christ is the Bridegroom of all: the church universal

(Eph. 5:25–33), the local church, and the individual Christian. The believer is united to Christ as a wife to a husband (1 Cor. 6:15–17). Therefore, to love or be devoted to anyone except the true Christ is to break the marriage vow.

The Christians in Corinth can no longer claim independence or autonomy. They belong to Christ now (1 Cor. 3:23). He is their one Husband, and in anticipation of the coming of the Bridegroom they are under obligation to preserve unsullied their virginity (cf. 1 John 3:3); and Paul, their father in the gospel, jealously desires to present them as a pure and faithful bride to Christ on that great day. To break this marriage vow through a relationship with anyone except the true Groom, is viewed by Paul as losing one's spiritual virginity. A pure bride is primarily a symbol of pure doctrine, which then leads to holy living,[39] and this pure doctrine is the essence of maintaining pure devotion to Christ.

Paul's assumption that the Corinthians have pure virginal status before God is an amazing testimony to the power of the gospel. Those who had previously been sexually immoral, idolaters, adulterers, practitioners of homosexuality, thieves, greedy, drunkards, revilers, and swindlers (1 Cor. 6:9–11) now stand as pure brides before God. The gospel's power to justify and sanctify the believer (1 Cor. 6:11) is what Paul jealousy seeks to preserve in the lives of the Corinthians.

Paul's divine jealousy burns for the perfect union of Christ with His bride. The passage in 2 Corinthians 11 intimates His deity and ultimacy, for it is because of Christ that the covenanted people are to be preserved faithful. Paul's godly jealousy for the Corinthians is based in the same deep covenant love that God feels for His people.

As the Corinthians' devotion to the true Jesus decreased as shown in their increasing sinful behavior, Paul's jealousy for their devotion increased. "For those souls are jealous which burn ardently for those they love, and jealousy can in no other way be begotten than out of a vehement affection."[40]

No love of the natural heart is safe unless the human heart has been satisfied by God first. The tragedies of human lives can only be solved by an understanding of the one great fundamental truth that Jesus Christ alone can satisfy the last aching abyss of the human heart.[41]
—Oswald Chambers

Although divine love is fully operative in this jealousy, and the well-being of the Corinthians is in sight, God's glory is also a motivator for Paul. The welfare of His people is a driving motivation for Paul, but his jealousy is also like God's in that the honor of God's name always remained his ultimate goal.

Paul's jealousy must also be considered within the tender pastoral heart that he had for his people. When he rebuked them for their unfaithfulness, it was done so in the context of the holistic loving ministry he had with them. It is safe to say that for Paul the primary focus of shepherding people was in the realm of truth. He realized that the most important way to love his people was to help them to know and live the truth. However, Paul balanced this hard passion for truth with the compassionate heart of a pastor. Paul is jealous for God's glory and the fidelity of His people, but he also has a deep love and affection for His people (Rom. 9:2–3; 1 Thess. 2:7; 1 Tim. 5:23; Philem. 1:7). He did not express his jealousy with self-righteous detachment, but as a loving father.

Unfaithfulness to God, according to Paul, was to believe in anything but the true gospel and the true Christ. Like the Old Testament prophets, Paul understood the marriage metaphor to be at the core of the covenant and the gospel, and therefore recognized any compromise of the gospel to be spiritual adultery. Religious pluralism was not an option for Paul.

He not only recognized the idolatrous implications of false belief, he also saw the fundamental connection between God's honor and obedience to Him. A Christian who lived as a friend of the world was an enemy of God. This unfaithfulness brought about an intense jealousy from Paul. Paul's love for the people to whom he ministered, and his devotion to their apprehension of the true gospel, was grounded in his ultimate goal in everything he did: the glory of God (Rom. 15:7; 1 Cor. 10:31; 2 Cor. 1:20, 4:15; Phil. 2:11).

Because jealousy is such a central characteristic of God and godly people, it should be understood as an emotion that needs to be cultivated and felt by godly Christians. If the limitations and qualifications we have discussed are heeded, this emotion should be encouraged and appreciated in the church and in marriage. True love responds with deeply felt jealousy whenever one in covenant relationship expresses infidelity.

God will allow no rival to Him in the lives of his people, and godly men and women will share in this jealousy for the faithfulness of His people, and ultimately, for God's eternal glory.

Loving our spouse starts with loving God

Love and faithfulness to Christ is fundamentally expressed in obeying Him. Jesus said, "If you love me, you will keep my commandments" (John 14:15), and loving others is the main way we keep His commandments.

Love for others is meaningless if it is not found in our closest relationships. For married followers of Christ, the starting point of love for others needs to be with the one with whom we are one flesh. Christlike, Holy Spirit–enabled, gospel-empowered love for our spouse needs to be at the top of our list of priorities as we seek to be faithful to Christ.

Dave, a dear friend of mine, had a counseling practice in which he primarily worked with Christian married couples who were having major relational conflict. One of the most disconcerting things he often experienced generally took place in the initial session. Dave would ask the two how things were going, which would open up a bevy of complaints from both the husband and wife, frequently expressed with vindictiveness, spite, and sinful anger. After listening to the couple trash each other for a while, Dave would typically turn to the husband and ask him how his relationship with the Lord was going in the midst of all this marital strife. Dave was often amazed by how often the answer was something like "Oh, glad you asked, actually it's never been better. Actually, all the struggles with her have really brought the Lord and me much closer."

Our capacity for self-deception and duplicity can be staggering. What Dave would do at that point would sometimes cost him any further appointments with this couple. He would open his Bible and read 1 John 4:20: "If anyone says, 'I love God,' and hates his brother, he is a liar; for he who does not love his brother whom he has seen cannot love God whom he has not seen." Dave would then close his Bible and have to inform the husband that "not only are you having marriage problems, you also have a lying problem. No matter how you may feel, your relationship with God cannot be in a good place if you are treating your spouse with disdain."

Devotion and love to Christ must be expressed through devotion and love for those we are called to love, most especially the one with whom we are one flesh. Keeping our wedding vows for life honors Christ.

Jesus said, "Whoever loves father or mother more than me is not worthy of me, and whoever loves son or daughter more than me is not worthy of me. And whoever does not take his cross and follow me is not worthy of me. Whoever finds his life will lose it, and whoever loses his life for my sake will find it" (Matt. 10:37–39). Even our greatest devotion on a human level should pale in comparison to our devotion for Christ. This does not diminish our love for others; it establishes it in Christ's love for us (1 John 4:19), which is the foundation of our love for Him and everyone else.

What fidelity involves

When we think of faithfulness in marriage, we think of keeping the seventh commandment, which prohibits adultery. While we need to be vigilant in guarding against the attitudes, thoughts, and actions that lead to adultery, sins of omission deserve equal attention along with sins of commission.

Our faithfulness starts with being kind and unselfish in our decisions and actions, even in the mundane details of daily life. It is expressed in listening well, asking how we can serve our spouse better, praying for each other, and tending to our own souls so we can be generous with our time and attention. It means we strategize about how to be better servants and build one another up. When we habitually neglect any of these, whether from indifference or lack of awareness of our spouse's needs, we eventually become guilty of sinning by omission.

As a pastor of a church with a lot of young adults, I have had the privilege of officiating many weddings. It is a great honor to stand before a congregation and an energetic, excited couple as they embark on a major new chapter of their lives. When we get to the point in the wedding vows when I hear them say "for better, for worse, for richer, for poorer, in sickness and in health, to love and to cherish, as long as we both shall live," I'm usually thinking something like, "Oh, dear young ones, you have no idea what you are getting yourselves into when you say that." I know that usually they are thinking that keeping that vow will mean being patient and caring when the occasional stomach flu hits or when money is tight. But I know that it won't be long before far greater challenges—both major life events and those more ordinary—will threaten their determination to be faithful. Then what? They will be tempted to take the easy way out—to pursue comfort, convenience, and independence. If they give in to those temptations, they may even have the gall to say something like "I feel a peace about leaving this hard marriage because I know God wants me to be happy."

Thank God for His amazing grace and patience. We certainly need it. If any married couple is going to rise above the easy way out, they will need a compelling vision and purpose for their lives and marriage that transcend shallow worldly values—and that depends on resources that only God can provide. That vision is a God-glorifying life, and the source of strength is the power of the gospel through the transforming work of the Holy Spirit.

We think of missionaries who serve in areas resistant to the gospel as displaying heroic faithfulness, but heroic faithfulness also takes place quietly in homes where husbands and wives are staying faithful through the steady stream of daily challenges that come their way. God is honored whenever we are faithful to Him, even if He is the only one who knows.

A great example of faithfulness to God through fidelity to his spouse was Robertson McQuilkin. He and his wife, Muriel, had raised six children and served as missionaries in Japan for twelve years. Muriel, who taught at Columbia, began to suffer from Alzheimer's disease. It got so bad that she was terrified whenever her husband was not nearby. He realized that he needed to resign from his job as president of Columbia International University, where he had served for twenty-two years, and also to step away from the many boards he served on and curtail his substantial writing and speaking ministry. From a practical standpoint, he was at the most influential and productive chapter of his ministry. Some of his friends encouraged him to place Muriel in a care facility—and in many situations, that indeed is the most loving act. But McQuilkin knew that the greatest way he could honor God would be to stay home and care for his wife. Here are some of his powerful words from his resignation speech:

> "It is clear to me that Muriel needs me now, full-time. . . . My decision was made, in a way, forty-two years ago when I promised to care for Muriel 'in sickness and in health . . . till death do us part.' So, as a man of my word, integrity has something to do with it. But so does fairness. She has cared for me fully and sacrificially all these years; if I cared for her for the next forty years I would not be out of her debt. . . . Duty, however, can be grim and stoic. But there is more: I love Muriel. She is a delight to me—her childlike dependence and confidence in me, her warm love, occasional flashes of that wit I used to relish so, her happy spirit and tough resilience in the face of her continual distressing frustration. I don't have to care for her. I get to! It is a high honor to care for so wonderful a person."[42]

Robertson McQuilkin's example stands out as a model of Christlike, joyful, servant-hearted, love for God in the way he loved his wife.

This is my commandment, that you love one another as I have loved you. Greater love has no one than this, that someone lay down his life for his friends. (John 15:12–13)

CONTINUING INSIGHT:

LOVING LIKE JESUS IN OUR MARRIAGE

by Darryl DelHousaye

In the simplest possible statement, the purpose of Scripture is to lead us to Jesus. Do not interpret that, however, as simply being born again. Deliverance from the penalty of sin is only the beginning of the salvation transformation Scripture aims to lead us into. We are expected to become like Jesus in every way as Scripture inculcates in us the very love of God, which in turn will lead us to love like Jesus (1 John 4:7–11).

With this context in mind, we can look at one of the best examples in the Bible of how human beings warp Scripture, and examine what Paul really said in those infamous verses about submission and obedience. He first speaks to wives:

Wives, be subject to your own husbands, as to the Lord. For the husband is the head of the wife, as Christ also is the head of the church, He Himself being the Savior of the body. (Eph. 5:22–24 NASB)

These words are often isolated or misinterpreted, but nothing in this passage warrants forcing a wife into a subservient role. The Greek word for "be subject" is *hupotasso*. Its primary meaning is to arrange oneself or to order oneself in such a way that you are helpful to the team. It is a word used in military terms to refer to a formation of soldiers. *Hupotasso* meant to stay in your position in the formation so that everyone can support each other.

Two things should especially be noted in this passage. First, the word for submit, *hupotasso*, is the same word Paul uses in reference to the church being submitted to Christ. In Ephesians 5:24 (ESV), he wrote, "As the church submits to Christ, so also wives should submit in everything to their husbands."

Second, the command for wives to be subject is in the middle voice. There are three voices in Greek grammar that describe the interaction of the subject of a sentence with the object.

Active voice means that the subject of the sentence performs the action, as in "I am talking."

Passive voice means that the subject of the sentence is the object of the action, as in "I am being talked to."

But when the middle voice is used, it means that the subject of the sentence is performing the action toward itself. "I am talking to myself" is an example of the middle voice.

> *Between a man and his wife there is a far closer relation; for they not only are united by a resemblance of nature, but by the bond of marriage have become one. Whoever considers seriously the design of marriage cannot but love his wife.*[1] —**John Calvin**

In Ephesians, the middle voice means that the wife performs the action of being subject, not the husband. She performs the action in regard to herself, not to anyone else. In other words, she chooses to arrange herself in her relationship with her husband. She is not forced into that position by the actions of her husband. This certainly leaves no justification for abuse or control on the part of the husband.

A woman's choice to support is consistent with the role of a wife as described at the creation of woman. Eve was to be a "helper suitable" for Adam, or literally, a helper corresponding to him (Gen. 2:18).

The word "helper," in Hebrew, is *ezer*. It does not even imply subjection. The word is used thirteen times in the Old Testament to describe God as our helper. The Hebrew word is not used in the sense of a servant who helps, that is, the hired help. Not once in the Hebrew Bible does the word refer to a servant. Rather it connotes the kind of help that comes when you are in serious trouble and you shout, "Help!" Eve was created because Adam needed help badly. His helper was suitable for rescuing him from being without a suitable partner.

The word "suitable" in Genesis 2:18 is *kenegdvo*. It is a compound of three Hebrew words. The prefix is simply the Hebrew letter kof, or a "k" in English.

It indicates a comparison, that is, it shows how "helper" compares to "him" or Adam.

The second part of the word is *neged*, which means opposite, counterpart, in the presence of, before, or over against.

The last part is *vo*, which refers to "him," meaning Adam.

Taken together, this compound word implicitly asks the question, what is the comparison between helper and Adam? The answer is that the comparison is *neged*. Literally, Eve was made to be a helper who stood opposite or in front of Adam, facing him. It presents a picture of two equals working together to perform a task. For example, if they wanted to move a table, they would have difficulty picking it up if the wife stayed in a subservient role under or behind her husband. They are only effective when she stands on the other side of the table and lifts her half. They have to stand opposite each other on equal footing, facing each other and working together as equals. Remember that the initial command to the man and woman was to fill the earth with others who would bear the image of God (Gen. 1:27–28). Neither could do this alone.

What does this mean for our understanding of Ephesians 5:22–24? It means that when a wife is imitating God, acting in Christlike love, she will attempt to order herself into her husband's life in such a way that she supports him and works in unison with him to accomplish the goals of the marriage. She will do this by her own choice, not because she is forced into subjection, but because that is what Christ would do.

HUSBANDS TO WIVES

The instructions to wives leave no room for the husband to impose on her right to make her own decisions. Paul gives clear direction that ensures he will have more than enough to do without worrying about how his wife acts.

> Husbands, love your wives, just as Christ also loved the church, and gave Himself up for her, so that He might sanctify her, having cleansed her by the washing of water with the word, that He might present Himself the church in all her glory, having no spot or wrinkle or any such thing; but that she would be holy and blameless. (Eph. 5:25–27)

Paul's instructions to the wife imply a life of love, but he doesn't take the chance that husbands will miss the importance of love. He begins with the blatant command, "Husbands, love your wives." There is no ambiguity here. Love is the only option.

Just to be sure, however, that husbands do not fail to grasp what this love means, he clarifies. No doubt men were just as self-serving then as we men are today. Paul's description, however, does not leave any excuse for the types of definition that often are given.

- Love does not mean jealously isolating one's wife under the pretense of protecting her.
- Love does not mean dictating decisions to her.
- Love does not mean forcing her to submit to a husband's will.
- Love does not mean demanding sex just because the husband feels like it.

The list could go on, but the point is clear. Loving one's wife is reflected in six characteristics that she will manifest when a husband is loving her biblically. She will be: sanctified, cleansed, spotless, without wrinkle, holy, and blameless. And all those things must be accomplished without dictating anything to her, since how she submits to her husband is her business, not his. For a husband to love his wife, he must act in a way that encourages her cooperation with him, not in a way that requires or coerces it.

What does it mean to be sanctified? The word itself is *hagiazo*, which is usually defined with terms like "set apart" or "consecrated." It does mean that, but the word speaks to regard or reverence. In Ephesians 5:26, the verb form implies that a husband will consciously choose to regard his wife as holy. One does not abuse what is holy. One cares for it. Loving one's wife means approaching her as a person would approach anyone of great worth—by exercising reverence and respect.

"Cleansed" is the word *katharizo*, and it means to clean by removing dirt. In this case, however, Paul specified the type of cleansing agent to be used— "the washing of water with the word." By this time, we should be able to imagine what that looks like. If we understand the Scripture correctly, it will make us more like Christ and it will bring us life.

In other words, husbands love their wives by applying the principles of Scripture in a way that helps them become more like Christ, reaching the full measure of their potential in life. A wife who is fearful rather than joyful, timid rather than bold, sullen rather than outgoing, or cold rather than loving has not been washed very well with the Word. A husband who lives in love will seek to do all he can to see those godly qualities blossom in his wife.

The same can be said of the other characteristics that Paul states, "having no spot or wrinkle" and "holy and blameless." The evidence that a husband is loving his wife well is that she grows into what God created her to be. Wives who are constantly trying to hide who they are have not been given the kind of environment in which they can be themselves. They are too ashamed of the flaws they perceive in themselves. Loving husbands bring encouragement and validation that takes away shame and replaces it with confidence.

The man who loves most will love best. The man who thoroughly loves God and his neighbor is the only man who will love a woman ideally— who can love her with the love God thought of between them when He made male and female. The man, I repeat, who loves God with his very life, and his neighbor as Christ loves him, is the man who alone is capable of grand, perfect, glorious love to any woman.[2]
—George MacDonald

CONTINUING INSIGHT:

MARRIAGE AND MUSIC IN THE EARLY CHAPTERS OF GENESIS

by James F. Coakley

There has always been a close relationship between romance, marriage, and music. Love has been associated with poetry and song for time immemorial. What may not be readily recognizable is that this relationship is even evident in the early chapters of Genesis. One of the ways to heighten a message's content is to set it to music, so it should not be surprising that the greatest book of all time uses that tactic to foreground certain points. One practice that astute Bible readers discover is that one must pay attention not only to the individual words of a text but to the overall shape of a passage.

Early on, the placement of poetry/songs in the Bible makes a statement. These poetic insets are placed at key points to add punch to what has been stated earlier in the text. This structural shape and pattern exist in the early chapters of Genesis on a microscale, but this shape is also used on the macroscale in the first five books of the Bible, the Pentateuch. That pattern is a narrative text followed by a poetic/musical interlude, which is then followed up by a brief epilogue. What is particularly interesting is how music and poetry, which are embedded in the text, help accentuate the main points of the narrative, serving as a peak, thematically speaking.

Genesis 1–4 Micro Pattern

	Narrative	Poetry	Epilogue
Genesis 1	1–26	27	28–31
Genesis 2	1–22	23	24–25
Genesis 3	1–13	14–19	20–24
Genesis 4	1–22	23–24	25–26

Notice that the first poetic inset is found in Genesis 1:27 and extols in song-like verse that male and female both are made in the image of God. We have dignity because both genders reflect the image of God and we are the pinnacle of God's creation activity! That is truly something to sing about and celebrate!

The next chapter looks at creation from a little different vantage point by focusing on humanity and its relationship to the world that God made. As a peak in this narrative, Adam joyfully exclaims in another poetic inset that the woman God made especially for him is now "bone of my bones and flesh of my flesh" (Gen. 2:23 NIV). Marriage is the peak of Genesis 2 and it is evident by the invocation of poetry/song embedded within the narrative. However, the next chapter details the fall in the garden, and this time the poetic inset is in the form of a curse placed upon the serpent, the woman, and the man for their disobedience. For the man and woman, what should have been a blissful life is now sadly tinged with sin and curse. Interestingly, the curse on man and woman is connected to their point of origin. In a poetic wordplay man (Hebrew *adam*) who was made from the ground (Hebrew *adamah*) is now

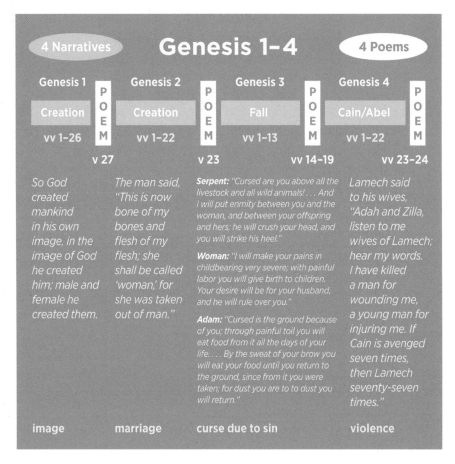

Genesis 1–4

4 Narratives — 4 Poems

Genesis 1	POEM	Genesis 2	POEM	Genesis 3	POEM	Genesis 4	POEM
Creation		Creation		Fall		Cain/Abel	
vv 1–26		vv 1–22		vv 1–13		vv 1–22	
v 27		v 23		vv 14–19		vv 23–24	

| So God created mankind in his own image, in the image of God he created him; male and female he created them. | The man said, "This is now bone of my bones and flesh of my flesh; she shall be called 'woman,' for she was taken out of man." | **Serpent:** "Cursed are you above all the livestock and all wild animals! . . . And I will put enmity between you and the woman, and between your offspring and hers; he will crush your head, and you will strike his heel."

 Woman: "I will make your pains in childbearing very severe; with painful labor you will give birth to children. Your desire will be for your husband, and he will rule over you."

 Adam: "Cursed is the ground because of you; through painful toil you will eat food from it all the days of your life. . . . By the sweat of your brow you will eat your food until you return to the ground, since from it you were taken; for dust you are to to dust you will return." | Lamech said to his wives, "Adah and Zilla, listen to me wives of Lamech; hear my words. I have killed a man for wounding me, a young man for injuring me. If Cain is avenged seven times, then Lamech seventy-seven times." |
| image | marriage | curse due to sin | violence |

going to experience friction with the stuff from which he is made. The ground will now be hard to work due to his disobedience. The woman, whose point of origin was from Adam's side, is now going to experience tension with the one from whose rib she was fashioned. Woefully this change is cast in mournful poetic language to commemorate how sin has affected the relationship between husband and wife.

The next chapter contains some clear examples of the fact that sin has now drastically affected the family structure and marriage. Sibling rivalry led to fratricide when Cain killed Abel. At the end of the chapter in a poetic boast (Gen. 4:23), Lamech speaks to his two wives (another evidence of how quickly sin has infiltrated the institution of marriage). Gleefully, in what is known as synonymous parallelism—a literary form that is clearly evident later on in the poetic books of Psalms and Proverbs—Lamech sadly but melodiously states to his two wives Adah and Zillah:

Adah and Zillah,
Listen to my voice, You wives of Lamech,
Give heed to my speech,
For I have killed a man for wounding me;
And a boy for striking me.

Now it is interesting to see the progression of the poetic songlike insets embedded at the end of these first four chapters. The first song in almost hymnlike fashion extols the fact that both men and women are made in the image of God and heightens our majestic status on the earth. The second song, sung by Adam, extols in a love ballad the wonders and beauty of marriage and foregrounds that relationship as one of the greatest gifts that God has given to humanity in the garden of Eden. But then sin enters the world and even poetry is affected because now instead of love ballads extolling marriage, mankind is singing the blues due to disobedience.

But the downward trek continues even more deeply in the next chapter when Lamech is glorifying violence done to a fellow human being made in God's image. So we go from a hymn, to a love ballad, to the blues, and ultimately to what sounds like heavy metal. Music not only foregrounds some of the thematic peaks in these early chapters of Genesis but also mirrors the sad effects of what devastation sin has brought into the world, especially as it relates to family and marriage.

It is to be hoped that the lessons in this book can begin to bring us back to where we are more Edenic in our marriages and in our songs. Marriage is the certainly a major theme early on the Bible and one worthy of celebrating in song!

CHAPTER 3

THE FOUNDATIONAL LANGUAGE OF MARRIAGE IN SCRIPTURE

by Darrell Bock

Marriage has fallen on hard times. Not only has the public debated about what a marriage actually is, but many people are no longer "signing up" to enter into marriage. The distinct handling of the institution of marriage is part of a social revolution that stems from many factors: the invention of the Pill, greater openness to divorce, social and legal availability of abortion, changed social mores, the prevalence of cohabitation, children born to parents who are not married, and more. There is no shortage of data that corroborate what is evident: marriage is becoming less common in the United States, and the impact is not just personal, but societal.

It is no accident that the the creation of man and woman in Genesis 1 and 2 is accompanied by the union of the man and woman and presented as one of the most significant of human relationships. Marriage is foundational, and is more than the two people in it—the institution functions as a key building block for society by, among other things, providing a stable home and environment for children. Marriage models cooperation across genders for those children and also for society at large.

Defining marriage in Scripture gives us a major window into a core human relationship and why Scripture presents the state of marriage as so central to human flourishing.

BEGINNINGS IN A GARDEN: HUMANS AND THEIR MISSION

In Genesis 1 two key terms need attention: image/likeness and subdue. One term tells who we are. The other tells us what we are to do.

What humans are

Early on, Scripture places marriage in high esteem. God's forming of male and female humans is the high point of His creation, and in many ways, marriage is the capstone of the creation narrative. On the sixth day, God creates humans in His image as told in Genesis 1:26–31. "In our likeness" (Hebrew, *demūth*) in verse 26 is not so much a physical attribute, however, since an incorporeal God is in view contextually, but in terms of certain attributes of person and relating that also connect to a sense and awareness of presence. God can be present—and is—without being seen. Likewise humans, through our character can and do stamp our existence and leave an impression whether or not we are physically in a particular location. Then verse 27 makes three statements: (1) God created humans in His own image; (2) this creation was in the image of God; and (3) they were created male and female. The double mention of humankind being made in God's image is clearly for emphasis in the text. No other creation of God is so closely associated with Him. In Genesis 1, the text has been building to this moment when God makes a mirror of Himself.

On this day, as God viewed His *entire* creation, which now included human beings, it is uniquely said of what He created that it was *very* good as opposed to the good of previous days.

What humans are to do

The creation commission and mandate God gives in verses 28–30 is given to both the man and the woman. Together they will carry out the calling God has given to humanity as the steward of creation, the instruction being to multiply, fill the earth, and subdue (*radah*) it, or bring it under control. Unlike other creatures, humans can rule and subdue by planning, discernment, and reflection, with an awareness of past and future. Man and woman are to accomplish this goal together. In effect, God has equipped people to be stewards of the creation. To manage the creation well is a core calling of life for each of us.

Genesis 2 zeroes in on the relationship of man and woman as originally designed before the fall. In verse 18 we see God recognizing that it was not good for Adam to be alone. This led into a process of identification that also produced an awareness of a need that the creatures already present could not fill. The goal was an *ezer k'negdo*, the translation of which has been a topic of discussion, even debate. The *ezer* describes a quality God demonstrates in numerous texts (Ex. 18:4, by delivering; Deut. 33:7, helping Judah against his enemies; 33:26, 29, by protecting and delivering; Pss. 33:20, help and shield; 115:9–11, protector; 121:2, protector; 124:8, by deliverance; 146:5–6, as Jacob's help).[1] As God helps us, so the one corresponding to (*k'negdo*) Adam is to help.

Since every person is a part of the human race and human nature is something social and has in itself the power of friendship as a great good, God willed for this reason to create all humans from one person, so that they might be held fast in their society not only by likeness of descent, but also by the bond of relationship. Thus the first tie of natural human society is husband and wife. And yet God did not make each one separately and then join them as if they were strangers to each other. Rather, He created one from the other, yet He put a sign of their union's power in the side, from which the woman was drawn forth and formed (Gen. 2:21-22). For they were joined to each other from the sides, they who walk side by side, they who together look where it is they walk.[2] **—Elizabeth Clark**

The picture of this second word is of one who fits or complements Adam. It is a word both physical and relational, as the idea is that she is an opposite match.[3] This one made to be like Adam, yet also distinct from him, is the match, the help. No such *ezer* existed for the man Adam until God created woman from the man. The result in 2:23–24 was a recognition and celebration that the counterpart had been found; indeed, the first time a person speaks in Scripture, it is Adam rejoicing in the bone of his bone and the flesh of his flesh, the one taken from him to be a team player with him. It is in this context that the text that defines marriage is presented as a pinnacle of creation, its concluding and climactic note. Genesis 2:24 (NIV) reads, "That is why a man leaves his father and mother and is united to his wife, and they become one flesh."[4]

THE DISRUPTION TO GOD'S DESIGN

As we have determined, God defined marriage to Adam as the forming of a home with a counterpart who is called to be a help and support as a team member in stewarding His creation well. The celebration is of completion of the unity that comes as Eve joins Adam as one both different from and yet like him. They are to work in the creation as stewards together, each as a reflection of the image of God, forming a home unit where mutual support can be found.

Break in mutual support

The design for marriage faced a severe disruption with the fall of Adam and Eve into sin in Genesis 3. Due to their choice to disobey God—something Eve initiated (Gen. 3:1–7) but that Adam was held responsible for as the recipient of the original command (Gen. 2:16–17)—the original design of their relationship was disrupted.

The consequences of the disruption are soon evident. When God confronts Adam about his disobedience, the man is no longer celebrating Eve's presence with him, but blames God for giving her to him, calling her "the woman you put here with me" (Gen. 3:12 NIV). When God confronted Eve, she blames the serpent for deceiving her. Neither of them takes responsibility for making a destructive choice, a choice they were free to make but that had consequences.

The entire sequence shows that freedom to choose does not necessarily mean freedom will be exercised wisely. In Genesis 3:16, the result is a battle and a rivalry between the man and woman in marriage. This text speaks of the husband dominating the wife. The Hebrew term here is *mashal*. It refers to a dominance in negative terms as part of a judgment oracle. The term can connote either a negative or positive tone depending on the context. For example, Genesis 37:8 involves a complaint by Joseph's brothers about Joseph's arrogant desire to control them, while Deuteronomy 15:6 is about Israel's rule over nations seen as an expression of God blessing the nation. The judgment context here in Genesis 3 points to the more negative sense of *mashal*, as everything else in the oracle also has pain and difficulty tied to it. The unity of the original creation with its mutual support has become a rivalry about power.

Something very subtle is also present in how the fall is portrayed; it is only when the team fails that the consequences come. Adam and Eve failed each other in their act of disobedience. Eve's act leads Adam into a bad choice, but Adam failed as well in not responding in line with the command God had given directly to him. As a result, the pattern God had designed to bring stability and support in a family led to devastating results for the entire creation. So strategic was the design of marriage that its brokenness spills over into creation at large, disrupting the very stewardship humans were created to exercise.

Non-monogamous marriage

The brokenness, then, does not stop with this failed start, but has permeated into every culture throughout human history. For example, consider the surprising amount of polygamy one sees in the Old Testament. This is clearly illustrated in the way Abraham, as the husband in a barren marriage, sought to provide for a descendant through another child bearer outside of Sarai, his wife. These events are almost described as a matter of fact and seem to have been cultural givens, especially since the scheme was Sarai's idea. However, though the activity was common, it is not an indication of the acceptability or advisability of such practices, nor did it imply God's sanction on the custom.

One can say that the consistent portrayal of such activity in Scripture is decidedly negative. The result of Abraham's effort to move outside of his marriage to provide for family descent through the slave Hagar led to intense jealousy and the emergence of a family line that yielded generational conflict. This is but the first of many such outcomes from an approach to life where multiple partners led to instability in the home and brought consequences of intense jealousy. The history of Solomon's many wives (1 Kings 11) is a paradigm for this broken model of marriage. Not only did Solomon follow these wives into idolatry, but his disobedience and unwise decisions resulted in God's choosing to divide the kingdom. The commandment not to covet another's wife is rooted in the sacredness and uniqueness of the singular male-female relationship (Ex. 20:17).

Faithful God and unfaithful people

The image of a faithful God married to His people is a picture pointing in the same direction (Ezek. 16:8). In the book of Hosea, the counterportrait of Israel as a bride unfaithful to her husband, the God of Israel, shows the image again of the consequences and pain that come from unions pursued without loyalty. The protection and support marriage was designed to offer, when broken or ignored, damages all who experience it.

By the time we come to the New Testament, references to marriage include the admonition to keep the marriage bed undefiled, which is a call to faithfulness in marriage (Heb. 13:4). From a mirror of the call of creation comes the importance of managing the household well, and a man who can do so as well as being the husband of only one wife becomes the example for selection of elders in the church (1 Tim. 3:1–5). Marriage is certainly not something to be forbidden, as some suggested; attempting to teach such a thing is seen as a departure from the faith (1 Tim. 4:1–4). Underlying these principles is the recognition that stable marriages lead to a more stable community, a healthy environment not only for children but for our neighbors and communities as well.

This is why divorce is so painful. It is the ripping up of something far more profound than a legal contract or social arrangement. It is the tearing apart of a relational fabric that had been sewn together into one flesh, now torn asunder with damage and fallout in all directions. The rupture of a marriage touches far more than the two people in it. No wonder marriage is lifted up in Scripture as a core relationship—it is because the institution of marriage does touch us relationally at our core. It prepares us for life in a world made up of men and women. It prepares us to steward well not just in terms of the things of life but with others relationally as well.

> God made man and woman. The first balance that was given was before sin entered into the relationship, a perfect balance of being one, spiritually, intellectually, and physically. All the imbalances have come as a result of sin upsetting the perfect balance. Anytime there is any "danger" (in Satan's way of looking at it) of anything having a possibility of being back in balance, Satan, of course, would strike out to destroy that balance.[5] —**Edith Schaeffer**

JESUS AND THE NEW TESTAMENT ON MARRIAGE

Causes for divorce

In parallel passages (Matt. 19:1–12; Mark 10:1–12) an issue is placed before Jesus for resolution as He is asked about divorce.[6] The question under consideration is whether it was lawful for a man to divorce his wife.

This was a matter for discussion because Deuteronomy 24:1 allows for divorce for something "unseemly." On the surface, the phrase appears vague. The Hebrew phrase *ervat davar* usually refers to some type of sexual impropriety, as the expression's use in other texts points to a range of issues from exposure of nakedness to adultery, even incest (Lev. 18:6–18; 20:11, 17, 20–21; Isa. 47:3; Ezek. 22:10; Hos. 2:10).

In Jesus' time, something "unseemly" had expanded among some Jews to include almost anything offensive a wife may have done. The more conservative rabbinic school of Shammai limited divorce to immorality, but the school of Hillel extended the list of acceptable reasons for divorce to things as innocuous as a poorly cooked meal (and later, Rabbi Akiva's teaching could even allow divorcing a woman for her loss of beauty). It is unclear if the separatist Qumran community took a view that prohibited divorce or only prohibited polygamy (Dead Sea Scrolls, Damascus Document 4:19–21—which in discussing Israel's faithfulness invokes the principle of one wife). When Jesus is asked this question, it is because a wide range of views existed, including a full array of options for divorce.

In addition, a situation had arisen that made the question especially pertinent. The ruler Herod had left his first wife to marry Herodias, the wife of another brother; and Herodias had also left her husband, so two divorces were part of the sequence of these events (Mark 6:18).

The divorce process stated that a man in Judaism would present the wife with a certificate of divorce saying she was free to find a new husband (Mishnah *Gittin* 9.1–4). The noted instruction in the Mishnah did not allow the husband to limit who the woman could remarry within the confines of the law.[7] Although on occasion, a woman could seek a divorce in Judaism, such circumstances were rare and usually involved women of high social status; or it occurred in a few communities that permitted it such as the Jewish Elephantine community. In Greco-Roman society anyone could get a divorce.[8] The ancient world, much like our world today, gave a wide open door for divorce.

Jesus' response goes back to the root issue of what marriage is. He states that divorce was permitted by Moses because of hardness of heart. In other words, divorce is undesirable. It is the product of a broken relationship and sin. Jesus goes back to the beginning and invokes the origin of marriage as the reference point for the question about divorce.

Purpose from creation

In His return to Genesis, Jesus' point is that the goal of marriage is not to enter into it with the hopes of getting out of it. He begins with the fact humans were created as male and female, an allusion to Genesis 1:27. He then cites Genesis 2:24, which instructs that a man leave his mother and father and cling to his wife and the two will become one flesh, a fresh unit connected to function together. The Greek term for clinging (*kolláō*) means to bind together or attach.[9] The implication is that here is a newly formed unit capable of contributing to creation, which may include producing and raising children. It is also here that Jesus makes it clear that marriage is designed to be between one man and one woman.

In a mysterious way this union is so intimate that two bodies become one entity, matched and paired up, together facing life's situations. This design is not merely a contract or an arrangement of convenience; it is a bonding of body, spirit, and soul, making a new entity out of two entities. That bringing together is sacred, not secular, as it is God who makes them one and sees them in a sense as one. The unit is a sacred one. This is why Jesus' remark that what God has put together should not be put asunder is the key part of His answer to the question. In marriage God forms a unit that is to exist, at least in its goal and design, until death breaks it apart. The Greek term for put together (*suzeugnumi*) refers to a yoking together, fusing to a unit something that was previously in parts.[10]

Jesus evokes creation here to show the core elements of what marriage is about. It is the bonding of male and female, not merely in a chosen relationship to take or leave, but as a unit designed for support and protection, one part of God's design for stewarding the creation. Marriage is to be the ideal place where children can be raised with a kind of mutual support and exposure to both genders, who are working in supportive cooperation.

In saying this about marriage, Scripture is not insisting that everyone be married. First Corinthians 7 makes it clear one can function as a steward in the creation and honor God while single, and this passage actually affirms that there are advantages to being single. Jesus Himself was unmarried yet noted that not everyone is prepared to be single (Matt. 19:1–12). Nor is this to argue that a couple is required to have children. It is simply that the family home with a mother and father is intended to produce an ideal environment for a child. The thrust of Jesus' reply in appealing to Genesis is about the design of marriage as a place where a male and female can experience a relationship that offers support. Jesus was saying that because God made humans into male and female from the beginning, a one-flesh union was also formed to provide a means of support for those contributing to the creation. That relationship was a part of the pinnacle of what God had created and needs to be honored in a way that fits its divine intention.

Mutuality in marriage

Mutuality in marriage is illustrated powerfully in a text that often is misunderstood with regard to its emphasis. The roles of husband and wife are described in Ephesians 5:22–33 and Colossians 3:18–19. Often when these texts are treated, it is the issue of power and authority between spouses that is highlighted. The text does raise this theme and teach it, but it also reshapes it. The husband is said to be the head of the wife and is called to love her. Wives are called to be submissive to their husbands as to the Lord. Several aspects of how this is said point to the fact that this is not primarily about power and authority in the way our culture often discusses it.

First, the Ephesians passage is framed by the discussion about being filled with the Spirit and being mutually submissive to one another (Eph. 5:16–21). The Colossians passage is similarly framed by wearing the clothes of character that reflect being part of the new man or new creation God brings to us when we come into relationship with Him (Col. 3:1–17). We see a relational mutuality in how we live that is highlighted in the framing that comes in Colossians; as Christians we live differently from those of the world. The last link in that character chain is love—compassion, kindness, meekness, patience, forbearance, and forgiving are also included for how each of us should carry ourselves (Col. 3:12–17). The love called for from husbands is to drink out of this deep, Spirit-shaped character well.

Second, Ephesians spends three-and-a-half verses on the response of the wife (Eph. 5:22–24, 33b) and eight-and-a-half verses on the role of the husband (Eph. 5:25–33a). More importantly, when the carrying out of male headship is described, the ideas tied to it are the example of Christ's love, His giving of Himself, how He presents her (the church) with splendor, loving her as His own body, cherishing her like His own flesh, and culminating in the citation of Genesis 2:24 where the unity of the couple is highlighted. So we see that headship involves caring for and serving one's wife in ways that lift her up and allow the couple to function as a unit. In this emphasis, Paul draws on the example of how Jesus described those who lead (Mark 10:35–45)—those who lead are to serve, not lord their position over others. In taking the time to describe how the husband should love as head in the home, Paul flips the way the world thinks of power and he describes a different kind of character, one that comes from being indwelt with the Holy Spirit. All this drives to the picture of the couple being one flesh, a team called to experience and steward life well together as man and woman.

THE MEANING OF MARRIAGE

A sacred bond

We have surveyed the definition of marriage in Scripture. We have seen that it is rooted deeply in the creation, coming as it does at the very start of the divine journey with human beings. It is even rooted in the gender differentiation that God provided for in the creation. The man and woman, male and female, were made in the image of God. In biblical terms, this lays the groundwork for marriage and the interdependence that comes from fusing this differentiation. This designed oneness of body, soul, and spirit is a part of what makes marriage a relationship unique from all others between individuals.

What we also saw in the Genesis text was the formation of a teamed relationship. Together a couple forms a shield of mutual support and protection in the midst of a call to steward the creation well. The man celebrated the arrival of the woman as a suitable complement to him. God provided the woman as a supportive completer of what the man brings to the creation. In that same differentiation and teamwork is provided an environment for children to grow, be nurtured, and flourish. A child, whether a son or daughter, gets to see both genders at work, side by side and mutually supportive. This is the design Genesis affirms for marriage.

Then came the fall. As we have discussed, because of the couple's choice to take the fruit of the tree God had forbidden, the mutual support of each member of the couple was let down in both directions. The woman became deceived and led the man into thinking they could be like God. The man, despite being the direct recipient of the command of God, also partook of the error. The consequences came not when one of them failed, but when both of them failed. The cooperation that was to come from either side was missing with devastating consequences. The couple decided to act autonomously from their relationship to God in light of the serpent's invitation to reject what God had called them to be, so in seeking to become what God alone is, their act was one not only of rebellion but idolatry.

Their action encapsulates many of the failures that plague humanity when life is pursued independently from God. This disruption led to the emergence of a rivalry between the man and the woman with blame for failure coming from each of them and direct responsibility being denied by both of them. The original design was disrupted and needed restoration.

Despite all this, Jesus affirmed the value of marriage and underscored its starting point. Jesus affirmed that divorce is an affront to what God does when He brings a couple together. It is the breaking not only of a vow between the two people but a sacred bond God creates. This is one of the reasons divorce is so painful. It tears at the soul of each partner and screams in a very public way the failure it represents. That is also what makes divorce so tragic and damaging, especially when children are in the mix.

Marriage is more than a mutually agreed upon arrangement between two people to be taken or left at one person's will. It is a sacred act, a bond involving three not two. It exists to help people carry out the divine call of being good stewards in a world that cries out to be managed well. A stable marriage has an important role in this calling, this mandate, a key piece in a much larger puzzle. Marriage was designed to be a foundation for the raising of children in a way that the child also could sense both a protection and the presence of people who care for their presence and livelihood.

Jesus also affirmed the nature of marriage as between a man and a woman. Consistently in Scripture, the idea of a same-sex union is never described in positive terms, not even in neutral tones, though we know that many today, motivated by a genuine desire for intimacy, are pursuing the sorts of relationships that are outside of God's design for human relationships. The church needs to be a rallying point for those caught in this tension that is part of our fallen world, a tension that stems from seeking unhealthy substitutes for marriage.[11] The brokenness we see in the world, even in heterosexual relationships, is also seen in a desire to go our own way in marital agreements. The "has God really said this" approach to the marital design issue or an approach that does not even care to consider the issues of design in marriage echoes the very kind of question the serpent raised in the garden.

The bond held together

The bond that is to hold a marriage together is of two strands. One strand involves recognition that a marriage is not merely a voluntary act of two people, but is a bond formed by and established by God. Of course, one of the reasons marriages struggle today is that many in the world never see the sacred dimension in marriage—marriage is considered to be the product of a merely human act, so therefore it should be subject to the whims and foibles of human life. A marriage relationship according to this worldview can be entered into or escaped from by the stroke of a pen. And for some couples, cohabitation is a way of experimenting before entering into a marriage to see if it will work for them. This placing of the toe in the water, so to speak, really cannot fully replicate the commitment and bonding God gives to a marriage and that marriage really requires.[12]

A second strand is a commitment to love and respect, something the passage in Ephesians raises. The powerful example of how Christ loves the church points to the selflessness and giving in marriage, traits that often are

God created man and woman directed to one another. God does not desire a history of individual human beings, but the history of the human community. However, God does not want a community that absorbs the individual into itself, but a community of human beings. In God's eyes, community and individual exist in the same moment and rest in one another.[13] **—Dietrich Bonhoeffer**

lacking. Simply thinking in terms of the other can serve as a corrective on the selfishness that impacts how we relate to each other. That selfishness produces the shrapnel that can damage a sense of union.

Oftentimes it is a loss of respect that eats away at the presence of love. This loss of respect, reinforced by actions, words, or a continuous combination of the two, leads a marriage to slowly die. The drift that sometimes causes someone to look to another outside the marriage loses sight of what created the original desire to bond. These pulls can come in many forms, but whatever their nature and origin, they represent a level of betrayal to original oaths given to each other and often made before God.

It is interesting that in Ephesians 5:32, Paul compares the bond of marriage to the relationship Christ has to His bride the church as a model for how the partners should relate to each other, with the call to the husband to love and to the wife to submit to and respect her husband. These roles also mirror to a degree the Trinity, where the Father directs and the Son mediates in a perfect partnership of communion and teamwork, where there is an efficiency of cooperation to make the creation function and salvation work. The genuine community in marriage is designed to show what relationships are built to be, a relationship made of diverse parts yet driving toward unity built on trust. That union is designed to reflect on and mirror both how the Trinity works as well as how Christ relates to the church.

The openness and unique nature of this relationship means that the intimacy of marriage is reserved to this one special person to whom a bonding before God has taken place. It means that nakedness involves no shame. One can be open and vulnerable because a bonding of heart, soul, passion, respect, and commitment has taken place. In the arms of this supportive relationship, a servant heart can drive each member of the couple as they mutually support each other.

OBSTACLES ON THE PATH TO MARITAL SUCCESS

A look at our modern world shows many obstacles to success in terms of marriage and its design. A lack of example, the wrong kinds of values, an excessive sense of shame, just plain selfishness, or an underappreciation of fidelity can destroy what marriage is designed to be.

That marriage has fallen on hard times is a reflection of the array of distractions that ask, "Has God really said?" The failure to appreciate what a marriage is divinely designed for and what its potential can be helps produce the off ramps from marital vows. Opting away from marriage leads to all kinds of side effects that impact not just the couple, but children and other family members. The results point to implications for all of us, not just the couple who is not married or who is divorced.

The observations in a chapter like this are not intended to be harsh, but instructive and descriptive. The pursuit of marriage is enhanced by an awareness of God's role in the marriage. It is made more secure by a complete commitment to mutual love and respect. Such a deep appreciation for marriage not only seeks to meet a divine design but also leads into a potential for human flourishing that the thin contemporary alternatives to marriage fail to provide. Scripture sets forth not a set of rules for life but a way of living, rooted in divine design, that leads to flourishing and aims at what is best for us. Such a lifestyle is beneficial to any person's personal and spiritual well-being and is also advantageous to a more stable society.

Love and respect set a tone for the resolution of conflict that does not result in resentment and a slow departure from relationship. Love and respect are a formula for marital recovery, looking to build out of and turn from momentary failure. In the context of a faith that exults in the role of mercy and forgiveness as seen in the example of Jesus, a platform is built from which human failure can recover from the common downfalls that frequently emerge in human relationships. An appreciation for what marriage is to be and how it benefits not just the couple but society can inspire us to become our better selves.

Especially in the context of human failure, an awareness of what Christian faith can supply by God's presence and the Spirit's power can bring an amazing reversal of direction. With God's ability to transform, one can pursue restoration and reconciliation. By following the divine example of service (Matthew 20:28 tells us that Jesus "did not come to be served, but to serve" NIV) and care, one can find ways to overcome the conflicts that inevitably creep into human relationships. We see where we fit when we embrace marriage as sacred. When we appreciate marriage as designed not just for our own lives but also for society at large, we understand that how we conduct ourselves in marriage extends far beyond our humble households. Still, the path to marital success is not easy.

Our culture's focus on what is good for me as an individual, with its sense of entitlement or an overwrought self-focus, gets in the way of building a bridge to the interdependence a marriage demands. What I get becomes more important and all-consuming, overshadowing what I can give. In a selfish society, the building of team can become challenging and the idea of self-sacrifice becomes counterintuitive.

Some people grow up without a good example to follow. Sociologists often chronicle the effects of children raised in broken homes or in contexts where they never knew a father and/or a mother.[14] In some families, a generational legacy of broken marriages is present, making it difficult for couples to assume the lifelong commitment that is God's design.

For others, a sense of shame about the body can undercut the giving that comes in intimacy, impairing one aspect of sharing that a marriage is designed to possess. When one or both partners has experienced abuse or trauma, the couple may need to seek help to overcome the damage. A person who has been seriously hurt may be more focused on an unhealthy notion of who they see themselves to be rather than on who they are and what they have to give and share. Being aware that one is with someone who cares about them as a whole person, someone with whom they are comfortable sharing the closeness of a unique relationship is a healthy step toward healing.

Our larger society's indifference to fidelity erodes the presence of examples that underscore what marriage can be and often is for many. The widespread portrayal of infidelity and access to it, which certainly is common in our world, in our arts and media, and a part of the reality of many lives, is rarely countered with anything but a "this is real life" feel. The inevitability of such constant images actually attacks the vision for a different kind of world and a different kind of marriage. Saying "it happens to everyone" dulls us to the impact of those regularly made choices.

CONCLUSION

The appeal of a look at marriage in Scripture is not a longing to go back to the good old days. The old days were not always so good either. Rather, it is a reminder that marriage was originally designed to be a safe haven for our children and for us. A stable home allows the creation to function better than the pieces of a dysfunctional world that emerges when families roam or get lost. Good homes in society come by one committed couple at a time.

That means that each couple needs to appreciate what marriage is as well as what it is for. They recall that truth is not just for their own sake but also for others, that their marriage is greater than the two people in it. It is an institution made by God and vowed before Him for a reason. God had in mind ultimate goals for our society as a whole when He designed marriage. It is at the very start of the human story because it matters for the human story. Regaining what has been lost and what is fallen is a core part of the biblical take on life and what God's design is all about. "Marriage is one" means God chose to allow us to steward our creation well. Because God knew what He was doing when He designed marriage, we do well to appreciate and follow that design. We are all served well when each of us in a marriage understands its uniqueness and the potential stability it gives to individual lives, society, and the creation. We do even better when that understanding is lived out with a partner and family who appreciate all that makes a marriage precious, special, and unique. A good marriage honors God and leads to a better, more stable world.

CONTINUING INSIGHT:

COHABITATION IN BIBLICAL AND THEOLOGICAL PERSPECTIVE

by David L. Woodall

Perhaps no other verse has been misused more than 1 Corinthians 6:12: "I have the right to do anything" (NIV). Anything? A history of the church could be written documenting the sinful actions that have been justified by citing the apparent freedom granted in this verse. The history begins with the Corinthians themselves. Modern translators place quotation marks around this saying to correctly identify it as a statement from the Corinthians (often called a "Corinthian slogan") articulating their erroneous theology. They justified two immoral actions based on this saying. First, a member of the church felt emboldened to cohabit with his stepmother in a sexually active relationship (1 Cor. 5:1),[1] and second, certain men in the church argued for the freedom to eat a cultic meal in an idol's temple and to be sexually active with the prostitutes provided as part of the after-dinner festivities (1 Cor. 6:15–17).[2]

A similar type of Corinthian error has invaded our culture today. In the spring of 1968, the *New York Times* revealed that a certain local college student was breaking the law.[3] Her behavior was illegal in New York and every state at the time, and her actions violated the ethical demands of the four-year liberal arts college where she attended. Her crime? She was living off campus with her boyfriend. The reporter was investigating a new cultural phenomenon that was birthed in the sexual revolution of the 1960s and fueled by the availability of contraception. Students called it "shacking up" or "the arrangement," but many Americans at the time called it simply "living in sin." Today we call it cohabitation—two unmarried members of the opposite sex living together in a sexually active relationship.

A 1968 *Life* magazine article suggested that a future anthropologist might consider this event as "a moment in which the morality of an era changed."[4]

And so it did. Today as many as 70 percent of first marriages among women aged 18–35 are preceded by cohabitation.[5] A 2016 Barna study revealed that the majority of Americans (65 percent) now believe that cohabitation before marriage is a good idea. Especially disturbing in this study is the conclusion that 41 percent of practicing Christians strongly or somewhat strongly agree that cohabitation is a good idea.[6] The Corinthian error, which justified sexual relations outside of marriage in the context of cohabitation, is being repeated. How should the church respond?

Paul's exhortation to the church in 1 Corinthians 5:2–13 outlines a proper response to a church member involved in cohabitation. The church first needs to repent of any pride (1 Cor. 5:2) and boasting (v. 6)—the type of attitude that looks the other way, caught up in the spirit of tolerance or the desire to not upset an influential member—and replace it with a period of mourning (v. 2). Our culture views cohabitation as a private matter between two individuals; Paul views it as an occasion for community grief.

The church must be fully convinced that cohabitation is an open rejection of biblical morality (vv. 3, 12–13)—an activity that impacts the entire church (v. 6) and should not be practiced by those who claim the name of Christ (vv. 9–11). The church should then intervene in the lives of cohabiting church members by exhorting them to turn from their cohabitation and reestablish purity.[7] The ultimate goal of the correction is the spiritual benefit that comes to individuals when their sinful tendency is changed into obedience (v. 5). If, however, the intervention fails (as it did in ancient Corinth), Paul repeatedly exhorts the church to no longer identify the unrepentant cohabitor as a member of the church (vv. 2, 4–5, 6–7, 11, 13). Christian lifestyle must match Christian confession.

Current research on cohabitation has also confirmed the practical benefits of living a biblical lifestyle. Cohabiting couples tend to have both difficulties within the cohabiting relationship and decreased marital stability after marriage.[8] The research is so conclusive concerning the negative impact of cohabitation that is has been labelled the "cohabitation effect." First Corinthians 5, therefore, unmasks the immorality of cohabitation and calls on the church to correct those who do not repent.

First Corinthians 6:12–20 identifies and reacts against the wrong Corinthian thinking that justified sexual relations outside of marriage. The main theological error centers around an incorrect view of the physical body. The Corinthians argued that what they did with their physical body was morally irrelevant. In addition to their general slogan in 1 Corinthians 6:12, they also claimed, "Food for the stomach and the stomach for food, and God will destroy them both" (v. 13a NIV). Their argument went something like this: the stomach has a craving for food, and food satisfies that craving. Likewise, the body has a craving for sexual relations, and a sexual relationship satisfies that craving. In both situations, a physical craving is satisfied apart from moral concerns. They also concluded that sexual relations are inconsequential because the body will ultimately be destroyed (v. 13b).[9]

Paul counters their wrong thinking with five arguments. First, any claim of freedom must always be limited by a concern for the benefit of others (v. 12).[10] The number one reason for entering cohabitation is to test compatibility for marriage, just like a person might test drive a car to see how it performs.[11] But human beings are created in the image of God with dignity and worth. They are not inanimate objects that can be discarded when no longer useful. The essence of marriage is an unconditional lifetime commitment to another person that transcends circumstances. Cohabitation is not marriage because, regardless of the level of commitment, it still lacks the permanence of a marriage commitment.

Second, the physical body is meant to be used for the benefit of the Lord, not for sexual freedom (v. 13). Third, the physical body is not destined for destruction; the physical body is destined for resurrection (v. 14). Fourth, the physical body of a Christian is joined to the Lord (vv. 15–17). This union means that sexual relationship must be compatible with the will of the Lord. Cohabitation, union with a prostitute, and any sexual relationship outside of marriage is a rejection of the lordship of Christ.

Finally, Paul summarizes his arguments by a single command—flee sexual immorality (v. 18a)—and by developing a Trinitarian theology: individual bodies are the dwelling place (temples) of the Holy Spirit (v. 19), purchased by the blood of Christ (v. 20a), and therefore must be used in a way that honors God (v. 20b).

Particularly instructive is Paul's quotation of Genesis 2:24 in 1 Corinthians 6:16. This reflects the biblical narrative of creation, fall, and redemption. The creation account identifies marriage as a permanent, public, committed relationship in which a male and a female establish a new family unit. The entrance of sin into the world gave birth to individualism and rebellion against the Creator and His design for marriage. Permanence was replaced with fleeting relationships; public declarations of intent were replaced by private encounters; covenant commitment was replaced by conditional arrangements; chastity in marriage was replaced with sex divorced from a permanent commitment.

Cohabitation is not marriage! Why is it wrong? The Genesis quotation gives us the reason: it has nothing to do with marriage and the creation of a never-ending covenant relationship with another person of the opposite sex. It is a willful rejection of God's plan for the creation of a family unit, in which sexual relations illustrate the complete oneness of a new and binding relationship. May the church seek to redeem this unbiblical trend by strengthening biblical marriage, rejecting cohabitation among church members, and developing a biblical view of the physical body.

CHAPTER 4

THE CHOICE AND HIGH CALLING OF MARRIAGE AND SINGLENESS

by Craig Blomberg

The American Psychological Association describes itself as "the leading scientific and professional organization representing psychology in the United States, with more than 115,700 researchers, educators, clinicians, consultants and students as its members."[1] Under the topic of marriage and divorce on their website, they adapt a statement from a major encyclopedia of psychology to begin their discussion with these observations:

> Marriage and divorce are both common experiences. In Western cultures, more than 90 percent of people marry by age 50. Healthy marriages are good for couples' mental and physical health. They are also good for children; growing up in a happy home protects children from mental, physical, educational and social problems. However, about 40 to 50 percent of married couples in the United States divorce. The divorce rate for subsequent marriages is even higher.[2]

The APA is a very secular organization. After these introductory comments in this article, the writers move immediately to how to make divorce as "healthy" as possible. So it is all the more telling that they recognize how valuable good marriages are for couples and their children alike.

Numerous sources decry the seeming parallels between statistics involving marriage and divorce among Christians and those from our society overall. But several years ago, Ron Sider observed that when one limits one's studies to theologically conservative evangelical Christians who consistently practice various spiritual disciplines, the percentage of marital breakups (and of numerous other compromises with worldly behavior) plummets.[3] Christian marriages today may face unprecedented challenges, but fidelity remains possible, and happy relationships can still be achieved. Much depends on couples' expectations and commitments. Are husbands and wives truly prepared to put others above self and to keep promises made for life, irrespective of those ever-so-transient feelings that are mistaken for true love?

Divorce, however, is just the tip of the iceberg in our culture's changed attitudes toward marriage. Not only do Christians turn a blind eye to those who have been divorced and remarried for reasons not even remotely linked to the genuinely exceptional situations in which the Bible permits these actions, but in many "evangelical" congregations, some couples live together as sexual partners without being married. Other Christians tolerate or even celebrate homosexual relationships, all the more so now that the Supreme Court has legalized same-sex marriage. The next development already unfolding outside the church is the normalization of polyamorous relationships—groups of men and women who agree to consensual sexual relationships, heterosexually or homosexually, within the group, but pledge not to have sex with others, thereby distinguishing the situation from simple promiscuity.[4] Some individuals, of course, know very well what the Bible teaches but choose to disobey it. Others, however, propose revisionist interpretations, believing that their behavior does not contradict Scripture after all. Still others are too unfamiliar with either the Bible's contents or competing interpretations even to know that there is a very good chance that God is quite displeased with their chosen lifestyles.

What does Scripture teach? More specifically, what does the New Testament teach? Christians must take both Old and New Testaments into account on any topic, but with the New Testament representing the fulfillment of the Old Testament, they cannot turn to Old Testament texts by themselves to determine God's will for their lives without asking how those texts have been fulfilled in Christ and therefore potentially to be applied differently today than before Christ came.[5] Readers of both testaments must similarly be alert for where culturally specific conditions colored first-century Scriptures in ways that make their applications today differ as well. But at least for the New Testament this is a more straightforward process of interpretation in that it does not first require assessing the relationships between the testaments.[6]

The traditional English-language wedding ceremony contains two clauses in it that summarize perhaps the two most important strands of New Testament teaching about marriage. First, it should "not be entered into unadvisedly or lightly." Second, it promises fidelity "till death do us part."[7] The first of these tends to get much less attention than the second, so it is important to address both themes. Both of them run contrary to today's secular "wisdom," which so easily infests the church. The rest of this chapter, therefore, unfolds each of these in more detail.

NOT TO BE ENTERED UNADVISEDLY: THE NEED FOR VALUING SINGLENESS AND CELIBACY

There are two sides to the church's historic emphasis on careful consideration before ever marrying. One is that even when God seems to intend for individuals to be married, they should consider carefully who they marry and how quickly. The second half of this chapter will return to this topic. Here we want to focus on what Roman Catholics have overemphasized, leading to a Protestant overreaction by underemphasis: the value of singleness and celibacy. Because some Christians in the early centuries of the church, drawing more on Greek philosophy than biblical teaching,[8] developed the idea that the highest levels of spirituality represented by their clergy and members of monastic orders occurred when people refrained from sexual relationships altogether, Protestants historically have undervalued the biblical teaching that God calls some people to a life of singleness and celibacy.

Too little reflection is devoted to the fact that the one, perfect, sinless man in the history of the world, Jesus of Nazareth, never married. When sexual desire is seen as itself sinful, this is understandable, but the Bible never teaches this ancient Greek notion. Adam, before the fall, was sinless as well, and yet God had declared that it was not good for him to be alone (Gen. 2:18). His initial relationship with Eve was both sexual and pure (v. 25). So why did God not exemplify the redemption of humanity by creating a second, sinless marriage? Of course, all kinds of complicating factors immediately rush in when one imagines God incarnate being married, which need not detain us here. The only point I wish to make is that Jesus, as a man who lived to be at least thirty-three years of age while remaining single and celibate, would have stood out dramatically in the Jewish culture of his day. Healthy young men were encouraged to take a wife by about the age of eighteen (Mishnah 'Abot 5.21). Not all marriages were arranged, but many were.[9] Do we ever imagine what it might have been like for Jesus trying to dissuade Mary and Joseph from seeking a bride for Him?

In this light, it is interesting to see how little is said about the spouses of any of Jesus' first followers. The only way we even know that Peter was mar-

> *For the sage says that parents provide goods and houses for their children, but a wife is given by God alone (Prov. 19:14), everyone according to his need, just as Eve was given to Adam by God alone. And true though it is that because of excessing lust of the flesh lighthearted youth pays scant attention to these matters, marriage is nevertheless a weighty matter in the sight of God.*[10] **—Martin Luther**

ried is because Jesus healed his mother-in-law (Mark 1:30)! Were the other disciples married? Odds are good that they were, but we hear nothing about it. Luke 18:29–30 may hint at it when Jesus declares, "no one who has left home or wife or brothers or sisters or parents or children for the sake of the kingdom of God will fail to receive many times as much in this age, and in the age to come eternal life."[11] As this quotation reminds us, however, just because the disciples had families didn't prevent Jesus from calling them to leave their wives and children for extended periods of time during the roughly three years of His ministry to go "on the road" with Him.

Elsewhere Jesus warns His followers that members of their own households may be divided against each other, especially when spiritual loyalties conflict (Matt. 10:35–36), and He insists, "If anyone comes to me and does not hate father and mother, wife and children, brothers and sisters—yes, even their own life—such a person cannot be my disciple" (Luke 14:26). Matthew's version reassures us that Jesus means that whoever loves family members more than Him is not worthy of Him (Matt. 10:37). The Greek and Hebrew words for "love" and "hate" in contexts like these can refer to "love more" and "love less,"[12] but the contrast remains jarring. One of the troubling realities of contemporary life is how many parents, including Christian parents, pressure their adult children to not move too far away from them, especially when grandchildren are involved, stifling the children's ability to follow God's lead to any part of the world, and this when technology gives us almost instant access to one another!

Other passages in the Gospels that relativize the importance of family relationships and traditional domestic arrangements include Luke 8:1–3 and 10:38–42. Imagine the potential scandal caused by a group of women, at least one of whom was married (Joanna—8:3), accompanying Jesus and the Twelve in their itinerant ministry, especially when they didn't always have supporters who would put them up for the night.[13] The pair of sisters, Mary and Martha, who lived with their brother Lazarus (John 11:2; 12:1–2), would have formed an unusual household for those days. We don't know if any of them were ever married, but apparently they were not during the years of Jesus' ministry. When Martha is preoccupied with domestic responsibilities, Mary adopts the traditional posture of the male disciples—sitting at Jesus' feet—in order to learn from him (10:39).[14] Jesus rebukes Martha and praises Mary (vv. 41–42) but the church has turned Martha more than Mary into the ideal role model for women in far too many settings ever since!

Mark 12:18–27 and parallel passages are usually avoided in Christian discussions about marriage vs. celibacy. There Jesus clarifies for the skeptical Sadducees, who did not believe in an afterlife, that the eternal state does indeed exist—"He is not the God of the dead, but of the living" (v. 27)—but will not include marriage and sex. Yet Jesus goes further and stresses that resurrection is embodied. Apparently, there are more wonderful pleasures in store for God's people than sexual release and even the exclusive interpersonal intimacy of marriage.[15] Whatever those pleasures are and whatever kinds of relationships we will have with other believers and with Christ Himself, who elsewhere calls us His bride (Rev. 19:7; 21:2, 9; 22:17), they will last forever, unlike the fleeting pleasures of even the longest and most wonderful marriage in this life. Single adults will not be able to complain that they missed out on anything!

Did Anna understand something of this? Luke tells us that "she had lived with her husband seven years after her marriage, and then was a widow until she was eighty-four" (Luke 2:36–37a).[16] As a very young widow, perhaps in her early twenties, she would have experienced considerable pressure in a traditional Jewish society to remarry. But Luke presents her, now in old age, as a long-standing model of piety, exercising a consistent ministry of prayer and worship in the temple precincts (vv. 37b–38). A very different kind of example, one who may well have repeatedly entered into marriage lightly or unadvisedly, is the Samaritan woman at the well, who has had five husbands and is now living with a man to whom she is not married (John 4:18). We do not know the circumstances that led to this tragic state of affairs; they may not have been entirely or even largely her fault.[17] But we do rejoice that with Jesus no one is beyond the pale when it comes to redemption.

Perhaps the most important passage in the Gospels that reminds us that not everyone should get married is Matthew 19:12. Here Jesus notes that there are three kinds of "eunuchs": those who were born with a deformity, those castrated or emasculated by others, and those who voluntarily choose a life of celibacy for the sake of undivided devotion to God's kingdom. Recent revisionist exegesis has tried to apply one or more of these categories to homosexuals,[18] but there is no genuine linguistic or cultural evidence to support such a link.[19] Even if some should emerge, it would not help the cause of those who want to justify endorsing homosexual acts because the whole point of the verse is to highlight that God calls some people to refrain from all sex. The point of Jesus' final comment in this passage—"the one who can accept this should accept it"—does not mean that Jesus' ethics are optional or that only some people are able to obey them. As the conclusion to verse 12, it refers back to the immediately preceding clause: whoever is able to live a single, and therefore, celibate life should do so.[20] The Voice clarifies by translating, "Anyone who can embrace that call should do so."[21] The converse does not logically follow—that a person who does not think they can live celibately is free to indulge outside of monogamous, heterosexual marriage. It just means they do not have to stay single if they get a chance to marry.

Paul elaborates on the decision between marriage and singleness in 1 Corinthians 7. This chapter has confused many readers before the growing consensus among contemporary scholarship to follow the oldest known commentary on 1 Corinthians (by Origen in about AD 200) and acknowledge verse 1b as a Corinthian slogan by a faction in the church in Corinth that was overly exalting celibacy.[22] Thus the CEB, CJB, ESV, HCSB, NAB, NET, and NIV all use quotation marks around the saying that the 2011 NIV translates as "It is good for a man not to have sexual relations with a woman." The Greek verb for "to have sexual relations" literally means "to touch," but touching in contexts like this was often a euphemism for sexual relations (just like "to know" in Hebrew could function similarly—Adam knew his wife, Eve, and children resulted!).[23]

All of 1 Corinthians 7 makes sense, then, as Paul's repeated "yes, but" approach to the pro-celibacy faction in Corinth.[24] The main point spans verses 1b–2. Paul can affirm the value of choosing celibacy but because so many people are already sinning sexually it is better for most people to marry or stay married and sexually active within the marriage.[25] He then applies this general principle to specific marital categories of couples. To those promoting celibacy within marriage, Paul says they may do so briefly, if both husband and wife agree and they do so to free up time for spiritual disciplines, but they must then come back together again sexually so that neither partner is tempted to look for sexual gratification with someone else (vv. 3–7). When he explains in verse 6—he says this "as a concession, not as a command"—as with Jesus that again does not make his instruction optional. Verse 7 clarifies: "I wish that all of you were as I am"—i.e., unmarried (see v. 8). But he understands that is unrealistic. His concession in verse 6, therefore, must refer to husband and wife coming back together again sexually—his last thought in verse 5.[26]

Our love has been anything but perfect and anything but static. Inevitably there have been times when one of us has outrun the other and has had to wait patiently for the other to catch up. There have been times when we have misunderstood each other, demanded too much of each other, been insensitive to the other's needs. I do not believe there is any marriage where this does not happen. The growth of love is not a straight line, but a series of hills and valleys. I suspect that in every good marriage there are times when love seems to be over. Sometimes these desert lines are simply the only way to the next oasis, which is far more lush and beautiful after the desert crossing than it could possibly have been without it.[27] **—Madeleine L'Engle**

Verses 8 and 9 address the *agamois* and *chērais*, literally to "the unmarried" and to "the widows." But Paul will address the never married beginning in verse 25, and a masculine form of *chēra* ("widow") was not used in koine Greek.[28] So it seems likely that Paul is using the masculine plural form of the "unmarried" to refer to widowers (see the NIV footnote). Because Paul identifies himself as someone who remains unmarried in this precise context, it may well be that he too is a widower. Advancing as far as he had in Judaism before his Damascus Road experience makes it very likely that he would have been married; only very rarely were rabbis, members of the Sanhedrin, or other Jewish leaders never married.[29] But, as a Christian, his values have changed. Marriage and family are not the virtual "be-all and end-all" of life as they were perceived to be by many within Judaism. He goes much further in supporting the pro-celibacy factions here by expressing his preference for widowers and widows not to remarry. But again he realizes he cannot absolutize this attitude.

Indeed, when faced in Ephesus with young widows who stir up trouble because they have not remarried and settled into family responsibilities, he encourages them to marry again (1 Tim. 5:11–14).[30]

In 1 Corinthians 7:10–16, Paul turns to those married who are contemplating divorce or have already divorced but not remarried. We will say more about these verses in the second half of this chapter, but for now the only point to note is what the pro-celibacy faction in Corinth would have said: in essence, "great—leave so you are not tempted to have more marital intimacy." Again, Paul allows this under one condition—if the partner who wants to leave is an unbeliever, the believing spouse is not bound to try to stop them at all costs (v. 15).[31] But otherwise Paul is clearly supporting the preservation of marriage.

Verses 17–24 form a kind of interlude in the chapter that may be summarized with the agricultural metaphor, "bloom where you are planted." In other words, don't feel you must change your marital status (or various other kinds of status also) just because you have become a believer.[32] Verses 25–35 then return exclusively to the issues raised by the pro-celibacy faction. To the never married—the "virgins" (v. 25)[33]—this faction would have urged perpetual abstinence, calling them to stay single and celibate throughout their lives. Once again, Paul can affirm that perspective up to a point. But he stresses that those who marry do not sin (v. 28). His reasons for supporting singleness, however, are quite different from those of the faction. They promote abstinence because they see the indulgence of bodily appetites as inherently sinful. Paul recognizes the advantages that singleness offers a person for undivided allegiance to Christ and His kingdom. The needs of a spouse, and children if present, even in the best of times can distract from wholehearted service to the Lord and the use of one's spiritual gifts (vv. 32–35). Some commentators have imagined that Paul would not have said these things to the church in Corinth in better days; after all, they were still not that many years removed from an empire-wide famine (Acts 11:28). Perhaps this is even what "the present crisis" in verse 26 is alluding to.[34] But in fact, Corinth was one of the wealthiest cities in Greece, able to rebound from such setbacks the fastest, and the actual reason Paul gives for his teaching is that "the time is short" (v. 29). Most likely, that is the "present crisis." Christ could return at any time.[35] That rationale is all the more true today as we are roughly two thousand years closer to the time of the second coming, whenever that should prove to be. So Paul's teaching remains as relevant as ever.

In verses 36–38 Paul finally considers the case of an engaged couple, wondering whether or not to go through with their marriage.[36] The pro-celibacy faction would have doubtless told them to be glad they had not finalized their vows, that they could still get out of this undesirable relationship that led to sex! For one last time, Paul agrees that it is possible to break an engagement if there is no resolve by both parties to move forward, but he steadfastly refuses to absolutize any call for the single life.

I am aware of the occasional pastor, youth worker, or other kind of Christian leader who properly stresses 1 Corinthians 7, especially verses 26–35, in instructing those contemplating marriage. A good way to phrase things is to ask someone, even while they are dating or courting a potential mate but before any kind of commitments have been made, "Is this someone with whom, if you were married, you would be able to serve God and use your spiritual gifts more effectively or less so?" But the majority of Christian ministries never couch things in these terms. Some even encourage Christians to marry considerably younger than they typically do today,[37] without acknowledging the widespread lack of maturity and availability of support systems that in other times and places in history made that more realistic.

In 1 Timothy Paul again has to address false teachers who are promoting celibacy as a moral absolute—forbidding people to marry (4:3a) as part of an ascetic agenda (vv. 1–4). Probably because Paul is writing Timothy directly and the church only more indirectly, he can use stronger words here than in 1 Corinthians.[38] He maintains that these ascetics are teaching doctrines of demons and have cauterized people's consciences (vv. 1–2). But this is not because Paul has suddenly changed his mind and is opposing all forms of restraint. It could be that the false teachers in Ephesus where Timothy was Paul's delegate (1:3) were insisting on abstinence from all sex and certain foods as requirements for salvation.[39] That would explain why Paul insists in 2:15a that "women [lit., "she"] will be saved through childbearing." Paul cannot mean individual women; he has already taught the Ephesians that salvation is by grace through faith, not any kind of good works (Eph. 2:8–9). Individual women will be saved "if they continue in faith, love and holiness with propriety" (1 Tim. 2:15b). But the gender as a whole must not capitulate to the call to stop marrying and bearing children. In other words, Paul may be countering the claim that salvation comes only through singleness![40]

Today's Christian singles repeatedly attest to feeling like second-class citizens in many evangelical churches. Preaching, adult Sunday school classes, small groups, and leadership roles of many kinds all seem to cater much more to the married. Unthinking peers, like older adults who are or have been married, regularly ask them why they are still single or how the quest for a partner is coming (whether or not they are looking for one)! There is next to no affirmation for any who might begin to wonder if God had called and gifted them for celibacy. Yet when we look at what a man like John Stott, the international Anglican statesman, was able to accomplish in his lifetime or what Lottie Moon, the indefatigable Southern Baptist missionary to China of a generation ago did in hers, both of whom believed they were called by God to remain unmarried, we see the wisdom in seeking out and encouraging young people to consider singleness as an honorable estate. Many other examples throughout church history could be cited as well.[41] I personally have single, celibate Christian friends of many different ages who attest to very fulfilling lives. They may be able to travel and minister in parts of the world that it would be next to impossible to bring a spouse or children into. They have the freedom to drop everything to meet hurting people's needs much more easily than others usually can. They have good small groups, supportive churches, and a cluster of close friends of both genders who meet their needs for fellowship in many different ways.

Marriage and sexual relations truly should not be entered into lightly or unadvisedly, no matter what our culture and even our Christian culture may say.

TILL DEATH DO US PART: THE NEED FOR LIFELONG COMMITMENTS AND PROMISE-KEEPING

When a couple does get married, they should move heaven and earth, so to speak, to stay married. If you can't trust someone to keep the most solemn and whole-life embracing promise they will ever make, how can you trust them to keep any other promises? This question sounds unbearably harsh but reveals just how out of sync our culture, and many of our churches, are with biblical teaching. We have fallen victim to Hollywood beyond our wildest imaginations. Try to envision someone in biblical cultures asking a young person, especially if his or her marriage was arranged by their parents, "are you in love with your fiancé(e) (or spouse)?" The result would probably resemble Golde's reaction to Tevye in *Fiddler on the Roof,* when he asks, "Do you love me?" and she exclaims, "Do I what?!" My wife and I were fortunate enough thirty-eight years ago to have a young pastor, guiding us through his first-ever premarital counseling sessions in preparation for his first wedding, whose initial question to each of us was, "why do you want to marry [the other one of us]?"[42] I had learned enough biblical teaching already by then to know I'd be in trouble if I simply answered, "because I'm in love with her." At best, he'd ask me to explain what true, Christian love was. At worst, he'd say, "Oh come on, Craig, you know that's not a good enough answer." In our young adults Monday night fellowship, as in our Sunday morning Bible class, he had stressed repeatedly that love was a commitment not an emotion.[43] If you can "fall" in love, you can fall out of it again! A promise to remain faithful for a lifetime cannot be based on feelings that come and go.

It is telling that arranged marriages in traditional societies have a far smaller divorce rate than marriages in modern Western cultures, including modern Western Christian cultures.[44] I am not advocating for a return to arranged marriages; I am a product of modernity as well, and quite happy with my selection of a wife! But I do sit up and take notice when a friend of mine who has spent his adult life with his wife as a missionary in a largely Islamic country and is raising four girls and one boy says completely seriously that he's glad he raised his girls in a moderate Islamic subculture rather than in America because the average dating experience of the Anglo young adult in the States is "practice for divorce"! In other words, relationships form and dissolve repeatedly in our Western culture, making it less difficult (even if usually still more painful) for marriages to break up as well.

The biblical foundations for marriage, of course, begin in the Old Testament, in the Genesis narrative, before the fall of the first couple into sin. Genesis 2:24 explains that "a man leaves his father and mother and is united to his wife, and they become one flesh." Both Jesus and Paul refer back to these foundations. Jesus does so in Mark 10:7–8, paralleled in Matthew 19:5, as justification for His command that no one should separate what God has joined together. In context, Jesus does not distinguish between certain marriages that God has joined together and others that He has not. Rather, He is arguing that because of the way God designed marriage as an institution, all marriages are intended to be preserved intact.[45]

With this Old Testament background established, we should not be surprised that New Testament vice lists regularly include *porneia* among those sins to be avoided (Matt. 15:19; Mark 7:21; 1 Cor. 6:13, 18; 2 Cor. 12:21; Gal. 5:19; Eph. 5:3; Col. 3:5; 1 Thess. 4:3; Rev. 9:21). *Porneia* was the broadest term for inappropriate sexual relations in the Greek language and included premarital sex, extramarital sex (which by itself could also be called *moicheia*—"adultery"), indecent exposure, homosexual sex, prostitution, polygamy, and bestiality; in short, any kind of sexual relations outside of monogamous, heterosexual marriage.[46] Contemporary English does not have any single word that embraces all of this; the King James Version "fornication" of Elizabethan English comes close but few people use that expression in common parlance.

Roman Catholicism has elevated marriage to the level of a sacrament, appropriate for the vast majority of humanity, even while stressing that a spiritually elite few can and should be celibate. Often John 2:1–12 is cited (as also in Protestant circles) as an example of Jesus blessing, dignifying, and even sanctifying a wedding ceremony. As a matter of fact, the text says nothing at all about Jesus doing something of this nature, only that He provided a large quantity of wine in miraculous fashion when the expected supply had prematurely run out.[47] We have to return to Mark 10:2–10 and Matthew 19:3–9 for His primary teaching on the topic.

The schools of the two major Pharisaic rabbis of the generation just before Jesus, Hillel and Shammai, debated the circumstances in which divorce was permitted. Both acknowledged that sexual infidelity required divorce and thus permitted remarriage, just as virtually every writer on the topic in the Greco-Roman world of the day did as well. In fact, in the ancient world, remarriage after divorce was expected.[48] But were there other permissible conditions as well? Hillel took a very liberal approach to the topic; Shammai a very conservative one. Intriguingly, both cited the same text from Deuteronomy 24:1—"If a man marries a woman who becomes displeasing to him because he finds something indecent about her, and he writes her a certificate of divorce, gives it to her and sends her from his house . . ." Hillel emphasized the Hebrew behind "something" and took it to mean just about anything that could be described as inappropriate or indecorous. Shammai, on the other hand, emphasized the Hebrew for "indecent," understanding it as limited to sexual immorality.[49]

Jesus cuts through all this casuistry. The Pharisees are trying to trap Him by getting Him to take sides in their debate so that someone will be upset with Him. In Mark He appears to make no allowance for divorce of any kind, but if the culture was all agreed on infidelity as the one legitimate justification for divorce, Mark's narrative may simply assume that understanding. Matthew, however, makes it explicit with what has come to be known as His "exception clause"—Matthew 19:9 (cf. also 5:32). But nowhere does Jesus mandate divorce. Even when the exclusive bonds of sexual intimacy have been broken, forgiveness and restoration remain the ideal. Permission to divorce is a concession to human sin, not an announcement of the divine will.

It is too easy, nevertheless, to spend all of one's time debating divorce in Jesus' teaching and miss the main point of His response to the Pharisees. God, from the beginning of the creation of human beings, intended for husbands and wives to stay together (Mark 10:6–9; Matt. 19:4–6). The time of the Law of Moses introduced a kind of parenthesis into God's plans for humanity, and God was more lenient with respect to divorce, because of people's hardheartedness (Mark 10:4–5; Matt. 19:7–8). But that was never God's permanent or ideal intention for humanity. While some Christians read these texts too carelessly and then appeal to hardheartedness as a reason for divorce today, Jesus is clear: that excuse ended with His coming, His death, resurrection, and sending of the Spirit at Pentecost, which together signaled the end of the period of the Law.[50] In many respects, the age of new creation returns to the original ideals of creation; in some cases it goes even further and anticipates the consummation of all things in the eternal state.

How does Jesus understand the commands of God to Adam and Eve? Mark 10:11–12 makes it plain that He is thinking reciprocally. What is permitted or prohibited for the man is the same as what is permitted or prohibited for the woman (cf. also throughout 1 Cor. 7). Both the Jewish and Greco-Roman worlds of Jesus' day had huge double standards that gave men all sorts of freedom to mistreat their spouses that women did not have.[51] Jesus banished these double standards. We may assume the same is true for Genesis 2:24. Of course, in days when extended families often lived together, the separation was not necessarily geographical.

It is better to stress that what in old-fashioned English was called "leaving and cleaving" denotes the transfer of one's most important human loyalty from parents to spouse.[52] "Becoming one flesh" then refers to the consummation of the marriage in sexual relations, but it is hardly limited to that. Everything that brings a man and a woman closer together—spiritually, emotionally, intellectually, socially—may come under its purview. The simple, old diagram still represents profound truths: if husband and wife are positioned at the two vertices on the base of an equilateral triangle and each makes a priority of moving closer to God, at the apex of the triangle, they will of necessity move closer to each other. Any claim that "God told me" to do something to my spouse that does not promote His revealed will and character, including repentance, forgiveness, reconciliation, and sanctification is a serious misunderstanding of God's will and communication. God does not command husbands and wives to do things that bring hostility, alienation, estrangement, or separation into a marriage.

If Matthew presents an "exception clause," 1 Corinthians 7 offers what has come to be known, somewhat strangely, as the "Pauline privilege." Many have thought that the key to this second exception to the general "no divorce" policy of the New Testament is that believers and unbelievers are "unequally yoked" (cf. 2 Cor. 6:14 ESV). This is no doubt true, but in light of Genesis 2:24 it may be that the key piece is the one spouse's desire to abandon the other with no intention of return. After all, if the two constituent elements of a marriage are transfer of interpersonal loyalty from parents to spouse and holistic intimacy, then abandonment ruptures the element of interpersonal loyalty, and sexual infidelity ruptures the exclusivity of the intimacy. So a Christian spouse who deserts his or her mate and marries someone else does not consign the abandoned individual to lifelong singleness. The mate who was abandoned is free to remarry, "only in the Lord" (just as with a widow; see 1 Cor. 7:39–40).

Again, however, there is no requirement that even a non-Christian and a Christian who are already married must separate. If the non-Christian is willing to continue living with the Christian, they are to stay together. The situation in Corinth was most likely where two non-Christians were already married and one converted but the other didn't. Paul recognizes spinoff blessings for the rest of the family if even just one parent is a believer (v. 14).[53] First Corinthians 7:16 is a notoriously difficult verse to translate because of a built-in ambiguity in the Greek syntax. It could mean, "how do you know if you will save your husband/ wife?" (a more negative rendering) or "for all you know you might save your husband/wife" (a more optimistic rendering). Either way, "the brother or the sister is not bound in such circumstances; God has called us to live in peace" (v. 15). The believing partner need not continue harassing the unbeliever to try to preserve the marriage when, after a period of time, it becomes clear that the unbeliever has no desire or intention of remaining in it.[54]

Are sexual infidelity and abandonment, then, the only legitimate grounds for divorce for a believer? If they are, then we have a very strange situation. Jesus is asked about a Pharisaic debate on divorce and acknowledges one and only one exception to the main point of staying in the marriage. Paul addresses a new situation of mixed marriages in Gentile communities that would not yet have been relevant to what Jesus would teach as a Jew before the establishment of the church. He, too, supplies one and only one exception to the main point of remaining married.

If either Jesus or Paul were intending to give a comprehensive list of exceptions, then one or both of them have contradicted the other and one or both of them have not acknowledged the other option! It is more likely that each was simply responding to the situation at hand without trying to offer a comprehensive treatment of the topic.[55] As a result, many Christians have added other exceptional circumstances when divorce could perhaps be justified: repeated physical abuse, prolonged addictions with no willingness to seek help to overcome them, life imprisonment without possibility of parole, irreversible mental illness, and so on.[56] Since the Bible does not explicitly address any of these situations, it seems better not to create lists of additional exceptions beforehand but adopt a case-by-case approach.

I have never heard any portion of 1 Corinthians 7 read at a wedding. Some parts of it no doubt have been used somewhere, but Paul's seemingly negative approach to marriage makes it natural for most people to avoid it in the context of a wedding ceremony. Part or all of Ephesians 5:21–33, however, is certainly one of the most frequently read passages at weddings. In the last century of evangelical preaching, a disproportionate amount of attention has been given to Paul's commands to the wife to submit to her husband and not nearly as much to the husband's responsibility to love his wife as Christ loved the church. When one studies the standard privileges granted to Jewish husbands and fathers and the enormously sweeping freedoms given the Roman paterfamilias, what stands out as countercultural in this passage are hardly the commands to the wives. No one would have batted an eye at them. What was radical, even shocking, was the picture of the self-giving love required of the husband, compared to Jesus giving up every privilege He had in order to die for the sins of the world.[57]

Of course, a husband cannot atone for the sins of his wife; only Jesus can do that. But apart from this one difference, the comparison Paul makes is simply stunning. Husbands must love their wives by giving themselves up, by doing that which will help their wives become more holy, in order to present them to God with as spotless and blameless a character as possible (vv. 25–27). Husbands must love their wives as they typically do their own bodies, caring for their various physical and mental needs (v. 28a). Paul is not considering the pathological masochist here but normal human behavior! In fact, when one sacrificially loves one's spouse, one is loving oneself because husband and wife have become one flesh (v. 28b).[58] More practically, if your spouse isn't happy, you aren't going to be happy either, so it is important to care for each other's needs. Philippians 2:3–4 generalizes from the marriage relationship to Christian friendships: "Do nothing out of selfish ambition or vain conceit. Rather, in humility value others above yourselves, not looking to your own interest but each of you to the interests of the others."[59]

Much has been argued in these biblical texts about privilege in marriage, but Paul is not speaking about privilege at all in these texts! He is speaking about responsibilities to sacrifice self for the sake of the other. If the husband has some unique role, it is to do what is in the best interest of his wife and to lay his desires aside if the two cannot come to agreement.[60] If the wife has some unique role, it is to submit herself to her husband. The last clause in verse 22 is cryptic, reading literally just "as to the Lord." The parallel passage in Colossians 3:18 sheds some light on Paul's probable meaning, with its expanded qualifier, "as is fitting in the Lord." Wives must never submit to their husbands (nor must Christians in general ever submit to human authorities) when they are asked to do something that contravenes God's expressed will. The numerous examples of civil disobedience throughout Scripture clearly demonstrate this—from the midwives in Moses's day refusing to kill Hebrew babies (Ex. 1:15–20), to Daniel refusing to worship Nebuchadnezzar (Dan. 4), to Peter and the apostles refusing to obey the Sanhedrin (Acts 5:29). No wife may ever take refuge in the kind of logic that alleges that if she simply obeys her husband in everything, God will judge the husband for any sins he commits but let the wife off the hook. The death of Sapphira for agreeing with her husband Ananias in lying about how much property they sold (Acts 5:8–10) clearly demonstrates that point.[61]

First Peter 3:1–7 is the last major passage on marriage that merits brief comment in our survey of New Testament teaching. This time the typically disproportionate amount of attention usually given to the wife's responsibilities can at least be partially justified by the fact that six of the seven verses are addressed to her. But verse 7 is a long and detailed verse of the husband's responsibilities and dare not be neglected. The passage begins envisioning what were no doubt common situations in the provinces to which 1 Peter was addressed (see 1:1), where the wife in a pagan marriage had become a believer but the husband hadn't.[62] The only explicit motive for submission in this passage is an evangelistic one (3:1). In a culture where women were expected to defer to their husbands in a broad range of contexts, Christianity would never commend itself to the unsaved by flaunting these expectations.

The main point in Peter's instruction to wives is actually not about submission at all. The dominant principle of verses 2–6 is that women should focus on a godly character rather than outward adornment to model true beauty. Some problems haven't changed in centuries and the problem is by no means limited to women! When Peter refers to Sarah as a model of the submission, and even obedience, of godly women of old to their husbands, he cites the only place in Genesis where she ever utters the word "master" (or "lord")—

Gen. 18:12—and that comes in the same context in which she is laughing at the idea of having a child in their old age.[63] The main thrust again lies not in the submission or the obedience but in the fact that she did "what was right" and did "not give way to fear" (v. 6b). The Greek says, cryptically, "do not fear their *ptoēsin*." *Ptoēsis* (the root form) can mean "terrifying, intimidation," or "fear, terror."[64] The Common English Bible may capture the sense with its rendering "and don't respond to their threats with fear." In other words, just as in Colossians, Peter is reminding wives not to be afraid of the ways in which a non-Christian husband can hurt them even if they remain faithful to Christ. But verse 9 also tells people to return evil with blessing, and enabling an abuser is not blessing them. Jesus Himself fled hostility every time He encountered it except at the very end when He knew He had to die by crucifixion. So no Christian wife (or husband) should ever subject themselves to repeated violence if they have the opportunity to escape it.[65]

With verse 7, however, Peter presumably is including Christian husbands in his purview, since only they would necessarily be present in the churches when his epistle was read out. The text is worth reproducing in full, since it receives comparatively paltry attention. "Husbands, in the same way be considerate as you live with your wives, and treat them with respect as the weaker partner and as heirs with you of the gracious gift of life, so that nothing will hinder your prayers." The New American Standard Bible is more literal in the early part of the verse with its translation, "live with your wives in an understanding way." Attempts to answer the question "understanding what?" probably overly narrow Peter's focus. Husbands should understand as much as possible about their wives to live as considerately as possible with them.[66] "The weaker partner" is literally "weaker vessel." A majority of commentators think Peter is focusing on the generalization that women in the ancient world were typically weaker physically than men. But except for the pampered lives of the tiny minority of wealthy women, the daily existence of most people, both men and women, in the ancient Mediterranean world was rugged enough to make this interpretation uncertain (cf. Prov. 31). Possibly more likely is the approach that understands the weakness to refer to greater vulnerability, now that Peter has commanded the wives to submit to their husbands.[67] Husbands must in no way take advantage of that gracious choice on the part of their wives.

More liberal scholars love to point out the various people throughout church history who have claimed women were ontologically or inherently inferior to men, and skeptics love to claim that such a view is inseparable from Christian and biblical teaching. But Genesis 1:27 unequivocally declares both man and woman to be created equally in God's image, which does not allow for any inherent superiority or inferiority. So, too, here, Peter stresses that husbands and wives are co-heirs of eternal life. There is not one whit of our eternal happiness that one gender can claim more than the other. In this life, therefore, husbands must respect and honor (from *aponemō*) their wives by their behavior. If they don't, their prayers may be hindered. Put bluntly, if husbands don't treat their wives with deference and respect, they dare not count on God to pay much attention to them when they are praying!

It is easy to look back over a long life and play down the hard times while magnifying the "glory days." As of this writing, my wife and I have been married over thirty-eight years. There has never been a time when I have seriously worried about her leaving me, nor to my knowledge one when she feared me leaving her. We have had some struggles, common to most intimate, long-term relationships, but I can honestly say that overall marriage has not been hard but rather very joyful and rewarding. Every five years a solid core of more than thirty men and women who formed part of the Campus Crusade for Christ chapter on my undergraduate campus gather, often with their spouses if they are married, for a reunion hosted by our former director and his wife at their home not far from our college. When we met in 2016 for our fortieth-year reunion, only three had been divorced. Everyone else who had married (which was most of them) was still married to their original partners. A few had struggled considerably, but many would have cited issues with grown children as far more challenging situations to deal with than issues with each other. Overall, virtually everyone said the Christian model for marriage was proper, fulfilling, and ultimately well worth it. And ours was the generation that pioneered the sexual revolution!

CONCLUSION

Marriage should not be entered into unadvisedly or lightly. Many people should not get married as quickly as they do; some who do marry should not have gotten married at all. Singles should be encouraged to pray seriously to see if God might be calling them to remain single, and celibate, for the sake of serving Christ and His kingdom more wholeheartedly. Even those who do marry are often not truly ready to consider marriage until they have become content with singleness as a fulfilling lifestyle. Otherwise, they tend to look to their spouse to make up for their own deficiencies, which rarely leads to a successful marriage. One has to be able to serve one's spouse, content with one's own identity and gifting. In marriage, as in other matters in life, it is better to give than to receive (Acts 20:35).

A God-pleasing marriage, then, is one in which the husband and wife are each dedicated to the other's well-being, and one that pledges "till death do us part" and remains faithful to that pledge. True, there are exceptional circumstances in which divorce and remarriage are permitted—in the cases of adultery or abandonment. Potentially, following a process of case-by-case discernment, there may be a very limited number of other situations as well. God's desire nevertheless remains that a husband and wife become each other's most intimate friends to whom they give more loyalty than they do to any other human being. And that requires a commitment to permanence and to consistently putting the other's interests above one's own. When a couple shares this commitment, no matter how often they fail, the result can be one of deep gratitude, contentment, joy, and security.

CONTINUING INSIGHT

KEYS TO PREMARITAL TRAINING

Greg Smalley

I've heard that after the age of eighteen, some of the best opportunities for people to come to Christ are during major life events—marriage, birth, and death. When people get married, have a child, or lose a loved one, they often tend to start thinking about faith. This is why helping engaged couples prepare for marriage can be one of the top producers of evangelism and is a great time to connect young families into the church.

Sadly, I've heard many leaders in our churches say, "Why bother? Younger engaged couples are too idealistic to truly benefit from premarital training—and they're absorbed in planning the big day. Or, if they're a blending couple, they're so focused on helping their children adjust that they're not thinking about their own relationship." These are valid concerns; however, I think one of the best reasons to work with engaged couples is to give them a great experience at your church, expose them to needed relational skills, and pair them with mentor couples. These experiences increase the likelihood that they'll reach out when they go through hard times as a couple, as they inevitably will—you're seeding the importance of marriage enrichment, and you're helping them build relationships with people who will walk with them through the highs and lows of marriage and life.

My wife, Erin, and I just celebrated our twenty-fifth wedding anniversary. One of our biggest regrets is that we didn't do more premarital training. I was arrogant at twenty-three. I thought that since I grew up in the home of well-known relationship expert Gary Smalley and was getting my master's degree in counseling, I knew it all, and we didn't need any preparation! Certainly, I reasoned, our marriage would be a cakewalk—the kind that would lead to people writing poems or songs about our love.

Boy, was I wrong! Honestly, we really struggled during the first three years of marriage because, among other things, we didn't have the right skills to manage our conflict—something that a good premarital program would have taught us. A few years ago, I actually found the assessment that we took in 1992—three months before our wedding. We laughed hysterically as the report "strongly suggested" that we would struggle working through conflict. This is why I'm so passionate about premarital training. It would have made a huge difference in the early years of our marriage because it works!

Research conclusively shows that couples who succeed gain the knowledge and skills they need before they settle into destructive patterns that often lead to divorce. In fact, you're 30 percent less likely to get divorced if you get some sort of premarital training before you marry.[1] Another study by marriage expert Dr. David Olson reports that 80 percent of the couples who did premarital training report higher marital satisfaction.[2]

So, what's the secret to a thriving premarital ministry? What kind of knowledge and skills are necessary for couples to learn?

SEVEN KEYS TO A GREAT PREMARITAL PROGRAM

Don't discourage your engaged couples

We often give newly engaged couples a confusing message. On one hand, we are excited and congratulate them. "I'm thrilled for you guys!" And then we decide that to be responsible we need to inject a sense of reality into their starry-eyed outlook by saying things like: *Marriage is really hard work. Things will change after you get married. The first year will be the most difficult.*

Worse, our culture constantly devalues marriage through subtle and not-so-subtle messages. Just do a simple online search for marriage jokes and see what pops up: "I love being married. It's so great to find that one special person you want to annoy for the rest of your life."

It's no wonder our young couples might feel ambivalent: "We're excited, but what have we done?"

Don't misunderstand me. We need to prepare couples for lifelong marriages, but we don't need to discourage them in the process. Keep your words uplifting and positive as you teach them the skills needed for a successful marriage. We don't want to send mixed messages about marriage. Instead of, "Sure, God has created something amazing, but once you walk down the aisle, you're about to go through the most miserable year of your life," say this: "Marriage is an amazing journey." Think about it. God created something so incredible that its value is hard to put into words. I wonder if this was what the apostle Paul meant when he wrote that marriage is a "profound mystery" (Eph. 5:31–32 NIV). It's almost unfathomable to fully grasp the mystery of how God designed a man and a woman to be joined together as one.

Marriage is not only a great mystery, but it's also a great adventure. Next to loving God with all your heart, soul, mind, and strength, your marriage will be the greatest adventure of your life. Throughout your journey, you will have incredible times together—countless moments filled with love, friendship, passion, laughter, safety, fun, unity, joy, and security. You will face hardships—times that you feel disappointed, hurt, sad, angry, disconnected, upset, frustrated, and lonely. Any journey will have highs and lows. But this is the beauty and the mystery of marriage. Embrace all that's true about marriage—the incredible times and the hardships. You will experience it all, and this is a great thing because God will use every season of your marriage to His glorification and for your benefit. That is the promise you can carry with you on your adventure together. God is always with you, and He is always fighting for your marriage.

When working with a church marriage ministry or when I'm doing a training with marriage mentors, I encourage them to tell their engaged couples not to let anyone dampen or crush their excitement. I want these couples to be thrilled with their choice. We need to cheer on their decision to get married and to buck the cultural trend that pulls for cohabitation over marriage.

Current research shows that the marriage rate in the US has hit a record low and many couples are choosing to live together and have children outside of marriage. According to the 2015 US Wedding Forecast from Demogràphic Intelligence, millennials in the next five years will have more of its members at a typical marrying age than any previous generation. But they are also less likely to tie the knot than their predecessors.[3]

Thus, we need to celebrate their choice to honor what God created and gifted to us. We need to send a very clear message to engaged couples:

> You're getting married! You're entering into one of the most sacred relationships ever created by God. He thinks so highly of marriage that He opens the Bible with a marriage. God uses marriage to describe His relationship with the Israelites and Christ's relationship with the church. And He ends the Bible with a wedding celebration.
>
> Marriage is not only a big deal, but it's an amazing thing as well. Sure, God will use your marriage to help you to become more like Christ. But don't lose sight of the amazing feeling of being married. There are well-meaning people who will try to beat you down and rob you of your excitement. They'll tell you how hard marriage is or toss out divorce statistics. Don't be disheartened. You get to write your own story regardless of what might have happened to the marriages of those close to you.
>
> Our culture will continue to devalue marriage, and many others will forgo marriage and choose instead to cohabitate. But this is not what God wants. His desire is that "Marriage should be honored by all" (Heb. 13:4). One of the greatest ways to honor your marriage is to remain overjoyed about your upcoming marriage. Don't let go of your dream for a lifelong, passionate marriage. You and your spouse go with God . . . that's a powerful force. We want to join you as well. We want to help you get the marriage you've always dreamed of.

Understand God's purpose for marriage

One way of helping couples guard their future marriage is to show them God's purpose for marriage. First, marriage was God's idea, not ours, and it is a lifelong covenant with Him. "What *God* has joined together, let no one separate" (Matt. 19:6 NIV, emphasis added).

Encourage couples to remove the word "divorce" from their vocabulary. When hard times hit, our only choice should be to press forward and get help. Retreat is easy when it's an option! Help them remember that marriage isn't always about individual gratification or the pursuit of happiness. In the excellent book *Sacred Marriage*, Gary Thomas poses this question: "What if God designed marriage to make us holy more than to make us happy?" Although marriage does bring great joy, the purpose in marriage isn't ultimately to make each other happy. God's true purpose is to mold each each of His children into the image of His Son.

And yes, God also created marriage for us to thoroughly enjoy. "May you rejoice in the wife of your youth. . . . may you ever be intoxicated with her love" (Prov. 5:18–19 NIV). God also unites couples to do together what they could never do alone. Thus, your marriage has to be about serving and blessing others—blessed to be a blessing. If you're living with confidence in the Lord, you will be a blessing to others. You will be "like trees planted along a riverbank, with roots that reach deep into the water. Such trees are not bothered by the heat or worried by long months of drought. Their leaves stay green, and they never stop producing fruit" (Jer. 17:8 NLT).

Manage conflict in healthy ways

Many couples avoid conflict like the plague, but we need to teach engaged couples that the sign of a healthy marriage is not the absence of conflict, but how couples manage their conflict when it comes—as it will. Research consistently shows that one of the best predictors for marital success is when couples work through their problems in a healthy way. Because many patterns of behavior are laid in the first year of marriage, it is especially important to address handling of disagreements in premarital preparation. We need to remind couples of James's advice: When troubles of any kind come your way, consider it an opportunity . . ." (1:2 NLT). Conflict is always an "opportunity"—an opportunity to learn something about yourself, your spouse, and your marriage. Thus, view conflict as a gift instead of something that should be eliminated or avoided. Conflict, when handled in a healthy manner, can be the doorway to intimacy and can actually strengthen a marriage.

Proactively invest in your marriage

One of the main factors people cite as a reason for their divorce is a slow fade. There wasn't an obvious problem—the couple's love simply grew cold as they grew apart. French author André Maurois wrote, "A successful marriage is an edifice that must be rebuilt every day." He was right on the mark. Marriage is a lifelong process that we must commit ourselves to again and again.

Love requires action. The key is to teach premarital couples the value of continuing to invest in their marriage and equipping them with practical ways to make daily investments in each other and their marriage. Pursuing a shared spiritual relationship, having sex often in a way that you both like, going on a weekly date night are ways to invest in marriage that reap great benefits. Advise your couples to commit to regular conversations when they talk about their inner life—feelings, likes, hopes and dreams—instead of merely administrating their relationship (discussing schedules, to-do lists, and finances).

Marriage expert David Mace wrote, "One of the great illusions of our time is that love is self-sustaining. It is not. Love must be fed and nurtured, constantly renewed. That demands ingenuity and consideration, but first and foremost, it demands time."

Protect Your Unity

I've heard that it takes the average couple about nine to fourteen years for the two to stop thinking about themselves as "individuals" and to start thinking about themselves as "one"—to go from "me" to "we." It shouldn't be surprising that the average length of a marriage that ends in divorce is eight years.[4] I imagine these divorcing couples never learned how to protect their oneness.

Our "oneness" is the superpower in marriage. God unites couples to do together what they could never do alone. When a couple is unified they can accomplish impossible feats. However, we have an adversary against us and against our marriage—our oneness will always be under attack (1 Peter 5:8). It's critical that we help our engaged couples learn to protect their unity. Encourage them to understand that they are not adversaries and should never think of themselves that way—because they are on the same team.

Commit to being a healthy individual

One of the stranger mathematical concepts to grasp is that two negatives make a positive. Honestly, to this day, I'm not even sure why this is true. But unlike in math, this same logic doesn't work within a marriage. One of the greatest truths that I've learned about relationships is that two unhealthy individuals will never make a healthy marriage. A successful marriage requires maturity; immaturity is why many marriages fail. Both people have to be committed to personal growth and development.

Single men and single women often ask me what are some vital character qualities needed for a great marriage. One of the most important is teachability. This is when a person is capable of being instructed, trained, and coached by God, a mentor, and their future spouse. God calls this process of personal refinement *sanctification*, or becoming like Christ. When we're in Christ, we "are being transformed into his image with ever-increasing glory, which comes from the Lord, who is the Spirit" (2 Cor. 3:18 NIV).

One of the greatest gifts we can ever give our spouse and marriage is a life-long commitment to pursue personal maturity. I know that I will never reach perfection in this life and that I will always be dealing with my faults and sin nature. But I will continue to press forward and pursue Christlikeness: "So that we may no longer be children, tossed to and fro by the waves and carried about by every wind of doctrine, by human cunning, by craftiness in deceitful schemes. Rather, speaking the truth in love, we are to grow up in every way into him who is the head, into Christ . . ." (Eph. 4:14–15 ESV).

As my wife and I recently celebrated a milestone anniversary, one of the lines that I wrote in my card to Erin was, "Thank you for faithfully standing by my side as God continues to refine me." You see, part of our marriage story is how God continuously upgrades us as individuals and how He uses this maturing process to strengthen our marriage. At the same time, God uses our marriage to grow each of us as well. I love how King Solomon so eloquently put it: "Two people are better off than one, for they can help each other succeed" (Eccl. 4:9 NLT).

It takes a village . . . to keep a marriage strong!

One of the greatest truths I've learned is that it takes a "village to keep a marriage strong." Even the healthiest relationships go through conflict, disappointment, temptation, and difficult times. And it's in these dark moments or painful seasons that Satan will do everything within his power to isolate you and keep you suffering alone. But a "cord of three strands is not quickly broken" (Eccl. 4:12 NIV). We need community when our marriage is tested.

This is the moment that our loved ones, who vowed to support and fight for our marriage, can make the difference between relationship life and death. Thus, we need to help premarital couples be intentional about regularly connecting with other like-minded couples, both those who are around the same age and those who are more seasoned, further down the road than they are. This community involves both give and take. Spouses who share a healthy, vibrant relationship rely on their support system, but they also recognize that they have a responsibility to help other couples thrive—"as iron sharpens iron" (Prov. 27:17).

These seven points are key to include in your premarital program. Other important topics a good premarital program should include:

- How to "leave and cleave"
- Dealing with family-of-origin issues
- Finances and budgeting
- Creating realistic expectations
- Understanding biblical roles in marriage

Ideally, premarital training should be broken into a ten-session format lasting one to two hours long (research suggests that eight to ten hours total is the ideal). This could be accomplished by using both an individual and group (five couples at the most) format. The training should also include an assessment.[5]

As you equip premarital couples, you are investing in their future marriage and the future of your congregation. The benefits are endless.

"Therefore a man shall leave his father and his mother and hold fast to his wife, and they shall become one flesh" (Gen. 2:24 ESV). Wise words and words of great joy.

DESCRIPTION

CHAPTER 5

THE LANGUAGE OF "EMBODIED" DIFFERENCES IN MARRIAGE

by Gregg R. Allison and Jason E. Kanz

One of the most beautiful aspects of life in general, and of marriage in particular, is its physicality. Affirming and living this truth, however, has not always been easy for the church, as it has perennially wrestled with the negative influence of gnosticism. This heresy features, among many tenets, the belief that "spiritual realities are inherently good, while physical realities are inherently evil."[1] Consequently, gnosticism dismisses or denigrates the material world. An example of such deprecation of physicality is this ditty from C. S. Lewis: "The fact that we have bodies is the oldest joke there is."[2]

At the same time, the church has acknowledged and defended the goodness of the physical. Even as the early church fought against the blight of gnosticism, it affirmed God's good physical creation, human embodiment, the incarnation of the Son of God, His future physical return, the resurrection of the body, and the physical new heaven and new earth. Still, to affirm physicality while suffering gnostic influences has been quite a challenge.

Responding to this challenge, this chapter will affirm the goodness of physicality, particularly as that involves human relationships, because God designed human existence to be an embodied reality. Support for this thesis will be offered from theology and neuropsychology.

CREATION

The opening chapter of Scripture narrates the wonder of God's creation of "the heavens and the earth" (Gen. 1:1).[3] The eternal, immaterial God created a temporal, material world consisting of oceans and mountains, plants and animals, and human beings. The goodness of the original creation emerged progressively: six times, God assessed His handiwork and pronounced it "good" (Gen. 1:4, 10, 12, 18, 21, 25). Then, for the seventh time, after His creation was complete, He declared it "very good" (v. 31).

At the apex of this physical world was God's creation of human beings. Indeed, every preceding divine act of creation seemed to be in anticipation of, and in preparation for, this climactic moment. Following a divine deliberation—"Let us make man in our image, after our likeness" (Gen. 1:26)—God actualized His plan: "So God created man in his own image, in the image of God he created him; male and female he created them" (Gen. 1:27). Though much debate surrounds the nature of the divine image—it is some attribute like rationality, or it is the activity of exercising dominion, or it is relationality—what emerged from this creative act were physical creatures: human beings are divine image bearers, physical creatures in this physical world.

In the process of creating humans in His image, God's attention to detail was exquisite and multilayered. Not only was it necessary for Him to create the physics of the entire universe, He also paid considerable attention to the biochemistry, anatomical differences, and hormonal variability between men and women. To bear the image of God, then, appears not to be simply one thing. It involves the integration of multiple streams. With specific attention to existing as physical creatures in a physical world, it is evident that God paid careful attention to matters of physics, chemistry, biology, endocrinology (hormone systems), and psychology.

EMBODIMENT

The physicality of human existence is underscored in the complementary biblical account of the creation of the first man and the first woman (Gen. 2:7, 18–25). God formed the first human being, a man, "of dust from the ground": the material element of human nature. Into this "lump of clay," as Martin Luther called it, God personally breathed "the breath of life": not a soul or a spirit, but the energizing principle that enlivens all living creatures (Gen. 1:31; 7:22).[4] Accordingly, "the man became a living creature": Adam, who was embodied. Though the narrative presents the man as created from dust of the ground, his physicality is not maligned. Rather, this dusty beginning underscores that the man was no angelic or divine being; he was not a heavenly being cast down to the earth for punishment or rehabilitation. Rather, he was an earthy creature whose creation wholly depended on his Creator's free decision to create him, and his continued existence depended on God's sustaining work to keep him in existence. But this image of dust in no way dismisses or denigrates the man's physical aspect.

God then created the second human being by taking one of Adam's ribs and forming a woman: Eve, who was embodied. The beauty of her physicality was underscored in Adam's joyful exclamation: "This at last is bone of my bones and flesh of my flesh" (Gen. 2:23). Moreover, the wonder of the physicality of the marital relationship between this man and this woman is highlighted in this marriage principle: "Therefore a man shall leave his father and his mother and hold fast to his wife, and they shall become one flesh" (Gen. 2:24). Certainly, marriage is more than the couple's physical relationship, but Scripture emphasizes the union between husband and wife as they engage in sexual intercourse: through that physical act, the two become one.[5] That this physical union is the key point of this marriage principle, and that the physical act itself is good, is underscored in the conclusion of the Genesis 2 narrative: "And the man and his wife were both naked and were not ashamed" (Gen. 2:25). The human physical relationship is good.

Accordingly, the divine design for human beings created in the image of

For reasons known only to Himself, God honored man above all other beings by creating him in His own image. And let it be understood that the divine image in man is not a poetic fancy, not an idea born of religious longing. It is a solid theological fact, taught plainly throughout the Sacred Scriptures and recognized by the Church as a truth necessary to a right understanding of the Christian faith. . . . The fact of God is necessary to the fact of man. Think God away and man has no ground of existence. . . . Man for all his genius is but an echo of the original Voice, a reflection of the uncreated Light. . . . everything that exists is dependent upon the continuing creative impulse.[6] **—A. W. Tozer**

God is embodiment: the normal and good state of human existence is that of embodiment. Furthermore, the divine design for married people is a physical relationship, which is good.

As we know, creation as embodied image bearers is not restricted to the first human beings, but is true of all human beings since then. Human physicality is both a divine reality, as God superintends the in utero process of individual human development (Ps. 139:13–16), and a genetic/hormonal/physical reality, explainable scientifically. Indeed, in the creation of His image bearers, God specifically attended to the physical developmental process of each person. The twenty-three chromosomes present in each cell in the human body contain deoxyribonucleic acid (DNA), which holds the specific genetic blueprint for each person. The human genetic code is evidence of God's attention to detail. Though each person's genetic sequence contains over three billion bits of information, the total amount of variability in the genetic material between people is infinitesimally small (about $1/1000^7$). In other words, from a genetic perspective, image bearers are strikingly similar to one another (and quite different from other species). Humans are genetically unique, yet despite the high degree of genetic overlap, what appears to be a low level of variability accounts for much of the great diversity seen between humans.

Each person then, within their DNA, contains the genetic material that makes one not just uniquely human, but individually unique. During the physical act of procreation, a man's sperm, which contains his genetic material, joins with a woman's egg, which contains her genetic material. However, it is important to note that each individual sperm and egg contains not the full genetic material, but shuffled combinations, allowing for each child's uniqueness. The fertilized egg contains all the information that makes her or him unique and human.

Each child undergoes roughly the same developmental process in utero.[8] The original fertilized egg, containing twenty-three chromosomes from the father and twenty-three chromosomes from the mother, begins to divide. One cell becomes two, two become four, four become eight, and so on. Early in fetal development, cell differentiation begins to occur; inner and outer layers develop. By about three weeks, most organ systems begin to develop.

Just as God saw fit to create Adam and Eve with obvious sexual differences (Gen. 1:27), He also embedded a process for prenatal sexual differentiation into the human genetic code. The only difference at fertilization is whether the DNA mixture received from the parents contains two XXs or an X and a Y on Chromosome 23. The child's mother always contributes an X chromosome to the pair, whereas the father may contribute either an X or a Y chromosome. In other words, a child's sex is determined by the father.

The physical development of the embryo proceeds identically through about the seventh week of gestation when the structures that will become either male or female sex organs, which began to form around week four, begin to change.[9] If a Y chromosome is present, it typically contains a gene labeled SRY, which stands for "sex determining region, Y chromosome."[10] This gene directs the formation of the male gonads (testes); in its absence, ovaries form. Dependent upon what genetic program begins, a cascade of changes occurs. In males, not only do the testes begin to form, but instructions are sent to further differentiate anatomical and hormonal development. With males, increased testosterone production occurs, which in conjunction with the genetic program, forms the penis. For females, increased estrogen leads to the development of the female genitalia and sexual organs including the vagina and uterus (i.e., womb).

Prior to differentiation, all embryos contain two different types of ducts, Müellerian and Wolffian, which ultimately become the male and female sex organs. Interestingly, the genetic coding shuts off the Müellerian ducts in males and the Wolffian ducts in females.[11] The development of the gonads leads to production of sex hormones, primarily testosterone—dominant in males—and estrogen—dominant in females, which further facilitates the development of dimorphic sexual characteristics.

These changes that begin during the first trimester continue through pregnancy and are evident at birth. On average, boys are larger than girls at birth, evidenced as early as eight weeks.[12] The size discrepancy persists throughout life, becoming especially evident after puberty when secondary sex characteristics form, further differentiating boys and girls, preparing them for, among other things, procreation, which will be discussed below. However, it is worth mentioning that these biologic and hormonal differentiations become increasingly evident as children as young as three to four years of age begin to identify with their assigned sex, which for most people remains relatively stable throughout their lives.

The human brain, the primary relational organ, also begins to develop early. The nervous system begins simply, initially consisting of three fluid-filled sacs or vesicles that continue to differentiate and increase in complexity throughout prenatal development. Eventually, these three vesicles reveal the marvelous intricacy of design, becoming the different regions of the brain, which

121

allow the body to function and a person to receive information from and act upon the universe.[13]

Even to the untrained eye, it is clear that the human capacity for thought, emotion, and relationship differs from other animals, even other mammals. The human brain is thinking, feeling, and relating on a much deeper level than anywhere else in the animal kingdom. One of the primary ways in which people are unique is their capacity for relational perspective-taking, or attunement. People are able to put themselves into another's shoes, to imagine what another is thinking and feeling, which increases the sense of connectedness. In healthy environments, children and parents engage in mutually reinforcing activities, for example, eye contact and smiling, that strengthen relational ties, promoting healthy attachments.

Neurologically, human brains—specifically, brain cells, called neurons—are designed to facilitate interpersonal relationships. One type of these neurons is commonly known as mirror neurons. Mirror neurons are unique in that they activate, or fire, both when we engage in a behavior and when we observe another engaging in that behavior.[14] As an example, a mirror neuron may fire both when someone uses a fork and when someone is observed using a fork. It is hypothesized that these neurons help foster interpersonal connection and empathy, supporting the notion that even our capacity for relationship has a component related to embodiment.

A second type of cell in the human brain involved in relationship is called a von Economo neuron.[15] They are hypothesized to be involved in a highly integrative process, helping to bring together information about states of thought and bodily sensations, which are commonly associated with emotion. This integration of bodily states with perception and thought is essential to navigating personal and social environments. For example, the response to someone jumping out from hiding and yelling will vary depending upon whether it is related to a crime or a surprise birthday party. Von Economo neurons help to integrate all of the information to guide social behavior and relationship.

Both mirror neurons and von Economo neurons appear to reflect God's plan for the physical body, and especially the brain, to be relational. Although these cells are found in some mammals such as the great apes, the number and proportion in humans seems to be uniquely designed to foster relational connection. In His sovereignty, God not only created these physical structures but carefully attends to their growth and proliferation as well.

EMPLACEMENT

The divine image bearers were created as physical beings to live in a physical creation. Indeed, after forming the first man from the dust of the ground and creating him in the divine image, "the Lord God planted a garden in Eden, in the east, and there he put the man whom he had formed" (Gen. 2:8). Thus, the site of the first humans' emplacement was a garden, which was no mere utilitarian facility. On the contrary, it contained "every tree that is pleasant to the sight and good for food. The tree of life was in the midst of the garden, and the tree of the knowledge of good and evil" (Gen. 2:9). This Edenic location provided beautiful physical sustenance for physical life (the fruit of the trees) as well as beautiful physical sustenance for eternal life (the fruit of the tree of life). It featured another tree with beautiful fruit—the tree of the knowledge of good and evil—the eating of which was prohibited on pain of death. Moreover, from that garden coursed four life-giving rivers, one of which "flowed around the whole land of Havilah, where there is gold. And the gold of that land is good; bdellium and onyx stone are there" (Gen. 2:11–12). Eden, its garden, and its surrounding environs were beautiful. In that garden God dwelt with His image bearers, and the three enjoyed a full and open relationship. Human emplacement was a wonderful physical blessing.

God not only designed the human brain to follow a specific pattern of development, guided in part by genetic variables, but also to respond to environmental stimuli. The brain is not simply guided by nature, but also by nurture; not only by genes, but also by setting. It is probable that God's original creation, Eden, which He called "very good," was the ideal setting for optimal development of brain, mind, and relationship, what interpersonal neurobiologist Daniel Siegel calls "the triangle of well-being."[16] It was ideal for relational formation, neuronal development, and consciousness.

Scientific evidence continues to demonstrate the importance of place. In general, a mother's womb is the idyllic location for a developing child. In ideal circumstances, it provides safety, nourishment, and stability. Because of the unvarying proximity to the mother, the child is also placed in such a way that they are already developing important relational attachments. The baby responds to the mother's rhythms and begins to recognize her voice as well as the voices of those who are in the immediate vicinity, for example, the father. Even before birth, the baby exists within a certain place, primarily the womb, and secondarily wherever the mother lives.

According to the World Health Organization,[17] there are numerous environmental determinants of health. Access to clean water, food in sufficient amount and variability, clean air, shelter, and sufficient space to move about are all beneficial in terms of well-being. Given that God described the garden as "very good," it is safe to assume that there was access to all that was required from the place.

Yet, optimal human flourishing cannot take place apart from relationship. God placed Adam and Eve in relationship with creation, with one another, and with Himself. In Genesis 2:18, God said, "It is not good that the man should be alone." So it is important to think of emplacement not only in terms of physical location (i.e., map coordinates) but also relational location.

Several decades of psychological research have demonstrated the importance of human attachment. Optimal functioning presumes stable, nurturing relationships, especially early in life. How a parent responds to a young child has significant implications for how that child will enter future relationships, even well into adulthood. According to Daniel Siegel, "the pattern of secure attachment enables the child to go out into the world and reach her full potential, engage with others in meaningful ways, and be able to regulate her emotions well so that life is full and in equilibrium."[18] The effect of these early relationships cannot be underestimated, not only with regard to future relationships, but toward engaging with the world at large. Secure attachment allows one to flourish in physical, relational, and emotional environments.

MARRIAGE AND PROCREATION

God gave a charge to His created image bearers: "Be fruitful and multiply and fill the earth and subdue it, and have dominion over the fish of the sea and over the birds of the heavens and over every living thing that moves on the earth" (Gen. 1:28). Often called the "cultural mandate," this God-given responsibility involves the building of civilization, with a focus on two elements: procreation and vocation.

The aspect of procreation is expressed in the command "be fruitful and multiply and fill the earth." This element means that the majority of men and women will be married, and the majority of those married couples will have children. This physical reproduction mandated for husbands and wives leads to the multiplication of other human beings who are divine image bearers. The initial fulfillment of this mandate is narrated in due course: "Now Adam knew Eve his wife, and she conceived and bore Cain, saying, 'I have gotten a man with the help of the LORD.' And again, she bore his brother Abel" (Gen.

4:1–2). The genealogies listed in Genesis confirm the ongoing fulfillment of physical reproduction, as the phrase "and so-and-so fathered so-and-so" is often repeated (e.g., Gen. 5). While a growing number of contemporary men and women mock the idea of genderedness, heterosexual marriage, and child-raising, Frederica Mathewes-Green humorously rebukes us:

> For large segments of the world, gender differences are pleasant, appealing, and enjoyable, and practical application of theory—reproduction itself—is hardly a chore. (The subtitle of a Dave Barry book put it winningly: "How to make a tiny person in only nine months, with tools you probably have around the home.") Yes, most cultures note and highlight gender differences, because most people find them delightful, as well as useful in producing the next generation.[19]

Procreation is a divinely designed and mandated responsibility, and its fulfillment is filled with joy.

Though the early chapters of Genesis convince us theologically of God's procreative mandate, there is clear evidence of biological design as well. First, and most obviously, the anatomical differences between men and women are striking, yet mutually compatible. God paid exquisite attention to the physical expression of the procreative relationship between men and women. Looking at the wider creation, it is certainly conceivable that God could have ordained a different method for propagation of humankind. It surely would not be outside of His power to speak each individual into existence with no involvement of man or woman; each new person could simply pop into being. Each new person could also be derivative of a single parent. Like mushrooms, offspring could grow simply by a parent sluffing off spores. Nevertheless, God chose a more physical, more intimate approach to reproduction, evident first and most obviously in anatomical differences.

However, differences between men and women extend beyond gross anatomy. There are also significant hormonal differences, which is the purview of the field of endocrinology. Both men and women produce each of the primary sex hormones, most commonly testosterone and estrogen, though certainly in different proportions. Testosterone is commonly conceived as the primary male hormone. Throughout the lifespan, testosterone levels vary considerably. As a young man enters puberty, his levels of testosterone increase dramatically. These increases in testosterone are associated with significant physical changes and the development of secondary sex characteristics. Relationally, testosterone also has a significant impact. A man's exposure to a woman,[20] and especially to a woman who is ovulating,[21] results in significant increases in testosterone. Interestingly, development of deeper romantic bonds often results in lower testosterone levels in men but increased testosterone levels in women.[22] Because testosterone appears to contribute significantly to the human sex drive, the reduction in men may serve to facilitate relational stability, while the increase in women intensifies their sexual arousal, which may also serve the stability of the relationship.

In women, the primary sex hormone is estrogen. Like testosterone for men,

Now we know. Love is not a happening, but a discipline. It only grows by feeding on constant attention and effort. There have been times in the decades past that I wondered—even doubted—that I loved you. But doubt is not a sin in loving. Arrogance is the grand transgression, but arrogance presumes, and presumption loses all. Love is a pilgrimage, and pilgrimages have many destinations.[23] —**Calvin Miller**

the increase in estrogen levels contributes significantly to the development of secondary sex characteristics. Additionally, it appears to have a significant role in the promotion and maintenance of relationship. As we mentioned above, the sex drive of men and women appears to be tied to testosterone, though for women, estrogen is required for the testosterone to "work." In men, higher levels of estrogen were found in fathers when compared with nonfathers, again arguing for relational stability, given that estrogen appears to be important in preservation of relationship.[24]

A third hormone bears mentioning: oxytocin. Oxytocin is produced in the hypothalamus, a small brain structure in both men and women. It is important because it helps facilitate relational bonding and interpersonal trust. Increases in oxytocin are typically seen in the context of monogamous relationships.[25] When a man and a woman are engaged sexually with each other, there is a mutual increase in oxytocin[26] that facilitates romantic bonding, supporting the idea that there is no such thing as a casual sexual encounter.

It is clear that the physicality of relationships extends beyond simply anatomical differences. God created men and women in such a way that their anatomical and hormonal differences reflect His good design.

VOCATION

The aspect of vocation is expressed in the command "subdue it [the earth], and have dominion over" the rest of the created order. This element means that able-bodied men and women will work, with the purpose of helping to build civilization. The initial fulfillment of this mandate is narrated in due course: "Now Abel was a keeper of sheep, and Cain a worker of the ground" (Gen. 4:2). It continues: "Cain knew his wife, and she conceived and bore Enoch. When he built a city, he called the name of the city after the name of his son, Enoch. . . . Adah bore Jabal; he was the father of those who dwell in tents and have livestock. His brother's name was Jubal; he was the father of all those who play the lyre and pipe. Zillah also bore Tubal-cain; he was the forger of all instruments of bronze and iron" (Gen. 4:17–22). The initial occupations were shepherding, farming, city building, tending livestock, musical artistry, and tool making. Contemporary professions include health care, construction, business, education, politics, transportation, sports, hospitality, banking, and more.

In the garden of Eden, Adam and Eve engaged in the expansion of the human race through procreation and in the building of society through vocation. This was their mandate to "Edenize" the origin creation by multiplying the small human race and enlarging the small space and society into the entire world. Today, human beings build civilization through generating (reproducing and raising) about 130,000,000 new human beings each year, and by about 5,000,000,000 men and women working in myriads of vocations. Procreation and vocation are the fulfillment of God's design for His image bearers to be about place making.

According to design, therefore, embodied and emplaced human beings/divine image bearers engage in the material production of physical civilization through procreation and vocation. Physicality in its many facets—embodiment, emplacement, relationality, multiplication, work—is good.

According to God's creation, then, men and women were created not simply to procreate, but to have dominion. The human body, and the brain that controls it, was specifically designed to act upon creation. Image bearers have physical bodies capable of a wide variety of work. The brain modulates basic physiological processes, for example, breathing, sleeping, moving, and digesting. It is also uniquely designed to act on the environment. Men and women are able to think, reason abstractly, solve complex problems, plan into the future, design, calculate, and organize. Each of these skills is essential for having dominion as God's image bearers.

The contemporary warning against "all work and no play" reflects the final movement in the opening creation narrative: "Thus the heavens and the earth were finished, and all the host of them. And on the seventh day God finished his work that he had done, and he rested on the seventh day from all his work that he had done. So God blessed the seventh day and made it holy, because on it God rested from all his work that he had done in creation" (Gen. 2:1–3). Not because He was exhausted from overextending Himself for six days of labor did God take off the seventh day, but to establish a template for His image bearers. Indeed, as part of His covenant with the people of Israel, God set forth this pattern for them:

> Remember the Sabbath day, to keep it holy. Six days you shall labor, and do all your work, but the seventh day is a Sabbath to the LORD your God. On it you shall not do any work, you, or your son, or your daughter, your male servant, or your female servant, or your livestock, or the sojourner who is within your gates. For in six days the LORD made heaven and earth, the sea, and all that is in them, and rested on the seventh day. Therefore the LORD blessed the Sabbath day and made it holy. (Ex. 20:8–11)

The old covenant featured a weekly six-day work and one-day rest pattern, mimicking the original creation week archetype.

This pattern was purposeful: the physicality of vocation calls for physical rest. Whereas God is omnipotent and never tires, He created His embodied image bearers as limited in power and susceptible to tiredness. Accordingly, they require regular relaxation. The normal rhythms of this rest are daily (i.e., most people sleep each night), weekly (i.e., most people take a day off—sometimes more—each seven-day period), and yearly (i.e., most people have an annual vacation; for example, the month of August in France). What people do for recreation is quite varied: they sleep, read, play or watch sports, visit friends, engage in hobbies, garden, listen to or play music, and the like. For most, rest entails refraining from doing what they do for work (the infamous "busman's holiday") and avoiding anything that provokes worry and stress (e.g., scheduling the coming week's activity; paying bills).[27] Certainly, contemporary workaholics thumb their noses at such a limitation and do whatever they can to resist the physical need for respite (e.g., caffeine fixes through coffee or energy drinks). Work and rest, however, are the Creator's good physical gifts to His human creatures.

Unfortunately, rejecting God's design for rest can have untoward consequences. Despite the eloquence of its design, the human body lacks the ability to work without rest for long. Even more, it begins to break down in the presence of unrelenting stress. When people are sleep-deprived, for example, their thinking becomes muddled, their emotions frayed, and their alertness diminished. Brain-imaging research supports this need for sleep: functional magnetic resonance imaging (fMRI) reveals that in those who are deprived of sleep, blood flow and brain metabolism slows.[28] Even at a cellular level, dysfunction is seen in the neurons in the hippocampus, a brain structure highly involved in remembering.[29]

Although sleep is perhaps most salient to rest, the effects of chronic stress are also well established. Those who work excessively and even exercise too much end up experiencing stress effects. Failing to give our bodies an opportunity to rest leads to emotional changes, decreased attention span, and/or increased likelihood of illness such as heart disease or inflammation.[30] Sabbath rest is not a luxury anyone can afford to bypass.

DISASTER, DEATH, AND DISPLACEMENT

Following the opening narratives of Genesis, our discussion so far has focused on the goodness of physicality in the original creation. The divine image bearers are healthy embodied beings. They live and work in a pristine physical world. They enjoy a limpid relationship with one another that includes maximum physical intimacy, and a face-to-face relationship with their Creator. Tragically, Adam and Eve transgressed by disobeying the one prohibition that God had placed on them: "You may surely eat of every tree of the garden, but of the tree of the knowledge of good and evil you shall not eat, for in the day that you eat of it you shall surely die" (Gen. 2:16–17). Their faithless, disobedient, rebellious, evil, sinful act was a total disaster, not only for the two of them as perpetrators of this heinous crime, but for the entire human race that would emerge from them (Rom. 5:12–21).

Their sin brought utter disaster.

Moreover, the death with which they had been threatened for violation of the divine prohibition took place both immediately and eventually. Immediately, Adam and Eve experienced alienation from their Creator, the one whom they knew face to face: "And they heard the sound of the LORD God walking in the garden in the cool of the day, and the man and his wife hid themselves from the presence of the LORD God among the trees of the garden" (Gen. 3:8). Cut off relationally though not physically from their Creator, Adam and Eve sank into greater and greater estrangement from their source of life and flourishing. Eventually, the two would experience complete physical demise, succumbing to the divine curse: "By the sweat of your face you shall eat bread, till you return to the ground, for out of it you were taken; for you are dust, and to dust you shall return" (Gen. 3:19). The physical aspect of human nature into which God had personally breathed the breath of live, making Adam a living being, would be withdrawn. Without this energizing force, they would eventually die physically. So, too, would all those to whom they would give physical life (1 Cor. 15:21–22).

Their sin brought universal death.

Additionally, God punished His image bearers for their heinous sin by expelling them from the garden: "Therefore the LORD God sent him out from the garden of Eden to work the ground from which he was taken. He drove out the man, and at the east of the garden of Eden he placed the cherubim and a flaming sword that turned every way to guard the way to the tree of life" (Gen. 3:23–24). This displacement was further complicated by the divine curse imposed on the fertile creation so that it would no longer be bountiful (Gen. 3:17–19). The garden that once was a realm of abundant blessing was closed off to sinful human beings, who were banished into a wasteland of their own making. They were destined to wander in a cursed realm of nature until God would rescue them through the realm of grace.[31]

Their sin brought unbearable displacement.

Narratively, the tragedies—physical and otherwise—of disaster, death, and displacement are portrayed over and over again in Scripture. From Genesis 3 through Revelation 20, "the damage done" by Adam and Eve's rebellion is rehearsed in the lives of the disfigured image bearers who flowed from them and in the defaced place cursed because of them.[32]

Adam and Eve's expulsion from the garden and from the presence of God affected all of creation from that time forward. Physical bodies do not work like they should. Cognition and emotion do not work like they should. Relationships do not work like they should. Racially segregated communities, gridlocked governments, environmental pollution, and natural disasters all reveal the cosmic effects of the fall. God designed the human body, the human mind, and human relationships to function well and reflect His glory. The divine mind gave thought to the anatomic and hormonal differences between men and women. He gave thought to how the children would develop in utero and outside the womb. He considered the importance of relationship on human development. He planned the human brain in such a way that it would be able not only to receive information but also to act logically and wisely upon the world, thus exercising dominion. But image bearers bear the scars of the fall.

On a neurological level, neuronal structures that were specifically designed to facilitate and enhance interpersonal interconnection show the deleterious effects of the fall. Most prominently, conditions such as autism, where there is a lack of attunement and interpersonal connection, can be associated with dysfunction of the systems involving mirror neurons and von Economo neurons. The effect of sin on the biological substrates ends up having wider ranging effects. Beyond developmental impairment, the brain can also stop working optimally as we see in Alzheimer's disease, multiple sclerosis, epilepsy, even traumatic brain injuries, and others. These conditions also affect thinking and relating.

Hormonally, the effects of the fall can be seen as well. Excessive levels of testosterone can be associated with increased promiscuity[33] and exposure to pornography.[34] In addition to natural variance, intentional manipulation of hormone levels also happens. Both men and women use synthetic androgens (e.g., testosterone) to enhance physical fitness and muscular size, which unfortunately can also be associated with increased aggression.

The failure to develop close relational attachments also has chronic effects. Problems in early attachments can lead to significant relational problems later in life for some people. When early caregiving relationships are deficient, people have trouble "making sense"[35] of their stories and can end up with relational difficulties. In addition to problems with secure attachment, three other patterns emerge from dysfunctional attachment.[36] These patterns may result in a cool detachment and relational disengagement with others (i.e., dismissal); an anxious, insecure attachment that places unrealistic demands on others (i.e., preoccupation); or an unpredictable, sometimes agitated, response (i.e., disorganization). Each of these states can result in poor neurobiological integration. The overall flow of information from one side of the brain to the other, or from the body to the brain, becomes disrupted, resulting in diminished neural functioning.

Once again, the fall has wide ranging effects, but it is essential to understand that these effects are not isolated. The effects of sin on biology, biochemistry, and relationships do not exist detached from one another. The noetic effects of sin (negative changes in thinking) affect relationships. Relational difficulties affect the ability to think clearly. Relational stress can lead to biological changes, from the common cold to increased likelihood of cardiac disease.

RESTORATION

As dark as the disaster, death, and displacement of Adam and Eve were, the one who created them in His image would not give up on His disfigured image bearers, nor on the defaced creation that was intended to be a hospitable and fertile space for the flourishing of human civilization. While the story of this restoration usually focuses on the divine work of spiritual redemption, its physicality pleads to be appreciated.

The restoration of humanity and its home begins with a divine promise in the midst of the divine curse on the serpent/Satan: "I will put enmity between you and the woman, and between your offspring and her offspring; he shall bruise your head, and you shall bruise his heel" (Gen. 3:15). A pitched and prolonged battle between the forces of evil and the forces of good would ultimately lead to the demise of the former and the victory of the latter. The physicality of this protracted war of redemption included the following: God called the pagan Abram to move from his country and family of origin and go to a land of promise, to become the father of many nations and the source of blessing to all humanity. God liberated one of these nations—Israel—from enslavement in Egypt and established its people as His people in the promised land. For the forgiveness of His people's sins, God provided atonement through the bloody sacrifices of animals and birds. He Himself dwelt, first in the tabernacle and second in the temple: these constituted the dwelling place for His splendid, radiant glory. When His disobedient people reached the fullness of their rebelliousness, God thrust them into exile, then in His mercy brought them home to their land.

Ultimately, God accomplished redemption through the incarnation of His Son as an embodied and emplaced human being like all embodied and emplaced human beings (Gal. 4:4–6). Jesus' miracles of healing were manifestations of the invasion of God's kingdom into a sin-saturated world, as well as expressions of divine compassion for physical suffering. Eventually, the incarnate Son was physically beaten, nailed to a cross, crucified, and buried—an outcast from His own people whom He came to save. But disaster, death, and displacement did not have the last word, as the crucified Son was physically resurrected. In turn, the promised Holy Spirit descended on Jesus' disciples in miraculous, tangible ways, and gave birth to a new covenant people, the church. As the new creation, the people of God are newly emplaced in this community and given new signs of the new covenant: baptism and the Lord's Supper.

Accordingly, God is a complete restorer. The crucified Son was physically resurrected, and God, by His Spirit and through the church, continues to restore. In *The Return of the King*, J. R. R. Tolkien gives voice to Sam Gamgee:

> "Gandalf! I thought you were dead! But then I thought I was dead myself. Is everything sad going to come untrue? What's happened to the world?"
>
> "A great Shadow has departed," said Gandalf, and then he laughed and the sound was like music, or like water in a parched land; and as he listened the thought came to Sam that he had not heard laughter, the pure sound of merriment, for days upon days without count.

If we focus only on fallenness, we think like Sam, that we are dead ourselves. But Tolkien wisely reminds us that because of Christ, a "great shadow has departed" and "everything sad [will] come untrue." The process of restoration is underway!

As we begin to operate out of the mindset that Christ has accomplished our redemption and understand that we live "in the new way of the Spirit" (Rom. 7:6), we begin to see significant changes in our thinking, relationships, and communities. Indeed, the gospel changes everything! These changes are not fully realized until later, but living in light of Christ's finished work has a positive impact now.

In Romans 12, Paul underscores the importance of renewing our mind. Indeed, active attention to our minds can affect how we think. Neuroimaging research has demonstrated that changing our thoughts can lead to physical changes within our brains.[37] These changes may lead to increased intrapersonal integration, resulting in a deeper sense of peace and settledness. Ideally, the result of these internal physiological changes will create a deeper sense of relational connection and secure attachment within husband-wife and parent-child relationships, as well as within relationships in the church community.

In His High Priestly Prayer (John 17), Jesus asks the Father to make the disciples one as He and the Father are one. This deep relational connection for which Jesus prays is the purpose for which God's image bearers are created. It is how we are designed to function. When we begin to believe that the

Father hears Jesus' prayer, we will begin to experience a much deeper sense of relational connection, which is true biblically and biologically.

As sojourners and strangers redeemed by Jesus Christ, Christians in the community of the church live the reality of "already but not yet." They are a new creation, in part (2 Cor. 5:17). They live in a new place, in part (1 Peter 2:9–12; Eph. 2:19–21). They have new marriages and families, in part (Eph. 5:22–6:4). They have new work, in part (Eph. 6:5–9). They experience a new rest, in part (Heb. 3:7–4:13). Christians live in the hope of the actualization of the "not yet": the bodily return of Son of God, the physical resurrection of their body, ultimate replacement in the new Jerusalem, and the ultimate re-creation in the new heaven and new earth (Rev. 21–22).

> Then I saw a new heaven and a new earth, for the first heaven and the first earth had passed away, and the sea was no more. And I saw the holy city, new Jerusalem, coming down out of heaven from God, prepared as a bride adorned for her husband. And I heard a loud voice from the throne saying, "Behold, the dwelling place of God is with man. He will dwell with them, and they will be his people, and God himself will be with them as their God. He will wipe away every tear from their eyes, and death shall be no more, neither shall there be mourning, nor crying, nor pain anymore, for the former things have passed away." (Rev. 21:1–4)

The apostle John's language of hope underscores a new creation (the new heaven and new earth), a new embodiment (released from tears, mourning, and crying), a new emplacement (God dwelling with His people), a new marriage (between God and His people of the new Jerusalem, readied as a bride for her husband), a new vocation (the nations bringing glory and honor to God; Rev. 21:26), a new rest (released from the pain of labor), a new reality (eternal life, with no death), and a new restoration (the former things have completely passed away). We have explored the beautiful physicality of human life in general, and of relationships in particular, rehearsing each of these specific topics from our respective areas of expertise: theology and neuropsychology. Our hope, in language less lofty than that of the apostle John, is that we as image bearers of God, and as redeemed followers of Jesus Christ, and as living stones in the temple of the Holy Spirit, will live our embodiment, emplacement, and relationality for the glory of our triune God, the missional advancement of the church, and human flourishing in the world in which we live.

UNDERSTANDING WHY "EMBODIMENT" MATTERS

by Beth Felker Jones

If we want to think Christianly about sexuality, we'll need to understand that Christian faith confesses one steady teaching about embodiment: God made the body, God loves the body, God has good creative and redemptive intentions for the body. Our understanding of sexuality and of our male and female bodies has to fit within this basic teaching. Despite agreement through the ages that this is the clear teaching of Scripture, Christians continue to be uncomfortable affirming the bodies that God created and declared "good" from the beginning.

The reality is that sin has created this idea that bodies are a problem and something we ought to be rid of, that bodies are problems while souls are not. This thinking tries to pin sin on our bodies while imagining that our souls are not also groaning under sin's weight. In this dualist view, we begin to believe that our bodies are not significant to living a godly life. For example, we place value and attention on things we think have to do with our souls— quiet times, prayers, and other things we believe are more spiritual—while believing that it matters less if we struggle with our physical life. The clear teaching of Scripture is otherwise; we are to "present" our "bodies as a living sacrifice, holy and acceptable to God" as "spiritual worship" (Rom. 12:1 ESV).

Presenting our bodies to God is at the heart of our spiritual lives. Everything we do is both physical and spiritual. Our bodies and our souls both matter. The church needs to reclaim the teaching that God has good intentions for us in the body, for the body.

We live in a strange and contradictory space in which both gnostic dualism and reductive materialism are embraced by many, even though the two positions are both less than Christian and contradict one another. Gnostic dualism affirms that only the spiritual matters, and on this view, it doesn't matter what one eats or drinks or does in the body. In contrast, reductive materialism acts as though only the physical exists, in which case no spiritual reality would stop me from eating whatever I like or doing as I please with my body. Both points of view fail to realize that God made both body and soul and that both matter, and both points of view can allow for lack of moral care about the body. A Christian recognition that both body and soul matter will insist that we are embodied moral creatures and that what we do in the body has meaning in its relationship to God and in our human relationships with one another.

Our culture of both gnostic dualism and reductive materialism encourages us to put our bodies in unhealthy places. We may desperately punish our bodies at the gym, not in a healthy way but in a frantic and despairing way that seems to worship the body, acting as though only the size and shape of the body matters. This looks materialistic but it can also carry shades of gnostic dualism when the focus and treatment of the body makes the body a problem to be solved or beaten into submission instead of a good gift from God with which God wants to do good things. When we treat the body as merely something to make smaller, thinner, and tighter, we may go far outside of health into punishing and harming the body.

When we're tempted to agree with our culture that our bodies are problems to be beaten down, we need to be reminded instead of the truth of the Holy Spirit, the truth that our bodies are good, that God made them, and God loves them. We can begin to pray to be aware of and attentive to our bodies, and we can pray for the Spirit to help us to offer our bodies to God. I believe deeply that we should pray far more over bodily things, as an antidote to the world's misguided communication about the importance or unimportance of the body.

The theological categories of creation, fall, and redemption can help us to understand our bodies. Our bodies are part of the creation that He deemed "good." With the fall into sin, our whole selves, body and soul, took on the weight of sin. But sin is not the end of the story. Through the work of Christ, we are being redeemed, body and soul. God is redeeming that which has been affected by sin. We cannot stop with sin, as though that were the last or most important truth about our bodies. We need to lean into redemption here. We need to begin to live the new possibilities for our bodies that are ours in Christ. "Are we to continue in sin that grace may abound?" (Rom. 6:1) No! Because of the redemptive work of the triune God, we are able to live a new life, and that new life includes our bodies. A key text is 1 Corinthians 6:20, which says, "You were bought with a price. So glorify God in your body." This is not just a future hope but a present reality. We must always take the effects of sin into consideration, but we also need to claim the transforming power of God and believe that we can live differently, body and soul, in a way that gives glory to God.

It may help us to think in particular terms, to pay attention to specific parts of our bodies and specific things we do with our bodies. How can we glorify God with our skin, our hair, our souls, our hands, our time, our rest, our work, our play? How can we glorify God in the way we eat? How can we glorify God with our sexuality? How do we glorify God as whole embodied persons? How do we remember, every day, that God intends our bodies for glory? We don't achieve this by our own will or power. We as believers were bought at a price, and it is only because that has already happened that we are able, by the power of God's grace, to begin to glorify God with our bodies. Our bodies are full of hopeful possibility that does not depend on our efforts but instead depends on our vital relationship with the Son, who, through the Holy Spirit, unites us with the Father.

CHAPTER 6

THE BEAUTY AND DESIGN OF MARRIAGE: AN IMAGE FOR THE CHURCH AND ITS GOSPEL

by Curt Hamner and Rebekah J. Byrd

"Let Us make man in Our image, according to our likeness; and let them rule over the fish of the sea and over the birds of the sky and over the cattle and over all the earth, and over every creeping thing that creeps on the earth." God created man in His own image, in the image of God He created him; male and female He created them. God blessed them; and God said to them, "Be fruitful and multiply, and fill the earth, and subdue it;" . . . God saw all that He had made, and behold, it was very good. And there was evening and there was morning, the sixth day. (Gen. 1:26–28, 31[1])

God creates, and He places man and woman in the garden, the perfect eco-system for humanity to flourish. This is the story of human origins, before the effects of sin that resulted in, among other things, a scarred environment and complications in relationships ongoing from the garden as evidenced in society today.

The understanding of marriage in Western society has traditionally been affirmed as an exclusive, monogamous relationship between one man and one woman. In recent decades, we have witnessed a shift from that understanding. Now cultural mores have changed, resulting in a desire to qualify what comprises a marriage in an increasingly homogeneous culture—one that strives toward gender sameness rather than celebrates the beauty and distinction of men and women—and, in turn, many have largely embraced what amounts to a secular or humanistic view of marriage.[2] Thus, the social commentary of roles has shifted in terms of one's expectation of husbands and wives and what each brings to the marriage relationship. Where once we embraced the beauty and mystery of distinction brought together to form a union, we now applaud their replacement by social or cultural egalitarian structures and the elevation of autonomy. These shifts have contributed to the list of one's expectations of marriage partnership, leading a generation to be less interested in traditional marriage in order to pursue a lifestyle that encourages and honors individual rights. These changes in expectations have permeated the church. Therefore, the church must engage the culture with a compelling message driven by the love of God and love for one's neighbor, while acknowledging that marriage is hard, marriage is complex, and marriage is mystery.

MARRIAGE IS HARD

Most couples can remember the day or event they would describe as when the "honeymoon is over." It doesn't take much time for the rubber to hit the road, as they say, when couples realize that marriage is, indeed, not an easy undertaking. Two self-centered, autonomous personalities find themselves clashing, and the business of getting down to real life together begins. The coming to terms with the reality that marriage is hard is a stark awakening for an entitled culture.

Yes, certainly, marriage is hard. When one thinks about marriage and the roles both members of the couple hold, each spouse's point of reference is usually associated with one's familial and spiritual background, experience, and a particular set of expectations. This means there is bound to be conflict. Marriage is about melding together two individual people—who come with varying religious and social experiences and even with different worldviews— into something new. No longer is one person's significance and contribution valued higher or lower than the other's. The nature of relationships is altered in a new form of nakedness brought by their personal sin and their sin nature. The fading of the honeymoon phase reveals the complexity of this new merger. Hormones associated with the physical and emotional vulnerability one displays to the other indicate the beauty, struggle, and hard work that must begin. It provides the opportunity for two individuals to come to the end of themselves for the sake of the other, but sometimes it deters people to do the work, leading them to end the marriage out of fear as soon as it begins.

Motivation for marriage is much more complex in our contemporary world than when marriage was encouraged for the benefit of society (raising a family) or to stop or prevent "fornication."[3] Today's single person is bombarded with, for example, online dating sites or apps with quick hookup options, leaving the path to marriage a daunting endeavor. *TIME* magazine introduced a three-part series on staying married, the first of which was "The Science of Marriage." In the introductory material, Belinda Luscombe reported on a survey done by Karl Pillemer from Cornell University, who surveyed seven hundred older adults for his book *30 Lessons for Loving*. Pillemer reported, "Everybody—100%—said at one point that the long marriage was the best thing in their lives. But all of them also either said that marriage is hard or that it's really, really hard."[4]

"You are not my enemy" was a phrase my husband and I (Becky) learned to say to each other while attending a marriage conference. This event was a generous gift to us from the congregation where we began our first year of marriage and ministry. We joked about having to repeat these words to each other even during the conference, but over the years we have been married it has served as a helpful reminder—in the midst of daily living as well as the larger issues of stressful moves, finding work/life balance, and raising four kids—that marriage was created to express something relationally beyond itself.

In the beginning, we read that God first created an ideal environment for humanity to flourish. Creation of man and woman was pronounced "very good" (Gen. 1:26ff), after God had declared that it was "not good" for man to be alone (Gen. 2:18). Together, man and woman are blessed and given co-responsibility to care for and rule over the other creatures and to be fruitful themselves (Gen. 1:26ff). What makes Adam and Eve different from the other creatures God had created? The narrative reveals something unique in how man and woman are formed and fashioned in the image and likeness of God (Gen. 1:22–27). It is man and woman who are to bear in both their distinctiveness and likeness to each other something mysterious about their Creator. Marc Cortez agrees that there is more going on here than reproduction. He adds, "Genesis 1 climaxes not in reproduction but in the 'one flesh' of Genesis 2 and the introduction of the marital relationship . . . the narrative says nothing about the 'one flesh' union producing offspring—but actually expresses a transcendent truth, a truth about the nature of God."[5] The passage indicates a pair that worked together. Man and woman were not functioning against each other or God but for each other and for God.[6] The oneness of the Holy Trinity is reflected in the "one flesh" expression of marriage.

When both Adam and Eve chose to act independently with selfish intent, desiring to be not only close to God, but to be like God, knowing both good and evil (Gen. 3:5–6), the beautiful union shifted from communal purposes to individual consciousness and blame. It revealed a new nakedness in opposition to the security and safety Adam and Eve found in each other, their environment, and, more importantly, with their Creator. They bore great consequences individually and for all of humanity and the world that was to follow.[7] First Corinthians 15:22 says, "For as in Adam all die . . ." Adam and Eve were no longer in a world that was enabling them to flourish, but still, God had not abandoned them. God created coverings for them and explained the consequences of their actions, which resulted in a complexity that had not been present before. Individually and corporately they inherited pain and toil, and in addition, disunity was embedded into their new circle of life.

You have heard how important obedience is; you have praised and marveled at Paul, how he welds our whole life together, as we would expect from an admirable and spiritual man. You have done well. But listen to what else he requires from you; he has not finished with his example. "Husbands," he says, "love your wives, as Christ loved the Church." . . . And even if it becomes necessary for you to give your life for her, yes, and even to endure and undergo suffering of any kind, do not refuse. Even though you undergo all this, you will never have done anything equal to what Christ has done. You are sacrificing yourself for someone to whom you are already joined, but He offered Himself up for the one who turned her back on Him and hated Him.[8]
—St. John Chrysostom

MARRIAGE IS COMPLEX

Marriage in all its beauty and design outwardly display the complexity of two distinct persons becoming one. Yet, such differences are to be celebrated rather than absorbed by the other, as men and women approach life differently. Louann Brizendine describes how such differences impact how each one relates. "More than 99 percent of male and female genetic coding is exactly the same. Out of the thirty thousand genes in the human genome, the less than one percent variation between the sexes is small. But that percentage difference influences *every single cell in our bodies*—from the nerves that register pleasure and pain to the neurons that transmit perception, thoughts, feelings, and emotions."[9]

Because we are a society that depends on rational and scientific reasoning, mere linear lines of thought and organization can rarely contain the full measure of the spiritual and physical significance of marriage's origins and purpose. As Christians who adhere to God's sacred Word, we rely on biblical clarity over a cultural framework to understand its complexity. Especially in Western culture, relationships in society are less driven to reflect gender distinction or a complementary understanding of roles between men and women. The church has the opportunity to portray the beauty and design of marriage to such an increasingly egalitarian-affirming society, one that embraces a culture that celebrates blurred lines of sexuality and gendered cultural categories. Instead of grasping this opportunity, many churches have chosen to be silent out of fear or have adapted the mindset of "it doesn't matter who or how one loves." Doing so without thinking through the theological ramifications for the gospel cheapens the type of love we are all called to display because of Christ (John 15:12ff).

The complexity of marriage reveals the struggle to faithfully display this type of love.

Both men and women are created for the glory of God, and each bear His image with equal value. In Genesis 2, the sexual distinction between Adam and Eve played a significant role. Man and woman each were created out of the pleasure of a triune God, but they were also created intentionally for one another, to relate to one another, for the benefit of one another. Adam declares: "This is now bone of my bones, and flesh of my flesh" (Gen. 2:23). No other creature, not even another man, could fulfill what woman was created to be, a "helper," someone suitable as a complement for the man.

This perfect environment was, however, tainted with the disobedience of both the woman and the man, who acted independently of each other, and ultimately of God.

Beginning in Genesis 3 and ongoing throughout human history, the evil one has skewed what it means to be male and female. Perhaps this misalignment of culture is more apparent at present than ever before. Dan Allender and Tremper Longman explain the demonic intent this way: "Gender reflects something about the glory of God. And God's enemy, Satan, wishes to destroy glory. The evil one cannot destroy God; therefore, he tries to destroy the reflection of God: man and woman. His prime way of attempting to destroy glory is to make it too frightening to be truly a man or a woman and to offer counterfeit routes to live out gender."[10] The functional roles intended for man and woman to live out became more complex by sin, and by the consequences each individual was to bear.

Even today, marriage reflects this complexity. Man and woman are created for one another to relate spiritually, emotionally, and physically; yet because of sin, we seek alternative options to this reality or use Scripture against itself in an abusive way to fulfill what was initially declared "good."

It is from this point on that creation groans, longing for its created purpose to be fulfilled (Rom. 8:22). Instead, both men and women, as husbands and wives, respond from a place of brokenness, causing them to hide behind their fig leaves.

One individual act changed the trajectory, however, redeeming that which was severed, the union between creature and Creator. As George Ladd put it, "The final goal of Christ's redemptive ministry is to restore order and unity in the whole universe, which has been disrupted by sin. God's plan is 'to unite all things to him, things in heaven and things on earth.'"[11] It is out of this radical love a new community is created and the mystery of the "one flesh" union in marriage becomes an image of Christ's dynamic love for the church.

This dynamic love for the church is demonstrated first by Christ, and is what Paul chooses to call a husband to display for his wife, placing himself in a vulnerable position out of love. Likewise, the wife who chooses to follow her husband's leadership places herself in a selfless, vulnerable position. This is the "attitude of Christ" that Paul admonishes the Philippians church to pursue in restoring (redeeming) the oneness of the church (see Phil. 2). This is a redemptive glance to the history of marriage. One who pursues this kind of understanding of the distinctions of marriage is creating the ideal, God-ordained spiritual/emotional ecosystem for relationships.

Marriage was created to be complex, in the security of the garden, *naked and unashamed,* providing the environment for both man and woman to flourish. The fruit of Adam's and Eve's roles was intended be the celebration of this union created and fashioned by God (Matt. 19:5–6). The one flesh union of Genesis 2:24 is not the reflection of what they produced or accomplished but who they were intended to be together. It provides the opportunity for marriage to display a different type of love (Matt. 5:43–48), one that is selfless, costly, committed, and thus mysterious, as it is only God who can work such beauty in the midst of such brokenness in our understanding of what "love" truly is. The uniqueness of marriage is its visible witness, not a hidden one. It recalls and images what was, while proclaiming the active Word and presence of God in His creation.

MARRIAGE IS MYSTERY

The gospel of John accounts that Jesus did not just appear on the scene in first-century Palestine, but was in the beginning, when marriage was created (John 1:1–5). It's significant that His earthly ministry began with a marriage feast and that a marriage feast comes at the end of earthly things (John 2; Rev. 19:7ff). When He quoted Genesis 2:24, He affirmed divine participation in the "one flesh" union (Matt. 19:3ff). Therefore, marriage in its display of distinction and union is an image the church should protect, as it is a living organism that mysteriously mirrors in its "one flesh" union the type of love Christ demonstrated for the church, of which Christ is the head.

Mystery acknowledges that there are elements to our humanity and its outworking that are beyond our understanding. It also acknowledges God is mystery (Isa. 55:8–11) and that the fullness of who God is and His attributes are not fully manifest. Therefore, even marriage in the New Testament becomes a sacred and redemptive vehicle that Paul uses to describe Christ's love for the church in Ephesians 5:22ff. It is an agape love with reciprocity. One of the Greek words translated into English merely as love, agape, evokes such traits as faithfulness, sacrifice, benevolence, delight, goodwill, commitment. Paul develops his language around this dynamic love with selfless intent in Philippians 2 and uses the same root, agape, in Galatians 5:13–14. In each of these accounts, Paul is relating selfless action and love, led by the Holy Spirit in parallel to Christ's sacrifice on the cross. It is a unity that is being reclaimed, a new community being formed for whom Jesus made intercession. "The glory which You have given Me I have given to them, that they may be one, just as We are one; I in them and You in Me, that they may be perfected in unity, so that the world may know that You sent Me, and loved them, even as You have loved Me" (John 17:22–23).

As we've said, a marriage is made up of two separate individuals coming together, forming a union that makes the two one. The church is a community that is likewise ontologically and biologically diverse. Paul's letters to the churches in Rome and in Corinth (Rom. 12; 1 Cor. 12–14) reveal the diversity of the social statuses, genders, and races represented. These are not weaknesses but strengths of the church. Romans 12:4–6b says, "Just as we have many members in one body and all the members do not have the same function, so we, who are many, are one body in Christ, and individually members of one another. Since we have gifts that differ according to the grace given to us, each of us is to exercise them accordingly." To the church in Galatia, Paul writes, "For you are all sons of God through faith in Christ Jesus. For all of you who were baptized into Christ have clothed yourselves with Christ. There is neither Jew nor Greek, there is neither slave nor free man, there is neither male nor female; for you are all one in Christ Jesus" (Gal. 3:26–28).

The unity Paul exhorts the church to display is something it cannot accomplish in and of itself, as the flesh is hostile to things of the Spirit (Rom. 8:7; Gal. 5:16). Paul in his letters recognizes the high call of such exhortations. Brad Harper and Paul Metzger are in good company with other notable scholars to observe that these are eschatological exhortations to the church in Ephesus. They call the individual to a different community standard above and beyond the roles and social structures they were expected to exhibit.[12] In Romans 12:10, 18 Paul says, "Be devoted to one another in brotherly love; give preference to one another in honor. . . . be at peace with all men." These are not transactional exhortations but familial ones that Jesus used Himself in describing those who obey God (Matt. 12:50). It is not about setting oneself in a hierarchy for the sake of power or authority (for such roles and gifts are divinely appointed, Rom. 12:5–6; 1 Cor. 12:4–7). Paul is calling both men and women to "walk in love"

There is no influence more powerful than the bond of love, especially for husband and wife. A servant can be taught submission through fear; but even he, if provoked too much, will seek his escape. But one's partner for life, the mother of one's children, the source of one's every joy, should never be fettered with fear and threats, but with love and patience. What kind of marriage can there be when the wife is afraid of her husband? What sort of satisfaction could a husband himself have, if he lives with his wife as if she were a slave, and not with a woman by her own free will? Suffer anything for her sake, but never disgrace her, for Christ never did this with the church.[13] **—St. John Chrysostom**

(Eph. 5:1–2) by submitting oneself first to Christ and choosing to serve one another in a diverse and complex community for the sake of the gospel. Wayne Grudem agrees that the dynamic impact of this metaphor serves to exhort the church to increase one's love and fellowship with one another. With this image of Christ and the church (His bride), it should "stimulate us to strive for greater purity and holiness, and also greater love for Christ and submission to him."[14] What would marriage image, what would our churches image, if we were walking in those words by the power of the Holy Spirit? It was a countercultural exhortation in Paul's day and so it stands today.

Have you ever heard someone say marriage is about give and take? Or that marriage only works if each person gives 100 percent? Setting up measurable and sometimes ideal expectations can often create opportunities for disappointment. The reality is that no person can fulfill or meet another's expectations 100 percent of the time. Ask any couple or ministry leader in your church—yet our interactions with one another are incarnational opportunities to image God or demonstrate something more. Jesus took the time to talk to His disciples about such engagements.

"You have heard that it was said, 'You shall love your neighbor and hate your enemy.' But I say to you, love your enemies and pray for those who persecute you, so that you may be sons of your Father who is in heaven; for He causes His sun to rise on the evil and the good, and sends rain on the righteous and the unrighteous. For if you love those who love you, what reward do you have?" (Matt. 5:43–46).

This is the type of action and love Paul is describing for the church. Charles Wesley wrote the hymn "And Can It Be, That I Should Gain?" based on Romans 5:8, describing the amazing love that God selflessly demonstrated for the church. It is a cruciform love Christ chose to freely and selflessly give of Himself for something greater (Heb. 12:2). This is counternarrative to a society that advertises to our minds and bodies that life and relationship are about personal pleasure and advancement.

Unity of mind and praxis acknowledges the complexity in bringing together two individuals in a marriage. Selfless action between husband and wife frees the marriage to be what it was intended from the beginning. Such a thing is not possible unless the Spirit is at work in and through it. In the church, it is not only our work, but the work of the Spirit, alive and working through the church for the purposes of glorifying God. It's about being a communion of saints, a new creation, mirroring to the world an alternative to self-serving, self-centered living.

Dietrich Bonhoeffer, a Lutheran theologian and pastor martyred during World War II, wrote some of his primary thoughts on the sociology of the church that put to words this idea of love displayed with reciprocity:

> Love for our neighbor is our will to embrace God's will for the other person; God's will for the other person is defined for us in the unrestricted command to surrender our self-centered will to our neighbor, which neither means to love the other instead of God, nor to love God in the other, but to put the other in our own place and to love the neighbor instead of ourselves.[15]

We live first as unto Christ and then to our neighbor. The new community being formed in the New Testament out of Jesus' ministry reflects what marriage images in self-sacrifice for one another (Matt. 22:37ff). Jesus says to His disciples who were arguing about which one was the greatest among them, "It is not this way among you, but whoever wishes to become greatest among you shall be your servant . . . just as the Son of Man did not come to be served, but to serve, and to give His life a ransom for many" (Matt. 20:26–28).

It is this demonstration of Christ's dynamic love that should ethically motivate us toward relationship with one another. This is why we must talk about marriage with distinctive rather than homogeneous language. As the church, we need to recognize the complexity in living this out among the diversity of people represented. It seems normal to our flesh to live out of selfish motivation, but this only strips away at the gospel witness that a diverse yet unified church is to reflect. Therefore, we need to be careful and mindful of our own experiences and stereotypes and choose instead, because of Christ's love and sacrifice, to honor and love one another over the benefit and advancement of ourselves.

Wesley Hill recently wrote *Spiritual Friendship*, which dives deep into his thoughts on life within the body of Christ. He says:

> Friendship, in Christian terms, is all about giving up oneself for the sake of love and embracing the cost of such radical loyalty. Friendship, in a word, is cruciform. If Jesus is the ultimate author and exemplar of friendship, then we can't fail to remember that his own practice of friendship ended with him strung up on an instrument of imperial torture, made helplessly vulnerable and wracked by grief. Friendship

for him wasn't an escape route from self-sacrifice. It was the other way around; self-sacrifice was precisely the way he enacted a life of friendship.[16]

This is radical thinking for today's relationships. Whether one is single, married, part of a blended family, or a single parent home, the call for selfless living is the same. It is hard work in a culture that makes us fearful of making such connections. Thus, we need to remember that we were created out of love of a Creator who designed humanity for relationship.

The parallels of marriage and the people of God throughout the Scripture, especially in Ephesians 5, is beautiful and compelling. The comparisons are so bold, yet shrouded in the origins of marriage and community from the beginning, so that even Paul needs to draw clarity to reality of what it is saying. "This mystery is great; but I am speaking with reference to Christ and the church" (v. 32). The ultimate reality held in this mystery is that Christ will restore the union of His people, which is clearly illuminated by the original design of marriage from the beginning.

CONCLUSION

In this chapter we have argued that marriage is hard, marriage is complex, and marriage is mystery. Marriage lived out within this mystery becomes not just a social unit, but a metaphor that images the type of love Paul is calling the church to live out toward one another, demonstrated by Christ's cruciform love. This type of love is not something we can do on our own; we need God's intervention, His salvation. Adam and Eve needed divine intervention, and modern marriage requires divine intervention. The unity Paul exhorts the church to display is something in and of itself that it cannot accomplish without divine intervention. The union of marriage and the church is in its essence, not its efforts.

This is not an unattainable exhortation, as the same Spirit works in all those who are part of the body of Christ. It is a call to live with selfless motivation demonstrated for us first by Christ, imaged in marriage, and lived out in a community steeped in love and unity for the glory of our Creator. This is a compelling gospel message.

MARRIAGE—GOD'S DESIGN

by Timothy R. Jennings

God is the Designer, Builder, and Creator of all reality—not only physical reality, but also the human mind and relationships. As such, God built His creation to operate on unchangeable protocols, principles of life, also known as laws. These include the law of gravity, laws of physics, and laws of health, but God also designed laws into how our minds and relationships function.

Any deviation from God's design is inherently damaging or destructive. On a physical level almost everyone recognizes this reality—violate the laws of health (e.g., smoke cigarettes) and health is undermined. But many fail to realize there are laws just as real, constant, predictable, and reliable as the laws of physics, and that these laws govern how our minds and relationships function. Violations of these design parameters damage us individually and relationally. We can only experience health, wellness, and restoration to abundant living as we return to harmony with God and His design for our lives. Here we will explore God's protocols for healthy relationships: love, truth, and freedom.

LOVE

Love in God's universe is more than emotion or compassion or concern. Love is functional and operational. God, who is love, constructed His creation to operate in harmony with Himself and thus built into the fabric of reality the principles of love. In Romans Paul states, "God's invisible qualities—his eternal power and divine nature—have been clearly seen, being understood from what has been made . . ." (1:20 NIV). Functionally, love doesn't seek to promote self, but is other-centered, giving, benevolent, or outward moving

(1 Cor. 13:5). In all living systems, life requires that this law of giving must not be broken. With every breath we give away carbon dioxide to the plants and the plants give oxygen back to us—the principle of giving (love) is built right into nature. If you choose to transgress that law of nature and tie a plastic bag over your head, the wages of that choice is death. Throughout all nature this is true—how plants produce food for us, and in turn we produce by-products of digestion that then fertilize the plants, the water cycle of rain and evaporation, and even human economies (money must be in circulation or the economy dies). The law of love is the law of life for God's creation.

This understanding provides insight into God's design for human marriage. God is love, and God lives in a triune perfection of love. Comprehending the way love functions is one of the best evidences for the doctrine of the Trinity. Outward moving love requires an object to receive one's love. Functionally, love cannot exist in a singularity. And two individuals can exist in a relationship of mutual narcissistic reinforcement—both admiring and praising the other. But only with three do we see demonstrated genuine, other-centered self-sacrificial love. My point is that the sinful human heart is incapable of genuine love (*agape*) without the influence of the Holy Spirit, so it takes three: husband, wife, Holy Spirit. Clearly, nonbelieving couples can exemplify other-centered love. But this demonstrates, I believe, the Holy Spirit's working in their hearts even if they have not yet acknowledged Him (see Rom. 1:13–15; Heb. 8:10). God's presence is the third empowering influence of genuine love.

"The LORD God said, 'It is not good for the man to be alone. I will make a helper suitable for him'" (Gen 2:18 NIV). Adam was made in God's image and God is love. Therefore, Adam could not enter into the fullness of Godlike love without someone for Adam to serve, without someone for Adam to sacrifice himself for. Eve was created to be the recipient of Adam's self-sacrificial love and service, receive that love, and in a relationship with their Creator (triune), let the love flow back to Adam in her loving self-sacrifice and service to him.

Sadly, when Adam and Eve transgressed, God's design of perfect love was displaced and replaced with fear and selfishness, also known as "survival-of-the-fittest." God, then, pronounced what happens when other-centered love is replaced with selfishness in the heart—the strong dominate the weak and the weak long to be dominated by the strong. "Your desire will be for your husband, and he will rule over you" (Gen. 3:16 NIV). Human relationships, without the renewing of God's Spirit, now function out of harmony with God's design, and all types of injury have occurred both inside and outside of marriage because of selfishness in the heart. It is God's plan to remove fear and selfishness from the heart and restore His law of love in the inmost being so that we will again experience relationship in harmony with God's perfect design of love.

TRUTH

What caused the disruption of God's perfect love in the hearts of humankind? Believing lies! Just imagine what would happen in your heart if someone told you the lie that your spouse is having an affair. If you believe the lie, even though your spouse is loyal and faithful, something inside you may change. When we believe lies, the circle of love and trust has been broken, which in turn results in fear and selfishness. We no longer believe our spouse is for us, but instead has turned to be for another—we fear we will be hurt and exploited, and therefore instantly seek to protect ourselves.

Once the lie is believed, the only path of healing is the truth. Truth destroys lies and restores trust, thus opening the heart for reconciliation and restoration. This is the root of the problem that happened to human beings in our relationship with God. We have believed lies about Him, which broke our trust in Him, resulting in fear and selfishness and seeking to save or protect ourselves. But sadly, such a course leads only to further pain and suffering. One of the reasons Jesus came is to destroy the lies, reveal the truth, and win us back to trust. Then in that trust relationship with Him, we open our hearts and He pours His love into our hearts (Rom. 5:5). His perfect love casts out our fear (1 John 4:18), resulting in ever increasing peace, love, joy and the ability to experience relationship as God designed.

FREEDOM

The law of freedom is a design law on which God constructed His intelligent beings to exist in perfect love. Love can only exist in an atmosphere of freedom. If you doubt this, see what happens if you tell your spouse they cannot use the car, telephone, computer, TV, or leave the house without your permission. When you're at a restaurant, don't allow your spouse to order their own meal, but choose for them. Don't allow your spouse to speak without your permission or have friends you haven't approved of. I can assure you that your relationship with be seriously damaged if you should do any of these things.

When we violate the freedoms of others, three predictable consequences always occur: (1) Love is damaged, and if freedom is not returned love will eventually be destroyed in such a relationship; (2) a desire to rebel and get away from the controlling person is instilled in the heart; and (3) if freedom isn't reclaimed but instead one chooses to stay under the domination of another, then over time individuality is destroyed and the ability to think and reason for oneself is lost. One becomes an empty shell, thinking through the lens of the controlling spouse.

Only in an atmosphere of genuine freedom does love exist and grow, and relationships thrive. Relationships in which we seek to dominate, abuse, control, or dictate to others are always damaging—to all parties involved. Love is destroyed in both hearts; individuality is destroyed in the mind of the dominated, while conscience is seared and character is warped in the heart of the domineering.

Only as we return to our God of love and live in harmony with His designs for life and relationships can we experience healing for our minds, marriages, families, and communities. Let's consider God's design laws of love, truth, and freedom and prayerfully ask God to write His law on our hearts and minds and choose to live in harmony with God, practicing His principles in how we treat others.

CHAPTER 7

THE DANCE OF GENDER IN NEW COVENANT MARRIAGE

by Eric L. Johnson

Dancing is one of the great art forms of most complex cultures, and partner dancing has been practiced in the West for centuries, recently brought again to cultural prominence on television in *Dancing with the Stars*. In the best partner dancing, both sexes manifest their talents equally through a highly skilled, choreographed form of embodied interaction—similar to dialogue—except that the man typically takes the lead by subtly signaling the next move and the woman follows.

Yet, through much practice, these roles are played so deftly and collaboratively and the moves so smoothly executed that the leadership is virtually invisible, except to experts. Through this gifted reciprocal collaboration, the couple realizes a unique aesthetic good. Why is this art form still accepted in a culture that questions male leadership in so many other ways? Perhaps because the combined agency, skill, and mutual respect evident in the best dancing produces an undeniable beauty that is compelling precisely because of the gender roles they are enacting; if he were to dominate his partner or if she refused to follow his lead, it just wouldn't be beautiful. In what follows, it will be suggested that new covenant marriage offers even better aesthetic opportunities.[1]

UNDERSTANDING SEX AND GENDER CHRISTIANLY

To advance our understanding of gender in marriage, we must properly distinguish sex and gender and get right their relation. Both are normed by God, but in different ways; sex by biological laws and gender by natural law and social convention. The sex of persons is a physical reality, embodied and relatively easy to determine, externally by one's genitals and microscopically by chromosomes. Established by genetic laws and studied in biology (a natural science), in the vast majority of cases (intersexuals excepted), sex is a binary, material reality: male or female.

Gender is the *sense* one has of one's sex.[2] According to most cultures, including the West until just recently, that sense is supposed to be based on one's sex and its embodied reality, and relevant scriptural teaching suggests that this linkage has ethical implications and is part of God's design plan for human life. As a result, orthodox Christians have generally believed that gender norms are a reflection of natural law, written by God on the human heart (Rom. 2:12–13).[3] At the same time, God has so constituted human life that many of its potentials are necessarily and legitimately shaped by culture and social convention, such as language, art, and to some extent gender (and the cultural norms associated with gender). For example, skirts in most cultures signify female, but in a few cultures, male; and individual men within a culture can express their masculinity in different ways, as individual women may so express their femininity. In addition, gender is affected by hormones, personally experienced, and requires subjective identification and ownership.[4] Correspondingly, gender and its norms are part of immaterial reality and studied by the human (or social) sciences. Unfortunately, because of the fall, the sense of gender is also capable of being distorted, probably resulting from biopsychosocial damage;[5] and furthermore, humans can reject natural law regarding gender norms, as well as sexual behavior, and consent to their disordered desires (James 1:13–14; Rom. 1:24–27), the obvious trend in our day.[6]

To summarize: (1) sex and gender are both binary, bounded, and normed by God; (2) God's design plan allows for some legitimate variability within the bounds of what counts as masculine and feminine, culturally and individually; and (3) those bounds can be transgressed, so that humans sin when they violate God's design plan. From a Christian standpoint, therefore, gender should be understood as a binary *ideal* or archetype of masculinity or femininity, a calling toward which biological males and females, respectively, are to aspire (with a degree of flexibility built in by God). Legitimate generalizations, therefore, can be made about each gender, without their being mutually exclusive.[7] For example, to say that manliness is about taking initiative does not mean femininity entails passivity, or concluding that women tend to be caring of others does not mean that men have no responsibility to care.

Failure to appreciate the transcendent origins of sex and gender in the divine will, and the dependence of the latter on the former, has sowed enormous confusion in our day, for we live in a culture that is abdicating its

> *It is the beginning of disintegration and decay of all the orders of human life when the wife's service is considered a demotion, indeed, an affront to her honor, and when the undivided love of a husband for his wife is considered weakness or even stupidity.*[8] **—Dietrich Bonhoeffer**

responsibility to shape gender according to one's biological sex. Our culture instead teaches its members that gender is purely a matter of one's individual, disembodied preferences or intuitions.

What follows is an analysis of sex and gender norms interpreted through the lenses of creation, fall, and redemption, in order to help new covenant husbands and wives fulfill their unique callings; relate prophetically and compassionately to an increasingly anomic culture, particularly to those anguished individuals whose felt gender would seem to contradict their sex; and at the same time justify the formation of a counterculture, within which the dance of gender in marriage can be practiced and celebrated.

THE CREATED EQUALITY AND SIMILARITY OF MEN AND WOMEN

"The first clear teaching of the Bible is that men and women are equal in terms of value and dignity in creation and redemption."[9] Each are the image of God, and together they especially manifest the fullness of God's image (Gen 1:26–27). This reminds us that God essentially transcends sex and gender and has characteristics reflected in both sexes. Moreover, God blessed them both and directed them together to accomplish the creation mandate to be fruitful and multiply and fill the earth and subdue it and have dominion over it (Gen. 1:28). *Together* they are mandated to be productive in cultural life and reproductive in family life, the two paramount tasks given to all humanity, which will be labeled here, *agency* and *communion*. Expanding on Genesis 1:26–28, Genesis 2 underscores the ontological equality of man and woman by showing that only the creature "woman" corresponds fully to the creature "man"—"for Adam there was not found a helper fit for him" (v. 20b ESV)—so God made another human out of Adam's own body. Afterward Adam sings a song of recognition and correlation, symbolized by their "one flesh" union (v. 24b), which in turn points ahead to the ultimate goal of their relationship: difference in unity.

The equality of the sexes is also illustrated empirically by their similar abilities in uniquely human characteristics. The evidence is abundant that men and women have mostly overlapping abilities on most measures of cognition,[10] achievement motivation,[11] general social orientation,[12] mathematical ability,[13] musical ability,[14] personality,[15] and leadership effectiveness.[16] In light of the research, Hyde[17] has argued that "gender similarities" should be emphasized far more than the comparatively negligible "gender differences." Masculinity and femininity can only be rightly appreciated in the context of the fundamental equality and similarity of the sexes.

REVEALED SEX AND GENDER DIFFERENCES BASED ON ORDER

Scripture does not shed as much specific light on created sex/gender differences as we might wish. Yet this too is an implicit theme of the Bible's first chapters. Adam was created first, from the dust, and Eve was formed from Adam's body, to be a "help" (*ezer*) that complemented and completed him (Gen. 2:18). Then, though pertaining to the fall, rather than creation, we should note that Genesis indicates the serpent tempted Eve first and she succumbed, followed by Adam. As Lee-Barnewall points out, the sequence of these events in the narrative must have significance, even if it is difficult to determine precisely.[18] However, the apostle Paul picked up on this order in his directions to men and women in the church in 1 Timothy 2:11–14 and 1 Corinthians 11:8–9. We should also note that the apostle interpreted humanity's primal sin as Adam's responsibility (Rom. 5:12–21), rather than both Adam and Eve's, or even just Eve's, since she sinned first, suggesting that the man bore primary representative responsibility for the fall, according to inspired New Testament interpretation.

At least three points would seem to follow. First, sex and gender differences are fundamental to the biblical accounts of primal human history. Second, revealed gender distinctions based on the order of the events of creation and the fall tell us something of God's design for gender and justify identifiable gender differences. Finally, Adam held special responsibility for the joint primal sin of the first human pair.

EMPIRICAL RESEARCH ON CREATED SEX AND GENDER DIFFERENCES

To gain the most comprehensive picture of created sex and gender differences possible, we should also consult the available empirical literature. As noted in chapter 5, notable physiological and embodied sex differences distinguish men and women: chromosomal, hormonal, morphological, and gestational. As a consequence, the following biopsychosocial tendencies have also been identified: males are larger than females throughout life;[19] have greater physical strength (e.g., sprinting, throw velocity);[20] boys and men are characterized by a higher level of activity[21] and more kinds of aggression (physical and verbal, though not indirect) than girls and women;[22] boys' play style is rougher than that of girls[23] and boys are more likely to dominate one another than girls do;[24] both boys and girls are more likely to play with same-sex than opposite-sex peers;[25] boys prefer vehicles over dolls and are less willing to play with opposite-sex toys than girls[26] (though both boys and girls typically resist socialization to play across type[27]); men exercise greater cognitive control over their emotions;[28] are more socially oriented toward groups and more motivated by competition;[29] are more likely to take risks;[30] have a stronger sex drive;[31] and are somewhat more likely to use a justice orientation in moral reasoning than women.[32]

In addition, girls play more cooperatively than boys;[33] favor dolls over vehicles;[34] prefer one-on-one social relations over groups;[35] women more accurately identify emotions from facial expressions;[36] process emotions more bilaterally in the brain;[37] are more expressive about their emotions;[38] have greater social skills in relation to emotional intelligence;[39] value closeness in marriage more;[40] are more oriented to close relationships;[41] have friendships that tend to be more intimate;[42] better mobilize social support when stressed;[43] are more responsive when offering support to their spouses;[44] are somewhat more likely than men to use a care orientation in moral reasoning than men;[45] bear and nurse a couple's children; and a far greater percent of mothers keep the children after a divorce (82.5 percent).[46]

When reflecting on such findings, we need to remember that researchers only have access to fallen humans embedded in fallen cultures. Moreover, observed differences are vastly overlapping, and though statistically signifi-cant,[47] are generally relatively small (with a few exceptions: body size, strength, aggression, and sex drive)—and in some cases are growing smaller. Neverthe-less, after over fifty years of research—much of it conducted to undermine gender difference—we are faced with a subtle but substantial body of evidence of a created template of masculinity and femininity upon which cultures for millennia have built their various notions of manhood and womanhood and that the Scriptures take for granted.

The bodies of men, encouraged by their cultures, move them outward; to do, to initiate; to control their emotions; to prefer relating to others in groups than intimate settings; to compete, excel, and focus on justice; and to procreate. The bodies of women, encouraged by their cultures, move them inward and toward others, especially in intimate settings; to be more aware of their emotions and talk about them; to focus more on those in need, than strict justice; to be more collaborative; and to care for others, especially their children. To put it simply, men are generally more oriented toward agency and women more toward com-munion (though they mostly overlap in both capacities).[48]

In the past, especially the primordial past, a sharper division of responsibili-ties existed in which such gender patterns promoted reproduction and survival and provided an adaptive way of life in a harsh and threatening, natural and tribal world. Men and women, with their respective strengths, both contributed to the continuance of our race: the conception, sustenance, birth, nursing of, and caring for the next generation of humans, as well as the development of culture and the provision of food, security, protection from the elements, altogether leading to a prosperous, flourishing human life. Historically, their respective dispositions inclined men to lead in the home and to build a culture and women to concentrate on family life and relationships. Cultural advances in science and technology have made such a sharp division less necessary, but our countercultural challenge today is to respect this deep gender grammar, designed ultimately by God, in a more technologically advanced world.

Even more importantly, we recall that both men and women are created equally in the image of a triune God, who is both agentic and communal.[49] As a result, their overlapping similarity in both aspects and their respective ten-dencies toward one mean that together they best form a complementary pic-ture of the triune God. As a result, the fullest agentic and communal devel-opment of both men and women should be pursued, while also fostering the fullest realization of their respective strengths and gifts. This will entail encouraging boys and men to realize their agentic potential, and doing so for the good of others, for example, for family and community, rather than purely for their own purposes. Similarly, girls and women can be encouraged to realize their fullest communal potential, and doing so as vigorous personal agents. Embracing our common humanity *and* our sex means celebrating the respective configuration of agency and communion of men and women as "two different expressions of human nature,"[50] each having its own advantages (and limitations) that are therefore gifts to the other. Masculine initiative and feminine nurturance, rightly interpreted, are strengths to be shared and used for the good of each other, to help each become more fully an image of God. This happens naturally, for men and women become more alike over the course of their lives;[51] and husbands and wives become more like each other through the course of their marriage.[52]

Stereotypes are cognitive generalizations, the inevitable consequence of finite social minds, and are to be expected in contexts like gender, since there are only two, polar options. Nevertheless, according to creation, humans have two interrelated goals that are both part of God's design plan for their maturation: to become more fully a flourishing personal agent-in-communion *and* to become more masculine or more feminine. In marriage, this will mean, at its best, that husbands will tend to take initiative, will want to lead, and will take responsibility for the well-being of those under their influence; whereas wives will tend to be more concerned with the quality of the relationships, with caring for, getting along with, and promoting the well-being of those under their influence. At the same time, the goal symbolized by their one-flesh union suggests that God intends that their history together promotes their increasing unity. All of this sets the (creational) "stage" for the dance of gender.

FALLEN SEX AND GENDER DIFFERENCES LEAD TO PATRIARCHY AND CODEPENDENCE

Men and women, we are told in Genesis, live under a manifold curse upon their sex, as a consequence of their primal sin (Gen. 3:15–19). In concert with the foregoing, the curse with respect to Adam alone had to do with agriculture, a synecdoche for cultural responsibility; while the curse with respect to Eve alone had to do with childbirth, a synecdoche for familial responsibility. The joint part of the curse referred to gender relations themselves, when God said to Eve, "Your desire will be for your husband, and he will rule over you" (Gen. 3:16b NASB), reflecting a tragic distortion of their respective strengths.

The word used for the woman's desire can be translated "longing," and has strong relational connotations in Song of Songs 7:10.[53] Her originally good desire for communion with her husband will be chronically thwarted, and it likely implies that that desire will itself be corrupted, turning into what we call today "codependence." Her undifferentiated self gets submerged through an over identification with her husband and a corollary neediness for him that overwhelms him, leading him to pull away, which only intensifies her pursuit. Or, perhaps in unconscious reaction to her husband's sinful "rule," she may be inclined to go head-to-head with him, tyrannizing him more subtly through complaints and criticism.[54] Or, perhaps she may gradually despair and give up on the relationship altogether. Regardless, her desire for her husband will be frustrated.

The second half of the joint curse says the man will "rule over" the woman. For centuries, many have argued that this phrase is either a restatement of their created relationship or refers to a change in their respective status, now mandated by God; but both interpretations would seem to justify patriarchy, literally "rule of the father" (Latin *pater*), but will be used in this chapter to refer to the male-centered rule over women, as well as children, that emerged from the fall, and was a distortion of God's design plan for masculinity. It makes better sense, and fits better with the previous section on creation, though, to see this as corollary to the woman's desire for her husband, corrupting the man's created disposition toward agency and initiative, turning it into narcissism and relational autonomy, and therefore explaining the *origin* of patriarchy. It is a consequence of sin, after all. Sin is selfishness, becoming a law unto oneself, the opposite of a loving agency.

In your love you see only the heaven of your own happiness; in marriage you are placed and given responsibility within the world and the human community. Your love belongs only to you personally; marriage is something beyond the personal, an estate, an office. Just as it takes a crown to make a king and not just his will to reign, so it takes marriage and not just your love for each other to make you a married couple both in human and in God's eyes. It is not your love that upholds marriage, but from now on it is marriage that upholds your love.[55]

—Dietrich Bonhoeffer

In their abandonment of a God-centered way of being, legitimate male and female differences came to be motivated by self-centered dynamics. Patriarchy is the fallen masculine identity forged at the cost of others, rather than based on their flourishing. Perhaps the archetypal masculine sin is pride, manifested in domination, self-promoting competition, and sometimes overt aggression. Codependence, we might say, is the fallen feminine identity forged by the loss of oneself, through compromised agency and inhibited personal individuation. Of the seven deadly sins, some have suggested that the archetypal feminine sin is sloth, manifested in self-abnegation, passivity, and passive-aggression.[56] So, the fall turned male and female strengths—respective manifestations of the image and glory of God—into liabilities, even vices.

The above patterns also show up in different forms of psychopathology. Men are more likely than women to have externalizing disorders, reflected in more antisocial behavior and substance abuse, which disregard and hurt others. Shockingly, men have committed 90 percent of the violent crimes in America.[57] Socialization in most fallen cultures has also unfortunately conspired with fallen biology to incline males to deny pain and sadness ("Boys don't cry") and avoid empathy and relational vulnerability, leading to a kind of "emotional circumcision,"[58] technically called *alexithymia*.[59] Women, on the other hand, are more likely than men to have internalizing disorders, like depression, anxiety disorders, and eating disorders, which involve a focus on one's emotions or physical appearance.[60] Corresponding nature/nurture interactions also contribute to greater indecision among women.[61]

With their superior strength and greater overt aggression, males made patriarchy a cultural institution, so its forms became embedded into virtually all cultures and taken for granted as rights, affecting their economic practices, laws, and marriages. As a result, males more consistently got their way, forcing women to obey their agency, seen at its worst in rape, reflective of a stronger sex drive expressed by antisocial narcissists. This state of affairs became normative for most of history—including church history—so that both men and women were largely unable to see it. As a result, patriarchs did not see the self-serving bias in their leadership, and their wives did not see how they had surrendered their God-given agency to another; in the process, both lost some of their image-bearing potential.

The Christian community can benefit from the insights of feminism into the fallen and consequently distorted assumptions, motives, and attitudes that have simultaneously reflected and obscured patriarchal and codependent dynamics. This can be done without without rejecting created sex and gender norms, as equality feminism has done (in contrast to difference feminism and the men's movement of the 1980s, which affirm the valid contributions men and women uniquely make to culture). For greater gender reconciliation to occur, male repentance (in an ironic twist) will entail listening to those whom we have oppressed, if we are to gain the self-awareness necessary to undermine our unconscious tendency to the self-serving dominance of patriarchy, something occurring culture-wide in our day through phenomena like the #MeToo movement. Some Christians still seem resistant to understanding these fallen gender dynamics, particularly from those outside the faith. At the same time, the Christian community could bring greater balance to contemporary discussions by carefully articulating the good of gender differences.

REDEEMING MASCULINITY AND FEMINITY IN MARRIAGE IN THE NEW COVENANT

In His curse upon the serpent, God made a promise to put enmity between him and the woman (in particular), "and between your offspring and her offspring; he shall bruise your head, and you shall bruise his heel." This *proto-evangelium*, cryptically announced the coming of Christ and His atonement, which annulled the consequences of sin for believers. Christ eventually fulfilled that promise and made His blessings flow "far as the curse is found," extending to the end of patriarchy and codependence and the establishment of a new covenant order with respect to gender.

From a new covenant perspective, we are able to see today that some degree of patriarchy was accommodated in the Old Testament era, "because of [men's] hardness of heart" (Matt. 19:8). Most notably, circumcision was the initiatory rite of old covenant membership, a remarkable concession to male privilege. Moreover, polygamy was permissible within that covenant (Deut. 21:15, 17) and practiced by a number of the greatest Israelite leaders (Jacob, David, and Solomon, to name three of the most prominent).

Jesus Himself, however, overruled the patriarchy of that era: "Because of your hardness of heart Moses allowed you to divorce your wives, but from the beginning it was not so" (Matt. 19:8 ESV; see Deut. 24:1–4). There was no comparable right for wives to divorce their husbands. Alluding to God's pre-fall design plan, Christ acknowledged the accommodating ethic of the Old Testament and denounced patriarchal divorce. As the Son, with greater authority than Moses (Heb. 3:1–6), He came to fulfill God's design plan and bring in a new creation ethic, involving the reconciliation of the sexes (Gal. 3:15, 28).

The Bible progressively reveals God and His ethical norms for humanity. As a result, we can see more clearly now—this side of the cross and resurrection—that God was working in stages and reserved the final stage for the establishment of the new covenant, especially symbolized by its initiatory rite of covenant membership: baptism for both men and women. Consequently, new covenant Christians can now recognize the harm of patriarchy to us all, since it undermines feminine agency and prevents men from learning how to love better by listening to the voice and insight of women, especially their wives.

Gender equality and similarity in the new covenant

The initiation of the new covenant era was a spiritual revolution, which has resulted in a much slower series of corresponding cultural reformations. We can see the seeds of a gender reformation in Christ's novel relations with women when on earth (e.g., Luke 10:38; John 4:27); the prominent role women played at the cross and resurrection (Luke 23:27–31; 55–24:11; John 19:25–27; 20:1–2, 11–18); the text from Joel cited in Peter's Pentecost sermon, at the founding of the church, about the Spirit being poured out on sons and daughters, enabling them to prophesy (Acts 2:17); as well as Paul's own teaching that union with Christ overcomes gender division and brings about the unity of the sexes in the new covenant community (Gal. 3:28). With regard to marriage, Paul advocated equal conjugal rights for husband and wife (1 Cor. 7:2–4), a radical idea in his day. Such evidence provided the leaven necessary for an eventual transformation of fallen gender norms into a Christian model for marriage, derived from created sex differences, but fitted for the new creation.

Redemptive gender differences in marriage

Through Christ, God was reconciling the world to Himself (2 Cor. 5:18). He "disarmed the rulers and authorities" (Col. 2:15), died to the "elemental spirits of the world" and their "human precepts and teachings" (Col. 2:20, 22), and brought into being the new creation (2 Cor. 5:17; Gal. 6:15), consisting of a new humanity reconciled to God and each other and being redeemed from the condemnation, power, and consequences of sin.

> For he himself is our peace, who has made us both one and has broken down in his flesh the dividing wall of hostility by abolishing the law of commandments expressed in ordinances, that he might create in himself one new man in place of the two, so making peace, and might reconcile

us both to God in one body through the cross, thereby killing the hostility. (Eph. 2:14–16)

Given his location in redemptive history, Paul focused most of his attention regarding the reconciliation of Jews and Gentiles (see the above passage on Eph. 2), but Christ's work also pertains to the reconciliation of men and women and their emancipation from the fallen human rules that alienated them (Gal. 3:28).

Christ's redemption fundamentally altered all human social relations. Consider the radical implications of the gospel for the wise, the powerful, and the nobility, as well as the foolish, the weak, and the low and despised of this world (1 Cor. 1:20–28), since Christ has overturned the worldly standards of honor and preeminence. "For the foolishness of God is wiser than men, and the weakness of God is stronger than men" (v. 25), and "because of [God] you are in Christ Jesus, who became to us wisdom from God, righteousness and sanctification and redemption" (v. 30). Paul repeatedly elaborated on the ironic reversals Christ himself had said characterized the kingdom of God: "Many who are first will be last, and the last first" (Matt. 19:30). This too has implications for men and women in Christ, particularly husbands and wives.

The apostle specifically addressed their relations in the household codes of Ephesians 5:22–33 and Colossians 3:18–19. His remarks reflect both a respect for the cultural gender norms of that time, as well as the transcendent significance of gender throughout this age, by the respective verbs he used to guide wives and husbands in their relationship and especially the metaphor he applied to it. Wives, he said, are to "submit to" (Eph. 5:22; Col. 3:18) and "respect" (Eph. 5:33) their husband, whereas husbands are to "love" their wife (Eph. 5:25–29, 33; Col. 3:19), as her "head" (v. 23), suggesting that the husband-wife relation is analogous to the relation of Christ and the church (Eph. 5:23–32). This latter move also connects Christian marriage directly to the radical implications of all that Christ has accomplished for the human race, including the gender curse. Paul's teaching here shows indirectly that patriarchy and codependence have in principle been overturned. No longer will a Christian husband be allowed to rule over his wife; she shall be loved like Christ loved the church. And Christ has set her free from the fallen need to find her fulfillment in her autocratic husband's affections; she is instead increasingly to seek his true good. In the new covenant, both images of God are encouraged to take responsibility in a unique way for their mutual flourishing.

Gender directions for wives

We begin by noting that, in the Ephesians passage, Paul had just told all believers to submit to one another (5:21), before using the same verb to guide wives in how they act toward their husband. This encourages us to interpret the wife's respective ethical task within the larger context of the new order established by Christ, in which the greater honor is reserved for servants, rather than those in power, with the Son of Man as the chief exemplar (Matt. 20:20–28; 23:1–12). In *Celebration of Discipline*, Foster considers submission to be one of the great spiritual disciplines and defines it as "the freedom to give up our own rights for the good of others."[62]

Christians committed to patriarchy have confused submission with servility, but they are actually morally opposed. The polar opposite of servility in human relationships is dominance, and they are complementary vices. Submission in the new covenant is a spiritual virtue, in which one nobly acts out of one's strength for the good of the other, demonstrated in vocations like physician or teacher. By definition, such submission cannot be dictated or coerced by a supposed authority; it can only be initiated from within, by the Spirit and love of the other.

Redemptive submission to one's husband, then, cannot mean simply doing whatever he says—agreeing with his ideas; and deferring to his decisions, judgments, and wishes, especially regarding matters that affect her and the family: vacations, school decisions for the kids, her vocation, moving to another city. Such an interpretation would render her more like hired help or a home computer than a co-image of God, and would reinforce codependence, rather than agency-in-communion thus fulfilling the curse, instead of the creation mandate, to say nothing of the new covenant.

Instead, the Holy Spirit through Paul was advocating a glorious, ennobling submission derived from Christ's life, death, and resurrection, capitalizing on her full human capacities, as well as her feminine strengths, in a way that pictures the church's relation to Christ. But the goal is the *true* good of her spouse, helping him to become his true self, the virtuous, flourishing man that God is calling him to be. Mindful, rather than disdainful, of his sins and weaknesses, the new covenant submission of wives involves using one's relational and emotional wisdom skillfully to help him become more like Christ; discerning when to challenge his "remaining narcissism," when it is blinding him and compromising their mutual welfare; as well as sacrificing her preferences and rights when that would advance it or when nothing important is at stake. Wives growing into this virtue are learning increasingly to trust and affirm the good in their husband's initiatives and emotional stability, instead of criticizing, recognizing how chronic disapproval and disrespect compromises her goal to foster a fundamental relational stance of love and acceptance, "just as Christ also accepted us" (Rom. 15:7 NASB). At the same time, their generally superior relational discernment will alert wives when their husband is acting contrary to the family's well-being. Since new covenant submission to him and his ultimate good is agentic and expressive, as well as communal, it will incline wives to share with husbands what will be ultimately beneficial for all.

Wives, of course, are in the best position to help their husband become more conformed to Christ. Paul is simply encouraging them to treat him as they would want to be treated, the way anyone would who wished to influence another for good, implicitly appealing to and utilizing their feminine strengths of nurturance, emotion awareness, and care to help their husband harness his masculine energy and initiative to become more loving—that is, more relationally attuned, emotionally aware, and considerate; therefore, more like Christ. Her challenge will be to patiently (and repeatedly) invite, model, and midwife this growth into a fuller flourishing of virtue for both of them.

This stance of wives helps move marriages out of a transactional orientation—"I'll do my part, if you do yours"—based solely on an ethic of fairness and justice. A committed care orientation to marriage, based on agape love, grace, and perseverance conveys the higher commitment involved in Christian marriage: I'm for you 100 percent; I've got your back; and I require nothing from you in principle, in order to be on your side (knowing that promoting the flourishing of one's spouse ultimately promotes one's own).[63]

Of course, the great irony at the heart of Paul's admonition to wives is that Christ preeminently exemplified such submission in his ministry toward others, symbolized in his washing of the disciples' feet. Fallen women in all cultures will inevitably fall short of such a transcultural gender ideal, and its healthiest exemplifications will scarcely be possible without the joint participation of a kind and loving partner. But such feminine virtue is inconceivable apart from the development of an adequate sense that one is transcendently loved by God, an identity grounded in union with Christ, and an agentic-communal self that is fairly well differentiated from one's husband.

Who is sufficient for these things? Only the triune God can enable wives to make progress on the feminine path toward Christlikeness.

Gender directions for husbands

The metaphor of Christ and the church is even more pronounced in the Spirit's words to husbands, who are to love their wives "as Christ loved the church and gave himself for up for her" (Eph. 5:25). What could more powerfully discredit patriarchy among Christian husbands than the example of Christ, who though divine and human, gave Himself up for His merely human wife, since husbands are ontological equals with their wives? Paul radically redefined masculine leadership according to the life, death, and resurrection of Christ, especially associating it with cruciformity,[64] while still appealing to masculine aspirations for leadership through identification with Christ and being the head of the marriage relationship.[65]

As Paul argued elsewhere, all believers are to count others as more significant than themselves and look not only to their own interests, but also to the interests of others. He called this orientation "having the mind of Christ," who did not count his equality with God a thing to be held on to, but becoming a servant, he humbled himself to the point of death (Phil. 2:3–8). This passage must also apply to marriage. With Christ, husbands are to divest themselves of their metaphorical privilege as the head and consider their wife as more significant than themselves, looking preeminently to her needs and interests. As Paul suggested, this can only happen in marriage as the husband expands his interests, so that they truly encompass his wife's, and his fulfillment is seen as best realized through her flourishing (see Eph. 5:28–29).[66]

Consider further the implications for the husband of the following saying of Christ,

> The kings of the Gentiles lord it over them. . . . But it is not this way with you, but the one who is the greatest among you must become like the youngest, and the leader like a servant. For who is greater, the one who reclines at the table or the one who serves? Is it not the one who reclines at the table? But I am among you as the one who serves. (Luke 22:25–27 NASB)

Patriarchal Christian men have tragically misused the marital metaphor of Christ and the church and grossly overidentified themselves with Christ, as they have lorded over their wives like Gentile kings. On the contrary, having Christ as their analogy makes the most virtuous men shudder, aware of their unworthiness and incapacity.

The Holy Spirit through Paul is calling Christian husbands to a different kind of leadership—leading in love—a wonderful irony, since it turns the universal Christian ethic of cruciformity into a means of masculinity, encouraging men to harness and channel their agentic energy and initiative in the service of others (Luke 22:28–30). Christianity provides a novel way for men to become masculine: courageously taking relational risks over time to demonstrate one's manhood, not in self-promoting competition with one's wife, but by enduring hardship, pain, and suffering for the sake of another, and thereby becoming more like Christ. This transformation of masculinity is one of the greatest achievements of Christianity.[67]

Husbands probably need a special directive to love, since they are generally less relational than their wife. Wise husbands, therefore, will be open to learning about love from their wife and listening carefully to her and her concerns, not discounting her "relational logic" as substandard compared to their own, more "objective" standpoint, but trusting their wife's general advantages in this area. This too is a salutary irony. This love command challenges new covenant husbands to follow Christ to the death of their narcissistic, patriarchal old self in order to become a new kind of man, one who uses his masculine energy and initiative to promote the flourishing of those within his sphere of influence and responsibility.

Leadership without hierarchy entails perceiving and treating one's wife as an equal "heir of the grace of life" (1 Peter 3:8), being kind and gentle, privileging her opinions over his wants, incorporating her unique wisdom and perspective, and being willing to examine his motives when he might be taking advantage of others in the family for selfish purposes. Husbands can transpose their competitive edge into an agape orientation by aiming to be the first to ask for forgiveness, the last to hold a grudge, and the quickest to lay aside defensiveness for the good of the other.

Of course, disagreements will arise. But as husbands grow spiritually, they will feel less of a need to win and be right, making it more possible to establish and maintain an overall atmosphere of love and acceptance, even being willing to accept more blame than he thinks perfectly justified, because in doing so, he will be following Christ's example, who was condemned in the place of his wife. New covenant husbands will challenge their wife, but as they mature, they will increasingly do so when discerning it will be productive and helpful, and when she is best able to receive it.

The love of new covenant husbands will likewise move them beyond a reciprocal, justice stance toward their wife—I'll give 50 percent, so long as you give your 50 percent—and instead seek to act 100 percent of the time with persevering kindness and gentleness, reaching out in love again and again, seventy times seven, regardless of whether one's wife reciprocates, trusting that eventually such love will win out (Rom. 12:20–21), as it did in Christ's resurrection.

Agape leadership is best exercised through dialogical persuasion, that is, through listening and talking and listening some more. Genuine dialogue requires two equal conversation partners, each listening, each able to speak freely, aiming at the good of the other. As new covenant husbands learn to trust the insights of their wife, when unsuccessful in persuading her of a particular course of action, they will conclude that either their case is deficient or she is not ready. Either way, coercion is not an option.

Masculine development also needs solitude, communion with God, gratifying masculine outlets (whatever they are, from sports to art), but especially male friendship and structured opportunities for men to help men become men (women seem to do this together more naturally). The pursuit of masculine virtue described in this chapter is inconceivable apart from an adequate sense that one is complete and perfect in Christ, inseparable from God's love, and an agentic-communal growing self increasingly secure enough to move toward intimacy.

Who is sufficient for these things? Only the triune God can enable husbands to make progress on the masculine path toward Christlikeness.

CONCLUSION

We have seen that men and women were both created in the image of the triune God, agents-in-communion, equal in dignity and worth—though men are somewhat more oriented to agency and women to communion. In the marital relationship, this similarity-difference dialectic provided the ground for husbands and wives to exercise their respective strengths as equal partners in fulfilling the creation mandate to multiply and rule over the creation. But this also set the stage for some high drama. Because of the fall, men turned their strength into tyranny and women into subservience, hoping to be loved in return. New covenant redemption makes possible the realization of God's original intentions in a fallen world: the leadership of husbands demonstrated in reversing the fallen disorder by loving and giving up their life for their wife, so that she might best flourish as a co-agent-in-communion; while the submission of wives is intended to promote their husband's true good, supporting and challenging him to become the best co-agent-in-communion he can be. Both are imitating Christ, God helping them, but doing so according to their gender.

Ultimately, masculinity and femininity are two expressions of glory (a Christian synonym for beauty). God is manifesting His glory in creation, especially in humans, concentrating it in His Son, and secondarily in His people. A special part of that manifestation is the drama and dance of gender. God's infinite glory is best displayed through the greatest variety of human beings, in all their colors, ethnicities, strengths, and struggles. Gender based on sex provides an additional two-fold refraction—masculinity and feminin-ity—each with its own array of variation. Without gender differences based on sex, the human manifestation of the glory of God would be considerably impoverished.

Significant individual differences in genetics, socialization, and narrative guarantee some variance within the parameters of masculinity and feminin-ity of each culture, so that from a Christian perspective these archetypes are best understood as broad-based, yet normative gender ideals toward which biological males and females, respectively, are to aspire. In some marriages, husbands are better cooks and wives better understand the Bible. Such vari-ability is not a problem to be solved; it just demonstrates the diversity of gifts God has generously distributed among His people.

In marriage, men and women have a unique, gendered opportunity to become more like Christ, in relation to a person mostly like us, yet different enough to make life more enjoyable, challenging, and rewarding. In Christ, we need not be threatened by that similarity or those differences. The real problem is our own remaining sin and blindness that keeps us from pursuing the well-being of our mate as well as we might.

So, Christian marriages are a kind of dance, both partners utilizing their unique talents and skills to the fullest, with men leading in love and women corresponding in submission, so that their movements are increasingly col-laborative and their unique and mutual glory of agency and communion becoming more balanced and whole, as each grows better at fostering the beauty of the other, that is, the beauty of Christ. Every couple is different, of course, so Christian charity and an appreciation for Christian liberty will need to guide our view of the dancing of others, but every couple's beauty is to some degree a function of how well the respective gifts of husband and wife come together to realize a greater good than they could have done on their own. Without the respective leading and responding, the dance would fall apart; there would be two individuals, rather than a couple. Yet, the dance of Christian marriage is only a symbol of a greater dance—of Christ with His people—in which all Christians participate, as He leads us into His perfect, eternal glory.

CONTINUING INSIGHT:

UNCOMFORTABLE LOVE

by Brett McCracken

I had a lot of freedom in my single days. Decisions on how to spend my time and my money were completely my own. If I wanted to spend Saturday morning writing at Goldfish Cafe in La Jolla, I could. If I wanted to donate to a charity or political candidate, I could. No one stopped me when I decided to go explore China on my own. No one demanded my time on weeknights and weekends, so I often spent long hours writing, working on books and blog posts as ideas came.

Much of this changed when I started dating Kira, and especially when we got married. How I spent my time and money suddenly mattered to another person. And honestly it was a hard transition. In our engagement I worried that marriage would reduce the time I could spend reading and writing. I feared I could no longer watch every movie or TV show I wanted to watch, nor fly to Europe on a whim if I wanted to. I suspected my blogging frequency would take a hit.

On all these points, I was right. Marriage has meant sacrifice. I can no longer spend the entirety of my Saturdays writing in the coffee shop of my choice. Kira wants to go on walks or spend time in the sun. Not ideal for a fair-skinned Scot like me, but it's what makes her happy. Marriage is about putting the other first. It's about sacrifice, the meaning of love. The cross.

Love found its ultimate expression in Jesus Christ, who sacrificed everything for our sake. He traded His perfect heavenly home for the fragile human form. He endured shame, ridicule, torture, and death in our place. Why? Because God so *loved* the world (John 3:16), that He sent His Son, who loved us and gave Himself for us (Gal. 2:20). "Greater love has no one than this, that someone lay down his life for his friends," said Jesus (John 15:13 esv[1]), both describing His own action and challenging His followers to follow suit.

Self-effacing and others-serving. Sacrificial. This is the central idea of Christian love. "By this we know love, that [Jesus Christ] laid down his life for us, and we ought to lay down our lives for the brothers" (1 John 3:16).

This is the uncomfortable meaning of love. It doesn't lead to easier or sexier lives. It leads to sacrifice. That's the core idea, but it applies in different ways. The following are three facets of the uncomfortable, countercultural, self-giving love that Christ perfectly embodied and that His followers should strive after.

LOVE—NOT A FEELING BUT A COMMITMENT

"Love" is a touchy-feely word in today's world. It's about stomachs with butterflies and cheeks that blush. It's about passion, pain, highs, lows, subject to come and go as circumstances morph. It's a *feeling* as dynamic as the weather. But if there's one thing the God of the Bible demonstrates about love, it is that it is *not* just a feeling. It's a commitment.

In the Old Testament, God *chose* Israel as His people, and continually chose them, even when they didn't choose Him. He established a covenant with them and was a faithful Bridegroom, even when they were an unfaithful bride. Time and time again in the Old Testament, Israel is described as idolatrous and adulterous, choosing to worship idols instead of God (e.g., the golden calf in Exodus 32) and acting like a prostitute who "receives strangers instead of her husband" (Ezek. 16:32). And yet God still pursues His people. His love is steadfast. The prophetic message of Hosea captures the dynamic vividly. Played out in a real-life marital drama between Hosea and Gomer, the message of Hosea is that even when Israel is adulterous (symbolized by Gomer), the Lord (symbolized by Hosea) is faithful.

If God is our model, then love is clearly "not primarily emotion or affection, but rather a covenant *commitment* to another person," writes Scot McKnight. "Commitment does not deny emotions; commitment reorders emotions."[2]

This is not how contemporary Western culture conceives of love.

The saying goes, "First comes love, *then* comes marriage . . ." We see love as the emotional prerequisite for relational commitment, not the obedient outgrowth of it. Marriage is viewed as a ceremonial officializing of an already-existing state, a champagne-popping party that pays little heed to the sober vows ("for better or worse, till death do us part") that have become little more than trite phrases for romantic-comedy movie posters and bridal magazines.

Society's conflation of love and emotion has led to unhealthy expectations. We assume there must be immediate fireworks with a potential mate, for example. We buy in to Hollywood's ideas of love-at-first-sight, "soul mates," and finding *the one* who "completes me." In our work with young adults, my wife and I have seen how much of a burden these ideas can be. If there is only one out there who is *the* one for each of us, how much pressure is that? Young people become obsessed with compatibility, and relationships never get off the ground because there are too many fears about being the perfect fit for each other. But *the one* is as unbiblical as it is illogical. What are the odds that the *one* woman in the world for me just so happened to work a few cubicles over from me in the administrative offices of Biola University? As my pastor, Alan, says, we don't marry soul mates. We marry "suitable strangers."

Society today dislikes the idea that love is *learned* as a *result* of commitment. The notion that a relationship's longevity depends not on emotional vitality but on unflinching commitment is distasteful to us. This is why many people (sadly including many Christian churches) see nothing wrong with divorce. If love is emotion, then it can come and go as emotions do. If marriage is just about us feeling happy, then the minute a marriage stops delivering happiness it is easy to justify ending it.

Richard Hays wisely observes that the church's permissive attitude toward divorce "has developed within a wider cultural context that regards marriage as a purely private affair, based on the feelings of romantic love. One 'falls in love' and gets married; when the feeling of being 'in love' dissipates, so does the basis for the marriage."[3]

Critics are right to point out the hypocrisy of evangelicals who cling to the Bible's teaching on homosexuality but conveniently ignore its teachings on divorce. As one recent observer wrote, lax attitudes toward divorce demonstrate how "evangelical leaders appear increasingly comfortable jettisoning those parts of the Bible that might interfere with their ministry to contemporary America."[4]

If Scripture's clear prohibition of homosexual conduct is an uncomfortable truth for progressive churches, Scripture's clear teachings on divorce (Mark 10:1–12) should be an equally uncomfortable truth for many congregations with high divorce rates.

The uncomfortable principle at the core of both issues is that love requires sacrificing the sovereignty of our feelings. Love cannot survive on the basis of emotional satisfaction. It is *covenantal*. And this is a hard truth to stomach, because it requires faithfulness even when we're not feeling it, even when our "heart isn't in it."

Cruciform love doesn't always feel rewarding and it doesn't always look like progress. But it does look like sacrifice and servanthood. Which is to say, it looks like Jesus (Mark 10:42–45; John 13:1–17).

LOVE SERVES THE OTHER, NOT SELF

Cruciform love does not insist on its own way. It is patient, it bears all things, endures all things (1 Cor. 13). Note that this doesn't mean hating yourself or enduring abuse. It doesn't mean serving *only* others while you wither in loneliness and bitterness. Love is mutual, and relationships in which only one party sacrifices are unsustainable.

But love at its best only works when each party gives more than each takes, seeking the other's flourishing *first*. This may look like weakness to the world, and Lewis is right that "to love at all is to be vulnerable,"[5] but weakness is strength in the economy of Christ. It's vulnerable for foster families to love a child who will only be in their care for a temporary time. It's vulnerable to speak up to a friend about a damaging pattern you observe in their life. It's vulnerable to enter a potentially dangerous situation in order to help someone at risk. This sort of love is countercultural in a world of consumerism and self-preservation, where the default is to seek first what is easiest and best for me.

One way we can embody the radical nature of this other-serving, vulnerable love is by truly being present and all-in with our love. This goes for how we love God, with "an undivided heart" (Ps. 86:11 NIV), and how we love others, with our undivided attention. This means we love by being undistracted, by turning off our phones when having coffee with someone. It means we exercise humility by being good listeners, quicker to hear and slower to speak (James 1:19). It might mean being inconvenienced for the sake of prioritizing physical presence: taking time out of a busy schedule to have a meal with someone rather than settling for a text message or Facebook exchange. It will likely look like uncomfortable hospitality: inviting strangers and hard-to-love neighbors into your home, or including the awkward outsider on your party invite list, and then giving them the seat of honor.

This sort of self-giving love works because it is how God-in-three-persons functions. The other-serving love between Father, Son, and Holy Spirit is one in which each "magnifies the other, wants the other to have the glory, and wherever possible gives to the other."[6]

This is also how love in marriage should work. Ephesians 5 is clear that in their complementary difference and selfless postures toward the other, husbands and wives are meant to represent Christ and the church. "This mystery is profound," says Paul in verse 32.

What does married love as a metaphor for Christ and the church mean for us? It means that husbands especially have an uncomfortable responsibility. In the way we love our wives, we are representing Christ! Too often we represent Him poorly because we fall in step with the culture's posture of self-serving, pride-building, pleasure-seeking love. Yet we are called to sacrifice for our wives, as Christ sacrifices for the church.

The "mystery" is countercultural because it situates marriage as a signpost of something beyond the couple, something more important than the individuals. This is the opposite of the popular conception, which sees marriage as largely "a means of self-fulfillment accompanied by sexual satisfaction," according to David Platt:

> A man or woman's aim is to find a mate who completes him or her. In this view, marriage is an end in itself, and sexual consummation is a celebration of such completion. Yet the Bible teaches that God created marriage not as an end but as a means to an end . . . [Marriage] is a living portrait drawn by a Divine Painter who wants the world to know that he loves his people so much that he has sent his Son to die for their sins.[7]

This is all very counter to the self-focused, "just-the-two-of-us" view of love and marriage that "suffuses almost all of our cultural narratives," observes James Smith.[8] The extravagant spectacles of today's typical wedding, "in which we get to be centre stage, display our love, and invite others into our romance in a way they'll never forget," is case in point, says Smith. These picture-perfect parties often set up marriages to fail because they frame them as "privatized enclaves for romance" removed from a higher goal or common good. "When lovers are staring into one another's eyes," argues Smith, "their backs are to the world."

Yet love was never meant to be a hideaway experience. When it is, it invariably fails. When love is outward focused, with a mission beyond itself, it flourishes. Kira and I have seen this in our own marriage. We eschewed the "nesting" mentality of newlywed life as a "privatized enclave of romance." We opted instead to jump right into the ministry of hospitality, inviting other couples, singles, and college students into our home on an almost open-door basis. We knew from our combined giftings that hospitality was likely one of God's purposes for our marriage, and that has proven to be the case.

Little has done more to strengthen our marriage than this outward-mindedness. It has been taxing and uncomfortable at times, yes. For introverts like us it's easier to hunker down and live quietly in our own private space. But we know our marriage isn't for us. We know it will not last into eternity. But we also know it will help prepare us for that day, and hopefully others too.

UNCOMFORTABLE LOVE PUSHES US TOWARD HOLINESS

One of the uncomfortable things about Christian love is that it isn't always nice. It doesn't always look like tolerance. On the contrary, love is sometimes about discipline and speaking truth, even when it hurts. This again is about sacrifice; the sacrifice of potentially offending someone you care about. But even if it is met with shame or discomfort, this sort of love is undeniably loving, for it has the person's best interests in mind. As Aquinas scholar Josef Pieper says, "Love is not synonymous with undifferentiated approval of everything the beloved person thinks and does in real life . . . love is also not synonymous with the wish for the beloved to feel good always."[9]

Love hurts. It hurts because it doesn't sit idly by while the beloved destroys herself. Like Christ with the woman caught in adultery in John 8, we can lead with empathy and love ("Let him who is without sin among you be the first to throw a stone at her," v. 7) but also call a person to stop sinning ("Go, and from now on sin no more," v. 11).

Society tells us love means accepting others "just as they are," without asking them to change. But biblical love is not about solidarity in brokenness; it's about committing to each other's holiness (as well as our own).

Relationships that model this are modeling the very heart of God, whose covenantal love for His people is grounded in discipline and demands of righteousness. There is no contradiction between truth and love, mercy and judgment, grace and discipline in God's character. As David Wells puts it: "He is the source of all that is utterly good, and such is his holy nature that he will, in judgment, consume all that has reared itself against him and against what is good. He both judges and is loving simultaneously."[10]

Sadly, the church often favors one end of the spectrum or the other. Focusing on God's love without His holiness results in "a Christianity that is benign, culturally at home, racy, politically correct, and endlessly tolerant," argues Wells, while on the other extreme, "God's love gets eclipsed in practice by his holiness, and then his holiness gets reduced to the accountant's old ledger book."[11]

We need to hold the tension of truth and love. They are not mutually exclusive. I like how Biola University president Barry Corey talks about it in his book *Love Kindness*, as the tension between "firm centers and soft edges."[12] Compassion does not mean we give up our convictions, and holding firm to truth does not mean we live without love.

The church needs to model this better. We need to take cues from Paul, whose letters to problematic early churches (Corinth, for example) were filled with rebuke and discipline inspired by and grounded in profound love. Describing a painful letter he had written to the church in Corinth, which had struggled with sexual immorality, Paul says: "I wrote you out of great distress and anguish of heart and with many tears, not to grieve you but to let you know the depth of my love for you" (2 Cor. 2:4 NIV). Whether the people we love are unrepentant in their sin or "not acting in line with the truth of the gospel" (Gal. 2:14 NIV), we owe it to them to confront them, compassionately and not hypocritically (Matt. 7:4–5). Joshua Ryan Butler says it like this: "Our world is desperately in need of love that is more than *comfort*; we need love that is also a *confrontation*."[13]

This sort of love is risky and uncomfortable, to be sure. But it is necessary. To love someone as Christ loves is to meet them in their sin but to not let them stay there. It is to walk with them in their battles and struggles, urging them onward (and they you) in the renovation of the heart. This will be messy and painful at times, requiring grace and sacrifice on all sides. But the more love takes on a cruciform shape, the more powerful it becomes.

This material has been adapted with permission from "Uncomfortable Love" in *Uncomfortable: The Awkward and Essential Challenge of Christian Community* by Brett McCracken (Wheaton, IL: Crossway, 2017).

CHAPTER 8

RECLAIMING HOLY SEXUALITY ·

by Juli Slattery

I was a guest on a Christian radio program when the host asked me this question: "Sexuality has caused so much pain in marriage and problems for Christians. How do we manage this part of our Christian lives?"

This man's question represents for me a massive paradigm shift we must make related to our approach to sexual issues. Sexuality is not a problem to be managed but a territory to be reclaimed. Yes, for many Christian couples, sexuality represents a struggle . . . a battle with porn, a conflict in marriage, a cloud of shame. However, beneath all the symptoms of broken sexuality is a fundamental problem: we have a superficial view of sexuality and its place within marriage.

Our greatest conflict over sexuality isn't about how often to have sex or how to defeat the impact of porn. The battle lies within the answer to this one question: Does sex within my marriage display the metaphor of God's covenant love?

Throughout this book, you're being challenged to see the deeper spiritual meaning of marriage. Many Christians readily grasp the idea that marriage is a reflection of God's love for us and an expression of the unity within the Trinity. However, linking sexuality to God's love is a much greater leap. Sexual intimacy is, after all, quite earthy. It involves our physical bodies and far too often is associated with our carnal desires. How then, could our sexuality possibly have a positive spiritual connection for us, even within marriage?

As we look at the changing views of sexual ethics within our culture, the fundamental shift does not lie within questions about issues like same-sex marriage or cohabitation. Rather, the erosion of sexual morality is rooted in our confusion about why we are sexual people.

Don Schrador, a secular humorist observed, "To hear many religious people talk, one would think God created the torso, head, legs and arms, but the devil slapped on the genitals."[1] That's a rather crude way of stating what many of us at some level believe. We know that we are created in God's image, but His divine plan does not seem to extend to our sexuality. Many Christians perceive sexual passion as devil-ridden rather than a God-ordained aspect of humanity. As a result, our approach to sexual conversations is often to "swat away" or try to manage typical problems like sexual temptation, arguments about frequency of sex in marriage, and pornography. This strategy has proven ineffective because it is defensive in nature and limited in scope. We will never solve sexual problems until we first embrace a paradigm that helps us make sense of our sexuality.

The culture has done a phenomenal job of writing a narrative about human sexuality. We are continually told that sexuality is for the purpose of self-expression, identity, and connection. Popular culture is repetitive and insistent in teaching us this narrative, providing endless role models of how healthy sexuality results from self-exploration and free expression. In contrast to this attractive narrative, the Christian church has given a list of sexual dos and don'ts with very little context of how our sexuality is to be integrated with who we are as God's people.

Reclaiming sexuality begins with telling God's story of why He created us as sexual people. Tragically, many Christians see the gospel as antithetical to sexuality. It seems heretical to put the words "gospel" and "sexuality" in the same sentence. Ironically, God has created sexuality to be a physical, biological metaphor of the gospel. You might even say that the gospel message is written within our sexuality.

SEXUALITY AND COVENANT LOVE

Everything God has created has a spiritual purpose . . . to reflect God's character and His nature. The Scriptures are rife with examples of physical things that teach us spiritual truths. The stars declare His majesty and the seasons His faithfulness. Jesus taught His disciples by pointing to vineyards, sheep, and food. God also created our relational world to express His character. Every child is born to a mother and father. Whether these parents are good or evil, family is an inseparable part of being human. Likewise, every human institution possesses authority to which we submit. We biologically experience seasons of helplessness (infancy, old age, illness) to teach us healthy dependence on those who love us. Scripture teaches us about our relationship to God through connecting to our experiences within our God-ordained relational world. Likewise, the purpose of our sexuality is fundamentally rooted within what it reflects about the character of our Creator.

Karol Józef Wojtyła, who became Pope John Paul II, spent much of his pre-papal ministry studying and teaching what has become known as the "Theology of the Body." He believed that the message of God's love and faithfulness is written on our bodies, specifically within our sexuality. As we study sexual wholeness and brokenness, we see the testimony of our greatest spiritual needs: intimate knowing, passionate love, and fidelity.

Pope John Paul's work pushes into truths that we already know and acknowledge, but often fail to integrate into every day life. David Platt puts it this way: "When God made man, then woman, and then brought them together in a relationship called marriage, he wasn't simply rolling the dice, drawing straws, or flipping a coin. He was painting a picture. His intent from the start was to illustrate his love for his people . . . For God created the marriage relationship to point to a greater reality. From the moment marriage was instituted, God aimed to give the world an illustration of the Gospel."[2] Russell Moore, echoes this truth in his own words. "Ephesians 5 is not a collection of tips for a happier, healthier marriage. Paul wrote that he was declaring that marriage is a 'great mystery,' the mystery of Christ and his church. In Christ and the church, Paul was not searching for

Sex is involved in love; but sex by itself is not love. It is easy for people who are strongly attracted to each other sexually to assume that they are meant for each other and that this attraction is love. True love is never selfish.[3] —**Billy Graham**

metaphors for human love. Marriage is itself the metaphor, the embodied image of the pattern God had already set. . . . To dispense with marriage and family, as God defines them, is to dispense with a mystery that points to the gospel itself."[4]

We will never grasp the spiritual significance of sexuality until we understand its link to the gospel message.[5] The starting point of all conversations about sexual issues must begin with the understanding that God intentionally created our sexuality to tell the story of His covenant love.

One evidence of this link between sexuality and God's love is the dual usage of the Hebrew word *yada* in the Old Testament. This word *yada* implies deep knowing and intimate knowledge. The writers of the Old Testament used this word to describe both sexual intimacy between two people and spiritual intimacy between God and His covenant people.

In the book of Genesis, we are told that Adam *yada* his wife and they gave birth to a son (Gen. 4:1). Then in the book of Exodus, we read Moses's plea to *yada* God and His ways (Ex. 33:13). David praised how God intimately knew him when he said, "You *yada* when I sit and when I rise" (Ps. 139:2 [6]). God intimately knows us. He has created us with deep yearnings that cause us to seek Him and search for Him. Our sexuality is a reminder that we were not made to be alone . . . first here on earth, but ultimately for eternity. We were created to experience intimate fellowship.

God created you as a sexual person in order to unlock the mystery of knowing an invisible God. John Piper alludes to this in his assessment that "The ultimate reason why we are sexual is to make God more deeply knowable."[7] Embedded within human sexuality are echoes of eternal truths of a God who loves us passionately, sacrificially, and faithfully.

Passionate celebration of covenant

While youth and young adult pastors are working to convince single Christians to abstain from sex, marriage and family pastors seem to be working just as vigorously to encourage married Christians to enjoy sex. How ironic that one of the greatest struggles for married couples is the freedom to enjoy the sexual pleasure they formerly tried so hard to avoid! Most husbands and wives have disagreements about how often to have sex, what's okay in the bedroom, and how to make their marriage bed an emotionally safe place.

While many married couples resign themselves to a mediocre (or even nonexistent) sex life, Paul urged married Christians to make sexual intimacy a priority (see 1 Cor. 7:1–5). The fact that the Song of Songs is one of the sixty-six books of the Bible indicates that a healthy sex life between husband and wife is a spiritual, God-honoring pursuit.

Why would God care if a married couple pursues sexual passion in marriage? Isn't it far more important for them to serve their church together or focus on raising their children? God cares about sexual passion in marriage because of what it reflects about God's passion for His people. Just as worship is a passionate expression of our love for God, sexual intimacy is a God-ordained way to celebrate the passion of the covenant promise between a husband and his bride. God is a passionate God and has created us to be passionate people. In a sermon titled "Lust and Love," Timothy Keller describes it this way:

> When you use sex inside a covenant, it becomes a vehicle for engaging the whole person in an act of self-giving and self-commitment. When I, in marriage make myself physically naked and vulnerable, it's a sign of what I've done with my whole life. . . .
>
> Sex is supposed to be a sign of what you have done with your whole life. . . . If you have sex inside a covenant then the sex becomes a covenant renewal ceremony. It becomes a commitment apparatus. You're getting married all over again. You're giving yourself all over again. It's incredibly deepening and solidifying and nurturing. . . . In marriage when you're having sex, you're really saying, "I belong completely and exclusively to you and I'm acting it out. . . . I'm giving you my body as a token of how I've given you my life. I'm opening to you physically as a token of the fact that I've opened to you in every other way."[8]

Through sexuality, God has given us an opportunity to practice with our bodies the passionate devotion of covenant. The promise a husband and wife make to each other was never intended to be one of stoic duty, but of intimacy and vulnerability.

As we become more aware of our biology, we see that engaging in sexual intimacy within a covenant relationship reinforces fidelity, bonding, and positive feelings toward one's spouse. It's almost as if sex was designed to be a covenant celebration party within our minds and bodies. Sex within a committed relationship releases chemicals like oxytocin (a bonding hormone), dopamine (a neurotransmitter that makes us feel good), and endorphins (natural pain killers and stress reducers).

Unfortunately, some Christian couples don't feel the freedom or permission to enjoy the full celebration of sexual intimacy within their marriage. After years of hearing implied or explicit teaching that sexual desire is sinful, they have difficulty flipping that switch to "God wants you to have fun in marriage." Sex becomes restrained for one or both partners.

Thankfully, God has given us the Song of Songs to express His blessing on sexual passion within marriage for both the husband and the wife. Like the chorus said to the lovers in the Song, God says to a husband and wife, "Eat, friends, and drink; drink your fill of love" (Song 5:1). When a man and woman give themselves fully to each other in celebration of their covenant, they not only please God but participate in a spiritual metaphor reminding us that God's love for His people is passionate.

Frankly, it's not okay for a husband and wife to neglect sexual intimacy in their marriage. It's not okay for them to share their bodies (sexual activity) without intentionally working to share the sexual journey of heart, soul, and spirit (sexual intimacy). True sexual intimacy is not just giving your body to your spouse, but together building the trust and communication to celebrate as one.

I've met so many men and women who view sexual intimacy as a chore rather than a celebration of love. They don't think sexual passion is worth fighting for and pursuing together. Likewise, I've met many Christians who serve God out of duty and obedience but don't know how to love Him with passion. I happened to be one of them.

Several years ago, I met Linda Dillow. I had been asking the Lord to bring me a spiritual mentor to challenge me in my faith and for accountability in public ministry. When Linda and I met, we quickly formed a close relationship. As we shared about our respective spiritual journeys, I was captivated by how Linda talked about her relationship with the Lord. She described Him as her lover, her best friend, and her most trusted counselor. She used words like "sweet" in reference to the Lord's loving care toward her. While I had been a Christian since preschool, I had never experienced this type of relationship with God. A word picture came to my mind. God was in His holy temple and I was on the outside of the gate, dutifully serving Him, hoping that through eternity I would be in His presence. As I peeked over the gate, I saw Linda there with the Lord, worshiping and enjoying His presence. How did she get there? I felt a longing to have that kind of relationship with my God and Savior. I want to be more than a dutiful servant; I longed to be an intimate worshiper. God invites us into this passion.

Passionate intimacy is an important ingredient of a successful marriage, but it's also an expression of our response to God's love. The Lord asks us to love Him not with joyless obedience but with passion. Consider David's expressions of emotion in the psalms, which include both praise and lament. He wrote songs of his love for God and even celebrated Him with dancing, on one occasion "dancing before the LORD with all his might" (2 Sam. 6:14). When his wife criticized him for "leaping and dancing before the LORD" in public (v. 16), the king retorted, "I will become even more undignified than this, and I will be humiliated in my own eyes" (v. 22). David knew how to extol God and His love not only with his intellect but with his heart. We can learn to do the same. Many Christians "'appreciate' God's covenant love but . . . have never celebrated (or even know how to celebrate) covenant love."[9]

When Christian couples accept a mediocre sex life, they mute an important aspect of this metaphor of God's passionate covenant love. As a Christian husband and wife pursue true sexual pleasure and intimacy, they are restoring and participating in a holy metaphor of profound spiritual experience. In essence, they are reclaiming territory that had been previously conceded to the enemy to distort at his will.

Sacrifice in covenant

Single Christians will sometimes ask me, "Why would you marry someone you haven't slept with? How will you know if you are sexually compatible?" I find this question somewhat laughable because men and women are by nature sexually incompatible. For men, sex leads to feelings of love. For women, feelings of love lead to sex. Men are quickly aroused and satisfied. Women . . . not so much. Men want direct stimulation in one place, and women want to be touched everywhere, delaying direct stimulation. Men want sex in order to relax. Women must relax in order to enjoy sex. Men tend to be visually aroused while women are aroused through emotional connection and physical sensation. As a result, men and women are sexually incompatible by God's design.

Adam and Eve were created as male and female in the garden of Eden before sin entered the world. We can assume that these same differences were hard-wired within their bodies just as they are within ours. Sin did not create differences between men and women sexually—sin distorted our approach to these differences.

Imagine a husband and wife who *were* completely, 100 percent sexually compatible, who never had to communicate with each other about likes and preferences. They never had to work through disagreements and hurt feelings. They never had to compromise or understand each other. While we might wish for this compatibility, I believe such a situation would prevent us from learning a key aspect of the metaphor of God's covenant love: unselfishness and sacrifice. Because men and women are so different, they must learn to love in order to experience a great sex life.

God is not so concerned about how we have sex. He is far more concerned about how we love each other. The pursuit of sexual intimacy for many couples is the greatest test and refiner of their love for each other. Early in my marriage, I used to ask God why sexual intimacy was so difficult in our marriage. Why did we have so many barriers to enjoying this gift that God supposedly gave us? God answered my prayer by showing me that sex is a lot like Legos. When a child receives the gift of Legos, he doesn't expect to find the completed picture on the box. Instead, he understands that the fun is in building and creating. In the same way, God has given us the gift of sex that we might together work on building something. Sexual intimacy is all about teaching us to build true love . . . the kind of love that God has for us.

God's covenant love for His people required great sacrifice. The Father sent His Son to suffer and die because of how much He loves us. Why would God's picture of covenant love not also require that we learn to sacrifice for one another?

Whatever challenges a couple may be experiencing in their sexual relationship, they would do well to consider them as an opportunity for them to learn to truly love each other. By being honest about a porn addiction, by extending mercy and forgiveness, by being patient as a spouse heals from past sexual wounds, and by denying one's own desire for the sake of the other, the couple will learn critical elements of God's great love for them. It is impossible to honor God with our sexuality (as single or married Christians) without learning to be unselfish.

A single Christian can demonstrate love for others by protecting their sexual dignity and purity. They can determine whether their thoughts, actions, and motives toward others are consistent with God's call to sacrificially love others or whether they are fueled by selfish desires. The sexual temptations and battles in our world are about much more than following God's list of right and wrong. Ultimately they develop our ability to deny ourselves in order to love as our Lord Jesus has loved us.

Biblical sexual morality isn't about keeping a list of rules. It's about learning to channel our most powerful desires through the lens of authentic love. This is an indispensable element of the metaphor of God's sacrificial love.

Fidelity in covenant

Perhaps the most central characteristic of covenant love is faithfulness. In contrast to the majority of human relationships, the covenant of marriage asks for the commitment to loyal love. The promise of marriage was never intended to be based on feelings, romance, or desire but on the ambition to love and to be loved for a lifetime. In sickness and in health. For richer and for poorer. For better or for worse. We know the familiar words, but have we ever considered that they echo the promises we hold so dear from our Lord? "I will never leave you or forsake you." "Nothing can separate us from the love of God in Christ Jesus." "I will be with you even to the ends of the earth." (See Deut. 31:6; Rom. 8:37–39; Matt. 28:20.)

Divorce and infidelity are physical reminders of the waves of tragedy and loss that follow a broken covenant. We all know stories like Dan and Karen's. College sweethearts, they began their marriage confident in their love and their commitment to each other and God. As is common, the first few years brought the challenges of waning sexual attraction, financial stress, and a baby on the way. Soon after learning that Karen was pregnant, Dan second-guessed his decision to marry so young. He became attracted to a woman at work who flirted with him and encouraged him in ways that Karen no longer did. The flirtation led to much more.

Although Karen sensed her husband pulling away emotionally, she was totally unprepared for the devastating news Dan dropped on her one Saturday morning. "Karen, I'm not in love with you anymore. Marriage isn't what I thought it would be and I want out." In a moment, Karen's hopes and visions for the future evaporated. Heartbroken, five months pregnant, working part-time, and living in a town far away from family, what would she do?

The ripple effects of Dan's decision to pursue "love" rather than to hold to his covenant continued decades later. His son became a pawn between mom and dad, growing up in two households vying for his loyalty, and had trouble with commitment himself as an adult. Divorce and infidelity are so common today that we fail to acknowledge the painful consequences visited on family and friends as well as on the individuals themselves.

While sexuality within marriage is an incredible gift, the misuse of this gift creates waves of devastation. The tangible pain, anguish, and destruction of a broken covenant and betrayal here on earth teach us about the not-so-obvious consequences of unfaithfulness to God. The Old Testament prophets used very graphic sexual terminology to describe the spiritual adultery of the Jewish people. The book of Hosea clearly links the prophet's experience of sexual covenant, infidelity, and redemption with the drama of God's pursuit of His Beloved Israel.

Just as great sex within marriage teaches us about God's passion and sacrificial love, a broken vow teaches us how dangerous it is to turn our back on our Creator. Divorcing because we have "fallen out of love" and staying married only "until boredom do us part" have become so commonplace that the concept of covenant is totally lost within our modern understanding. Because we have not taken marital fidelity seriously, we have compromised the beautiful metaphor of God's promise to love us with an everlasting love.

God did not create sexuality as a random way to make babies. He intentionally created our sexuality to be passionate, intimate, and vulnerable. As Paul explains in 1 Corinthians 6:12–20, our sexuality is mysteriously linked to our spiritual identity as children of the Most High God. Every sexual choice is a spiritual choice because of the significance with which God imbedded our sexuality.

SEX AND THE SPIRITUAL BATTLE

When I teach the connection between spiritual covenant and sexuality at events, I sometimes have women say to me something like, "What you are describing is so far from my experience! Sex has always been dirty, oppressive, and associated with shame. I can't even begin to wrap my mind around the idea that it's holy." I suspect that many honest men would have a similar reaction. They learned about sex through pornography, which objectifies a woman's body, and then they experience waves of shame associated with their sexual passion.

We have an enemy who understands the incredible power of sexuality. Even if we can't grasp it, Satan knows that when we experience sex as it was intended, we will have a tangible picture of God's great covenant love. In my work with women, over and over again I see that as they heal sexually, they grow in their love for God. Satan will do anything he can to separate us from experiencing the fullness of holy sexuality. Human sexuality is a masterpiece embedded with spiritual significance, a masterpiece that is constantly under attack in the spiritual realms.

Scripture tells us that we can be prepared to stand against Satan because we are not unaware of his schemes (2 Cor. 2:11). In his attempts to destroy the masterpiece of sexuality, our enemy employs three predicable strategies. They are what I call the three Ds: distortion, doubt, and deception.

Distortion

If you've ever been to an art museum, you have likely noticed that security guards stand watch in practically every room. Their purpose is not simply to prevent theft, but also to protect priceless art from the destruction of vandalism. Why someone would want to throw paint on a beautiful Rembrandt or disfigure one of Michelangelo's sculptures is beyond me, but some people are driven to destroy. Satan has such a drive. Since he cannot create anything, he desecrates the beautiful gifts God has created.

Christopher West writes,

> If the body and sex are meant to proclaim our union with God, and if there's an enemy who wants to separate us from God, what do you think he's going to attack? If we want to know what's most sacred in this world, all we need do is look for what is most violently profaned. The enemy is no dummy. He knows that the body and sex are meant to proclaim the divine mystery. And from his perspective, this proclamation must be stifled. Men and women must be kept from recognizing the mystery of God in their bodies.[10]

The beautiful "canvas" of sexuality has been repeatedly vandalized to the point where many of us can't identify what it was originally created to represent. I think of a mature Christian woman I recently talked with who, because of horrific childhood abuse, believes sex is always dirty and tainted with lust and violence. Other Christians have no problem enjoying sex, but see it as completely devoid of relational meaning and significance.

Many of Satan's attempts to vandalize sexuality involve separating sex from its relational and spiritual purpose. Pornography, hooking up, and even having (or withholding) sex for the purpose of selfish desire are examples of this disconnect. I've talked to Christian couples who, while sharing their bodies sexually, nurture private individual fantasies or recall pornographic images. We must understand that this is a distortion of God's design for sexuality, even within the confines of marriage. Sexual purity is not just saving sex for marriage, but the wholehearted pursuit to honor the spiritual and relational significance of covenant love.

Every one of us bears the marks of Satan's distortion of sexuality. In this fallen world, it is a challenge for all of us, married or single, to grasp the beauty of this rich metaphor of covenant love. Some people grew up in a religious setting that reinforced the idea of sex as sinful and dirty. Others learned about sex through experimentation as a teenager. And even Christians may agree with the cultural narrative that healthy sexuality is primarily rooted in self-pleasure and personal identity. Each of these is the work of Satan's distortion.

A simple experiment is to, over a few days, pay attention to what is presented in entertainment, the media, conversations, images, and so on about sexuality. It is overwhelming how thoroughly Satan's attempts to distort sexuality have infiltrated culture, homes, and even churches.

Doubt

Satan's second strategy is using sexuality to cause us to doubt God's goodness. Countless men and women have walked away from a relationship with the true God because of what the Bible teaches about sex. How many individuals and churches have distanced themselves from God because they can't accept biblical teaching on issues like homosexuality and cohabitation? What began as a discussion about sexual morality resulted in a conclusion that the God of the Bible is not trustworthy.

Teaching an incomplete message about God and sexuality can cause people to walk away from Him. A few years ago, I read a blog post written by a woman who captured the doubt experienced by many who have found Christian teaching on sexuality to be confusing and restrictive. At the age of ten, her Christian church encouraged her to sign a purity covenant, promising to save sex for marriage. She found much of her identity and right standing with God in her ability to keep this pledge and was able to abstain from intercourse until her wedding night. But when she got married, she still associated her normal feelings of sexuality with guilt and shame. In her words, "I couldn't figure out how to be both religious and sexual at the same time. I chose sex."

We must understand that our enemy's desire is to do more than cause us to reject God's standard of sexual holiness. He also wants us to doubt God Himself.

When we look at Satan's first assault on humanity in the garden of Eden, we read three statements that represent the kinds of lies our enemy uses even today in his assault on holy sexuality: "Did God really say?" "You will certainly not die," and "For God knows . . ." In these three statements, Satan tempts us to doubt God's Word, the consequences of sin, and God's heart for our good. His strategy was successful many thousands of years ago and is still successful today. *Did God really say* sex should be reserved for marriage? That marriage should be between a man and woman? *You will certainly not* experience pain, punishment, and separation from God if you choose to indulge in pornography. God understands. *For God knows* that great joy is found through going after what you want. He's trying to keep you from happiness.

Deception

Jesus flat out called Satan a liar—the father of lies. He said that Satan is incapable of telling the truth (John 8:44). Whenever Satan is at work, we will see a trail of lies. His assault on sexuality is no exception.

A man who is same-sex attracted believes *God created me this way.* A woman who was promiscuous as a teen lives the lie *I can never be clean or forgiven. I deserve to be used by men again and again.* The woman who was exploited believes *men only want one thing. I can't trust any man, not even my husband.*

Beneath all of our wounding and sin are lies we've been told and believe. Often the lies feel more true than the truth.

One man sent me an email describing how Satan's lies kept him from honesty and healing, even while sitting in church every week:

> The first half of my life I didn't think God wanted me. Though I grew up in a deeply Christian home, attended church regularly, read the Bible and prayed daily, I had a secret. I had gone through nine years of sexual abuse as a boy but I believed what happened was my fault. I did not feel abused, I felt like a very dirty boy who no one would love if they knew who I really was. And it got worse from there. I became obsessed with sex by age eleven and by age thirteen had starting abusing younger boys.
>
> I remember hearing testimonies at church of people who had been alcoholics on the street, but when they accepted Christ they said they never took another drink and their lives miraculously changed. Instead of feeling encouraged, I wondered why God didn't help me when I begged Him to change me. By age fifteen I decided either my sin was too great even for God to fix, or I was so sinful He no longer wanted to. This is the lie Satan convinced me of. I was unforgiveable, unsaveable, and unlovable. Quite frankly, most people would have said the same about me if they knew what I had done.

Most of us know that Jesus declared that He is "the way and the truth and the life" (John 14:6). Jesus didn't just speak truth, He embodied it. When the enemy lies to us, he is keeping us not just from the concept of truth, but from the Man of truth who has come that we might have life.

RESTORING HOLY SEXUALITY

In 2012, Linda Dillow and I cofounded a ministry called Authentic Intimacy. Every day, my job is to write, speak, and teach about sexuality. Trust me, this is not a job I readily signed up for. I am a reserved person by nature and dislike conflict. There are many other topics that fit more within my comfort zone. However, there is nothing quite like witnessing God's redemption of a person's heart or marriage. I get letters like this one:

> In January 2015, I confessed my struggle with pornography to a lovely woman, to *you*! Juli, I received so much freedom; for the first time I put the sin to the light, and it was the beginning of this journey toward freedom!
>
> Thank you so much for listening to the voice of the Lord; because of your obedience to the Lord I am able to say that I am free from every sexual sin, I have a thirst for the Lord, that no man, no website, nothing can satisfy my thirst for Jesus! I am renewed and restored! I am loved by my King!

And this one:

> I want to thank you for the ministry of Authentic Intimacy. Growing up no one spoke to me about sex, and I went through some sexual trauma. I never had a safe place to talk about what happened to me because of the shame I felt. Once I got married, I didn't know how to enjoy sex. It still felt dirty and wrong somehow.
>
> God has been using your ministry and it has changed my life. You are speaking truth into silence. Your podcasts have brought me even closer to God and to my husband. Finally someone is talking about the secret things that so many women are struggling with.

God is in the business of redemption. When we speak His truth out loud, the enemy's lies are exposed and people are set free. Helping people embrace God's design for sexuality isn't just about helping them have better sex lives or encouraging them to "save themselves for marriage." It is about engaging the enemy in warfare—challenging God's people to take back the ground we have so readily conceded to the enemy's schemes.

When we talk about healing in the Christian church, rarely do we boldly proclaim that Jesus heals our sexual and relational wounds. We readily pray for our brothers and sisters to be healed from cancer and other physical diseases, but we never consider that God wants to bring healing to our sexual brokenness. Yet Jesus Himself ministered to sexually broken people when He walked on earth (e.g., John 4:1–42; Luke 7:36–50).

As we reflect our Savior, we need to show people that He not only cares about marriage and sexuality, but that He has the power to redeem this area of our humanity.

I pray that many churches and Christian leaders take up the challenge to begin speaking honestly, boldly, and biblically about sexual issues. We have inherited a tradition of silence related to sexuality . . . I've frankly been told that "these conversations don't belong in the church." I believe this is a grave mistake for which we are reaping the consequences in our present age. As a result of our refusal to talk about holy sexuality, we have in essence given a worldly culture the permission and authority to define healthy sexuality. We have conceded the entire conversation about sexuality to secular sources. Now, even mature Christians likely think about sexuality through a cultural rather than biblical lens.

It's time for us to break the silence and show a hurting world that God is the creator and redeemer of our sexuality. Allow me to suggest two ways that we can begin reclaiming this territory for our own marriages and for others.

View sexuality through the lens of the great commission

A fundamental reason why we don't address sexual issues within the church is that we don't see how such conversations fit within the biblical call to preach the gospel and make disciples of all nations. Preaching, evangelism, and discipleship are the spiritual work. Sexual issues traditionally have been relegated to medical or psychological intervention.

When Jesus left His disciples, He gave them a final charge, representing what they should be doing here on planet earth. He said, "All authority in heaven and on earth has been given to me. Therefore go and make disciples of all nations, baptizing them in the name of the Father and of the Son and of the Holy Spirit, and teaching them to obey everything I have commanded you. And surely I am with you always, to the very end of the age" (Matt. 28:18–20).

I believe in our day and age it is impossible to adequately fulfill this great commission while refusing to engage in sexual topics. Why? Because sexuality represents an incredible arena of human pain and brokenness. It also is a primary area of humanity in which the average Christian fails to *obey everything Jesus has commanded.*

Talking about God's design for marriage and holy sexuality, walking with people through the journey of healing from addiction or sexual abuse, standing lovingly upon the truth of God's unchanging Word . . . these are the roads on which we become the hands and feet of Jesus in modern culture.

Practically, addressing sexual issues like abuse, harassment, addiction and sexual shame provides a platform to engage people related to their spiritual thirst and need for a Savior. In John 4, we see Jesus intentionally engaging a woman related to her sexual brokenness rather than shying away from this sensitive area of her life. Why? Because, as John Piper noted, "The quickest way to the heart is through a wound."[11] Sexual confusion and wounds create for us perhaps the greatest opportunity to engage people in spiritual conversations.

We must remember that every sexual question is also a spiritual question. If God cannot be trusted to lead us, redeem us, and empower us within our sexuality, He cannot be trusted at all. To the extent that we continue to ignore Jesus' authority in these conversations, we allow the worldly culture to define not just sexuality but also the perceived character of God.

Make holy sexuality a priority

Sexuality is typically viewed as a "side dish" in marriage and in Christian circles. It's considered an optional aspect of humanity to engage in and to discuss. Churches can go years without ever teaching about holy sexuality or specifically addressing relevant sexual issues. In our world in which these conversations are so controversial, it is even more tempting to teach around passages that directly address sexuality. Likewise, Christian married couples go decades experiencing little to no sexual passion and assume that this is normal.

This "side dish" mentality is destroying marriages, lives, and congregations because we've neglected to teach biblical truth about sexuality.

Sure, we might have a sermon series every ten years on the Song of Songs and purity retreats for the high school group, but few Christians are encouraged to bring their true sexual questions to church with them. Questions like:

- I was exposed to porn when I was eleven and can't stop looking at it. Is that a problem? Does God hate me? Do I need to tell my wife about this?
- Before I became a Christian, I lived a very promiscuous life. I want to leave all of that behind, but I don't know how to get rid of the shame and the memories.
- My wife was sexually abused as a child. She hates sex and only does it with me out of duty. How do I help her work past the pain?
- My son is gay and engaged to another man. Both of them claim to

follow Jesus, and they go to a church that supports their relationship. I'm so confused about what to say and even what to believe about this! Can you help?

I assure you that these are common questions with which people are wrestling in every church, including yours. But they may not feel permission to voice them. Worldly sources are far more comfortable bringing up sexual topics and far more confident in their sexual advice. It's almost as if God's truth hits a wall as it approaches our sexuality; the Holy Spirit seems to be barred from the marriage bed.

In contrast to the church's squeamish approach to sexuality, the culture is fully committed to preaching and passing on a secular sexual narrative. From programing for preschoolers to state universities, we are bombarded with messages that sexuality within every context is to be explored and enjoyed. The culture has taught us how to think and what to believe about every sexual issue. In essence, we have been sexually discipled by the world.

For the tide to change, the Christian church must engage in a similar manner. We must be passionate about reclaiming the conversation, presenting a compelling narrative of biblical sexuality.

I have spent the past several years studying and teaching the integration of Christian truth and sexuality. What I've discovered is that even the most mature Christians struggle to apply their faith to sexual questions and struggles. Few Christian couples ever think to pray about their sexual relationship or ask God for sexual healing. The assumption is that there should be a brick wall between the "spiritual me" and the "sexual me."

Howard Hendricks once said, "We should not be ashamed to discuss what God was not ashamed to create." And yet we are. In what Christian settings is it normal to ask questions about orgasm, sexual pain, masturbation, whether God approves of married couples using sex toys, and how often a husband and wife should be having sex? Those are questions relegated to *Cosmo* or to a therapist.

God's truth extends into every arena of our lives, including sexuality. While we may be hesitant to address sexuality, God certainly was not. Think about all the times sexuality is addressed in the Bible. The Song of Songs, for example, is so explicit in its descriptions, that modern translators have toned down the language to make it "less offensive" as if God were embarrassed by our sexual passions. The Bible addresses practical issues like sexual abuse, prostitution, sexual infidelity, homosexuality, healing from trauma, making sex a priority in marriage, sexual temptation, and redemption from sexual sin. Faithfully teaching through the Bible means reflecting upon God's truth in all of these areas. So why are we so timid?

Both in a church community and family setting, reclaiming holy sexuality must be a priority, for sexuality certainly is a priority within the secular culture.

What if a church determined to integrate teaching on holy sexuality into every level of discipleship and church life? What if it became normal to talk about sex from the pulpit, in small groups, in family and singles ministries, and within youth curriculum? And what if married couples determined to reclaim true sexual intimacy? What if they determined to overcome barriers that keep them from experiencing true intimacy in their sexual relationship? They would confront pornography and other forms of counterfeit intimacy. They would seek out help and counsel to address pain from their past and actively address the selfishness and unforgiveness that keep them from building oneness in body, soul, and spirit. They would be intentional to study each other and learn how to become great lovers with the goal of creating a sexual relationship that is satisfying for the both husband and wife.

Rarely do we determine to make holy sexuality a priority. Yet if we understood the spiritual metaphor of sexuality, we would consider this a God-honoring, gospel-centered endeavor.

If we were to truly grasp the big picture of why God created us as sexual beings, it would fundamentally change how we approach sex in the marriage bed, how we combat the enemy's distortions and deceptions, and how we engage our own brokenness and that of the world around us. With every sexual choice, thought, action, or belief, each of us is either working to restore the holy metaphor of sexuality, or we are participating with Satan's schemes to vandalize it.

The wall between the spiritual and sexual has to be torn down. God created sexuality to be a powerful spiritual metaphor of His passionate, faithful, and covenantal love. It's time for us to rediscover the power of this dynamic truth.

CONTINUING INSIGHT:

SHAKING SOULS

by Mike Mason

I can never make love to my wife without thinking what a crazy, preposterous, utterly unlikely thing is this business of sex. Who could have dreamed up something like it? There's only one answer: the glorious God of the cosmos, whose essence is love. Of all the absurdities of atheism, none is more jarring than the notion that nature itself, through evolution, somehow came up with the staggering invention of human sex. If the sexual act were purely something mechanical or biological, one might possibly conceive of it as developing apart from an intentional Creator. But how much greater it is than that! Married couples enjoy an ecstasy, an orgasmic fusion of physical, mental, emotional, and spiritual bliss such as evolution never dreamed of.

When Adam and Eve, the first couple, were banished from the garden, the Lord installed cherubim and a flaming sword to guard the entrance, and He also "made garments of skin for Adam and his wife and clothed them" (Gen. 3:21 NIV). That these two events coincided is not coincidental. The sword, the cherubim, and the clothing all had essentially the same purpose: to bar the way back to Eden. Nakedness in marriage is the one place where it is still possible to witness, without guilt or shame, something of the original light of Eden. Actually, nakedness is a form of light—a spiritual light designed to irradiate the image of our Maker. Of course the rest of nature—all of it naked—also provides occasional glimpses into Edenic glory, times when we seem to see past the fallen creation into the unfallen, or perhaps even into the new creation. But the naked human body is more hauntingly revealing than anything else in nature, which is why all of nature may freely go naked except for humanity. Only humans wear clothes because we ourselves must stand with the cherubim at the gate of Eden, wielding the flaming sword, and the only place where that sword may safely be set down is the marriage bed.

When this happens, how healing it is! And prophetic—prophetic of the fact that we belong in Paradise and will surely return there.

We cannot speak of nakedness without discussing sex, because exposure of skin is only nakedness on the outside, while sex is nakedness on the inside, a coupling of one's interior being with another's. To be naked with another person is both a symbol and a demonstration of perfect honesty, perfect trust, perfect giving and commitment, and if the heart is not naked along with the body, then the whole action is a lie and a mockery. Paul says, "Do you not know that he who unites himself with a prostitute is one with her in body? For it is said, 'The two will become one flesh'" (1 Cor. 6:16 NIV).

The giving of the body but the withholding of the self is an absurd and tragic contradiction. Exposure of the body is like the telling of one's deepest secret: afterwards there is no going back, no pretending that the secret is still one's own or that the other does not know. This is, in effect, the ultimate step in personal relations, and therefore not to be taken lightly. It is not a step that establishes deep intimacy but one that presupposes it. As a gesture symbolic of perfect trust and surrender, it requires a setting or structure of perfect surrender in which to take place. It requires the security of the most perfect of reassurances and commitments into which two people can enter, which is no less than the loving contract of marriage.

Think about this: When God clothed Adam and Eve, why did He not also cover their faces? The face is arguably the sexiest part of the body, studded with bumps and curves, orifices and complexities. In fact, God did cover the face, but in a way that is different from the rest of the body. Moses was veiled when he gave the law of the old covenant to the Israelites, and a veil remains over the hearts of unbelievers (2 Cor. 3:13–18). This veil is whisked away when anyone turns to Christ, for believers are those "who with unveiled faces contemplate [reflect] the Lord's glory" (v.18 NIV).

This veil is further lifted in marriage, a phenomenon symbolized in some wedding ceremonies when the groom raises the bride's veil to kiss his new wife. You who are married, have a good look at your partner's face, especially in lovemaking. Is she not now even more beautiful? Younger? More innocent? Is her face not shining? After thirty or fifty years of marriage, are there not times in lovemaking when your partner is transformed back into the same fresh, youthful man or woman to whom you said "I do" on your wedding day? This is the mystical, forever-young miracle of nakedness in marriage, where face and body may be glimpsed as they were in youth, as they were in Eden, or even as they will be in heaven. For our God is not a God of the moribund but of those who even now are being raised to new life.

Images of heaven normally portray the citizens as wearing clothes, and Scripture speaks of a "white robe" (Rev. 6:11). But what is this "robe of his righteousness" (Isa. 61:10) if it is not the naked human body itself, finally redeemed and revealed in all its glory as the image of God? Naked we came into the world and naked we depart, for clothing is not needed where we are going. Christ on the cross was shamefully nude in order to defeat, not only death, but shame, so that in heaven we may be robed in our own resurrected flesh. This poor naked body of ours is the very mercy seat of God.

Will there be sex in heaven? No, because our insides will already be outside, and nakedness alone will be all the glory we can stand. No titillation in this nakedness, for in itself it will be fully satisfying, the culmination of intimacy: the entire revelation and self-giving of each person to every other. Now, upon greeting, we shake hands. Then, being already as intimate with one another as we can possibly be, we shall shake souls.

SECTION 3

CHALLENGES

CHAPTER 9

FROM SHAME TO WHOLENESS

by James S. Spiegel and Amy E. Spiegel

When the great American boxer Joe Louis was told that his upcoming opponent Billy Conn planned a "hit and run" strategy, Louis famously responded, "He can run but he can't hide." No doubt this unfortunate fact inspired fear in Conn as he considered the prospect of being trapped in a ring with the great champion. Although Conn did a bit of running that night in 1946, he certainly couldn't hide. And his back hit the canvas for good in the tenth round. While in most respects marriage is nothing like a heavyweight boxing match, there is this similarity: you cannot hide from your spouse either. However much I might try to conceal or cover myself, what I truly am will eventually be discovered by my spouse. And vice versa.

As we were originally created, such absolute intimacy or "nakedness" was nothing but good news, as it meant purely joyful and loving mutual disclosure. But alas, with the fall, marital nakedness suddenly constituted bad news, as sin transformed this intimacy into an occasion for fear, shame, and alienation. In any marriage, the presence of sin mars and disrupts at times. But if a husband and wife genuinely live in grace, trusting in Christ for their salvation and actively pursuing righteousness, the joy of marital nakedness as God originally intended it is possible. In this chapter, we will discuss the fact of sin and brokenness within marriage, noting its origins and some of the ways it is manifested in marriage. And we will explain how the gospel brings forgiveness and restoration to married couples, restoring relational wholeness and turning nakedness back into a profoundly hopeful thing.

GARDEN NAKEDNESS: ORIGINAL JOY AND SUBSEQUENT SHAME

The key to understanding the meaning and purpose of marriage lies in understanding our origins. Looking at the creation account in the early chapters of Genesis, we find that the first man and woman were made for each other, and God did so by creating the woman from the man. We are told that "God made a woman from the rib he had taken out of the man, and he brought her to the man" (Gen. 2:22).[1] Adam's response is significant: "This is now bone of my bones and flesh of my flesh; she shall be called 'woman,' for she was taken out of man" (Gen. 2:23). Scripture goes on to declare "that is why a man leaves his father and mother and is united to his wife, and they become one flesh. Adam and his wife were both naked, and they felt no shame" (Gen. 2:24–25).

Now what is the significance of this curious reference to the fact that "they felt no shame"? Well, what is shame? It is a sense of distress and embarrassed humiliation associated with the consciousness of one's guilt. Prior to their sin, Adam and Eve had no guilt, so they had nothing about which to feel ashamed. But then, after being tempted by the serpent, they ate of the forbidden fruit, and "the eyes of both of them were opened, and they realized they were naked; so they sewed fig leaves together and made coverings for themselves" (Gen. 3:7). It is noteworthy that once they sin, their shame is manifested cognitively as an awareness of their nakedness but also behaviorally in the action of self-covering. This suggests that there is something more to their shame than simple embarrassment about their sin. So why the impulse to cover themselves? To understand, we need to recall the vital concept of "one flesh" that the marital union was originally intended to achieve.

This notion of a married couple becoming one flesh is reiterated in the New Testament, both by Jesus (Matt. 19:5) and by the apostle Paul (Eph. 5:31). Gaining a richer understanding of the concept of oneness will enable us to better grasp both the original, blessed nakedness prior to the fall as well as the reason for the intense shame and the behavioral response of the first married couple. To do so we must go back beyond even the story of human origins in the book of Genesis. We must go back to the deep nature of God. As with all Christian belief and practice, everything flows from the Holy Trinity, and this is especially true of marriage and sexuality.

God is triune, which is to say that although He is one being, He exists eternally as three persons. Each person is equally divine, sharing the same divine essence though each has distinct features and roles. The Nicene Creed—the historic standard for orthodoxy—articulates this mysterious but critical doctrine noting that God the Father is "maker of heaven and earth, of all things visible and invisible" while God the Son is "begotten, not made; being of the same essence as the Father." Lastly, it says, "The Holy Spirit, the Lord, the giver of life . . . proceeds from the Father and the Son, and with the Father and the Son together is worshiped and glorified."[2] It is crucial to note both the unity and plurality of the Godhead. Though a singular being sharing the same "essence," God also exists as three distinct persons. Moreover, the relationship among the three persons of the Godhead is dynamic, one we would be at a loss to comprehend if we didn't have some tangible point of reference for grasping it. Fortunately, God has given us such a reference point, a point that stems from our very nature as human beings, specifically in the nature of our relationships, particularly marriage and family.

Consider these remarkable parallels. In the Genesis creation account, Eve "proceeded" from Adam and they were therefore of the same substance, hence "flesh of my flesh." They shared the same human essence, though they were distinct persons. And their sexual union, just as with men and women ever since, resulted in a child who, though again of the same human essence, nonetheless is a distinct person. Three persons, one human essence. The parallels here to the Trinity are striking and provide clues to the sacredness and purpose of human marriage, sexuality, and procreation. Indeed, marriage and sexuality are potentially keys for unlocking great mysteries. For each, in its own powerful way, reflects key aspects of the Holy Trinity. As Pope John Paul II has said, these truths are "capable of making visible what is invisible: the spiritual and divine. It has been created to transfer into the visible reality of the world the mystery hidden from eternity in God, and thus to be a sign of it."[3] And as Christopher West puts it, "marital union is meant to be an icon in some way of the inner life of the Trinity."[4]

Now working with these parallels, all of which reveal aspects of how human beings are made "in the image of God," what may we learn? First, human beings were created for communion between persons, a union and mutual disclosure by interpenetration. Of course, nowhere in human experience do we find a more intimate union and interpenetration than in sexual intercourse. Thus, nowhere in human experience is the dynamic union of the Trinity better imaged than in the sex act. So intercourse is profoundly sacred[5] and, we might say, even sacramental.[6]

A second thing we learn is that sex should be an experience of mutual giving, free sharing, and total vulnerability between a man and a woman. Just

Even within Christendom the significance of marriage and what it represents vary. Within the Roman Catholic tradition, marriage is viewed as a sacrament (ex opera operato) based on Ephesians 5:32 (mysterium), meaning that divine grace is upon the couple on declaring their marriage vows in the sight of God and the church. Orthodox traditions visually image their theology of marriage (also sacramental) through the betrothal and crowning service, which represents spiritually one coming into the kingdom of Christ as His bride. Protestant theology generally moves away from the view of marriage as sacrament, and interprets marriage as a symbol, image, or covenant established between Christ and His church, which God uses to extend His grace. Regardless of these variations, it is widely recognized that marriage, in its divine origin and design, represents the mystery of Christ's sole fidelity to His bride, the church.[7]

as the persons of the Trinity enjoy complete and abundant mutual giving, the human sexual union is designed to reflect this. Within the Trinity there is a joyful nakedness because of the perfect unity of the Father, Son, and Holy Spirit. And human sexuality is designed to reflect and even achieve something of that joyful nakedness and unity.

Third, and crucially as a complete reflection of the Trinity, human sexuality is meant to be a giving in the sense that it may be productive of life, the multiplication of joy and discovery through the emergence of a third person, the child who proceeds from this sacred union and shares the same human essence as his or her father and mother. And just as the dynamic intimacy of the father and mother bring about joyful mutual discovery, the relationship between the parents and their child brings yet more joy and discovery. The human family thus mirrors, if imperfectly, the Trinity as three distinct persons share the same essence and dynamically disclose themselves one to another. Even with this picture in mind, it's still important to note that an infertile couple is no less whole or no less a "family" than a couple blessed with children. We are made complete in Christ after all!

These are truly wonderful truths, and they powerfully declare the beauty and sacredness of human sexuality. They also suggest to us much about the joy of the original human nakedness, a joy that was tragically forfeited with the fall into sin recounted in the third chapter of Genesis. Let's now consider just how terrible the consequences of the fall were in terms of its impact on human sexuality. First, sin brings a loss of unity, personal alienation, and return to solitude. With the impulse to selfishness and pride that is inherent to sin, there comes also a loss of pure, selfless giving. This is displaced by threat of domination and interpersonal disturbance, which naturally gives rise to alienation and ultimately fear. The "other" who once shared subjectivity through the deepest conjugal union now becomes a distanced object, capable of being used for selfish pleasure or worse. Thus, it is no wonder that our primordial parents wanted to hide themselves and conceal, in particular, their reproductive organs—the sacred means of mutual giving and procreation. The aspects of their body that were created to be enjoyed freely and without fear are now a potential source of exploitation and unwelcome vulnerability.

A further consequence of sin's distortion and corruption of human relationship is defensiveness and accusation. When God asks Adam, "Who told you that you were naked? Have you eaten from the tree that I commanded you not to eat from?" Adam replies, "The woman you put here with me—she gave me some fruit from the tree, and I ate it" (Gen. 3:11–12). Note the implicit double accusation here, as Adam's response shifts the blame to Eve and, ultimately, God Himself. In one act of disobedience, the joy and blessed unity of the original human couple is turned to alienation, fear, and accusation. And not just regarding one another but also toward their Creator. Here we have in microcosm the story of the entire human race. Adam's moral failure shatters the harmony of Eden and ripples down through history, impacting every aspect of human relations, between parents and their children, children and their siblings, neighbors, friends, and beyond. But nowhere is the depth of human sin and its consequences more vividly apparent than in marriage. When corrupted, the greatest blessings often become severe curses. That is certainly true in this case. Let us take a closer look at some of the ways in which sin infects and corrupts marital relationships.

THE GARDEN FORSAKEN: OUR COMMON STRUGGLE

After the fall of humans into sin, the descendants of Adam and Eve multiplied and spread throughout the earth. But alas, their sin spread with them. In Genesis 6 we are told, "The LORD saw how great the wickedness of the human race had become on the earth, and that every inclination of the thoughts of the human heart was only evil all the time" (Gen. 6:5). Eventually the plague of man's sinful behavior became so great that God destroyed nearly everyone on earth through the worldwide flood. Still, the survivors, Noah and his family, carried the same moral poison of original sin, and so do we today. Like a patient who must admit to being ill before hoping to be cured, we must come to a recognition of the seriousness of our sin problem in order to understand how broken human beings are, why marriage is so difficult, and why the gospel is the only means of redeeming marriage.

The fundamental doctrine of original sin says that as descendants of Adam, human beings are born corrupt, having inherited both guilt and a tendency toward sin. This is why none of us had to be taught to lie, envy, or covet— sadly, these things come quite naturally to us. So original sin is not just about the fact that human beings, as a matter of universal fact, act (and think and speak) immorally from time to time. It concerns the fact that we have an innate disposition to do so. Jonathan Edwards sums up the matter when he says, "the great depravity of man's nature appears, not only in that they universally commit sin, who spend any long time in the world; but in that men are naturally so prone to sin, that none ever fail of immediately transgressing God's law."[8] Edwards underscores the severity of our sin problem here by noting that it is both universal and immediate in its effects. In every human life, as soon as we are mature enough to make voluntary choices, we in fact make sinful choices. The core aspects of our sinful nature are selfishness and pride—two tendencies that, to compound matters, make us oblivious to our own sin. John Calvin expounds on this vicious cycle:

> There is, indeed, nothing that man's nature seeks more eagerly than to be flattered. Accordingly, when his nature becomes aware that its gifts are highly esteemed, it tends to be unduly credulous about them. It is thus no wonder that the majority of men have erred so perniciously in this respect. For, since blind self-love is innate in all mortals, they are most freely persuaded that nothing inheres in themselves that deserves to be considered hateful.[9]

So not only does our sinful nature make us selfish and abjectly proud, it also blinds us to just how corrupt we are.

Given this situation, how can anyone be saved? Thankfully, through the gospel, God works grace in people's hearts, awakening us to our sin, prompting us to repent of that sin, and empowering us to obey Him. But even the regeneration of our hearts does not completely eradicate our sin problem, at least not on this side of paradise. Although we are completely justified in Christ and therefore free from God's condemnation, our sinful nature is not removed until heaven. In the meantime, we must still struggle with sin and strive to grow more virtuous and obedient through the process of sanctification. This can be exceedingly difficult and discouraging. In fact, at times we might even feel that we're making no progress at all because of the tenacity of sin in our lives. John Wesley says of the sin of believers:

> These continually feel [a] heart bent to backsliding; a natural tendency to evil; a proneness to depart from God, and cleave to the things of earth. They are daily sensible of sin remaining in their heart—pride, self-will, unbelief; and of sin cleaving to all they speak and do, even their best actions and holiest duties.[10]

So the Christian is simultaneously aware of her own sin and confident in God's complete forgiveness through Christ. At one and the same time, she recognizes her own rebellious inclinations and is fully committed to Christ. This is a strange, almost paradoxical moral condition, but it is the condition of every Christian on earth.

As arduous as the pursuit of righteousness can be for the individual Christian, it becomes that much more complicated and challenging when Christians marry. For marriage brings two sinners into the closest proximity, living together daily, each struggling with their own sin issues while at the same time facing the additional challenge of dealing with the other person's sin issues. Some young people think that marriage will automatically make their moral struggles easier. While there are many moral benefits to the conjugal partnership, it also presents new challenges as the relational impact of each person's sins are compounded. Also, pain from past relational wounds now impacts one's spouse as well as oneself. After nearly twenty years of marriage, we have certainly felt the damaging impact of sin and past wounds in our own relationship. Here are some personal illustrations of this biblical truth that we have experienced firsthand.

Pride

They say pride comes before a fall, but in the case of human nature pride came after the fall, and nowhere is this truth more evident than in the intimate, day-to-day interactions of married life. From the stereotypical male refusal to pull over and ask for directions (of which I, Jim, have often been guilty) to the more serious haughtiness of spirit that refuses to admit guilt or wrongdoing (of which we are both often guilty), marriage is a veritable breeding ground of examples of prideful behavior. Living with someone year after year offers endless opportunity to embarrass oneself, and a lack of humility can only bring about barriers to a true communion of body, mind, and spirit. In our relationship, as in countless others, pride has led to humorous "detours" that cost us precious minutes, and sometimes hours, in travel time, but has also led to sorrowful relational detours that have cost days of tension and stony silence. Failure to conquer one's pride has the same effect as continuing with an ill-conceived remodeling project. One is left in isolation, refusing to accept the grace being offered, and regardless of the innocence of one's spouse, he or she is left cleaning up the mess alone.

Selfishness

Standing before family and friends, aglow with hope for the future and lofty in their love for each other, few couples can imagine that in the not too distant future they will be arguing over who gets control of the television remote or whose responsibility it is to take the trash out tonight. With vows of being "soul mates" and "best friends" still ringing in their ears, married couples find themselves locked in battle between their desire to serve their spouse and a desire to please themselves. No longer is your future your own. Despite the fact that we spend years longing for someone to share our lives with, the reality of compromising on decisions, big and small, can be a rude awakening to many. Whether deciding what to have for dinner, where to locate your family, or how to discipline your children, in marriage, the opportunities to be selfish are as many as the day is long.

Resentment

One of the many truths regarding marriage that we have both learned over the years is that sometimes it is the small slights that are the hardest to forgive. Often it is the little things that can poison the relationship between husband and wife. Like a small splinter that festers just below the skin, a lack of forgiveness for past wrongs can fester just below the surface of a marriage, waiting to resurface at the slightest provocation. These resentments can be nurtured for years, allowing its caretaker a sense of moral superiority over his or her spouse. Resentment is a wound kept fresh, picked at by a refusal to let it heal. There are just as many chances for resentfulness as there are chances to sin against each other in marriage.

DAMAGED AND ASHAMED

Crippled by Past Wounds

Just as we all carry Adam's guilt and inclination toward sin with us from birth, so we all carry the consequences of others' sinful behavior toward us into marriage. Verbal or physical abuse by a parent, sexual assault by a stranger or boyfriend, etc.—the list goes on and can form the links of a strangling sinful chain to the past. Like Jacob Marley of Dickens's *A Christmas Carol*, we each drag the sins of others into our relationship with our spouse. In her irritated tone, we hear the voices of the past, belittling and demeaning us. In his playful pat, we feel the sting of humiliating violation. Facing past wounds in marriage must be a two-way street. On one hand, the wounded partner must learn to trust her spouse, not holding him responsible for the sins of another while on the other hand, she must work to be trustworthy, not rushing her spouse to let go of painful habits of thought he is not yet capable of moving past. Without mutual trust and respect regarding past wounds, partners can easily find themselves tearing one another apart rather than building one another up, creating fresh wounds and adding insult to injury and preventing either husband or wife from moving out of the pain of the past and into a healthy new chapter.

Haunted by Past Sins

Some of the sins we carry with us into married life are not those committed against us but rather committed by us. Haunted by mistakes or failures of the past, we can become handicapped in receiving God's free gift of grace, which must be the center of each Christian's life as well as the heart of a striving marital relationship. My ability to forgive another is based on my having experienced God's forgiveness of my sins. Scripture tells us that "as high as the heavens are above the earth, so great is his love for those who fear him; as far as the east is from the west, so far has he removed our transgressions from us" (Ps. 103:11–12). Just as God flings our sins from His memory and frees us from our feelings of guilt over them, He draws us closer to Himself, allowing us to feel the height and breadth of His love, which in turns allows us to love one another all the more.

THE GARDEN TRANSCENDED: A NEW NAKEDNESS

For all of the moral failure and psychological brokenness that we, like any married couple, have experienced, we have remained together and after almost two decades are more committed to each other than ever. How is this possible? In a word, grace. But let us unpack this. God has completely forgiven each of us, though neither of us deserves such mercy. And as recipients of such unconditional favor, we are motivated to pay that grace forward, to forswear condemnation to each other, as well as to our children, other family members, and anyone else we know. That is the way of the gospel and the kingdom of God, as the recurrent New Testament teaching of this idea makes clear. To the church at Ephesus the apostle Paul writes, "Be kind and compassionate to one another, forgiving each other, just as in Christ God forgave you" (Eph. 4:32). He repeats this message to the church at Colossae: "Bear with each other and forgive one another if any of you has a grievance against someone. Forgive as the Lord forgave you" (Col. 3:13). In these passages, Paul is simply reiterating the teaching of Jesus, though his original directive reverses the direction of the conditional and features a coupling of the positive message with a negative one. Jesus says, "if you forgive other people when they sin against you, your heavenly Father will also forgive you. But if you do not forgive others their sins, your Father will not forgive your sins" (Matt. 6:14–15). Jesus communicates the same sobering message in the parable of the unmerciful servant in Matthew 18. After declaring that the unmerciful servant will be tortured until he pays back all he owes, Jesus asserts, "This is how my heavenly Father will treat each of you unless you forgive your brother or sister from your heart" (Matt. 18:35). Given that we all have struggled to forgive certain people in our lives, these are frightening words!

Jesus thus warns us of the consequences of failing to forgive. Some people find this passage worrisome, but to those who really know Christ's forgiveness it should not be. John Piper explains:

If the forgiveness that we received at the cost of the blood of the Son of God, Jesus Christ, is so ineffective in our hearts that we are bent on holding unforgiving grudges and bitterness against someone, we are not a good tree. We are not saved. We don't cherish this forgiveness. We don't trust in this forgiveness. We don't embrace and treasure this forgiveness. We are hypocrites. We are just mouthing. We haven't ever felt the piercing, joyful wonder that God paid the life of his Son.[11]

So, as Christians, we absolutely must forgive one another. This is especially important in the case of married couples, since the husband and wife are "one flesh." Paul expounds on the theological foundation and practical import of this conjugal unity when he writes,

Husbands, love your wives, just as Christ loved the church and gave himself up for her to make her holy, cleansing her by the washing with water through the word, and to present her to himself as a radiant church, without stain or wrinkle or any other blemish, but holy and blameless. In this same way, husbands ought to love their wives as their own bodies. He who loves his wife loves himself. After all, no one ever hated their own body, but they feed and care for their body, just as Christ does the church—for we are members of his body. (Eph. 5:25–30)

Now to properly grasp the analogy Paul uses here, it is critical to remember that the church—the community of Christ followers—is regarded as the body of Christ.[12] So as Christians are purified by the work of Christ, we are in a sense simply taking part in His own purity and holiness. Given our unity with Him, His love for us is essentially an expression of divine self-love. Paul is suggesting that a husband should take a similar perspective in regard to his wife. Their unity is such that loving her is likewise an expression of self-love. And to fail to love one's wife is to fail to love oneself.

So, let us return to the topic at hand—forgiveness. Given a man's "one flesh" unity with his wife, to refuse to forgive her is effectively to condemn himself. And to extend forgiveness is to forswear condemnation and embrace mercy and grace for himself. Presumably this applies equally to a wife as well. Since she is one flesh with her husband, her forgiveness or condemnation of him will rebound upon herself in kind.

The point, then, is that a Christian marriage is supposed to be a bond of grace, a relationship in which mutual mercy and forgiveness is foundational to the relationship, mirroring the mercy and forgiveness that the couple has been shown by Christ. The beauty of this approach is that it is at once both profoundly realistic and hopeful. It is realistic because in a context of grace there is no reason to deny, avoid, or shrink from the reality of our extreme sinfulness and psychological brokenness. Since the grace of Christ is sufficient to atone for all our wrongs and heal all our wounds, there is no reason to hide behind our relational "fig leaves." Herein lies great hope, because grace, being an aspect of love, is a fear killer. As the Scripture says, "Perfect love drives out fear" (1 John 4:18). And without fear, we are able to be naked before each other in a way that was impossible before, to be completely honest and forthright about our own sinful ways and psychological weaknesses. The benefits here are numerous, as now a husband and wife are relieved from all sorts of relational anxieties and can enjoy more effective communication, which in turn has profound benefits in a marriage.

THE KENOSIS PRINCIPLE

Clearly, mutual grace is the essence of a strong marital bond, and the gospel is crucial for this. But it is important to dig down even further to see exactly what aspect of the gospel is the most powerful moral force for forging this bond. This consists in the paradoxical truth that there is power in weakness. With service and submission comes real strength. This point is crystalized by the apostle Paul:

> In your relationships with one another, have the same mindset as Christ Jesus: Who, being in very nature God, did not consider equality with God something to be used to his own advantage; rather, he made himself nothing by taking the very nature of a servant, being made in human likeness. And being found in appearance as a man, he humbled himself by becoming obedient to death—even death on a cross! Therefore God exalted him to the highest place and gave him the name that is above every name, that at the name of Jesus every knee should bow, in heaven and on earth and under the earth, and every tongue acknowledge that Jesus Christ is Lord, to the glory of God the Father. (Phil. 2:5–11)

What Paul articulates here is what may be called the Kenosis principle. This word derives from the Greek *keno*, empty. Because Christ lowered

Himself, He was exalted. Humility is basically voluntary weakness, and Christ demonstrated the most extreme form of humility possible, laying aside His infinitude to take on human flesh, and then living humbly even relative to the human condition. The radically ironic consequence of this, of course, is that humanity is redeemed and Jesus Christ is exalted to the highest. Now it is important to note that Paul is not just doing Christology here but ethics. Note that he prefaces this passage by extolling us to emulate Christ, to bring "the same mindset" to all our relationships. So extreme humility is a model for how we are to relate to everyone, and this includes one of the most important of all human relationships—marriage.

The Kenosis principle suggests that there is power in weakness. Paul indicates as much elsewhere when he says, "I will boast all the more gladly about my weaknesses, so that Christ's power may rest on me. That is why, for Christ's sake, I delight in weaknesses, in insults, in hardships, in persecutions, in difficulties. For when I am weak, then I am strong" (2 Cor. 12:9–10). Again, this is counterintuitive, a moral paradox. How could weakness be a strength? But perhaps this fact only seems odd when we consider it from a first-person standpoint. We tend to admire others' admissions of weakness, which is essentially vulnerability, as a positive trait. Psychologist Brené Brown has pointed out that "I want to experience your vulnerability but I don't want to be vulnerable. Vulnerability is courage in you and inadequacy in me. I'm drawn to your vulnerability but repelled by mine."[13] So this same trait we admire in others is something that we abhor in ourselves. How is this possible?

Again, the explanation, it seems, goes back to the garden. Vulnerability is a kind of nakedness, which, since the fall, we naturally fear. And it is precisely this fear that is transcended when we choose vulnerability or any other form of humility. When we do so in marriage, the strength this begets takes many forms. For one thing, it enhances marital intimacy. We connect with our spouses at a far deeper emotional level when we are honest about our weaknesses. But there are further benefits that humility brings, including the reciprocity it tends to beget. Humility is contagious. Perhaps this is where the "power" of humility lies, in its tendency to inspire others to be more sympathetic with our personal desires even as we voluntarily surrender them or de-emphasize them. Here is another paradoxical dimension to this principle: In putting others' desires before our own we are more likely to get what we want. But, of course, one must put this ironic dynamic out of mind when putting on the mind of Christ, lest we deploy the Kenosis principle just as a means of manipulating others, which is really not to put on the mind of Christ at all.

Finally, the Kenosis principle is the practical cure and inoculation against the deadly moral vices, discussed earlier, that plague all marriages: pride, selfishness, and resentment. This is because humility is the moral opposite of pride and selfishness. To take a humble attitude is simply incompatible with those vices. And since resentment is built upon pride and selfishness, humility likewise drives out a resentful spirit as well. As simple as it sounds, then, it is probably true to say that the key to a healthy marriage is for both spouses to practice Kenosis, to humble themselves and put the others' needs and desires first, to seek to serve rather than seek to be served. Of course, it should be no surprise that this is the key, for this attitude is the moral essence of Christlikeness, and marriage is essentially an image of Christ and the church.

Marriage is the hardest context of all in which to apply the Kenosis principle, precisely because it is the most intimate of all relationships and therefore the most intimate and constant abutting of human wills. Mike Mason notes,

> Even the closest of couples will inevitably find themselves engaged in a struggle of wills, for marriage is a wild, audacious attempt at an almost impossible degree of cooperation between two powerful centers of self-assertion. Marriage cannot help being a furnace of conflict, a crucible in which these two wills must be melted down and purified and made to conform.[14]

The call to Christian humility is a fundamental challenge to the innate impulse of the human will to assert itself and dominate others, what Nietzsche called the "will to power." To follow Christ is to crucify that Nietzschean instinct and to receive in exchange far more benefits than you might have obtained even if your will to power had completely dominated your spouse. For humility brings mutual submission and cooperation, which is a source of joy, while the tyranny of will only brings resentment and fear of reprisal.

Too often we think that the goal of marriage is to make us happy and therefore our view of our spouse can become rigidly utilitarian. If they can keep making us happy, we will keep them around. If they stop making us happy, there must be something wrong. But as much as it flies in the face of our culture, we might say that our spouses are designed by God sometimes to be a thorn in the flesh (Paul's familiar metaphor as in 2 Cor. 12:7–9). Not that they should be viewed as a trial to be endured—rather, living with any human being no matter how wonderful they are is a trial, and it should not surprise or discourage us when there is conflict. It should humble us, as Paul's thorn humbled him, and drive us to Christ, who is the only true source of happiness that we can find. It should also humble us because it works both ways. We are the thorn in our spouse's flesh just as they are ours. Whatever annoying habits or true character flaws we find exasperating about them, we can be sure that they have an equally long if not longer list about us.

One might think that this mutual irritation might be what makes a marriage weak, frustration and conflict causing cracks in the marital relationship that will eventually lead to it crumbling, but Paul tells us that the exact opposite is true if we will follow Christ and the example He has set. God's grace and mercy, shown both to us and by us, will fill in those gaps and create a bond that will last for eternity if we will rely on His power rather than our own. This also should lead us to be honest, not only with each other but with those around us, rather than whitewashing our marriages, using Photoshop to smooth out the flaws, and presenting a false picture of married life. Instead we should glorify God by making Him and the gospel the center of our marriage, privately as well as publicly. We shouldn't use this as an opportunity to air our spouse's faults to others (e.g., "I could never stay married to Bill if it wasn't for the love of Jesus") but rather celebrate God's goodness in bringing us together in our weaknesses to sanctify us for His purposes. The beauty of marriage is not captured in the wedding day photo, with everyone looking their best and on their best behavior. It is captured in quiet moments of prayer and forgiveness that drive us again and again to the cross that we might be like Paul, content in the face of hardships, made strong by being weak, and by boasting in Christ alone.

MARRIAGE AS AN ONGOING WORK OF GRACE

It is important to keep in mind that, like all works of grace, the Christian marriage bond is not one that can be passively sustained. Rather, as in the individual Christian life, it must be actively pursued and developed. Paul tells us to "work out your salvation with fear and trembling" (Phil. 2:12). And in the book of Ephesians, immediately after reminding us that our salvation is a gift of God, "not by works, so that no one can boast," he adds that this salvation was for the purpose of doing good works. As he puts it, "We are God's handiwork, created in Christ Jesus to do good works, which God prepared in advance for us to do" (Eph. 2:9–10). So, although we were not saved by our good works, God has saved us to do good works. Accordingly, it is helpful to reflect on some of the "works" of marriage, tasks that Christian married couples can and should be doing as an outworking of grace, which reinforces the couples' individual and shared faith commitment and serves as well to pay it forward to others.

One of the ways the gospel redeems and restores marital work is by making the husband and wife moral-spiritual confidants. Throughout the week, we share theological insights and discuss biblical truths, especially as these relate to current events, work-related issues, and personal friendships. These are usually unplanned conversations triggered by, say, a news event or pressing life situation, the aim of which is to enhance one another's understanding and provide mutual counsel. We don't typically think of these as constituting a dialogue about "practical theology," but that's what it really is, and we both benefit immensely as a result. Life regularly throws curveballs at us all, including some challenging moral dilemmas. Helping each other with such challenges is an act of grace. Married couples should recognize this as such and be intentional about this mutual service.

Another way that married couples engage in works of grace is by being allies in redemptive service, such as by actively encouraging and helping others. Every married couple has their special gifts and strengths as far as this goes. We like to encourage through hospitality, such as by having students over for dinner, dessert, or a game night. These times create opportunities for students to share their stories and struggles, which in turn helps us to know how to minister to them. Our united focus on this sort of outreach takes our eyes off ourselves in a healthy way, and it strengthens our bond as a couple as we work together for such redemptive ends.

The most obvious form of shared service for married couples is family stewardship, especially the rearing of children. There is nothing more challenging or rewarding for a married couple than this, because the training one must do to prepare a child for life in this world is so vast, from personal hygiene to social skills to monetary matters to athletic skills to all the subjects in school. In all these areas, they must be endowed with a strong work ethic, and on top of it all they must be taught to develop a distinctly Christian perspective on all of it—seeing the things they are learning through the lens of a theology of creation, fall, and redemption. Whew! If that seems overwhelming, that's because it is. But it is the challenge of Christian parenting to succeed as much as possible in these things. The whole endeavor is obviously life-forming for the children we raise. But the devoted teamwork this demands from couples can also be profoundly unifying, another powerful dimension of the bond of marital grace.

There is also a couple's cultural stewardship, by which we mean the ways in which a husband and wife share projects of productive work outside the home, whether professionally or personally. For many couples such work constitutes a significant divergence of interests, and this does not naturally invite mutual support or teamwork. If he is at the office, and she is at school or at home with the kids, it can be difficult to stay mutually abreast of one another's current challenges and achievements. But doing so is critical and an act of grace. For other couples, work projects may naturally converge that can reinforce their "team" mentality, though it can create problems as well. In any case, couples must strive to understand and support each other in their various forms of work. This too reinforces the bond of grace.

Lastly, there are the spiritual disciplines—the exercises that we undertake for the sake of moral-spiritual growth, such as prayer, Bible study, fasting, sacrifice, confession, solitude, fellowship. Christian couples should be engaging in prayer and mutual confession, but they can also be intentional about achieving some togetherness when practicing some of the disciplines that are most naturally pursued individually. In addition to mutually encouraging one another to, for example, engage in fasting, frugality, and sacrifice, they can go about these disciplines side by side, as it were. For example, the two of us like to fast together on various occasions, especially with a particular prayer focus, such as the healing of a friend or family member. Not only does God bless with answered prayer but the practice also gives us a sense of participating in the same spiritual battle, which further enhances the bond of grace and reinforces our "one flesh" unity.

CONCLUSION

In his 1904 poem "Adam's Curse," William Butler Yeats decries the notion that any work of beauty—whether in art or human relationship—comes easily or naturally. On the contrary, he insists, "It's certain there is no fine thing / Since Adam's fall but needs much labouring." A good marriage is surely a "fine thing," as Yeats would put it. And since Adam's fall, that goodness only comes with much hard work, as we must deal with the sin and shame that threatens to make marital intimacy a threat rather than a blessing. The key to a Christian understanding of marriage, however, lies in recognizing that this hard work must be a consequence of grace, not a prelude or means to it. The only real means of grace is Christ's work and our personal surrender to God's application of it to our lives. Then, and only then, can our hard work be effective.

In the context of the bond of marital grace, a married couple's mutual nakedness can be completely redeemed. Where once there was guilt and shame, there now can be forgiveness and acceptance. Where once there was fearful vulnerability, there now can be joyful disclosure. And where once there was relational fracture and alienation, there now can be relational wholeness. The gospel nakedness goes beyond restoring the original nakedness of our foreparents in the garden. It heals marriages and equips couples to pay grace forward in profoundly redemptive ways. And that is a fine thing indeed.

CONTINUING INSIGHT:

"WAITING" TO MOVE TOWARD FORGIVNESS

by Deborah Gorton

For many, the biggest challenge faced in the pursuit of forgiveness is a misplaced expectation that has to do with "waiting." We wait for our readiness to forgive another, and often we're waiting for the conditions of forgiveness to be perfectly laid before us before we act.

This waiting narrative has such a strong presence in our lives. The unfortunate consequence is often a false belief that waiting equates to idleness, that our approach to something is passive rather than active. We fail to see "wait" for the verb it is. In Scripture, we see that waiting includes three things: expectation, readiness, and the continuum of action that exists within our waiting. For example, consider the familiar passage of Isaiah 40:31 (ESV), "But they who wait for the LORD (expectation) shall renew their strength (readiness); they shall mount up with wings like eagles; they shall run and not be weary; they shall walk and not faint (action)."

Movement toward forgiveness will always exist within the boundaries of brokenness. Until Christ reestablishes His kingdom, we are perpetually navigating an earthly world and all its fallen consequences. Yet, it is precisely because of God's promise that He Himself will one day "restore, confirm, strengthen, and establish you" (1 Peter 5:10 ESV), that we are free to approach forgiveness *through* the pain of our brokenness as opposed to waiting for the pain to subside or disappear.

Yet to experience this freedom requires a radical acceptance of the discomfort and imperfection that surrounds the practice of forgiveness.

The incidents that lead to a need to extend or receive forgiveness can result in deep emotional and psychological hurts. Recognition of this truth and validation of the experience (both emotional and perceptual) are critical steps forward in the process. Many people believe that for forgiveness to take place, both the absence of emotional pain and its residual hurts—as well as the expectation that the person who hurt us will initiate the steps of forgiveness—must be present first, i.e., before forgiveness is initiated. Yet when the offending party doesn't "move" or take action, we can be left feeling hopeless and helpless.

Further, we often misplace the order of feelings and actions. I see this in my own life when I confront the need to forgive loved ones or clients. I tend to think I need the feelings first before I can take action to initiate. Once I experience confidence, comfort, happiness, contentment (the list could go on and on), I tell myself, only then I will act.

But what if forgiveness is actually gained by moving in the other direction? Emotions certainly can provide insight. They can give meaning and definition to the people and experiences in our life. However, in my experience, they were never meant to be the launch indicator for our best decisions.

Unfortunately, we often function in the false perception that healthy decisions require an accompanying positive emotion. Something that falls in the category of "pleasant." Think about it. How often do you fail to move toward something because it feels uncomfortable? Our feelings become a self-perceived insurmountable barrier, and we stay stuck in the deceitful "comfort" of our own curated discomfort.

Embracing the truth of Scripture necessitates a radical acceptance of the reality of forgiveness. We accept that God is helping us, even calling us in His strength, to be comfortable with the uncomfortable.

In the gospel of John, Christ states, "I have said these things to you, that in me you may have peace. In the world you will have tribulation. But take heart; I have overcome the world" (John 16:33 ESV). We avoid initiating forgiveness because we're seeking earthly justice; we fail to see that forgiveness will *always* take place within tribulation. Waiting for peace that comes from a change of heart on the part of your transgressor can be a misguided hope, a hope placed in the righteousness of humanity. Righteousness comes from God and God alone (Phil. 3:9). Moving toward forgiveness while embracing the mess and clinging to the peace only God can provide is radical acceptance in action. This approach to forgive has the power to transform us from the inside out, bleed into our relationships and revolutionize our communities.

CHAPTER 10

RECLAIMING BEAUTY AMIDST BROKENNESS

by Andrew J. Schmutzer

As honor has its greatest showcase in marriage, so does shame have a unique ability to cripple a marriage. In fact, is any relationship paralyzed by the effects of shame quite like a marriage is? Both of these—honor and shame—live on a spectrum of relational freedom and health. So dynamic is this continuum that shame is evident both objectively in social disgrace ("let them be clothed with shame and dishonor," Ps. 35:26[1]), and subjectively in the feeling of personal shame ("the man and his wife were both naked and were not ashamed," Gen. 2:25). This is the last observation of the Eden couple, and it is stunning to us because it is written for all of us who have grown up "south" of Eden, where nakedness is basic to feelings of shame.

Personal shame commonly follows a shameful action. In the relational dynamic of marriage, shame not only follows an act done, but shame can also occur from a wrong suffered. Partners can hurt each other. The lack of shame, then, can indicate the need for serious steps toward sorrow and repentance. At one point, Paul even writes, "I say this to shame you" (1 Cor. 6:5 NIV; cf. 2 Thess. 3:14). But a post-Christian culture that prizes autonomous self does not accept these moral "vital signs" of shame, guilt, honor, or repentance.

Shame is not only part of the profound brokenness that married couples can encounter, it is part of the baggage they also bring to their marriage. Our study aims to unpack some of the complex effects of marital sexual brokenness by returning to the Creator's design for relationships in Eden (Gen. 2).

Our discussion will consider the glorious design of marriage within creation, trace the unique unraveling of relationships in Genesis 3, and then consider how the reality of external disgrace and internal shame are illustrated in the pandemic of sexual abuse that affects two in every ten marriages.

THE RELATIONAL ECOSYSTEM

Our relational God has constructed creation to function relationally. In the "first exposition" of Genesis 1, humankind is the zenith of the creative week (1:26–28). In the "second exposition" of Genesis 2, humankind holds the middle place in the chapter (2:5–18). Whether culminating or centering, God's image bearers are surrounded by a vibrant relational ecosystem. We can identify five key associations that comprise this relational ecosystem:

1. God with humankind—binding of royalty (Gen. 1:26; Ps. 8:5);
2. Humankind with the ground—binding of origin (1:24; 2:7; Ps.146:4);
3. Humankind with the animals—binding of domain (1:28; Jonah 3:7–8);
4. Man with woman—binding of mission (1:28; 2:23);
5. Humankind with self—binding of honor (1:26; 2:25).

These are the "core bindings" in which marriage functions, the relational pylons of creation theology. Creation theology shows us that relationships are primary to the divine-human encounter, and human relationships therefore have a functional outworking that stems from a God who is known in relationship. Anthony Thiselton puts it well: "God created humankind because God loves us and chose to reach forth, as it were, out of himself, to create beings 'other' than himself, to commune with them and enjoy fellowship with them."[2] Such fellowship comes with responsibility and consequences.

For God's part, His faithfulness is evident in the very laws of nature that sustain His creation (Ps. 148:5–6). But God does not impose Himself on the first couple, forcing them to make certain choices, nor does God suspend moral laws today so that relational pain can be avoided. Instead, God continues to work within the relational ecosystem He designed, honoring the integrity of human choices for the sake of ongoing relationship. Throughout this relational ecosystem, humankind serves in several arenas. People are accountable to God (their commissioner), honored in marriage (their partner), developing the ground (the cultivated), protecting the animals (the ruled), and granted dignity and glory (God's representative). In a very real sense, work is worship (1:28; 2:5, 15; 3:23). Marriage is a call to cultivate numerous relationships, and the image of God makes this possible.

IMAGE BEARERS AND RELATIONSHIP

In creation theology, being an image bearer is primarily functional—the creation mandate immediately follows to be: "fruitful, multiply, fill, subdue, have dominion" (1:28)—but is also relational. Throughout Scripture, all these core bindings of the relational ecosystem are meant to work together like instruments in a symphony. So while image is tied to "ruling" (1:26b *radah*), it is significant that there is no mandate to rule other people. This "ruling" is important, because it envelops this entire passage. The divine discussion about rule (v. 26 NASB) then echoes in God's audible blessing (v. 28) for humankind to rule. Humankind serves as God's under-king, charged with the care of creation and protection of all. It is this royal image that gives humankind the moral vision and functional capacity to achieve an order worthy of their Creator. They co-create with God (4:1), as Adam has a son in his own "likeness, after his image" (5:3).

Marriage, intimacy, and God's priestly blessing for reproduction can only be understood in the wider context of God's royal commission for His image bearers. Before continuing, we must make several important observations that sharpen our focus on God's design and priorities for marriage and intimacy. First, notice that the pronoun "our" (Gen. 1:26a) underscores a theomorphic perspective (i.e., humans in the form of God), as "our image" and "our likeness" fix their point of reference in God, not in "him" or "herself."[3] This truth calls out the idolatry of autonomy and self-sufficiency, bringing an antidote to our inordinate preoccupation with "I."[4]

Second, notice that this text (1:26–28) also portrays a holistic personhood. We do not *have* God's image, we *are* God's image. Gender is not image, and the language here is that of sexual differentiation as "male and female" (1:27), not gender as we think of it. Sexual difference is the prerequisite for reproduction in 1:28. This passage culminates in language of collective unity ("them," v. 27c). Throughout Genesis 1–2, God addresses them as persons, not genders.[5] In fact, once it is declared that God made gendered image bearers, the text refers to them only in the plural.[6] Gender as we think of it ("man" and "woman"), does not occur until 2:23. This holism corrects our culture's growing gender fluidity, which is isolated from accountability to the relational ecosystem. A theology of sexuality is not found in neutralizing or synthesizing gender but, as Miroslav Volf explains, "affirming gender difference while at the same time positing one gender identity as always internal to the other."[7]

Third, we should understand the danger of a disembodied personhood. We lose all basis for addressing physical boundaries, sexual intercourse, as well as sexual abuse of the body when the image of God is defined without embodiment. The issue is this: If image is cognitive capacity, then image is reason; if worship is central, the image is spiritual; if the aesthetic is primary, then image is creativity; if image is Trinitarian, emotion-filled relationship, then image is relational.[8]

The net result of all these is locating the image in the interior of the person. This is a serious misstep for a theology of sexuality in marriage, where the partners' sexed bodies are held in love, mutual respect, and availability (1 Cor. 7:3–5). The difference in sexed bodies of men and women actually grounds their intricate interdependence.[9] Clearly, in order to address sexual violence, one must have an embodied anthropology. Marriage can surface forms of shame long buried: shame that lives on in our minds, souls, and bodies. In the words of Robin Stockitt in *Restoring the Shamed*, "The shame is likened to a foreign object, something alien, alive perhaps, but with the smell of death about it. It has its own separate yet toxic existence within the physical being of the sufferer."[10] If marriages are to address their complex forms of shame, then embodied realities, not just ideas, must be understood.

While certain aspects of the interaction between men and women manifest depending on time and place, such fluctuation nonetheless "stands in marked contrast to the stable difference of sexed bodies."[11] Both representing (via relationship) and resembling (via corporality) are vital to a theology of image. Recall, it is the body, not the soul, that is the temple of the Holy Spirit (1 Cor. 6:19–20). Marriages don't merely suffer from boundaries broken prior to marriage. It is the ongoing reality of memories embodied in traumatic ways that couples must address.[12] Nor is embodied living only for earthly life. A strong argument can be made that heaven for the believer will still be realized as a gendered reality, since gender is a part of personhood. Mary will still look like Mary and Joseph, like Joseph. The role of sexuality may be different (cf. Matt. 22:30), but as Volf explains:

> Paul's claim that in Christ there is "no longer male and female" entails no eschatological denial of gender dimorphism. . . . The oneness in Christ is a community of people with sexed bodies and distinct gen-der identities, not some abstract unity of pure spirits or de-gendered persons.[13]

SEXUALITY IN CELEBRATION

The second exposition (Gen. 2:4–4:26) is a "close-up" of the relational, covenant making "Lord God," who "forms" the man from the dust (2:7). God did not rest from creating by withdrawing from creation or dominating it. Rather He genuinely fills a need in the man's life (2:18). God "allows himself to be affected, to be touched by each of his creatures. He adopts the community of creation as his own milieu."[14] The relational ecosystem of creation assumes from the start that it is only together and always together that human responsibilities can be carried out,[15] in community rather than individually. It is together that Adam and Eve find their identity—and it is together that their identity will be fractured. But first, we hear the man speak! (author's translation)

> This one (*zo't*) is finally bone of (*min*) my bone,
> and flesh of (*min*) my flesh;
> this one (*zo't*) shall be called "woman" (*'isha*),
> for from man (*min 'ish*) was taken this one (*zo't*)

It is not until there is someone like him that we hear the man speak—in poetry! Notice that his words are exuberant joy, a poetic celebration in the presence of his attending Creator and possibly to his creative Lord. The man highlights their unity from a shared source (*min*, three times). From 1→2→1, marriage is portrayed as a reunification of an original unity. To the man's great delight, the woman (*'isha*) now forms a crucial bond in the relational ecosystem, and he puns on her emergence from the man (*'ish*). Using "bone and flesh" are terms of kinship that mean the other person "is as close as one's own body."[16] Notice that this is the man's evaluation. This time the Creator gives the assessment of His creation to the man. The serpent got it wrong: God does not hoard His power (3:5). Instead, He shares necessary power for the sake of interdependent relationship.

What the reader hears is the man's sacrament of surprise. "This one" (three times) celebrates a definiteness that is vital to healthy sexuality in marriage. This core binding includes sexuality and means that what affects one, affects the other. Hurting one will hurt both (Eph. 5:28–29).[17] The man "is saying yes to God in recognition of his own sexual nature and welcoming woman as the equal counterpart to his sexuality."[18]

The voyeur, adulterer, and abuser are on a spectrum at the opposite end of surprise, in which people become faceless pawns to be moved at will, devoid of any sacramental delight. In sexual deviance, it is precisely the lack of creational boundaries that no longer brings "this one" delight. The personal encounter of the couple highlights a deeper intimacy.

FACE INTIMACY

In the Old Testament, the face (*panim*) could be the most important part of a person's body. The face was a relational concept that referred to the entire person.[19] So in the Song of Solomon, one hears the "lover" declare: "Let me see your face, let me hear your voice" (2:14). As these texts illustrate, "The embodied subject is what we see in the face."[20] A primordial intimacy has been stirred in these gardens (cf. Song 4:14; 6:2). Genesis 2:23 is a benchmark of intimacy and celebration—the man (*'ish*) for the unique presence of the woman (*'isha*). This is precisely the creation standard of "male and female" pairing that Jesus refers to—citing Gen. 1:27 with 2:24—as foundational to the original blessed plan of God, rising above all exceptions and protests (Mark 10:6–9; cf. Deut. 24:1–4).[21] When Jesus passed over the divorce laws

> There was not guilty shame. Dishonest shame of nature's works, honour dishonorable,
> Sin-bred, how have ye troubled all mankind with shows instead, mere shows of seeming pure,
> And banished from man's life his happiest life, simplicity and spotless innocence!
> So passed they naked on, nor shunned the sight of God or angel; for they thought no ill.
> So hand in hand they passed, the loveliest pair that ever since in love's embraces met;
> Adam the goodliest man of men since born, his sons, the fairest of her daughters Eve.[22] **—John Milton**

of Deuteronomy for the narrative of Genesis, he placed the Creator's ideal will above God's concessionary will in order to curb further domestic abuses.[23] God can make allowances to reduce the sting of consequences, but Jesus anticipates the coming kingdom that will restore the bonds of relationships to their original created form.

But how could they be naked, and yet have no shame? Sexual vulnerability and safety is a barometer of relational health. So long as the trust and harmony with God remained undisturbed, the first couple enjoyed an innocence and lack of shame.[24]

NAKEDNESS, SHAME, AND EXPLOITATION

The couple's nakedness, with absence of shame (2:25), seems fanciful to us, now. But it was written for us who know shame. This illustrates the use of implied contrasts: nudity and safety, exposure and acceptance, don't make sense to us. Nudity is a powerful condition, biblically, because it speaks of vulnerability (cf. Gen. 9:22; Isa. 47:1–3). Some of humankind's deepest relational dignities and social boundaries are at stake, so stripping someone was intentionally degrading and profoundly humiliating (2 Sam. 10:4–5; Isa. 20:4).

For kings and nobles, rich clothing showed their dignity, but slaves wore little and prisoners of war, often nothing. The poor struggled against exposure and nakedness.

> Clothing is also such a boundary for the physical body, which is a microcosm of the social system. Nudity means the complete absence of boundaries; the body is accessible to any and everyone, thus destroying its exclusivity as something "set apart." . . . nudity erases social clues and so is unclean.[25]

Shame is inherently relational. To aggressively expose someone is to shame them (Matt. 27:28, 31). Unlike the Western cultures that view nudity as a form of protected "speech" or art, ancient cultures still use nudity and stripping as a social tool to shame control behavior. In our biblical context, however, "shame" implies physical exploitation and humiliation—"to be ashamed before one another" (cf. Gen. 2:25). Not surprisingly, moral shame can be viewed metaphorically as "nakedness" (Ezek. 23:28–29; Rev. 16:15). But for the sexually abused and raped, shame and humiliation are not some sectarian custom or ancient Bible story—it's their story! It is the couple's mistrust and rebellion that will dismantle their naked vulnerability (Gen. 3:7, 10).

The biblical notion of "self" is always a relationally embedded self, rooted in an extended web of relationships.[26] Whereas the Western ideal is the unembedded self, here we encounter another "core binding" of creation that will be affected by sin. The biblical person is always a being-in-relationship. But the mistrust of rebellion breaks apart the relational ecosystem.

The "core bindings" break apart

Arriving at Genesis 3, the couple serve God as His royal representatives. They have power for dominion, not a dominion of power. They certainly do not have an autonomous rule, but exercise their dominion under the "LORD God," who is the Cosmic King.[27] The serpent begins to dismantle another "core binding"—the couple's trust in their caring Creator. Observe the following steps in their rebellion.[28]

The temptation begins when a creature brings deception (3:1a, 13), which raises doubt in two key areas: God's goodness (vv. 1b, 5) and sin's repercussions (v. 4). With her perspective reoriented, the woman has made some stunning changes to the "LORD God's" original command (2:16–17). In her attempt to correct the serpent's claims: she belittles their privileges (vv. 2–3a), qualifies God's generosity (v. 2), alters key terms (v. 3a), employs vague language (v. 3a), expands the prohibition (v. 3b), and minimizes the penalty (v. 3c).

Devastation done and dialogue over, the narrator describes a pathetic scene. Observe the following process. Doubt led to an inordinate desire to possess something forbidden (v. 6a). This desire led to actions of mistrust and rebellion (v. 6b). This disobedience spread to immediate relationships (v. 6c). Their relationship experiences debilitating shame (v. 7). Shame brought fear (vv. 8–10), and these factors brought relational dissolution (vv. 7–13).

With the formal entrance of shame into the couple's relationship, several points should be noted. The woman gave some fruit to her husband "who was with her" (v. 6)—he was there the whole time, and she clearly needed him! If words can be deceptive, silence can be deadly. This point is further confirmed by a point of grammar: in verses 1–7 there are about twenty plural verbs and pronouns, but these plurals all go away in verses 8–19 that follow, a devastating clue to a community now shattered. Combative language now takes over. Further, the "LORD God" laid down a "Thou shalt not" kind of law before there ever was sin or disobedience (2:17). Law promotes relational flourishing. What she could only describe as a "saying" (v. 3a), the "LORD

God" reasserts as His "command" (vv. 11, 17)—twice to the man. When God comes calling, they are not only hiding from the "LORD God" in shame, they are also hiding from each other! Relational fracture is now evident in every part of God's "very good" creation: spiritually, socially, environmentally, and even with the personal self.

Estrangement in the relational ecosystem

In truth, "sin" is not even mentioned until Cain's exile (4:7, 13–14). Instead, it is rebellion and mistrust that shatters relationships, bringing shame and devastation. The loss of relational trust fractures the harmony in the "core bindings." This brings God's judgment on all domains of relationship. They follow the order of the transgression: serpent → woman → man (3:1–7). Both functional and relational, what follows in 3:14–19 can be described as compensatory judgments. Nahum Sarna helpfully observes that the judgment for each party not only: (1) affects what is of central concern in the life of that entity, but also (2) regulates an external relationship.[29] It is common to hear that only the ground is cursed (3:17), and the woman receives no punitive word at all. This is an overstatement. In fact, the woman is the only party mentioned in all three judgments: "and the woman" (3:15), "to the woman" (3:16), "the voice of your wife" (3:17). Additionally, her "pain in childbearing" (3:16b) is repeated in his painful toil (3:17). Finally, the set of three judgments are bracketed by the same temporal phrase: "all the days of your life" (3:14, 17), with "dust" and "eat" (3:14, 19) defining the entire oracle from God. The woman is the bridge between the judgment on the serpent and the man. The entire passage hangs together. Isolated verses cannot be pulled out of this entire unit.

There is some measure of correspondence between the offense and the judgment, between their point of origin (i.e., ground, man) and their future struggle in life. Relational hostility will now exist between humans and the serpent (v. 15). For her part, the woman will pursue fertility amid relational antagonism with the man (3:16b). Similarly, the man now pursues the soil's fertility amid its antagonism (vv. 17–19). In other words, their points of origin no longer offer security or fulfillment.

The judgments meted out don't declare what must happen, but what does happen. Many are rightly concerned that abusive or violent action against women is sanctioned here. This is not a prescriptive "doom" on how any party must act but a description of what will happen. "Whatever the interpretation, the relationship is spoiled" and their intimacy has been diminished.[30] It is pain and alienation that bind relationships now (Gen. 5:29; Eccl. 2:23).

It must be realized that every core binding has now been broken. The collective pain of the man and woman and suffering is staggering. The man's "painful toil" (*'tsabon*, v. 17) working the ground repeats her "pains" (*etseb*) surrounding birth (v. 16a). A final bond is ruptured when the couple is "banished" from the presence of the LORD (v. 23), and the duty of "guarding" (2:15) the garden is now given to cherubim (3:24). As guardians of the glory of God (Ex. 26:1), the cherubim now keep the man and the woman out of the garden sanctuary, rather than welcoming them into it.[31] Once Abel's blood soaks into "the ground" (4:10), it "will no longer yield its strength [crops]" for Cain (4:12). But it is a pervasive wickedness in the human heart (6:6) that stunningly connects the LORD's grieving "heart" (6:6) with his own "pain" (*atsab*). From Creator to creature, the entire relational ecosystem now suffers in enmity (6:7; Rom. 8:22). This is the ongoing context of married life for all people. How shame can live on and strangle the health of a marriage needs to be considered.

HOW SHAME REIGNS

Shame has a theological architecture.[32] Struggling marriages must find their way against the backdrop of a groaning world. Because creation itself is marred, marriages can struggle to find hope and a safe place. As William Brown puts it, "Every text in which creation is its context, the moral life of the community is a significant subtext."[33] Brokenness can come from systems in society, entrenched social patterns, and also from difficulties in one's personal life. We may wish to separate these out, but Scripture does not distinguish between nature, culture, and community. What is obvious, however, is that shame has ingrained itself in our broken world.

In the biblical account, the couple not only hide from God, they hide from each other in shame. Their actions point to the way shame can present itself in rising forms of intensity:

1. Healthy Shame—reminds us of relational responsibility and the danger of diminishing others.
2. Perfectionist Shame—attempts to hide our sense of unworthiness by socially conforming or using a performance of acceptable values.
3. "Identity-based" Shame—enforced belief and behavior by a dominant group or culture toward a "lesser" group (e.g., racially, socially, gender).

4. Toxic Shame—experiences that result from another's violating or abusive behavior, like sexual abuse.

5. State of Shamelessness—when someone lacks a natural remorse for violence and betrayal of others.[34]

If spouses are going to address the effects of a partner's sexual abuse, then they will have to "unpack" Toxic Shame (#4). This addresses abusive behavior that includes everything from domestic neglect to sexual abuse.

Our experiences of life are stored within our physical selves, not merely in a "mind." Shame has its own existence, yet inhabits the body of the shamed individual in complex ways. "Shame is an expression of separation, division, the tearing apart of that which was always intended to be held together in harmonious beauty."[35] What makes sexual abuse so toxic is that accompanying forms of shame pervade the senses and pollute one's interpretation of life and self. Sexual abuse is a potent source of embodied shame. In the same sense identity and sexuality are interconnected, the strands of shame and sexuality are intricately knitted together.[36]

COSTLY BROKENNESS OF THE ABUSE WOUND

Holistic sexuality can be holistically broken. The body is massively complex for abuse survivors. Either one idolizes the body in iconic images of appearance and desire or one disdains the body though a life of physical disorders. Both are disorienting, whether embodied life becomes narcissistic or the enemy of one's very existence.[37] But ironically, it is the unspoiled paradigm of marriage in Genesis that helps us interpret the destructive effects that sexual abuse can have on the marriage relationship.[38]

1. Sexual abuse fractures the unity of personhood.

Whereas God created a holistic being, a *nephesh* (Gen. 2:7), sexual abuse effectively tears apart the *nephesh*—wholeness of a person. It un-creates because it depersonalizes and dismantles the symphony of human parts. Abuse violation deadens life along a spectrum of security and terror, respect and shame, wholeness and brokenness.[39] Survivors need people to model healthy perspectives toward the body that don't divide the body into "pieces and parts." Healing for this marriage can include a discipleship of the body that lives through the body, rather than using a body.

2. Sexual abuse impairs sexual expression.

Whereas God rooted sexuality within the creation mandate (Gen. 1:28a), sexual abuse stymies this blessed calling of sexuality. Victims of abuse often become hypersexualized. Many act out their sexual conditioning or what they have come to associate with sex and the expectations of the "other." God defined sex with an accountable function, intended for bonding and reproduction. But abuse is a poisonous contact that leaves debilitating physical, emotional, and psychological toxins to ferment in the mind-body complex. Tragically, sexual abuse is enacted against another image bearer. Many catastrophes can cause emotional trauma, but sexual abuse uniquely undermines the person's sense of self. Survivors need marriage partners who are patient with a victim's sexual triggers. Healing for this marriage requires reconnecting sex to a sense of real agency for the survivor.

3. Sexual abuse distorts delegated authority.

God's vice regents were given a derived authority as caretakers over His creation (Gen. 1:28b; Ps. 8:6), the intent being for the benefit of creation. We do not think of "subduing" and "ruling" as something a king or other leader does *against* his own people, but for their well-being (Ps. 8:6). However, around 80 percent of victims of sexual abuse are abused by family members,[40] so sexual abuse—and incest by a parent in particular—may be the most profound example of malicious leadership. In sexual abuse, the divine "coronation" for nurture is exchanged for a reign of terror. The abusing family epitomizes the corruption of social order through control, perversion, and unpredictability. Survivors are often incompetent trustors, and will be so for the rest of their lives. Marriage is a place for survivors to learn the skills of trust, maybe for the first time. Non-abused spouses need to understand that healing does not remove suspicion. But marriages can learn new ways of talking and touching, without authoritarian demeanor and general power differentials.

4. Sexual abuse disfigures the "face-identity" of others.

What the narrator reports in Genesis 1:27 and the LORD "builds" in 2:22, the man celebrates in audible poetry (2:23). Sexual abuse robs what is meant to be protected—sexual particularity. The victim loses Adam's "sacrament of surprise." When victimization is tied to a guardian figure, the poetry of intimacy is doubly shredded. Sexually ambushed, victims cannot help but view the "face" of others with deep suspicion. Survivors need to learn how keep the wrong people out and the right ones in. Marriage must be a safe place for heart-forming bonds. But various relationships along the intimacy spectrum can be paralyzing for the victim, because they must engage another's face, the most intimate part of a person. Beyond just "losing face," abuse introduces a world of shame to nakedness that even Adam and Eve did not know. From a simple touch to the marriage bed itself, triggers (e.g., smells) are often discovered unintentionally. What is healing for victims requires the non-abused spouse to help the victim to relate intentionally, "gazing into the face." Not only can the victim feel defaced, but overtures of deep relationship can restore faces of others, too. Marriage can be a place to heal sexual brokenness. The lover's "face" in their spouse will only reappear with painful healing. Full spiritual intimacy in "God's face," however, may have to await another wedding (Rev. 19:7).

5. Sexual abuse isolates the "self" from community.

Surrounded by dignifying speech (Gen. 1:26a), human beings were made in community for community (2:18), where we find purpose. Sadly, abuse poisons a person against community. It severs relational ligaments connecting the "who" of personhood from the "what" of embodied life. The ability to read social interactions are cut. In the words of Volf:

> The self, however, is always a social self, and a wrongdoing intertwines the wrongdoer and the wronged as little else does. For the mistreatment consists not just in the pain or loss endured, but also in the improper relating of the wrongdoer toward the wronged—and remembering it not just with our mind but also with our body.[41]

Through debilitating shame and self-hatred, a victim undergoes a crushing alienation. The affirmation they desperately need they can no longer risk. Healing for the survivor reconnects a disembodied view of sexuality to personhood, and self to community. Marriage can help translate care into community for the survivor. The survivor needs theological healing; a reintegration into a nourishing faith community. I say theological, because spiritual healing is the rarest and most difficult to achieve. Reconnecting with a God, who didn't show up to prevent the abuse in the first place, can be a crisis of faith that returns to haunt a marriage and child-rearing. A supportive community is a healing antidote for the isolated survivor.

6. Sexual abuse destroys family relationships.

Familial ties and terms are used throughout Gen. 2:18–25. God is pictured as the loving and active Provider who: observes the need, finds an appropriate mate, brings her to the man, and presides over Adam's excitement in covenantal language. Even in shifting loyalties from parents to spouse, family language saturates 2:18–25. Being naked without shame elevates the familial virtues of innocence and trust (2:25). Sexuality is rooted in the biblical prescription for marriage, one that celebrates the nuclear family (2:24; Prov. 5:18–19).

But an abused child begins to wonder if their abusing father, mother, or older sibling is their guardian or their lover. Abuse subverts relationships celebrated in creation because a child cannot give or receive as an equal. Abuse is relational cancer, attacking vital organs of relationship, destroying relational tissue, and collapsing family structures. In fact, the ability of abuse to obscure internal and external relationships makes it a cosmic affront to the Creator and the orders of His creation (cf. Gen. 6:1–3). Healing for the survivor requires learning to transform toxic patterns before they are transferred. Though not all abused people abuse their children, many abusers were, themselves, abused. While key relationships for survivors have brought unimaginable pain, it is also relationships that help heal. Marriage for this survivor can help establish fresh boundaries inside and outside the home.

7. Sexual abuse mars connecting metaphors for God.

In the garden-sanctuary of Eden, God is portrayed as a cosmic King, master artisan, attentive father, gracious provider, and just protector. Naturally, the reader is invited to look for corresponding relations in their own world: God as parent (Hos. 11:1), midwife (Isa. 66:7–9), mother (Isa. 66:13), and protective fortress (Ps. 31:2). But for the abused, their "bridging" metaphors for God have also been violated—particularly the nurturing metaphors for God as father and protector. Should we be surprised that scriptural language for "presenting your body a living sacrifice . . . your service of worship" (cf. Rom. 12:1) might be distasteful to an abuse survivor? The overwhelming incongruity between the earthly and heavenly Father causes many victims to abandon their faith altogether. God as a loving parent is a beautiful truth, but the concept can be perverted due to the wrongs heaped upon the abused. Healing for the victim requires them to find a new collection of metaphors that reconnect God to their painful story and His wider creation. The church—Christ's visible body—must plan for this dissonance among survivors, when up to 20 percent of its congregation has experienced abuse.

As the author, I conclude with several observations relating the wonder of our Creator and Redeemer to the marriage of an abuse survivor and the complexity of their healing process. But as a survivor myself, I also part with some recommendations and encouragement.

Prepare for the rigors of a journey

We started this chapter with creation, because shame did. But the expulsion of the man and the woman from God's presence places us on the journey into redemption. Marriages reflect the cost of both embodied brokenness, but also the created intention to nourish the other. For marriages marred by abuse, there is a journey to be embraced for both partners. Love, patience, and understanding are needed from each person in the marriage, but how these play out will look different. Pursue quality counseling, support groups, and help in parenting. It's about care during the healing process, not about an easy or absolute cure. The entire person needs healing, that is, becoming whole. And every part of marriage must be up for the challenge. Be sure to walk the healing path together, struggle together, and grow together—or you can grow apart—but the survivor sets the time frame, not those going along. Healing is a family project. Scruton sums up some crucial points we've made:

> Persons can be harmed in ways that are not adequately summarized in the ideas of a violation of rights. They can be polluted, desecrated, defiled—and in many cases this disaster takes a bodily form. If we don't see this, then not only will sexual morality appear opaque to us and inexplicable; we will lose sight of the ways in which the moral life is lived through the body and displayed in the face.[42]

Exchange a "defaced" perspective for that of lovers

A healing marriage has comfort in each other's presence, not mere function. I'd like to include "joy," but healing can be a tough road that tempers some emotions altogether. A healing marriage, especially for survivors, is a striving one, a courageous one, but not one that ever arrives. That said, even broken lovers can learn to see beauty in scars. They must learn to "look *into* each other, and search the eyes and face of the beloved for the thing to which they seek to be united . . . not a thing but a perspective, defined for all eternity as *other* than mine. C. S. Lewis puts the point nicely with his remark that friends are side by side, while lovers are face to face."[43]

Weed out the survivor's surrogate attachments

The celebrated partner "is accountable to others, and sees him or herself from the outside, as an other in others' eyes."[44] Sexual shame, however, collapses one's vision, fractures relational bonds, and fixates on the self, just to survive. For survivors, the first community of marriage forms the epicenter of their healing. The marriage relationship must help the survivor avoid surrogate attachments, whether workaholism or destructive habits. Instead, survivors should be encouraged to take up a constructive hobby and, as much as possible, some form of exercise. This community of accountability is a preparation for the deeper experience of God.[45]

Distinguishing between guilt and shame

Though related, guilt and shame are not the same. While shame hides behind façades, it also twists our view of God. Shame does not have a legal solution, but guilt does.[46] True guilt does not live in feelings, but in knowledge.[47] Relationship has a role here. Sin is not the failure to achieve a certain moral standard; it is the choice to turn one's back on a loving relationship.[48] In Genesis, Adam and Eve illustrate this well. To bring redemption, Jesus went utterly public—on a cross! There was no greater shame-making debacle than the cross. Jesus did this "so that our shame could be absorbed in him."[49]

Survivors can wear a form of shame on their face that complicates a marriage. Faces tell stories, some very debilitating stories. In marriage, however, the defaced victim can become the restored beloved. The surviving spouse needs a vision and a partner, not a timetable and an agitator. A redemptive vision says: "Those who look to him are radiant, and their faces shall never be ashamed" (Ps. 34:5).

Empower the non-abused spouse to "aid" the survivor

When the victim's violation can feel like contamination, the non-abused spouse must learn to converse in the "languages" of toxic memories, childlike grief, and relational betrayal. The non-abused spouse is the primary agent for their partner's healing. For the survivor who is struggling with the effects of their abuse—yes, some effects will last a lifetime—a loving marriage can be a place to help absorb the shame, by sacrificial stooping to the level of the other's weakness. This is loving the survivor on the level they need, similar to the way Jesus lowered Himself to the plane of the woman caught in adultery, then showed her a new path, with accountability. The stooping work of Christ can bring new meanings to old wounds. The survivor is struggling to become a someone, not a something, and tender aid can bring deep currents of healing.[50] Remember, Jesus belongs to a unique line of shamed prophets, as He hung naked on the cross. Exactly—they took His clothes, too!

The survivor's marriage celebrates an intimacy restored by Christ

Marriage is a unique commitment for life in face-presence of another. Those sexually hobbled through abuse will struggle to look into another's face without help. While God uses agents of healing, He is the ultimate Healer. The work of Christ restores the sacrament of surprise and excitement, even for God: "I have singled you out by name. You are Mine" (Isa. 43:1 JPS[51]). Believers are Easter-marked by Christ. Donald Hagner explains that the new kingdom reality in Jesus involves "the restoration of the perfection of the pre-fall creation," which reflects the new ethics of the kingdom.[52] Then, the relational ecosystem will be reinstated. The glory of God is restored in the face of the crucified.

Honor is restored in the risen Christ

There is a vision for healing marriages crippled by past abuse. Abuse, and its accompanying shame, is an intensely personal experience, so it needs an intensely personal remedy.[53] Wounds are required to heal wounds. This is a wonderful paradox that survivors can lean into! The risen Christ restores honor to all those wounded and broken who gaze upon His face (cf. 2 Cor. 3:18). It is the glorified face (Rev. 20:11) of our Lord that will give new meaning to his abused face (Matt. 26:67).[54] The face of God gazing upon us is nothing other than the experience of salvation itself.[55] Here is a deep well of connections between Jesus' suffering and survivors' struggle to find wholeness. Jesus, the perfect human, became a "victim" and in the process, showed Himself honorable by how He "shamed shame" for all mask makers, hiding from community.[56] In His family, the toxically shamed are released from their disgrace. The slain Lamb grants us fellowship in a new society that is defined by His scars (Rev. 5:6).

CONTINUING INSIGHT:

SHAME: CREATING/FINDING A HEALING MARRIAGE

by M. Ashley Schmutzer

As Andrew has stated in his opening paragraph, shame has a "unique ability to cripple a marriage." And an abuse survivor may experience toxic shame "that result from another's violating or abusive behavior, like sexual abuse." When the abuse survivor enters into marriage, they are being asked to become one with their spouse. This can be a frightening, difficult experience. The survivor may experience triggers and may not know in any way, yet, what "safe touch" is all about. What is needed in this is understanding, patience, and selflessness on the part of the non-abused spouse. This may sound like an endeavor no one would want to try—but there is something very beautiful about coming alongside someone who has been hurt and showing them how to feel safe, to trust, and to experience wholeness in a way that is right and good. Not in a codependent, dysfunctional way, but in an innocent, nurturing, cultivating, dependable, trusting way.

Abuse survivors need someone who can love them unconditionally and be gracious when they feel triggered. They have been *used* in the past. Now they can be *treasured*. They need a consistent reminding from their spouse that they are safe, that they are protected, that they are loved and cherished. As Andrew stated, "Healing requires reconnecting sex to a sense of real agency for the survivor." Sexual intimacy for a survivor when they are safe, protected, and cherished can help heal the wounds that have been caused by past perpetrators. Often, the survivor may need to guide and help the spouse know what scares them, and what feels safe. Making new memories and learning together can heal like nothing else can.

It's also possible that some triggers haven't even surfaced yet. When those come, being patient, kind, reminding the survivor that you love them and care for them, and *showing* that can go a long way. Find out what does trigger them. Learn about your spouse, study them, care for them. Healing can occur through sexual intimacy in a way the survivor has never known. Where they once were used and abused, they can heal and find delight.

Andrew also states, "Survivors are often incompetent trustors and will be so for the rest of their lives. Marriage is a place for survivors to learn the skills of trust, maybe for the first time." Trust is built through time and proven commitment. When an incompetent trustor sees the commitment of a spouse for days/weeks/months/years, it has the ability to help heal what has been wronged. Bridges of trust can be built where none have existed in the survivor's life before. The committed spouse can reassure, build into, and love unconditionally in a very healing way.

The journey of marriage and healing needs to be prepared for. It's important that one doesn't go into a marriage trying to just be the survivor's savior. The surviving spouse needs a partner who has their back, who builds into them, and comes alongside them when they are hurting. It is someone who listens and says, "I'm so sorry. I know this is difficult." But there also need to be other supporters. It is not meant to all be on the survivor's spouse. The spouse can be the main encourager, but not the sole encourager. They can be the most trusted, and most unconditionally loving and supporting, but not the only one in this difficult walk. No one can be the only support of someone who has been through this tragedy. It is likely that counseling and support through individual counseling and support groups may be necessary on and off throughout married life.

One also needs to go into the marriage without a timetable for their partner to heal. Look at it as walking a journey by the side of someone you love. Your partnership can give them hope and endurance and trust that there is a light at the end of the tunnel. Research has shown that we can do almost anything when someone commits to walking by our side. But everyone's journey is different, and there is no template for healing. The best we can do is commit to continuing to move forward, and to commit to each other.

Our spouse needs to hear from us that we are in for the long haul, and we are committed to growing together through the triggers, the fears, and the joys. It is also important to realize that as the supportive spouse we are not just there to endure. As Dan Allender states, "The supportive spouse, however, is not merely there to endure the turmoil and provide stability . . . Instead, it is a time for both husband and wife to be transformed. One person may be more focused on the path toward healing, but both partners must be open to deep change."[1] While the survivor may struggle to find their footing, and may, at times, lash out, this should not be the norm. Being a supportive spouse doesn't mean taking abuse or harshness but calls for respect and care to go both ways. Being open to deep change means growing through those difficult times and continuing to be supportive and encouraging and trusting. "Our deepest loyalty must be to being formed in the image of Christ, to become the person we are most deeply created to be. This exceeds the legitimate desire for happiness; it must prevail against every inclination to seek safety, an absence of pain, or false comfort."[2]

Finally, there is an added silver lining, if you will, to coming alongside an abuse survivor in marriage. We will be challenged, and we will come out stronger and more understanding of pain and why a sinful world so needs Christ. To look deep suffering and shame in the face, to provide comfort and care, to come beside and help our partner bear up under deep pain is like walking on holy ground. What if so much of what Satan has tried to ruin can be turned around for healing and helping others? What Satan sets out to destroy, God can heal and make more beautiful. "The thief comes only to steal and kill and destroy; I [Christ] have come that they may have life, and have it to the full" (John 10:10 NIV).

CHAPTER 11

WHEN MARRIAGE FALLS SHORT OF THE CHRISTIAN IDEAL

by Eric L. Johnson and Jonathan T. Pennington

Ted and Mary met in class at the Bible college they both attended and began to date the following year. On the surface, they came from very different backgrounds—she was raised in a fundamental Christian home and went to church three or four times a week; he had grown up in a nominal Christian family, becoming an outspoken atheist in high school who, surprisingly, converted a year after graduation. But their stories shared a deep commonality: they both had grown up in unhappy families.

By the time they met, they had similar conservative values and ended up at the same Christian college because they each wanted to understand the Bible better. After dating for a few months, they began to have significant conflict, which led to a breakup that lasted for a few weeks. However, their strongly ambivalent affection for each other (which to some extent masked their respective relational insecurities and fears) made it impossible to end the relationship. So they continued dating and eventually became engaged. During that time, they read some of the best Christian marriage books of that day and thought they had a good sense of what the ideal Christian marriage would look like. They each tried hard, even prayerfully, to become the kind of person who would make a good spouse. They married shortly after Ted's graduation, and the numerous disagreements they had throughout the honeymoon were a foreshadowing of their rocky first year. Their frequent clashes culminated in Mary's suicide attempt around their first anniversary.

Thus began their journey of mutual unhappiness, conflict, and dismay that continued for many years, despite a strong commitment to Christ, involvement in the local church, holding solid theology, and adhering to Christian ethical norms that forbade divorce for merely irreconcilable differences. Indeed, among the first hurdles they had to overcome was Ted's tendency to turn their disagreements into a lecture on biblical truth and his demands, when he felt threatened, to remind Mary of her obligation to submit to his headship. These tactics were especially exasperating to her, because though she had been raised in a home environment that affirmed the husband as the head of the household, Ted seemed to her to be uncaring about her thoughts, feelings, and desires. In addition, he was controlling and self-centered (in retrospect, she realized, much like her father).

Perhaps their worst memories are those infrequent times when, in the midst of a "lecture session," Mary would start hitting herself in the face out of desperate frustration. Whenever that happened, Ted would quickly wrap his arms around her to prevent the blows, usually while continuing to scold her, one time threatening to take her to a mental hospital if she did it again.

During the early years of their marriage, they went to some pastors for marital counseling but, aside from some sound advice about confronting their sin and how to get along better, they received little lasting help and fumbled along in a marriage they couldn't get out of. Though they admitted it to no one, they both secretly despaired about their future together.

Our marriage was ours, belonged to the two of us, and was full of wonderful things, terrible things, joyous things, grievous things, but ours.[1] **—Madeleine L'Engle**

As you might expect, the names of this couple are pseudonyms. But the husband is one of the authors of this chapter (Eric). My wife and I have known throughout our marriage that our sins against each other have been a major source of our difficulties. Indeed, this knowledge has been one of the heaviest burdens of our journey. At the same time, we can say today, after nearly four decades together, that we are not where we used to be—thanks to God and His grace—though we still fall short of the ideal!

The other marriage represented by the authors of this chapter also falls short of the ideal. Now twenty-four years and six children in, I (Jonathan) am just now waking up to see the profound and sobering ways that my own woundedness from my fatherless upbringing has tainted how I relate to the world and especially to my wife. This awareness is in addition to my own sin and pathologies, which continue to frame my perspective and motivate my self-centeredness. Unknowingly, for most of our marriage, I have engaged in a program of convincing myself and my wife that I am a victim of *her* pathology and that she was the cause of all of my unhappiness.

Over the decades that both authors have been married, many books and sermons have been produced describing what the ideal Christian marriage looks like. Many Christian couples have been helped by such works, in large part because of the biblical values they espouse and the biblical goals that shape their agendas. However, we suspect that this literature has had a lesser impact on more troubled Christian marriages. Christian marriage books generally do a good job of describing the ideals of a Christian marriage and challenging couples to engage in practices that promote those principles, but for the most part, these resources are aimed at the healthier majority of couples and often assume the operation of a fair amount of creation grace (usually called "common grace"[2]) during childhood development. As a result, relatively little consideration tends to be given to addressing the special needs of marriages in which the spouses have relational styles that were significantly compromised by growing up in a dysfunctional family of origin.

To help the more troubled minority of Christian marriages, we are convinced that more is needed than pointing to the Christian ideal and offering strategies that work for relatively healthier individuals. To supplement their creation grace deficiencies, couples in distressed and conflicted marriages will benefit from meeting periodically with a therapist trained in negotiating the complex labyrinth of the internal and relational dynamics at play. In addition, they should also be part of a local church that is explicitly welcoming of such marriages and, depending on their size, offer various kinds of help; and most importantly, the inexhaustible redemptive resources available through union with Christ and communion with God.

UNDERSTANDING DISTRESSED AND CONFLICTED CHRISTIAN MARRIAGES COMPREHENSIVELY

When we consider Christian marriages characterized by distress and conflict, we should seek to understand them as comprehensively as possible. A Christian framework will include sin—original sin, personal sins, and vices; the ethicospiritual psychopathology[3] that is the special focus of Scripture; as well as biopsychosocial[4] damage, which is the special focus of modern psychopathology, as found in the American Psychiatric Association's guidelines;[5] and suffering. Original sin necessarily affects all marriages, whereas distressed and conflicted marriages involve suffering by definition, as well as some measure of personal sin and vice, and often are a function of biopsychosocial damage.

As a result, Christians have available to them two distinct languages of psychopathology that describe different classes of problems from very different standpoints. The goal of a unified, comprehensive Christian framework for psychopathology is to resemble, as fully as possible, God's holistic, omniscient understanding of psychopathology, resulting in a single diagnostic system that includes biopsychosocial and ethicospiritual disorders, and their combinations.

SIN AND DISTRESSED/CONFLICTED CHRISTIAN MARRIAGES

As with other social forms of distress and conflict, the marital kind reflects the works of the flesh: enmity, strife, jealousy, fits of anger, rivalries, dissensions, divisions, and envy (Gal. 5:20–21). "What causes quarrels and what causes fights among you? Is it not this, that your passions (Gk. *hēdonē*) are at war within you? You desire and do not have, so you murder. You covet and cannot obtain, so you fight and quarrel" (James 4:1–2 ESV[6]).

Marriage is a microcosm of human relationality, where the joys and sorrows and the virtues and vices of humanity are found in their most concentrated form. Civility is far easier to practice with acquaintances than with those with whom we live. In marriage the self-aggrandizing drive of pride that unconsciously promotes one's sense of superiority, virtue, and rights is constantly challenging and being challenged by each other, which tends to manifest itself in conflict. Even more insidious is when one spouse's pride is complemented by the other's "sloth" or passivity,[7] which collaborate to constitute a relational kind of sin that makes tyranny possible. Similarly, two spouses can collude in mutual pride and passivity by not challenging each other to take responsibility for themselves and become more like the persons they are called to become in Christ.

Sin affects marriages in a very different way in the banality of indifference, boredom, and distraction, leading to an often inchoate distress that manifests itself more indirectly than conflict in unfulfilled created longings and the gradual death of the self of one or both parties.

Sin in marriage can also be considered as disordered love. If love consists in delighting in one's spouse, desiring his or her well-being, and desiring comprehensive union with him or her,[8] then we might suppose that marital sin is manifested in focusing especially on the sins and weaknesses of one's spouse, rather than on his or her goodness and strengths (given by God). Marital sin also includes desiring (usually unconsciously) the diminishment of the well-being of one's spouse and acting in ways that inhibit his or her flourishing; and resisting union with one's spouse, which is promoted in such ways as not spending time together, and sharing together thoughts, feelings, desires, plans, and story.

All this is to say that, according to a biblical view of marriage, normal spouses who are relatively healthy bear responsibility before God and each other for how they treat each other, for their actions and inactions, and for the underlying state of their hearts toward their partner. God's design is for each marriage partner to move away from an external ethical orientation that blames the other for the state of the marriage and toward a more relational/internal ethicospiritual orientation. This orientation is based in one's union with and perfection in Christ. Spouses take increasing responsibility for themselves and for their contribution to the state of the marriage. Apart from union with Christ, and the forgiveness, justification, and adoption one has in Him, it would seem impossible to go very far in grasping one's marital sin very deeply.

Finally, by relying more and more on communion with God, rather than one's spouse, to meet relational needs, spouses can focus more of their attention on learning how to love their spouse better.

ATTACHMENT THEORY

An understanding of attachment theory is helpful in discussing the effects of biopsychosocial damage on marital distress and conflict. Basically, attachment explains how a child's earliest relationships result in a sense of security or insecurity, which usually continue throughout childhood and into adulthood, and thus into marriage.

Most of the theory and research in this area has been done by secular physicians and psychologists,[9] though many Christians have utilized its insights.[10] According to attachment theory, individuals vary in their attachment style: secure attachment and three kinds of insecure attachment: preoccupied/anxious/ambivalent, dismissive/avoidant, and unresolved/disorganized/disoriented.[11]

These attachment styles result from the organization of the child's brain that occurs during parent-child interactions, especially in the first few years of life, shaped reciprocally by the parents' relational style (including their beliefs, emotions, and relational skills) and the child's temperament. The following summarizes the findings.

Preoccupied/anxious/ambivalent

Preoccupied parents of *anxious/ambivalent* children are generally not consistently available, sensitive, perceptive, and effective with them. Such parents desire to connect, but they lack discernment regarding their child's state of mind, so the engagement is non-contingent and not consistently responsive to the child's signals. Instead, parents "intrude" on the infant's mind and seemingly arbitrarily impose their agenda on the child. As a result, the parents meet their infant's emotional needs sporadically and unpredictably.

Infants appear to deal with this somewhat erratic relational world by focusing intensely on the relationship and their own experience, seeking as much connection as possible. Gradually, such children form a false self, which is disconnected from their own actual experiences, as they learn, based on parental cues and preferences, how to please their parents. When grown, these individuals have difficulty regulating their own recollections/thought processes and tend to experience frustration in their close relationships, functionally reenacting their prior experience, which has been influenced by their own perceptions, expectations, and preferences. As we might expect, they tend to be hyperaware of the negative emotions of their spouses and get quickly distressed in relational conflict.

Dismissive/avoidant

Dismissive parents of *avoidant* children are generally emotionally unavailable, neglectful, and rejecting, and so also tend not to be attuned to their children's state of mind and emotions. The children's emotional needs, then, tend not to be met. These parents have difficulty relating to their children according to their level of development, and they are likely to express negative emotions to their child and practice physical punishment, sometimes even constituting abuse.

The children learn that relationships are painful, so they must "live on their own." Researchers hypothesize that the children's strategy in such a relational environment is to minimize proximity and reduce their expectations of a satisfying relationship. Such children may dissociate[12] and disconnect from their own mental life. When they grow up, they remember few warm, caring experiences with parents, but their memory of their early relationships is generally poor. In adulthood, they tend to have low self-awareness, be unable to attune to the emotions of their spouses, and move away from them in relational conflict.

Unresolved/disorganized/disoriented

Unresolved/Disorganized parents of *disoriented* children are fearful, distracted, and frightening. They are frequently emotionally and sometimes physically abusive. They send mixed messages to their children: "Come to me." "Get away from me." The parents, therefore, are a source of anxiety and confusion, rather than comfort. The children cannot make sense of these paradoxical communications, and they seem stuck between approach and avoidance, leading sometimes to dissociation.

All this hinders the proper development of the children's mind. "The sudden shifts in these children's states of mind yield incoherence in their cognitive, emotional, and behavioral functioning."[13] As a result, the children have very poor self- and emotion regulation. When grown, they become confused and disoriented when recalling their early relationships and manifest symptoms of dissociation. Their relations with their spouses are confusing, unpredictable, and can be very painful emotionally, and in some cases physically.

CHILDHOOD ATTACHMENT STYLE EXPOSURE

The proverbial wisdom that "the apple doesn't fall far from the tree" has been meticulously documented empirically over the last century. One example is the highly replicated finding that the attachment style to which one is exposed in childhood is usually reproduced with one's own children. John Bowlby, the originator of attachment theory, hypothesized that attachment experiences form "internal-working models" in the mind of the child, a cognitive-affective structure of self-and-other that gets reactivated in one's future social relationships.[14] Internal-working models are a part of what has been termed *implicit memory*, since they are formed prior to language acquisition and episodic memory, in contrast to *explicit memory*, which can be verbalized and consciously accessed. As a result, adults are generally unable to describe their attachment style in words; internal-working models are activated automatically, and in most people they operate outside of conscious awareness. Abundant evidence shows that early attachment experiences shape the developing child's memory and attention; emotion experience and regulation; self-representation and narrative; social perceptions, expectations, and communication; and the underlying neural architecture of all these psychosocial processes.

Attachment styles have been studied in over fifty countries, and researchers have discovered some cultural variation. But when averaged across cultures, roughly a third of the samples have some form of insecure attachment.[15] Generally speaking, insecure attachment is associated with a higher incidence of psychiatric disturbance, including anxiety and mood disorders. In addition, attachment research has found significant effects lasting throughout childhood and adolescence and on into adulthood. Attachment style has been found to affect sibling relationships and childhood friendships, and relationship security in early adulthood, most importantly, marital relationship—though there is also evidence of some people moving from insecure to "earned secure status."[16]

ATTACHMENT STYLES IN MARRIAGE

When couples enter into marriage, each has an attachment history that they bring with them into the relationship. James Fisher and Lisa Crandell[17] distinguish three common types of insecurely attached couples: (1) dismissive/dismissive couple attachment: both partners are characterized by detachment and emotional distance and resist depending on one another; (2) preoccupied/preoccupied couple attachment: both partners feel deprived emotionally and come to believe that their partner is unwilling or unable to satisfy their needs; and (3) dismissive/preoccupied couple attachment: one partner expresses most of the distress and the other believes the only problem is the other's distress.

In addition, some couples have only one person with insecure attachment, either preoccupied or dismissive. Judith Crowell and Dominque Treboux report a 50 to 60 percent concordance rate of the attachment status of married couples.[18] Some have noted a gender pattern of anxious females paired with avoidant males.[19] Mention should also be made of those whose attachment style alternates between avoidant and anxious, depending on their mate's behavior. As might be expected, couples whose marriages are characterized by mutual secure attachment style are more likely to report marital satisfaction.[20]

Mention should also be made of patterns of interactions that characterize distressed and conflicted marriages. Likely rooted in attachment experiences during childhood, conflicted couples often engage in self-perpetuating interaction loops like "pursue-withdraw" or "criticize-and-complain responded to with defend-and-distance."[21] Such "strategies" to promote attachment by anxious spouses and to reduce pain by avoidant spouses prove to be counterproductive to their desires, since over time these patterns can increase distance and frustration between the spouses and cause additional emotional wounds that make the relationship more difficult. Such wounds usually have to be addressed and trust has to be restored, before they can collaborate on strengthening their marriage.

> Over time, as we both grew as individuals and as we sought counseling together, we began to experience healing in our marriage. Yes, we faced many rough patches over the decades of our marriage, but I'm so glad we stuck it out through our painful first few years. God has worked in our life together—and He's used our marriage struggles and failures to draw us closer to Him and to each other.[22] —**Kay Warren**

This effort can be facilitated by repair attempts and transparency regarding unmet needs, as well as forgiveness. Spouses can learn to pay attention to *all* that their partner is actually communicating, rather than just what it *feels like* they are communicating. Attachment therapy begins with helping the spouses find a safe haven and secure base—perhaps with a therapist or with God or both. From that safe place they reevaluate their patterns of interaction and initiate and learn to practice new patterns of interaction that are more likely to foster well-being. Doing so will enable the couple to eventually form a more secure attachment bond with each other.[23] Ideally, they become mutually reinforcing of each other's healing.

Christians will want to interpret this vast, mostly secular literature according to their worldview.[24] The fact that early childhood suffering has caused significant damage to the biopsychosocial dynamic structures is of immense concern to God (Matt.18:6), since He has great compassion for those with any kind of weakness (Matt. 9:36; 14:14; Luke 7:12–14). At the same time, as humans develop into personal agents before God, they become responsible for the current state of their character and actions with others, and therefore they are to seek appropriate remediation when necessary, whether or not they were responsible for causing that state.

In addition, as personal agents, they also commit personal sins, which will undoubtedly be shaped by the particular form of their character and its limitations. Consequently, as insecurely attached Christians become aware of their attachment status in early adulthood (due to relationally impoverished families that had less creation grace than is desirable), they are called by God to embark on the journey of "inward deepening."[25] This involves personally taking responsibility for themselves and their actions, confessing their sins to God and those they sin against, and seeking help from Him and mature others to get the psychospiritual healing they need, in order to obtain "earned-secure attachment" in Christ and in relation with others through redemptive grace.

WHAT IT MEANS FOR THE CHURCH

Though we are not aware of any research on percentages of different attachment styles in the Christian community, it seems likely that since insecure attachment affects roughly 33 percent of the population in cultures around the world, about the same percent would be found in the church.[26] So, while most Christian marriages experience some degree of marital distress and conflict, we might expect that about a third of Christian marriages are characterized by more substantial challenges due to at least one spouse having insecure-attachment status. That amounts to a significant minority of Christian marriages (and families). What is the church to do with this portion of its body?

Since the days of the early church, Christians have recognized the need to instruct church members on the basics of Christian teaching, ethics, and spiritual practice. Back then the process was called *catechesis*: evangelicals today term it *discipleship*. Perhaps basic instruction regarding marriage should also become a part of church life. Such instruction is sometimes done in larger contemporary churches, particularly in premarital counseling and marriage seminars, and there are fortunately many books on Christian marriage available today.

However, the vast majority of this kind of teaching and writing on marriage generally consists of relevant biblical and ethical teaching or common sense principles (e.g., love and respect) or both; it presumes relatively healthy biopsychosocial functioning, because it is sensibly aimed at the two-thirds majority who grew up with "good enough" Christian parents and had secure attachment. Typical Christian instruction may be sufficient to enable securely attached believers to make the adjustments needed to lead to a satisfying marriage, with some discipline, practice, and the Spirit's help; and that may be all the majority of Christians need in order to develop relatively healthy Christian marriages.

However, those of us with insecure attachment will likely find that such education, combined with well-intentioned attempts to follow through are not enough to change one's relational style, and that more is needed. *This is because the deep, implicit, biopsychosocial dynamic structures responsible for attachment cannot be modified by mere education, discipline, and good intentions.*

Someone close in heart to me should know something about things that records do not record: the dreadful sufferings of our childhoods, from which we rescued one another, but could not wholly heal the wounds that later often proved disabling; the sufferings that we endured after our love began—all of which (over and above our personal weaknesses) might help to make pardonable, or understandable, the lapses and darknesses which at times marred our lives—and to explain how these never touched our depths nor dimmed our memories of our youthful love.[27] **—J. R. R. Tolkien**

Those who did not come from "good enough" families and so have relatively damaged brain/souls (leading to difficult relationships) still need teaching and discipleship in order to provide the cognitive, ethical, and spiritual framework within which to do the deeper reconstructive work necessary to become more mature Christians. Moral education alone will not be enough. Such people also need healing relational experiences with God and others, healthier than their original attachment figures. Otherwise, their largely unconscious insecure-attachment dynamic structures will guarantee that they continue to repeat the form of their past relationships in the present, *even though their explicit theology of marriage may be excellent*!

Functionally, the above state of affairs has often led informally to the coexistence of three groups of married couples in local churches:

(1) the ideals—those in fairly healthy marriages characterized by secure attachment, who have comparatively little distress and conflict, some of whom may serve as marriage role models to the rest of the church;

(2) the seekers—securely and insecurely attached couples with comparatively greater distress and conflict than the first group, but who nonetheless strongly identify with and aspire to have a marriage like the "ideals," but who therefore have difficulty acknowledging consciously and publicly their marital struggles;

(3) the disenfranchised—couples with at least one insecurely attached member (and usually two) who, because of significant marital distress and conflict, have come to the conclusion that the ideal Christian marriage is out of reach, but who feel they have no one in the church with whom they can talk about such difficulties, since they feel such shame for falling short of the ideal.

Partly sustaining this social configuration is a tendency of the church's less-than-perfect members (all of us) to divide humanity into two groups, the righteous and the wicked, or us versus them. Of course, on the one hand, this ethical hierarchy reflects actual differences in virtue and vice, as well as brokenness and woundedness, which Christians must recognize and affirm or fall into ethical relativism. God's moral law *is* holy, righteous, and good (Rom. 7:12). It reflects the character of God and His design plan for human beings. Healthy Christian marriages will be more conformed to that template than conflicted marriages. The gospel never undermines the law, but fulfills it (Matt. 5:17; Rom. 8:3–4).

Yet, the law can create strong personal and social shame and send lawbreakers into hiding. Worse than that, according to the apostle Paul, sin takes the law and kills us with it (Rom. 7:8), in at least three different ways—leading to more law-breaking, despair, or self-righteousness—while reinforcing our tendency to divide humanity into the righteous or wicked, better or worse.

However, the gospel is good news, in part, because it is the great equalizer of God's people, since *everyone* falls short of God's glory and only Christ's perfection corresponds to the law's absolute standards, making it possible for *anyone* to stand before God without condemnation, clothed in *His* righteousness. So the gospel alone undermines any self-promoting, unconscious divisiveness based on human difference in ethical performance, whatever the cause. Unfortunately, this higher, transcendent, gospel perspective often gets obscured in the life of the church, since it is easy for believers who still live in the flesh to forget the ongoing need we all have for the gospel, and to regress back to merely ethical ways of thinking, living, and viewing one another in our everyday lives.

Creation grace

One way to interpret the differences among the healthier couples found in the church and those from a dysfunctional family of origin is to consider the degree of creation grace (or common grace, as noted earlier) that has characterized their respective development. As Christians know, "Every good gift and every perfect gift is from above, coming down from the Father of lights, with whom there is no variation or shadow due to change" (James 1:17). Christians in the Reformed tradition have labeled this activity a form of grace, because, first, it all comes ultimately from God. Second, He *owes* no one anything, so *all* His goodness is a gift; and third, as we previously noted, the human race is contaminated by sin and therefore worthy of judgment, rather than blessing, from God (Ps. 51:4; John 3:36; Rom. 1:32; 3:1–23; Eph. 2:1–3). Consequently, *all* the benefits everyone enjoys in life are gifts of God's kindness, who, in His sovereign mercy, bestows His goodness on whomever He wishes and however He sees fit (Dan. 2:21, 38). The apostle Paul pointed out that the true God "did not leave himself without witness, for he did good by giving you rains from heaven and fruitful seasons, satisfying your hearts with food and gladness" (Acts 14:17).

So, the Bible teaches us that God is the ultimate source of *everything* good that humans enjoy. Creation grace, then, refers to God's blessings outside of those directly related to his special revelation and redemption (called redemptive or saving or special grace), so creation grace includes medicine, technology, and the arts, as well as the benefits of having loving and wise parents, leading to the blessing of secure attachment.

A synthesis of redemptive and creation grace

The redemptive grace that only Christians enjoy builds on and enhances creation grace, so that whatever creation grace blessings one received in one's family-of-origin are capable of further enrichment/fulfillment by union with Christ and communion with God. At the same time, relatively healthy families are found in all cultures, irrespective of their particular religion or worldview and the direct influence of Christ's redemption. So, in addition to the redemptive grace mediated to Christian families through the faith of family members who believe in Christ—which undermines sin more fundamentally than mere creation grace alone—creation grace is also continuously being mediated to Christian families, as well as non-Christian families, without their necessarily being aware of it. This truth manifests in such things as brain development, a healthy body, mental and emotional health, proper nutrition, sufficient resources to meet the basic needs of the family, and common virtues. In addition, the kindness, wisdom, and loving affection of parents is present, some of which is passed on through a well-functioning attachment system and makes one's own marriage and parenting easier.[28]

Creation grace, then, provides the "infrastructure" for redemptive grace and works in conjunction with redemptive grace. Consequently, it is difficult, if not impossible, for Christians to distinguish the operation of creation grace and redemptive grace in their lives. How much of being a loving parent is due to the love that one received in one's family-of-origin (creation grace) and how much is due to one's personal relationship with Christ by the Spirit? These distinctions are rendered even more obscure when one is raised in a loving Christian family.[29]

The point here is that it is possible for beneficiaries of God's creation grace either to be simply unaware of it or to take some credit for their goodness unconsciously, and conversely to judge harshly those who have less of it. "For who regards you as superior? And what do you have that you did not receive? But if you did receive it, why do you boast as if you had not received it?" (1 Cor. 4:7 NASB). Christian marriages are a mysterious synthesis of creation and redemptive grace, far beyond the grasp of human understanding. Consequently, no Christian has the right to judge another brother or sister. Yet such judgment seems almost axiomatic in church, particularly in churches that take the moral law of God most seriously.

The foregoing discussion, we must concede, could provide excuses for the bad behavior of some spouses: "My insecure attachment made me do it!" However, conscientious believers cannot be satisfied with the blame-shifting exemplified by our first parents. Understanding attachment difficulties does not *excuse* misbehavior—there is no excuse for sin—but it does offer a partial *explanation*. And such explanations can help insecurely attached Christians acknowledge, confess, and repent of their sins, and come to terms with their faults and weaknesses in Christ.[30] Understanding these issues can help them appreciate why they (and their spouses) are so slow in the process of conformity to Christ, particularly compared to the more securely attached and those who have had less disadvantaged lives. God certainly takes such factors into account, and so can we, His people.

BIBLICAL THEMES THAT INFORM OUR UNDERSTANDING
OF MARRIAGES THAT FALL SHORT

Thus far we have examined the importance of recognizing the role that bio-psychosocial factors have on the experience of marriage and the importance of the church coming to terms with this. The arguments above operate within a Christian worldview, and assorted references to biblical and theological truths have been offered. It will also be beneficial to examine a few biblical themes that inform the preceding discussion: human flourishing through suffering, the virtue of wholehearted imperfection, and union with Christ.

Human flourishing through suffering

The universal question of human flourishing has driven religious and philosophical reflection for as long as we have historical records. The Bible is no exception, presenting God as the Creator who sets the apex of His creation, humans, in a place of flourishing and satisfaction.[31] But their rebellion and foolishness has severely compromised this flourishing and will ultimately lead to death. The long biblical story is the narrative of God redeeming and restoring humanity to the flourishing that we long for, centered in the work of Jesus and culminating in the new creation, a place of life and shalom. The final stage of the Christian story of the world will be the flourishing of believers with God and each other forever.

The Christian understanding of the desire for human flourishing has a unique and unexpected twist on the idea and one that relates to the reality of imperfect marriages. Namely, Jesus and the New Testament Scriptures teach that true human flourishing is found in the midst of and even through the pain of suffering. Herein lies one of the great paradoxes of the biblical witness: that happiness, blessedness, joy, and life itself can be found during suffering, loss, and pain. This is counterintuitive, to say the least.

In the Beatitudes in the Sermon on the Mount (Matt. 5–7), Jesus redefines flourishing (Greek *makarios*) in terms of ways of being in the world that appear to be the *opposite* of what will bring happiness—poverty of spirit, hunger and thirst, humility/humiliation, making peace rather than making sure one's rights are honored, and even persecution (Matt. 5:3–12).

The apostle Peter offers similar encouragement, teaching that even in the midst of trials Christians can rejoice, because of the certain and imperishable future awaiting us (1 Peter 1:3–9); we follow Jesus' example in the same (2:19–25), and we are not surprised at our difficulties and trials because it is precisely in this space that we find God's blessings and the presence of His Spirit (4:12–14).

The apostle Paul is a witness to the ironic and unexpected experience that precisely through knowing God's comfort in our trials we are enabled to sympathize with and comfort others (2 Cor. 1:3–7), and the true place of strength and contentment is in weakness and difficulty because through Christ's power "when I am weak, then I am strong" (2 Cor. 12:10). Thus, Christianity teaches that human flourishing is something that we rightly long for and will ultimately experience at our full redemption in the new creation (Rom. 8:18–25; Rev. 19–22), but that is experienced now as well in the midst of suffering precisely because it is this pain that forces us toward self-awareness and our need for God's loving presence.

The application to imperfect and disordered Christian marriages is not difficult to see. No one wants, nor are we encouraging, the pursuit of a deeply flawed, broken marriage that inflicts pain on oneself and one's spouse. Teaching on Christian suffering is not meant to inculcate a martyr syndrome or glorify suffering as a good in itself. Nonetheless, rather than interpreting and approaching such deeply broken marriages (such as those of the "disenfranchised" discussed above) as failures to be fixed and the simple result of sinners being outside of God's will, we can instead see by faith that God uses such suffering, pain, and difficulty precisely to awaken and deepen the self-awareness and compassion for others that is part of Christian maturation.

If it is true that God's people have experienced God most deeply and profoundly and sweetly in their places of suffering, then a deeply flawed marriage that is, at least in part, a result of one's upbringing and biopsychosocial damage can be exactly the space and the means by which God brings to His people healing and life. Thus, those with conflicted marriages can take courage and have hope that God is present and at work in the midst of their suffering. Indeed, flourishing, life, love, contentment, and peace can be experienced there and can contribute to its resolution. God in His sovereignty and wisdom chooses different means to advance uniquely His glory and our well-being. Distressed and conflicted marriages provide a particularly powerful context for such manifestation.

The virtue of wholehearted imperfection

Another biblical theme that can be found woven throughout both the Old and New Testament is God's valuing of the virtue of being wholehearted yet imperfect people. At the core of all biblical ethics is the idea that God's creatures should be *like* Him, that we should be imitators of God. The under-lying logic is straightforward: Because humans are creatures made in God's image, we will only experience flourishing, wholeness, and virtue to the de-gree that we are aligned with God Himself, functioning as His image bearers, in accord with His nature.

Biblical ethics is not just a matter of external conformity to His laws but rather is whole-person behavior, postures, habits, affections, values, and at-titudes that align with and mirror God's own. The function of the Bible in God's redemptive work is a program of resocialization and reorientation of our values, habits, thoughts, and actions. To be godly is to be *like God*, which is in fact the intended etymology of "god-ly."[32]

This deep vein of *imago Dei*–imitative biblical ethics finds its clearest out-croppings in texts such as Leviticus 19–20 which exhort God's people to "be holy, for I am holy" (19:2; repeated in 1 Peter 1:16). "Holy" in Old Testament teaching does not mean in the first instance moral or ritual purity but dedicat-edness, or singular devotion. This holiness does *result* in a kind of purity and morality that accords with God's character and His moral law, but purity in ac-tions is a function of the root idea of holiness as singularity and wholehearted-ness. Such devotion to God brings about holiness, as fruit from a healthy tree.

It is important to note that while God does care about morality and ethical choices and behavior, He does so only to the extent that this is the fruit borne from a good and dedicated heart, the inner person. The definition of hypoc-risy in the message of the prophets and in the New Testament is God's people having external obedience while their inner person or heart lacks dedication and love for God (cf. Isa. 29:13; Matt. 6:1–21; 15:8; 23:13–36). Thus, God does not seek our moral perfection—something unattainable by His fallen creatures—but the transformation of the inner person that then bears fruit of morality in its season and increasingly over time.

The point of unpacking this biblical ethical idea of whole-person dedicated-ness is that it helps us give moral and psychological space for imperfect, flawed, and struggling marriages. When we think of holiness in idealistic and moral-perfection terms (the perennial Christian temptation), then we can only look down on and even reject those whose marriages are deeply flawed and troubled. If the instrument for evaluation of our own or others' marriages is some kind of idealistic standard—which is almost certainly heavily arbitrary based on our own personal and cultural expectations—then the reality of imperfect marriages (our own or others) can only be interpreted as bad or wrong morally.

But a biblical ethical view inclines Christians not to evaluate ourselves in terms of the attainment of a certain ideal marriage-state but to the pursuit of greater humility, sincerity, and honesty in our journey toward God's wholeness, even if our exemplification of it is flawed. A sound and healthy living tree will bear fruit, even if that fruit may be weaker and not as robust and delicious due to external factors such as soil quality, nutrients, amount of sunshine, and blights of disease. So too, the church must have space for marriages that are alive and dedicated, even if their glory-manifestation is far from the ideal because of negative factors, like sin and biopsychosocial damage, that affect the marriage.

Union with Christ and its impact on imperfect marriages

One of the most significant and unexpected practical doctrines of the New Testament is the Christian's "union with Christ." Christianity does not merely teach that believers in Jesus have been forgiven of their sins or even merely that they are now legally justified to stand before God. Much more profound, intimate, pervasive, and effectual is the deeper truth that believers have been transferred out of death and darkness and bondage and have been re-placed and re-positioned mysteriously and mystically *into* the life of Jesus (Col. 1:13–14).

Based largely on the New Testament teaching (especially of Paul) that believers in Jesus have been put "into Christ," and live "in Christ," they have been given a new identity, kinship, standing before God, lineage, future, and metaphysical reality. This "union with Christ" teaching has been called "theological shorthand for the gospel itself" and "a key image that pulls together numerous motifs in the biblical witness."[33]

This beautiful Christian reality has a direct impact on imperfect marriages. A distressed/conflicted marriage consists of two wounded sinners. Born in sin, both spouses suffered more or less in childhood, experiencing some degree of biopsychosocial damage—in some cases, the development of insecure attachment—and as they grew, they learned sinful and unhealthy ways to relate to others, seeking in some degree to advance their own supremacy and meet their attachment needs improperly. From a Christian standpoint, what they both need, more than anything else, is union with Christ and communion with God.

The New Testament teaches that this is precisely what has happened through the Spirit's work for believers, enabling believing spouses to cultivate a healing, love relationship with their heavenly Father and with Jesus, their ultimate spouse and brother. Based on their union with Christ, believers are also baptized into Christ's body of believers—the church of Jesus Christ—where they can practice healing communion with one another (1 John 1:3). In addition, they have been incorporated into the suffering of Christ (Rom. 8:17; 2 Cor. 1:5; Col. 1:24; Phil. 3:1). Finally, since Christ was crucified in weakness (2 Cor. 13:4) believers have also entered into a mystical solidarity with Him through whatever biopsychosocial damage they might have.

In all aspects of their psychopathology, believers are united to Christ, so that their lives are already perfected in Him, positionally, and they are now on a journey of incorporation into the triune God's holy, healing love, which will be completely perfected in the *eschaton*, where an eternal weight of glory will be given them, proportional to their suffering on earth (2 Cor. 4:17). Things are more complicated when only one spouse is a Christian, but the believing spouse, at least, can utilize these theocentric/therapeutic resources, helping them develop a different attachment style than what they grew up with, now that they have a secure base in the triune God and His people. Now they are able to recognize and disidentify with the insecure relational style that they grew up with, which tends to be activated automatically. Eventually they can become more of a provider of safety and security, as well as friendship and love, to their spouse, based on the everlasting safety, security, friendship, and love they have with God in Christ.

HELPING DISTRESSED/CONFLICTED COUPLES IN THE CHURCH

In light of the foregoing, how might the church do a better job of helping couples who experience significant distress and conflict? We conclude with a few suggestions.

To begin with, depending on where they are in their own journey of self-awareness and maturation, pastors and counselors in local churches can help by recognizing the differences between securely and insecurely attached marriages, learning how to address the distinct needs of the latter—who are far more likely to seek counseling—and creating safe, sacred spaces for both groups to work on their marriages with a more skilled and loving mentor.

Second, churches themselves can communicate both the marriage-relevant aspects of the law (biblical standards for healthy, Christian marriages), as well as the necessity of the gospel for all their (less-than-perfect) couples. The church can become increasingly saturated with grace, its members' engagement with the law thoroughly mediated by Christ and His redemption, so that the law becomes "gospelized"—no longer a standard by which we compare ourselves, but a goal toward which we all aspire in Christ. Over the long haul, this will result in a change in the tone and atmosphere of a church from perfectionism and anxiety to greater mutual transparency, vulnerability, and gratitude to God. With the Spirit's help, there will be no diminishment in the ethicospiritual standards of the Bible, but there will be a palpable diminishment in arrogance and judgmentalism, on the one hand, and shame and envy, on the other.

Third, churches can learn to become more sensitive to individual differences in marriages, exemplified in the pastoral care of the apostle Paul and the history of the church, regarding individual believers.[34] Rather than simply promote the ethicospiritual ideal of a healthy Christian marriage, churches might offer marriage seminars that include material aimed at both securely attached and insecurely attached couples. This would help both groups appreciate the existence of marriages different than their own, and their respective strengths and liabilities, as well as their common calling to glorify God. In addition, they could be encouraged to recognize their respective advantages and disadvantages, while learning to view each other in Christ in a spirit of mutual acceptance and love. This could involve highlighting the tendency toward perfectionism, arrogance, and judgmentalism of the more securely attached and the tendency toward shame, envy, and despair of the more insecurely attached and conflicted. But both groups would be challenged to overcome the fleshly tendency to divide the church based on ethical performance.

The securely attached have comparatively less exposure to chronic suffering and the impact of biopsychosocial damage and will benefit from getting to know those who have suffered more. Ideally, this would help them become more grateful to God for their blessings and more understanding of those less advantaged. Conversely, the tendency of the insecurely attached to feel shame and hide from others is best undermined by the love and acceptance of kind, healthier people. Perhaps, at first, this unifying agenda would require separate meetings to address the respective struggles of the different kinds of couples. Then both kinds of couples would be better prepared for joint meetings; particularly so that the more distressed/conflicted couples could be encouraged to be more transparent about their struggles, without concern about being judged by the less distressed and conflicted. But this would have to be temporary. Research is needed to determine the benefits of this proposal, including whether such training is best done jointly or separately. But we already know that God desires that His church become a unified body (Phil. 2:1–4; Eph. 4:1–16).

Finally, because the healing of brokenness and growth into flourishing seem to be directly proportional to one's depth of self-awareness, God's people need safe places where the latter can be fostered. Because of our sin and shame, moral lecturing and judging one another generally inhibit honest self-assessment and vulnerability. Therefore, churches are needed that can train group leaders how to create groups where members can explore their sinfulness and brokenness in a fellowship of humility and compassion, as well as holiness, so that members are more inclined to open up, rather than hide.

CONCLUSION

In this spirit of openness, both authors of this chapter have "come out of hiding" to acknowledge the limitations of our marriages (with our wives' approval!). We have been encouraged through our respective journeys that God blesses marriages that are "poor in spirit," and hope to encourage others to be more open about their marital struggles. Through union with Christ, communion with God, and the Spirit's enablement; confession and repentance; understanding one's attachment style, the impact of one's relationship with one's parents, and differences in personality types;[35] the healing of attachment style through God and others; and the overt support of local churches, may the triune God increasingly bring Christian marriages that fall short of the ideal to a place of greater acceptance, harmony, and love.

CONTINUING INSIGHT:

SELF-PROTECTIVE FAÇADE IN MARRIAGE

by Tony Wheeler

Individuals can revolutionize their marriage by choosing to intentionally move toward their spouse in love through, and in spite of, the walls of self-protection.

Most of us have invisible walls that we have placed around our hearts to protect us from pain. Because we all experience disappointment and pain early in life, most of us developed these walls at a young age, based on pain and circumstances beyond our control. We don't have the power to change our childhood circumstances, so the only thing we can control is how we react to the pain and to others. We intuitively create a way of protecting how we relate to other people, seeking security behind what we'll call a self-protective façade but as we get older, the façade meant to protect can easily become a barrier to intimacy and authentic relating within a marriage.

Recognizing the self-protective façade in marriage

Because this barrier—these rigid walls—dictate our actions toward our spouse in marriage, we will always move toward self-protection before we move to love our spouse, unless we are aware of what is fueling our self-protective façade; and, most people are unaware how much self-protection, pain, and burdens from the past are affecting their marriage in the present. Within a marriage, our self-protective façades control the level of defensiveness and intimacy we have in our relationship because they either allow our spouse to know our heart or they create a wall to keep our spouse out and defend our heart.

Façades are also based on our core desires and emotional pitfalls. We all have unique core desires that drive the way we desire to be treated by our spouse. Some examples of core desires are the desire to be loved, accepted, respected, appreciated, significant, and secure. Whether we're aware of it or not, we have a strong core desire that is driving our marriage as we strive to get our desires met through our spouse. If we crave respect, we will attempt to act in a way that gains respect from our spouse—on a daily, sometimes hourly, basis. He or she is probably unaware how deeply we feel we each need respect and, most likely, is not meeting our desire.

Knowing how to become aware of what is beneath the surface in our hearts—rather than moving through life controlled by the fear of being exposed—will have a positive effect on how we view our spouse and increase our ability to love God, others, and ourselves.

Many of us struggle with one or more emotional pitfalls that include anxiety, depression, shame, fear, and anger, any of which can also control and negatively affect a marriage. One person may struggle with managing one or more emotional pitfalls, and their spouse might struggle too, thus increasing the stress on the marriage. If one person in a marriage struggles with shame, for example, it is highly likely that their self-protective façade includes anger, arrogance, or attempting to appear intelligent. All these façades attempt to cover shame. Core desires and emotional pitfalls contribute to the façades we choose, and these affect every aspect of life, especially our marriage.

A husband's and wife's façade often complement each other: a strong one matched with a weaker one, a funny one matched with a depressed one, a controlling one matched with a shy one, a perfectionist one matched with an uninhibited one, for example. The downside is that the person we marry also has unhealed trauma and pain in his or her life and is also struggling to present a good enough façade to the world to have his or her deep desires met in order to be loved, admired, respected, and significant.

As married couples face the trials of life together, the painful truth of who they really are as individuals behind the façade will surface. As individuals in a marriage are unable to communicate behind each of their façade and find the truth in a situation, they struggle to get their core desires met, which are the hoped-for results of a great façade. They struggle to communicate on a vulnerable, authentic level. They struggle to continue to present their self-protective façade to their spouse and feel respected, secure, loved, understood, admired, getting their core desires met, etc., because now their spouse has seen behind this façade and knows some of the truth.

Historically, the average year for divorce for most couples used to be around the seven-year mark. More recently this has been lowered to the fourth year of marriage. Our façades are crumbling at ever faster rates, the point when a person no longer feels his or her spouse will ever be able to understand them or meet their needs and desires. These people usually feel there is no hope for true authenticity within the relationship, the point when the façade is lowered and truth from the heart emerges. Individuals in a troubled marriage often feel they are not being understood, and they usually aren't, because their façades are so strong and the truth is still to be found behind them.

As individuals no longer feel the safety and love they once felt at the beginning of the relationship, they reason that they can find the happiness they long for either alone or in another relationship—it is the fault of the other person in the dissolving marriage. Most of the time, it is the result of faulty thinking about who we are to be within a marriage covenant and a misunderstanding about how our façades work within a marriage.

Pushing through the self-protective façade

Awareness of the specific ways in which self-protection was created for the past can help people recognize when their façade is causing relational problems in marriage in the present. In order to overcome the fear associated with connecting with others, it is helpful to identify areas of pain in our lives and from our past that helped create our specific façades. Most of us must do the hard work of finding healing from past pain, burdens we carry, and behaviors we are stuck in. If we do not become aware of what is controlling us, we can go through our entire lives never really loving ourselves or others or sharing our heart with others.

For example, if as a part of our façade we decided we would be invisible, then, most likely, for years we have sent an invisible, yet real message to people through our body language and our words: "Don't see me. I'm not here." Most people comply and ignore us, if we present this self-protective façade long enough. If we become aware that we are overlooking a person because of how they are presenting, we can intentionally begin to break through this barrier of invisibility and recognize that the person is there. Being seen can bring great life to a person. If someone is married to a mate who presents as invisible to others, they can begin to push through this façade and encourage their spouse, speaking to their heart at opportune moments.

Within a marriage, these shells become barriers to connecting and intimacy. If we are not willing to expose the truth about ourselves to our spouse, we will stay stuck in a place of isolation and pain. It feels like death to expose the truth to our spouse and risk feeling the shame, depression, anxiety, fear, or whatever our emotional pitfall may be, but the result of sharing the truth will bring the opposite effect we believe it will: we will typically find that a new closeness and intimacy develops by being honest and dropping our walls, if even momentarily.

As another example, many people protect themselves in marriage through anger or even arrogance, and project the message "I'm stronger than you. I'm superior to you. I'm more intelligent and will always win over you." Although bullying or pride might make the person initially feel good and seem to protect their heart, the truth is that pride comes with the backlash of disgrace. Proverbs 11:2 (NIV) predicts, "When pride comes, then comes disgrace, but with humility comes wisdom." When we see this façade, the person's emotional pitfall is most likely shame. Covering themselves with superiority and power makes them feel protected from the backlash and sting of shame.

We can move toward a person struggling with the self-protective façade of arrogance with compassion for the trap their façade brings into their lives. We tend to dislike and avoid these people, when the truth is they need and crave a core desire such as respect, significance, or acceptance just as much or even more than the next person. Once we're aware of a façade, we can learn to recognize it for what it is and choose to ignore it and connect anyway. After pushing through the initial presentation, most people, over time, open up and desire true and lasting relationships. In marriage we might have to work for years to continue to love a person in spite of their incredibly strong self-protective façade.

Believing truth and declaring freedom

After understanding the devastating effects of their self-protective façade on their own life, a person might have many epiphanies within their marriage such as:

> I'm aware I don't want to be rejected. I was bullied and rejected in elementary school and even in my family. Whenever I'm aware that someone is going to reject me, I lash out at them or reject them first. Now I can see I am doing this to my spouse. My self-protective façade includes anger, arrogance, and being invisible. The emotional pitfalls and definite obstacles of shame and fear control my behavior when I am with my spouse and in my self-identity. I send the message to my spouse through my words and body language that I don't want to belong— when the truth is that I desperately want to be connected and belong. I'm aware now that I do this, and now I'm declaring I don't want to do this anymore. I'm uncovering the lies I have been believing in this area and working to believe the truth instead. I declare that I do belong in this marriage and that I will no longer allow the obstacle and lie that I don't belong to control me. I want to achieve this goal of being known and loved, understanding that Christ is the only one who can and does unconditionally love me.

> My spouse, being human, will never be able to totally, unconditionally, perfectly love me, yet we can work together in this difficult time by sharing the truth of our pain and past. Instead of being distant or lashing out or presenting pride and rejection to others, I am declaring that Scripture says that I am safe in the shadow of God's wing. I am a friend and heir of Christ Himself, and He has adopted me into His family. Nothing can stop His love from reaching me. I belong in the body of Christ, as these people are my brothers and sisters in Christ.

> Scripture states that I can always find grace and hope in Jesus. I've been rejected and hurt in the past, but Psalm 34:18 explains that "The Lord

is close to the brokenhearted and saves those who are crushed in spirit." God is my refuge now. I no longer want to be arrogant and angry at people, making them feel little and low. I want to belong and walk in humility, learning to help others feel loved and accepted, like they also belong in the body of Christ, because they do. I want to reconcile with my spouse now that I understand how my own self-protective façade has created this dynamic within our relationship.

As we become willing to allow our hearts to discover the truth of our lives and become aware of the true state of our hearts and share our hearts with our spouse, we can find freedom and improve marital satisfaction. In John 8:31b–32, Jesus said, "If you hold to my teaching, you are really my disciples. Then you will know the truth, and the truth will set you free." Jesus never asked us to pretend we were okay. He never asked us to tell our spouse that we are fine and then cry ourselves to sleep or engage in sinful distractions to avoid really thinking or feeling about the truth in our hearts.

John 8 begins with the story of the woman caught in adultery. She stood before a crowd who was ready to stone her. Jesus provided a way out for her. He protected her from the people who accused her. These same people wanted to trap Jesus and accuse Him, but Jesus brilliantly turned it around on them by writing on the ground with His finger, possibly writing specific sins the people in the crowd had committed. One by one they dropped their stones and left. They knew they couldn't accuse this woman anymore because Jesus knew the truth about their lives. He knew they were sinners, just like the woman caught in adultery. After the last person left the crowd, Jesus said to her, "Woman, where are they? Has no one condemned you?" "No one, sir," she said. "Then neither do I condemn you. Go now and leave your life of sin."

Just as Jesus protected the woman caught in adultery, we can protect our spouses as they lower their façades in order to be known, extending grace and forgiveness and mercy. We can intentionally work to love and encourage our spouse as they expose their heart to us.

Many of us are hiding the truth of our lives, and it is keeping us from finding freedom. I frequently have people ask me, "How do I find hope and peace with my spouse? How do I find freedom and healing in my marriage?" Before this truth can be discovered, we must become aware of the true state of our hearts. Before a deeper level of connecting and intimacy in marriage can occur, people must become willing to become aware of three areas: what is occurring in their own hearts, what is occurring in the hearts of their spouse, and what is occurring in the atmosphere around them through the Holy Spirit. What does God want to happen in a conversation between a husband and wife?

Self-protection can be fueled by fear, anxiety, shame, and pride, emotions controlling our ability to reach out and really see and care for our spouse. These emotions are also, in some ways, a by-product of our incredible need and ability to protect our hearts from pain. Our self-protective façades are also usually created by a strong core desire within our hearts to be seen in a certain light, with love, respect, significance, security, etc., creating the need for a false self to exist in order to get this need met.

Self-protection might be holding a person back from entering into the amazing gift of consistent and true fellowship, intimacy, and connecting with one's spouse, but it need not.

CONTINUING INSIGHT:

A SOCIAL SACRAMENT

by Jared Pingleton

Life is relational. We were designed by the Creator in loving relationship, through loving relationship, and for loving relationship. Without the reality and reciprocity of loving relationships—the supremely designed prototype of which is marriage—life itself could not begin or continue.

But when reading the short distance from Genesis chapter 1 to chapter 3, we are taken proverbial light-years from idealized theory to realistic practice. Sin changed everything. Along with the rest of the cursed creation, marriage became a lot harder. Since then, the cold, harsh reality is that we all inevitably marry someone with baggage, issues, unresolved hurts, and possibly unrealistic romanticized expectations about how marriage will "complete" them. Thus, we typically spend lots of emotional energy trying to *find* the right person, rather than dedicate ourselves to *becoming* the right person!

Marriage dynamics are classically complex. The unvarnished, denial-shattering truth is that we are all broken, and our spouse is likewise broken (hey, I know my wonderful wife, Linda, isn't perfect because her mate selection capability is inherently flawed!). Furthermore, we reap what has been sown into our spouse's life before we showed up. This subconscious phenomenon of being impacted by our mate's previous relationships is called, in psychodynamic theory, transference. Obviously this is completely unfair: others hurt our spouse and we suffer the effects. And yet at the same time when you think about God's redemptive plan, what could feel more "unfair" than helping our spouse heal from what we didn't hurt and helping them fix what we didn't break? More than our primitive concepts about "fairness," God delights in transforming blessings out of our, and our spouse's, brokenness!

So God is not unfair; He is a redeemer and a reconciler. What if He is more concerned with cultivating our holiness than creating our happiness? What if He has designed blessings to be transformed from our (and our spouse's) brokenness? What if God designed marriage for much more than gratification of our infatuatory fantasies and impulses?

Because marital systems are classically complex, convoluted, and conflictual, it seems the better questions become: "How can we in the church healthfully minister to these realities?" "How can we drastically reduce the divorce rate—especially among Christians?" "How can we speak persuasively into the rampant cohabitation epidemic in our society?" "How can we positively impact the traditionally low satisfaction rates in American marriages?" and "How can the church become more relevant as we deal with people and their real needs?"

To begin with, we must face the fact that the church at large has frequently avoided dealing with the delicate topics of mental and relational issues. We already know that people's problems are messy and complicated, and can be costly in terms of time, money, and energy. We hear words such as conflict, dysfunction, and psychopathology and feel uncomfortable, and sometimes subconsciously threatened in case our own issues might be exposed. Thus, people in many congregations avoid facing relational and emotional pain by means of the unholy trifecta of silence, shame, and stigma.

Therefore, the church must *end the silence, eliminate the shame*, and *erase the stigma* surrounding mental and relational health problems. We must normalize the fact that all humans have problems and that there has never been and never will be a perfect marriage. We must not only accept the truth that marriage may be one of the hardest things to do well, but that it is also one of the most important things to do well.

Just because we are Christians doesn't mean we are immune to or exempt from unhappiness or afflictions. Rather, Jesus stated bluntly that we will have troubles in this life (John 16:33), but that we should be encouraged because of His mighty transcendence: "Take heart; I have overcome the world." Orienting and educating the church and its leaders about these issues may be the most effective key to help hurting persons and marriages, as will implementing premarital counseling, marriage mentoring, and marriage enrichment ministries.[1] We must speak truth and shine light, and spread salt into our deluded, darkened, and decaying world.

Moreover, to minister effectively to Christian marriages in this country, we need to examine the enormous discrepancy between a biblical understanding of the nature of marriage, compared to the secularized model perpetuated by Hollywood and Hallmark. Our culture subtlety brainwashes us about relationships in ways that are antagonistic to Scripture and are actually in conflict with the development and maintenance of a healthy marriage. The church needs to understand these erroneous suppositions that permeate our culture, and teach correct concepts about love and commitment from a biblical worldview.

Certainly everyone longs to love and be loved. Love is the universal human language; it is the ultimate expression of caring for someone beyond ourselves. Unlike anything else, the rosy and romantic topic of love has inspired poets, artists, and thinkers down through the ages as they have extolled its virtues and vicissitudes. But more important than marrying the one we love is loving the one we marry! It is intriguing that the epic saga of the almighty Creator of the universe's intimate disclosure of Himself to His creation—the Bible—begins and ends within the concept of human marriage. From the first chapter of Genesis (1:27) to the last chapter of Revelation (22:17), God's love story to us unfolds within the context of marriage.

This profound mystery (Eph. 5:32) of the marriage relationship in many ways expresses the essence of God's kingdom. It should be no surprise that the Giver of Life chose to disclose Himself to us, His beloved bride (Rev. 21:2, 9) by means of the greatest love story ever told—and use the paradigm of marriage to convey it. Love, the deepest yearning and need of the human heart, mirrors the magnificent expression and reflection of the Creator's heart!

Some people are easier to love than others. The Roman poet Ovid famously concluded, "If you would be loved, be lovable," stating an obvious human condition on loving others. Yet, the almighty sovereign God—who is love personified (1 John 4:7–12)—loves us unconditionally as the ultimate expression of His everlasting love for us (Jer. 31:3). God loves us because of His lovingness, not because of our lovability.

Jesus turned our natural tendency of human nature upside down when He asked rhetorically, "If you love those who love you, what reward will you get? Are not even the tax collectors doing that?" (Matt. 5:46 NIV). What's harder —and therefore requires an unconditional commitment—is to care for and love someone who isn't always easy to love, or who doesn't always return your love. It is at this level of depth that involves a mature, realistic love for one's marital partner, not a conditional romantic feeling.

One of the most frequently voiced complaints I hear as a marital therapist is something along the lines of "I just don't have any feelings for him now," or "I'm not in love with her anymore." After empathizing with that client's disappointed expectations and likely narcissistic injury and loss, I will inno-cently inquire as to what that has to do with their marriage vow. As previously stated, this is an incredibly important point for both theology and psychol-ogy: God loves us because of His lovingness, not because of our lovability.

God is proactive; He is not reactive, as we so often are. God loves us un-conditionally because of who *He* is, not because of who *we* are. Jesus cannot love us any more or any less than He does right now, because He loves us fully and without condition. Agape love is an eloquent expression of God's char-acter and an exemplary extension of His integrity. God is love: that's simply who—even how—He is.

Therefore, in the same way, I believe *true love is more about the character of the lover than the characteristics of the beloved.* Think about it: this basic con-cept is both countercultural to what our surroundings typically tell us about love, and it is revolutionary. The idea of love being more about the lover than the lovability of the beloved dramatically alters our relationship paradigms and has the potential, if lived out, to permanently transform marriages.

How does mere romantic love fall short of having this potential? Roman-tic love is always generated by the other person and focused on us. We have been conditioned to expect the other person to initiate the first move—thus other-generated—and then meet our needs to fulfill us and make us happy —self-focused. That is the stuff of which romantic fantasies, cheap novels, pornography, and chick flicks are made.

But the exact opposite is what is true; it's real love that is mature and fulfilling. *Mature, agape love is both self-generated and other-focused, not the other way around.* When people recite their marriage vows, they are entering into a lifelong, unconditional covenant to love their spouse on days that end in "y," as long as they are breathing, no matter what. We are to love our spouse regardless, and we are to be committed to doing what is best for their welfare no matter what it costs us. Genuine love always has an altruistic attitude and agenda. This is not very romantic, but it is verifiably realistic.

It is our personal character, not the other's personal characteristics that is to motivate our love for our spouse. Mature love is not based on warm fuzzy feelings—feelings are the result, not the cause, of love. Most of us get married wishing *to be loved* like this, not *to love* like this!

When we expect the other person to make us happy, we are eventually bound to be disappointed. By hoping our spouse will make us happy, we subconsciously idolize them in the place of God. As with so many other things, we may be unintentionally and unwittingly tempted to worship the creation instead of the Creator. We can confuse the vehicle (marriage) with the destination (God's will for our lives). Our spouse is not our ultimate source for our soul, God is. Consequently, we tend to expect more from marriage than God intended it to provide. And when troubles, even heartaches, come, as they inevitably will, God wants us to turn to divinity, not divorce.

The church needs to step up and more effectively teach and preach the essence and power of a covenantal marriage commitment. Vows are a curious thing. The truth is that if humans were faithful by nature then vows wouldn't be necessary! It is precisely because we are not inherently faithful or honest or loving that we must stand up before our family and friends and declare that we will be. And although this accountability can help support our intentions, that doesn't mean we will not break the vow, because everyone does in some way(s). As imperfect people we all necessarily marry another imperfect person. And if these realities are properly understood, it requires us all to become forgiveness experts.

Obviously we need to look to the Lord at this point; not only for mercy and grace, but also for inspiration and example. God's love for His children is absolutely unconditional and altogether unilateral (e.g., Rom. 5:8; 1 John 4:10, 19). Our marriage vow is a sacred oath, a holy pledge, and a solemn promise.

The sacrament of marriage vows, properly understood and lived out, constitute the closest picture of the Father's covenantal love for His children. Yet our society dismisses the powerful theological implications of the marriage covenant, referring instead to the arrangement as contractual. A covenant and contract are not the same things. There are actually at least ten ways in which the notions of covenant and contract are completely antithetical.[2] For one thing, a legal contract is written on pieces of a dead tree. It has no life, vitality, or energy. In contrast, a marriage covenant is written on our hearts and is lived out daily as we decide to faithfully love one another, warts and all . . . whether we feel like it or still are "in love" or not.

For couples who no longer feel they are "in love" today, I would submit that it is because they quit investing in the relationship and unselfishly extending themselves yesterday. My marital vow has less to do with my wife than it has to do with me. The depth and degree to which I exercise it is the degree to which I keep my integrity intact. My wife and I promised we would love each other no matter what, even when we feel least like doing so. We have chosen and promised to love each other in an other-focused manner . . . as God loves us, because He *is* love, not because we are always loving, lovely, and lovable. As such, that is a profound horizontally lived out microcosm of the gospel.

CHAPTER 12

DIVORCE AND REMARRIAGE

by William A. Heth

The heart of the good news in the kingdom of God is the redemption of fallen humanity. This includes the redemption of broken relationships between God and people, people and people, and structures in society inhabited by imperfect people. At the core of the most enduring of these relationships—the marriage relationship—is the concept of covenant, and the New Testament compares the loyal love that husbands and wives pledge to one another to Christ's sacrificial love for the church (Eph. 5:25–32). This is why a book that seeks to elevate marriage to the beauty and glory of its original design needs to include a chapter on divorce and remarriage. Divorce is about broken commitments in the relationships of broken people, and remarriage is about new commitments made by broken people.

The topic of divorce and remarriage is not a happy one. People don't read chapters like this unless they are considering remarriage after divorce, contemplating getting out of a very difficult marriage, or have themselves been divorced against their wishes. Counselors, pastors, and friends of those facing such questions want to offer the best biblical counsel possible. I hope to provide that in what follows.

Let's begin by highlighting some central passages affirming the permanence of lifelong marriage. We know that God hates divorce. Married couples should rule out the possibility of divorce from the outset, especially since research shows that seeing divorce as an option and talking about it increases risks for a breakup. Jesus' statement in Matthew 19:6, "Therefore what God has joined together, let no one separate" (NIV), suggests that God is involved in some way in the joining of every man and woman in marriage. Who would not want to partner with God in every way possible in something that He is involved in? Then, in Ephesians 5:22–33 Paul draws an analogy between the husband and wife's marriage relationship and Christ's relationship with the church, His bride (cf. 2 Cor. 11:2; Rev. 21:2). The implications this has for marriage as an enduring covenant and the accompanying sacrificial love, respect, and commitment through thick and thin that this encourages is profound.

Yet the following list of New Testament passages that directly speak to our topic reveals two things. For one, there is a tension between God's design for lifelong marriage as described in the preceding paragraph and two situations that might bring that marriage to an end. For another, Matthew and Paul seem to be at odds with Mark's and Luke's record of Jesus' teaching. Neither Mark nor Luke mentions any exceptions to Jesus' saying that to divorce and remarry is to commit the sin of adultery. These two tensions are the main reasons people hold different views of what the Bible teaches on divorce and remarriage.

> "But I say to you that everyone who divorces his wife, *except on the ground of sexual immorality* makes her commit adultery, and whoever marries a divorced woman commits adultery." (Matt. 5:32,[1] emphasis added)

> "And I say to you: whoever divorces his wife, *except for sexual immorality*, and marries another, commits adultery." (Matt. 19:9 emphasis added)

> And he said to them, "Whoever divorces his wife and marries another commits adultery against her, and if she divorces her husband and marries another, she commits adultery." (Mark 10:11–12)

> "Everyone who divorces his wife and marries another commits adultery, and he who marries a woman divorced from her husband commits adultery." (Luke 16:18)

> To the married I [Paul] give this charge (not I, but the Lord): the wife should not separate from her husband (but if she does, she should remain unmarried or else be reconciled to her husband), and the husband should not divorce his wife. (1 Cor. 7:10–11)

But if the unbeliever leaves, let it be so. *The brother or the sister is not bound in such circumstances*; God has called us to live in peace. (1 Cor. 7:15 NIV, emphasis added)

Does Scripture teach that no one should ever divorce, and if a divorce occurs there should be no remarriage? Or does Scripture stress the permanence of marriage while also recognizing that certain situations would make the continuation of a marriage inadvisable or intolerable?

VIEWS OF REMARRIAGE

For years I defended the view that even though a married couple might separate or get a legal divorce in some situations (e.g., persistent adultery, physical or verbal abuse, incest, desertion by an unbeliever, etc.), no one should ever remarry after divorce.[2] I have heard some go so far as to say that anyone who remarries after divorce is living in a continuous state of adultery, but I have always found that stance scripturally and practically problematic. There are two major reasons why I encourage the church to reject this extreme. First, when Paul preached the gospel in Corinth and many placed their faith in Christ for the forgiveness of their sins, there were obviously couples who had been divorced and remarried for a variety of reasons. Yet Paul never tells those couples to dissolve their marriages. In fact, Paul specifically includes adulterers and the sexually immoral in a list of sinners and then says this about them: "And such were some of you. But you were washed, you were sanctified, you were justified in the name of the Lord Jesus Christ and by the Spirit of our God" (1 Cor. 6:11). Second, when the gospel writers talk about Jesus' teaching on divorce,

There is no indication that a second marriage, even following an illegitimate divorce, is seen as permanently adulterous. Divorced Christians who have remarried should not commit the sin of a second divorce to try to resume relations with a previous spouse (see Deut. 24:1–4) but should begin afresh to observe God's standards by remaining faithful to their current partners.[3]

The view that no one should remarry after divorce is attractive among some Christians, given our permissive and commitment-challenged culture. We would not want to permit what Jesus forbids; but neither would we want to forbid what Jesus permits. Yet I have come to the conclusion that the three no-remarriage views I once defended—the incestuous marriages view, the betrothal view, and the early church fathers' view—cannot adequately explain the total biblical picture on divorce and remarriage.

The unlawful marriages and betrothal views unnecessarily restrict the meaning of the Greek word *porneia* when Jesus says those who divorce and remarry commit adultery "except for sexual immorality (*porneia*)" (Matt. 19:9; cf. 5:32). One viewpoint argues that *porneia* is a reference to marriages with close relatives,[4] and the other viewpoint thinks *porneia* is referring to an act of marital unfaithfulness during the Jewish betrothal period such as what Joseph suspected of Mary (Matt. 1:18–25).[5] Both try to defend the view that Jesus did not permit remarriage after divorce once a lawful, consummated marriage has taken place.

But nothing in the context of Matthew 5:32 or 19:9 suggests the reader should narrow his or her focus to these precise situations. Modern Bible translations correctly translate *porneia* as "sexual immorality" (ESV, NIV), "immorality" (NASB, NET), and "unchastity" (NRSV) in the broad sense of the term. Deuteronomy 24:1 is in the background of both Matthew 5 and Matthew 19, and that Mosaic text is about divorce among lawfully married couples. Further, when the Pharisees try to trap Jesus and ask Him in Matthew 19:3, "Is it lawful to divorce one's wife for any cause?" the debate going on at the time was between the more liberal view of rabbi Hillel ("for any cause") and the more restrictive view of rabbi Shammai ("except for sexual immorality"). This was a debate about grounds for divorce among married couples, not unlawful marriages or unfaithfulness during the betrothal period.

But what about the early church fathers' view? This no-remarriage view does understand *porneia* in Matthew's exceptions just as all modern translations do. This view permits divorce on the grounds of sexual immorality, but forbids remarriage. All Greek writers and all Latin writers except one in the first five centuries of the church believed Jesus taught remarriage following divorce for any reason is adulterous.[6] Nor did the early church fathers allow remarriage after divorce in the 1 Corinthians 7:15 case where a believer is deserted by an unbelieving spouse. How seriously should we take this early consensus about what the New Testament teaches?

History tells us that there was a growing asceticism in the early church.[7] This strain of thinking could helpfully promote abstinence from worldly pleasures and goods to achieve spiritual goals; but it could also negatively forbid that which Jesus or Paul may have permitted. For example, the apostle Paul was already correcting ascetic tendencies in several of his churches (1 Cor. 7:1, 8, 36; Col. 2:21), even addressing false teachers who wrongly forbade marriage (1 Tim. 4:3). In 1 Corinthians 7, Paul is largely correcting an abstain-from-sexual-relations perspective of a group of ascetics at Corinth. Though Paul clearly permitted remarriage for widows and widowers (1 Cor. 7:8–9, 39), several church fathers even disallowed second marriages after the death of a spouse (Athenagoras, Tertullian, Clement of Alexandria). Athenagoras (ca. 177 CE) actually referred to remarriage following a spouse's death as specious adultery! It is easy to see in a climate like this that if prominent teachers forbade second marriages after the death of a spouse, how much more they would most likely forbid remarriage after divorce for sexual immorality.

In what follows, I want to defend the growing consensus among evangelicals that the New Testament *permits* but does not *require* divorce and remarriage for unrepentant sexual immorality (Matt. 5:32; 19:9) and desertion of the marriage by an unbeliever (1 Cor. 7:15).[8] We will also consider what our response should be to those who divorce and remarry for reasons other than the two Jesus and Paul specifically address. Following this chapter are two articles that further address the issue from a more pastoral perspective.

THE IMPORTANCE OF UNDERSTANDING CULTURAL BACKGROUND

To fully grasp what the Bible teaches about marriage, divorce, and remarriage, we need to consider more than just the words in the Bible; we also have to consider the sociocultural context or framework in which those words were spoken. This is where the work of Craig Keener and David Instone-Brewer come in. Both have done extensive research to help re-create, as closely as possible, the framework of shared assumptions that first-century readers would bring to their understanding of the New Testament teaching.[9] This will help us explain, for example, how to harmonize Mark's and Luke's seemingly absolute prohibition of divorce and remarriage with the exception that Matthew includes.

Early readers would have known that Jesus' sayings were general statements against divorce, never intended to be taken as absolute statements that allow for no exceptions. We will unpack this more below, but the fact that both Matthew and Paul contain exceptions to the general statements proves this point. Matthew's "except for sexual immorality" clause (5:32; 19:9) and Paul's words in 1 Corinthians 7:15, "The brother or the sister is not bound in such circumstances" (NIV), would have been readily recognized as indicating a justifiable or valid divorce.

In the parallel passages Matthew 19:4–6 and Mark 10:6–9 Jesus cites two references from the first two chapters of the Bible to ground His teaching about the permanence of the marriage relationship:

> He answered, "Have you not read that he who created them from the beginning made them male and female [Gen 1:27], and said, 'Therefore a man shall leave his father and his mother and [cleave] to his wife, and the two shall become one flesh' [Gen 2:24]?
> So they are no longer two but one flesh. What therefore God has joined together, let not man separate."

When we read in Genesis 2:24, "For this cause a man shall leave . . . and cleave . . ." we are reading the language of biblical covenants. These are commitment terms that occur throughout the Old Testament. The word *leave* refers to the abandoning of one loyalty for the sake of another, and *cleave* refers to one's commitment to the marriage partner, which takes precedence over all others.

This is beautifully illustrated in the book of Ruth. Ruth was a Moabitess, not an Israelite. Her God was not Yahweh, the God of Israel, but she had married into Naomi's family when Naomi and her husband and two sons moved to Moab to avoid the famine in Israel. Over time, tragedy struck: Naomi's husband died, and both Ruth and her sister-in-law lost their husbands, who were Naomi's sons. Now destitute, Naomi decided to move back to Israel, but she gave her two daughters-in-law the freedom to stay in Moab and look for new husbands. The text says Ruth's sister-in-law "kissed her mother-in-law good-bye. But Ruth clung tightly to Naomi" (Ruth 1:14 NLT). That is our word cleave. Now listen to Ruth's expression of loyalty and love, one that is a model for the kind of covenant commitment one would expect in marriage. Ruth says to Naomi:

> Do not urge me to leave you or to return from following you. For where you go I will go, and where you lodge I will lodge. Your people shall be my people, and your God my God. Where you die I will die, and there will I be buried. May the LORD do so to me and more also if anything but death parts me from you. (1:16–17)

Scripture indicates that marriage is a covenant (cf. Ezek. 16:8, 60; Mal. 2:10–16) to which God is a witness (Gen. 31:5; Prov. 2:17; Mal. 2:14); when a husband and wife pledge their faithfulness to each other and consummate their marriage, they have voluntarily entered into a covenantal relationship. Unfortunately, because human beings are fallen and sinful, covenants are sometimes broken, but that is not God's intent when He joins a man and woman in marriage.

The author of one of the most extensive Old Testament studies on marriage as a covenant affirms that covenants in biblical times could be both violated and dissolved.[10] Covenants in the ancient Near East had the goal of establishing a relationship through a volitional commitment that included obligations with someone who was not a flesh and blood relative. Covenants were the means used to extend the loyalties inherent in kinship relationships to relationships where people were not related.[11] When Genesis 2:24 says, "They shall become one flesh," this does not literally make husbands and wives as closely related as they will be to their own flesh and blood children. The primary sense of "covenant" (*bᵉrît*) is that it is an "elected, as opposed to natural, relationship of obligation established under divine sanction."[12] This means that Jesus' statement in Matthew 19:6, "'What therefore God has joined together, let not man separate,'" does not mean "no one can separate," but rather means "it is possible to separate, but you should not."[13]

JESUS' TEACHING IN MATTHEW 5:31–32

Deuteronomy 24:1–4 is the Old Testament passage on divorce that lies in the background of Jesus' teaching on divorce in the Sermon on the Mount (Matt. 5:31–32) and in His debate with the Pharisees (Matt. 19:3–12; Mark 10:2–12). Here is the text:

> When a man takes a wife and marries her, if then she finds no favor in his eyes because he has found some indecency [*ʿerwat dābār*] in her, and he writes her a certificate of divorce and puts it in her hand and sends her out of his house, and she departs out of his house, and if she goes and becomes another man's wife, and the latter man hates her and writes her a certificate of divorce and puts it in her hand and sends her out of his house, or if the latter man dies, who took her to be his wife, then her former husband, who sent her away, may not take her again to be his wife, after she has been defiled, for that is an abomination before the

LORD. And you shall not bring sin upon the land that the LORD your God is giving you for an inheritance.

This passage recognizes that divorce is an existing practice in the ancient Near East; it does not command or legislate it for God's people. The actual law that is instituted in this passage occurs in verse 4: the primary purpose is to prohibit the restoration of an original marriage after the intervening set of circumstances mentioned in verses 1–3. The relevant facts of the case provided in verses 1–3 need not concern us here.[14]

Matthew's goal in recording the Sermon on the Mount is to present Jesus as a new and greater Moses. Like Moses, Jesus ascends the mountain to teach His disciples the ethics of the kingdom (Matt. 5:1; cf. Ex. 19:3). What Jesus says in Matthew 5:17, "Do not think that I have come to abolish the Law or the Prophets; I have not come to abolish them but to fulfill them," indicates we should not think of Jesus as standing in opposition to what Moses wrote in the Old Testament; rather, Jesus is setting the record straight about what Moses meant contrary to the misinterpretation or "convenient" interpretations of His Jewish contemporaries (cf. Matt. 15:1–9).

Jesus says in Matthew 5:31–32: "It was also said, 'Whoever divorces his wife, let him give her a certificate of divorce.' But I say to you that everyone who divorces his wife, except on the ground of sexual immorality (*parektos logou porneias*), makes her commit adultery, and whoever marries a divorced woman commits adultery." What can we learn from this? First, Jesus' opening statement in verse 31 indicates that Deuteronomy 24:1 was read as a command by Jesus' contemporaries (cf. 19:7). Jesus tempered this interpretation by saying in Matthew 19:8 that Moses permitted or allowed divorce because of hardness of heart.

Second, Jesus is the first Jewish teacher to introduce the notion that divorce followed by remarriage is a violation of the seventh commandment, "You shall not commit adultery" (Ex. 20:14). This sets Him apart from the Jewish teachers of His day. Divorces were viewed as either valid or invalid (i.e., ones where the husband would incur financial penalties for a socially irresponsible divorce) by Jesus' contemporaries, but remarriage after the giving of a bill of divorce was never forbidden.

Third, the Greek words behind the clause "except on the ground of sexual immorality" (*parektos logou porneias*) correspond precisely with the way the school of Shammai transposed the two Hebrew words for "some indecency" (*'erwat dābār*) in Deuteronomy 24:1 in their debate with the permissive

Hillelites. This means that Jesus is making an exception that is similar to the more restrictive view of Shammai. Shammai allowed divorce for some kind of sexual misconduct, including adultery, and with this Jesus agrees.[15]

Could Jesus possibly be teaching the notion that someone could divorce for immorality but then forbid remarriage? This is unlikely for several reasons. The Old Testament makes a distinction between valid and invalid grounds for divorce. Valid divorces were recognized when some socially recognizable violation of the marriage vows had occurred. This is indicated in Deuteronomy 24:1 by the phrase "some indecency," the wording of which corresponds with the exception Jesus cites in Matthew 5:32.[16] Invalid divorces, on the other hand, occurred for frivolous, selfish, or other unjustifiable reasons and resulted in financial penalties for the husband. He had to pay divorce money, and the wife received back the dowry, a gift, monetary or material, given by her father for her future security in the marriage. Invalid divorce is indicated by the word "hates" in Deuteronomy 24:3 and possibly the phrase "hates and divorces" (ESV margin) in Malachi 2:16a, translated idiomatically by the ESV this way: "For the man who does not love his wife but divorces her, . . ." Though still debated, this might mean, contrary to most translations of Malachi 2:16, which have God say "I hate divorce" (NASB, NLT, NET, and the footnote in the NIV), that God is not opposed to all divorces.[17]

Further, we should also remember that Jesus' divorce saying in the Sermon on the Mount in Matthew occurs with other teachings that emphasize them by overstating them. If these were interpreted literally, they would wreak havoc in peoples' lives. Jesus says things like, "But I say to you that . . . whoever says, 'You fool!' will be liable to the hell of fire" (5:22); "But I say to you that everyone who looks at a woman with lustful intent has already committed adultery with her in his heart" (5:28); "And if your right hand causes you to sin, cut it off and throw it away. For it is better that you lose one of your members than that your whole body go into hell" (5:30); and "But when you give to the needy, do not let your left hand know what your right hand is doing" (6:3). Reading literally, "and whoever marries a divorced woman commits adultery" (Matt. 5:32b//Luke 16:18b), ignores Jesus' teaching style, conflicts with Jesus' other sayings, and brings Jesus in conflict with Moses. Read as an overstatement (i.e., rhetorically),[18] Jesus makes the powerful point that one must do everything within one's power to be faithful to one's marriage partner and avoid divorce at all costs.

Because this passage is so well-known and we have touched on aspects of it already, we will simply quote it here in full and then highlight the main points.

> And Pharisees came up to him and tested him by asking, "Is it lawful to divorce one's wife for any cause (*kata pasan aitian*)?" He answered, "Have you not read that he who created them from the beginning made them male and female, and said, 'Therefore a man shall leave his father and his mother and hold fast to his wife, and the two shall become one flesh'? So they are no longer two but one flesh. What therefore God has joined together, let not man separate." They said to him, "Why then did Moses command one to give a certificate of divorce and to send her away?" He said to them, "Because of your hardness of heart Moses allowed you to divorce your wives, but from the beginning it was not so. And I say to you: whoever divorces his wife, except for sexual immorality [*mē epi porneia*], and marries another, commits adultery."
>
> The disciples said to him, "If such is the case of a man with his wife, it is better not to marry." But he said to them, "Not everyone can receive this saying, but only those to whom it is given. For there are eunuchs who have been so from birth, and there are eunuchs who have been made eunuchs by men, and there are eunuchs who have made themselves eunuchs for the sake of the kingdom of heaven. Let the one who is able to receive this receive it."

In this face-off with the Pharisees over grounds for divorce, the religious leaders try to trap Jesus with a question they think will discredit Him in the eyes of most well-thinking people: "Is it lawful to divorce one's wife for any cause?" (Matt. 19:3b). However, the Pharisees are caught off guard when Jesus cites Genesis 1:27 and 2:24 as the basis for what God has to say about the nature of the marriage relationship. This leads them to counter Jesus' citations from Genesis (in Matt. 19:4–7) by appealing to the Mosaic provision for divorce in Deuteronomy 24:1.

The views of the two rabbinic schools with respect to the Mosaic permission for divorce in Deuteronomy 24:1 are well-known.

> The School of Shammai say: A man should not divorce his wife unless he found in her a matter of indecency [*dbar 'erwāh*], as it is said: *For he*

finds in her an indecent matter [*'erwat dābār*]. And the School of Hillel say, Even if she spoiled his dish, since it says, *For he finds in her an indecent matter* [*'erwat dābār*] (Mishnah Gittin 9:10).[19]

Both Hillel and Shammai read Deuteronomy 24:1 as commanding the giving of a divorce certificate (cf. Matt. 5:31) if the husband found "some indecency" (literally, "nakedness of a thing") in his wife. The school of Hillel focused on the word "some" and sanctioned divorce for a variety of reasons. The school of Shammai stressed the word "indecency" and limited divorce to adultery or similarly severe offenses. But no Jewish teacher or court ever prohibited remarriage after divorce, no matter the reason for the divorce.

The "for any cause" phrase in verse 3 reflects the popular Hillelite view, and the "except for sexual immorality" clause in verse 9 alludes to the position of Shammai as we saw in the wording of Matthew 5:32. No doubt, most of the Pharisees sided with the more lenient view of Hillel as reflected in their question in verse 3. Jesus' disciples almost certainly did too. Notice how they responded after Jesus says what He does in verse 9: "If such is the case of a man with his wife, it is better not to marry" (v. 10). This is an emphatic way of saying they would rather get out of a difficult marriage than stay in and work on it! Wrong response, guys.

So how did Jesus differ from His contemporaries? First, Jesus says that Hillelite "any cause" divorces are invalid. Whoever divorces and remarries for unjustifiable reasons commits adultery. Second, Jesus' own view is closest to that of the Shammaites when He made an exception for divorce and remarriage for the innocent party in the event of sexual immorality. Adultery was a very serious violation of marriage promises throughout the ancient Near East and in the Old Testament (Gen. 20:6–10; 39:7; Job 24:14–15; Jer. 9:2; 29:23; Mal. 3:5; cf. Heb. 13:4). That's why we should not be surprised that Jesus, God's Son, takes a similar view of that violation of the marriage covenant and makes an exception for it. However, Jesus only permitted divorce, whereas Shammai may have required it (Mishnah, *Sotah* 5:1) while also forbidding an unfaithful wife to return to her husband.[20] Jesus' teaching of forgiveness up to seventy-seven times (Matt. 18:21–35) encourages wronged spouses to forgive and restore the marriage if at all possible. Finally, the disciples' stunned reaction in verse 10 to Jesus' divorce saying in verse 9 suggests that Jesus' view is more conservative than even Shammai's. Jesus implies that spouses should work on seemingly undesirable marriages.

God makes distinctions between the different kinds of love, and shows that love of a man and woman is (or should be) the greatest that the love of a man and woman is (or should be) the greatest and purest of all loves. For he says, "A man shall leave his father and mother and cleave to his wife" (Gen. 2:24), and the wife does the same, as we see happening around us every day. Now there are three kinds of love: false love, natural love, and married love. False love is that which seeks its own, as a man loves money, possessions, honor, and women taken outside of marriage and against God's command. Natural love is that between father and child, brother and sister, friend and relative, and similar relationships. But over and above all these is married love, that is, a bride's love, which glows like fire and desires nothing but the husband. She says, "It is you I want, not what is yours: I want neither your silver nor your gold; I want neither. I want only you. I want you in your entirety, or not at all." All other kinds of love seek something other than the loved one; this kind wants only to have the beloved's own self completely. If Adam had not fallen, the love of bride and groom would have been been the loveliest thing. Not this love is not pure either, for admittedly a married partner desires to have the other, yet each seeks to satisfy his desire with the other, and it is this desire which corrupts this kind of love.[21]
—Martin Luther

THE BASIC STRUCTURE OF JESUS' DIVORCE SAYINGS: MARK 10:11–12 AND LUKE 16:18

Why are Matthew's exception clauses missing from Mark's (//Matt. 19:3–12) and Luke's (//Matt. 5:32) records of Jesus' teaching? We know that Mark is writing for a Roman audience where there would be no interest in the specifics of the Hillel-Shammai debate. Mark omits not only the phrase "for any cause" in the Pharisees' opening question (Mark 10:2//Matt. 19:3) but also the "except for immorality" clause in Jesus' divorce saying (Mark 10:11–12//Matt. 19:9). Mark also includes the application of Jesus' teaching to women who had the option to divorce in the Roman context: "and if she divorces her husband and marries another, she commits adultery" (Mark 10:12). As noted above, I believe Jesus' divorce sayings in Mark and Luke should be viewed as generalizations that admit of exceptions or rhetorical overstatements that drive home what Jesus is saying about the covenantal nature of marriage and the loyalty required of marriage partners;[22] either way, I do not believe Mark and Luke wanted their readers to think Jesus prohibited divorce for any and every reason. Why?

First, Paul did not interpret Jesus' saying this way. He makes an exception for divorce and remarriage in a new situation (1 Cor. 7:15) after citing what the Lord taught (1 Cor. 7:10–11). Second, Roman law expected a spouse to divorce an adulterous partner, so Mark and Luke need not specify this. Third, the basic structure of Jesus' divorce saying in all the synoptic accounts is this: "Whoever divorces his wife and marries another commits adultery" (Mark 10:10–12//Matt. 19:9 and Luke 16:18//Matt. 5:31–32). The only way first-century readers could make sense of this teaching is to assume that the divorce Jesus envisions was not valid. In other words, yes, it is true that "Whoever divorces his wife and marries another commits adultery," unless the divorce occurred for a valid, justifiable cause like sexual immorality. Everyone would have agreed with this point.[23] Matthew's "except for sexual immorality" clause makes this assumption explicit and answers the Pharisees' question in Matthew 19:3 by interpreting the "some indecency" in Deuteronomy 24:1 in line with Shammai's more restrictive position (yet only permitting, not commanding, divorce).

What should we make of Jesus' additional remark at the end of Matthew 5:32//Luke 16:18: "and whoever marries a divorced woman commits adultery"? Taken literally, this would mean that Jesus viewed marriage covenant as unbreakable in God's sight; even the innocent party would not be free to remarry after a valid divorce (i.e., "except on the ground of sexual immorality" [Matt. 5:32a]). John Murray says "There can be no question but it applies to the person divorced without the proper ground."[24]

On the other hand, throughout this chapter I have recognized the reality that covenants, including the marital covenant, unfortunately, are broken and may therefore eventually be dissolved. We know this from the culture context in which Jesus and Paul were teaching, and we know it from present day. When Jesus said, "What therefore God has joined together, let not man separate" (Mark 10:9), He knew it was possible that a breach in a marriage *could* occur, though He adjured against it in the strongest terms. Jesus, like the case law in Deuteronomy 24:1–4, recognizes the validity of subsequent marriages, for He says to the woman at the well, "You are right in saying, 'I have no husband'; for you have had five husbands, and the one you now have is not your husband" (John 4:17–18). And Paul says to former adulterers converted under his ministry in Corinth, "such were some of you" (1 Cor. 6:9–11). Thus Jesus' saying that "whoever marries a divorced woman commits adultery" is a graphic image exhorting husbands to be faithful to their marriage vows at all costs.

Finally, how do we respond to the teaching that only the innocent party in a valid divorce is free to remarry, but not the guilty party? If the marriage covenant is broken or violated by a spouse's betrayal, then "it is difficult to see on what ground the contracting of another marriage on the part of the guilty divorcee should be considered adultery."[25] Yet this seems to conflict with Paul's teaching that when two Christians divorce for invalid reasons, both "should remain unmarried or else be reconciled" (1 Cor. 7:11). Paul's command that the "guilty" spouse should not remarry does not seem to be a punishment—Matthew 12:31 says there is only one unforgiveable sin—nor a consequence of the invalid divorce, "but a practical way in which they can try to reverse their mistake, and the command only lasts as long as this might still be possible."[26] If all attempts possible to restore the marriage fail, however, would Paul have required the invalidly divorced spouses to remain unmarried for the rest of their lives? I do not know if there is any way to answer this question with confidence, but I would err on the side of saying "No" where true repentance for failure to reconcile has taken place. If one of the spouses decides to file for divorce, whether or not they remarry, then it seems they have failed to keep their promises and the marriage covenant is broken.

This is where the notion that divorce is a kind of "adultery" might prove instructive. Blomberg may well be correct when he states, "Jesus maintains that the divorce *itself* creates adultery—metaphorically, not literally—through infidelity to the lifelong, covenantal nature of marriage (cf. the characteristic Old Testament use of 'adultery' to refer to breaking one's commitments to God—e.g., Hos 2:4; Jer 5:7; Ezek 16:32)."[27] And if divorce is covenant-breaking, i.e., adultery, then the primary focus in Jesus' saying about committing adultery is not the sexual aspect itself but the covenant breaking and betrayal that sexual immorality signifies whether a remarriage occurs or not.[28]

As we will see next, sexual immorality may have nothing to do with the divorce and remarriage situation Paul addresses in 1 Corinthians 7:15; it has to do with covenant breaking and unfulfilled obligations. When one spouse abandons another—whether a believer or unbeliever (one's faith is ultimately not the crucial issue there either)—the covenant loyalty promised in marriage is forsaken.

When Paul evangelized the city of Corinth on his third missionary journey (Acts 18:1–17), he ran into a problem when only one of the partners in a marriage received the gospel. Here's how he dealt with it:

> To the rest I say this (I, not the Lord): If any brother has a wife who is not a believer and she is willing to live with him, he must not divorce her. And if a woman has a husband who is not a believer and he is willing to live with her, she must not divorce him. For the unbelieving husband has been sanctified through his wife, and the unbelieving wife has been sanctified through her believing husband. Otherwise your children would be unclean, but as it is, they are holy.
>
> But if the unbeliever leaves, let it be so. The brother or the sister is not bound in such circumstances; God has called us to live in peace. How do you know, wife, whether you will save your husband? Or, how do you know, husband, whether you will save your wife? (1 Cor. 7:12–16 NIV)

Paul, "as one who by the Lord's mercy is trustworthy" (7:25c), wants new believers in Corinth to know that they should not divorce their unbelieving mate (vv. 12–14). Yet if the non-Christian spouse wants nothing to do with the believer's faith and leaves, Paul says, "The brother or sister is not bound (*ou dedoulōtai* [from *douloō*]) in such circumstances; God has called us to live in peace" (1 Cor. 7:15 NIV).

The crucial statement in the Jewish bill of divorce was, "You are free to marry any man" (Mishnah *Gitten* 9:3). Paul's "The brother or the sister is not bound in such circumstances" (1 Cor. 7:15b) makes this exact point. It is the negative formulation of the Jewish bill of divorce. Given Paul's Jewish background, it is virtually certain that Paul permits the remarriage of the deserted party if they so choose. This is also the most natural reading of the exception: it frees or "looses" the believer from the obligations of his or her marriage covenant. This is considered a valid or legitimate divorce.

Some believe that Paul is adding a second exception for divorce and re-marriage (the so-called Pauline privilege) to the one found in Matthew, and that he does so under the leading of the Holy Spirit (cf. 1 Cor. 7:40b; 14:37). However, it is more probable that Paul is simply applying what was always the case in Old Testament marriage law. Exodus 21:10–11 states that a husband must give a wife food, clothing, and marital rights (i.e., sexual relations). Both the rabbis and Paul applied these equally to the wife and the husband, and the three provisions of Exodus 21:10–11 "became the basis for the vows in Jewish marriage contracts and in Christian marriage services via the reference in Ephesians 5:28–29."[29] Paul's exhortation in 1 Corinthians 7:3–5 that spouses must mutually render regular sexual activity to one another is also an application of the principle of Exodus 21:10. The desertion of one spouse by the other is added: to not provide physical, financial, emotional, and spiritual support is a violation of the marriage covenant. Paul says abandonment of one spouse by another is a justifiable ground for divorce and remarriage.

The teaching of Paul in 1 Corinthians 7 strengthens our point that Matthew's exception clauses function along the same lines. This reinforces the view that Jesus' divorce sayings were never intended to be understood as absolute statements that admit of no exceptions. We should also be willing to consider the possibility that because Jesus is answering a specific question in Matthew 19//Mark 10 related to the ground for divorce and remarriage in Deuteronomy 24:1, there may be other causes for divorce and remarriage that Jesus did not address. But that topic must be approached very cautiously.

WHAT ABOUT 1 CORINTHIANS 7:10-11, 39 AND ROMANS 7:2-3?

The only remaining texts we need to briefly comment on are these:

> To the married I give this charge (not I, but the Lord): the wife should not separate from her husband (but if she does, she should remain unmarried or else be reconciled to her husband), and the husband should not divorce his wife. (1 Cor. 7:10–11)

> A wife is bound to her husband as long as he lives. But if her husband dies, she is free to be married to whom she wishes, only in the Lord. (1 Cor. 7:39)

> Accordingly, she will be called an adulteress if she lives with another man while her husband is alive. But if her husband dies, she is free from that law, and if she marries another man she is not an adulteress. (Rom. 7:3)

These passages could be used to defend a no-remarriage understanding of the New Testament teaching on divorce and remarriage, but I believe that would be a misuse of their intent. Where 1 Corinthians 7:10–11 is concerned, we simply note that Paul goes on in 1 Corinthians 7:15 to make an exception for divorce and remarriage in the case of desertion. He sees no contradiction here. Corinth was under Roman law, and in that system either husband or wife could initiate a divorce just by walking out. Paul's directive to "remain unmarried or else be reconciled" in verse 11 must be referencing an invalid divorce.

With respect to the other two passages—one of which is an illustration—we really should admit that it is most probable that Paul just does not have in view the other valid grounds for divorce and remarriage, namely divorce for sexual immorality or desertion by an unbeliever.

CONCLUSION

So what unites the exceptions cited by Jesus in Matthew 19:9 and Paul in 1 Corinthians 7:15, and might there be additional exceptions beyond these two? Here I stand with Keener's affirmation of Blomberg's analysis:

> Blomberg (*Matthew*, 293) rightly points out that exceptions beyond those stated in Scripture must be governed by the principle that unites the two biblical exceptions: (1) both infidelity and abandonment destroy central components of marriage; (2) both leave an innocent party unable to save the marriage; and (3) both use divorce only "as a last resort."[30]

We sometimes hear pastors and teachers say Jesus teaches that marriage is "more binding" than His contemporaries taught, and this is certainly correct. However, knowing that marriage vows can, unfortunately, be violated and promises broken should not focus our attention on the impossibility of "breaking" an indissoluble bond formed by sexual union. Rather, marriage is formed by means of a conditional, volitional covenant. Covenants are relational commitments, and the most important goal one should have in building a strong marriage is to grow in one's passion for the person with whom they are bound in the new covenant, namely Jesus Christ. And Jesus our Lord said: "If you love me, you will keep my commandments" (John 14:15). Thus our application of the biblical teaching of marriage should put the stress on covenant commitments, on loyal love, on mutual responsibilities, on integrity, on ethical living, and on the maintenance and care of spouses and children (cf. Ex. 21:10–11; Eph. 5:25–29). All this we will want to live out in accordance with the character of a life lived with the desire to please the One who "loved us and gave himself up for us" (Eph. 5:2).

CONTINUING INSIGHT:

PASTORAL CONSIDERATIONS

by Chuck Hannaford

There are other resources that address various divorce and remarriage situations,[1] but in this article I want to take a different approach: Why do relationships deteriorate, and how can spouses be the best marriage partners they can be? The reality of divorce is all around us, and the pain associated with the dissolution of marriage affects millions of people. Consequently, for those who are created to be in relationship, remarriage is an evident certainty. So the church first should do all it can to help couples avoid divorce. The sad inevitability is that many couples give up too easily. Significantly, "longitudinal studies reveal that two-thirds of unhappy marriages will become happy within five years if people stay married and do not get divorced."[2]

And for those who have been through a divorce, the church needs to work out how to help the married-again succeed and even flourish.

Blame shifting

Fallen people inherently focus on others' failures, magnify their flaws, and justify our "right" to be angry or believe it is our spouse's responsibility to make us happy. Blaming each other for personal shortcomings has been around since the beginning. "The man said, 'The woman whom you gave to be with me, she gave me fruit of the tree, and I ate.' Then the LORD God said to the woman, 'What is this that you have done?' The woman said, 'The serpent deceived me, and I ate'" (Gen. 3:12–13 ESV). This dynamic of blame shifting and avoiding personal responsibility is the antithesis of relational health, conviction, and repentance.

The very nature of "self" is going to be challenged because marriage is designed around selflessness, not selfishness. Yet Jesus tells us if we are to follow Him, we are to deny ourselves (Matt. 16:24), which is only possible when the Spirit of Christ controls us (Eph. 5:18; Col. 3:16). While we are instructed to deny "self," it can be dangerous to deny pain, hurt, rejection, betrayal, and other emotions that arise from living with another broken human being. We must confront these emotions; otherwise they take root and serve as justification for the maltreatment of others. Thankfully, forgiving, continually wiping the slate clean, and repentance are God's methods of dealing with these powerfully destructive feelings. If we live in the "light" of our individual brokenness instead of blame shifting, we will have the right kind of fellowship, redemptive fellowship, with our loved ones (1 John 1:7).

Unresolved negative emotions

Each person brings into marriage baggage related to their family of origin: expectations, dreams, and hopes. Past emotional, physical, or spiritual trauma colors one's view of themselves, marriage, and God. These often unconscious forces impact the way a spouse relates to the other and can have a detrimental impact on the marriage. They need to be addressed in the dating and engagement phase of the relationship. In a remarriage situation, there is additional baggage—the original issues plus what led to the end of a previous marriage and the trauma of divorce. Each of us must assume personal responsibility for the state of our own soul. This can occur through prayer and Bible study, counseling, relationships with close friends we have asked to speak into our lives, and reading helpful books such as the *The Meaning of Marriage*.[3]

Anger, as an example of baggage, is almost always a secondary emotion. When the cause of anger goes unresolved it grows to resentment and eventually becomes bitterness. Anger is both an offensive and defensive emotion. The primary emotions that usually lead to anger are hurt, rejection, betrayal, fear, and a host of others.[4] When we experience these primary emotions, anger serves the purpose of overcoming the immediate sense of feeling vulnerable and it gives us a false sense of control.

Anger is sometimes also used as a mechanism for manipulation and keeping others away from unresolved sensitive areas. Telling your spouse you are angry because he or she said or did something that makes you angry does not resolve the issue. This is where many couples get stuck. However, if you are able to communicate in a loving or respectful manner that when such-and-such is said or done, or that it is hurtful, makes you feel rejected, or creates fear, then you are getting to the heart of the matter. Further, if you communicate that the reason for your reaction is that you love them and desire their affirmation, the defensive dynamic is taken out of play.

Whether we're doing all we can to make a first marriage work or entering into another, we know we have these unresolved issues when we overreact to minor situations.

Imagine someone stepping on your foot and what your physical reaction would be. You immediately pull the foot back and push the other away. If your foot is injured, you may find yourself protecting it for some time after the injury. Emotions are similar. In fact, we try to protect areas where we have been hurt previously by keeping those who love us most at a distance, even if they were not the ones who originally hurt us.

Consider how this might play out in those who remarry after being wronged by a hurtful divorce. Again, we see the importance of personal responsibility and being aware of strongholds we have developed over time that prevent us from being able to give or receive. This is critical in foiling the enemy's plan to divide us. Whether a first or second marriage, we cannot expect to enter into a successful relationship when we import negative emotions into the relationship.

The power of a biblical focus

Consider a marriage in which the husband assumes correctly that loving his wife is an act of worship and the wife respects and appreciates her husband (Eph. 5:22–33). If we understand that Paul, under the inspiration of the Holy Spirit, is speaking directly to every married couple, the dynamics of our personal interactions would be dramatically transformed. We would begin to ask questions that identify elements within us, which hinder our expressions of love or respect. Issues such as unforgiveness, resentment, and unresolved anger destroy our ability to love or respect another. Identifying and dealing with unresolved wounds will alter the relational dynamic, since the other's behavior will not define our reaction; God's redemptive power will. Our response patterns shift from selfish defensive reactions to selflessly searching for the only thing each person can control—his or her reaction. The question to ask when there is disagreement is "Does my spouse's perspective align better with God's than mine?" This makes submission a desired positive and helps us take responsibility for our former misalignment.

To keep a marriage healthy as God intended, each person must have a growing and intimate relationship with Christ in which pleasing their Lord determines everything (John 14:21; 15:15; Ps. 51:4). Apart from one's connection to Jesus and their love for Him, there is little motivation to work on a hurting marriage (or remarriage) or to implement changes in one's own life. It has been said that one can only give what he or she has. Again, we see the importance of a vibrant spiritual life so that each person has something to give the other. If a husband is to love his wife as Christ loved the church, he should submit to the needs (not necessarily wants) of his wife and use all his resources to meet her needs to the point of death, even as Christ sacrificially loved the church (Eph. 5:25).

If the wife, as an act of worship, respects her husband's position even when he does not love her sacrificially, it would create a desire for him to earn her personal respect. This example creates a positive feedback loop within the relationship, husband and wife each taking responsibility under God for themselves. Our focus then is primarily between us and God and any impediments that harm our fellowship with Him. Changing others is the work of the Holy Spirit and not that of a spouse who takes it upon himself or herself to point out the other's faults.

When a husband loves his wife, even when she does not act in a lovable manner, and a wife respects her husband, even when he acts disrespectfully, the Holy Spirit has room to adjust each individual's attitude through conviction as we abide in God's Word. With time, work, and a submitted heart to God, we stop defending our bad behavior and begin building the other up. It is never too late to begin this process. The bottom line is that no matter how many times a person has failed, their patterns in relationships won't change until they themselves do. Following God's principles puts a primary focus on guarding your heart (see Prov. 4:23) and not allowing the sun to set "while you are still angry" (Eph. 4:26 NIV).

How far to go to save the marriage?

Marriage was designed by God for our sanctification, not merely our satisfaction. Sanctification is difficult in marriage, but it is where we must live out the gospel. We cannot hide from our spouse; this person sees us as we really are. Marriage forces us to get serious about what Scripture says about sanctification and the selfless love we are called to by Christ.

In order to heal a broken marriage, or prevent the dissolution of marriage, a few enemies of marriage should be addressed. Couples can develop a deadly form of passivity, and the problems facing them build while they do nothing.

It has been said that marriage is something that exists while we are busy doing other things. This is patently false, and that is why when children, jobs, or other activities are at the top of the hierarchy, marriages suffer.

When problems become too big to ignore or other interests become too great, we begin to separate from one another more. This type of passivity leads to compromise. There are times when well-meaning friends and family attempt to get us to compromise our covenant for their comfort. We must be careful from whom we seek advice. Some individuals move from passivity to a sense of defeatism and start to give up.

What about situations where attempting to save a marriage seems impossible, short of a miracle? When there are violations of covenant promises such as abuse, unrepentant adultery, alcohol or drug abuse, or any situation where one partner (or the children) is in some form of danger, protecting well-being becomes the priority. Some continue to put themselves in danger because their need to be in a relationship is greater than the desire to be healthy or see themselves as the Father's beloved son or daughter. For marriage or remarriage to flourish, there must be a mutual pledge from both husband and wife to actively fight against anything that does not belong in the covenant with God and commitment to each other.

What constitutes a reasonable attempt to save the marriage? There is no general answer to this question that fits all scenarios. Each individual must answer this question based on a vital relationship with the Lord, and the church can guide. Has the person done everything within his or her power to identify personal contributions for relational dissonance, repented of them, taken steps to change, and sought forgiveness for those offenses? The Newtonian law can pertain to relationships: for every action there is an equal and opposite reaction. Personal change sometimes effects a change in the other, and the person seeking to end a marriage should examine himself or herself to ensure that all possible has been done to save the marriage.

A pastor and the church should do all possible so help a couple heal their broken marriage. When a couple or one partner considers ending a marriage, the church must lead the spouse through these questions: Have I confronted the challenges to sanctification in my marriage or have I allowed these challenges to lead me to separation? Have I been as committed to building my marriage and honoring my spouse as I have to finding fault and justifying my decisions? Have I worked on the "enemies" of my marriage and taken responsibility for the ones I let in?

Perhaps one way to answer the question "What constitutes a reasonable attempt to save the marriage?" is best answered by addressing and honestly answering the questions above.

MINISTRY, REMARRIAGE, AND GOD'S REDEEMING POWER FOR THE NEXT GENERATION

by Ron L. Deal

God's design for the home is perfect. The homes of God's people, however, have never been—nor do I suspect ever will be—perfect.

"Go call your husband."

"I have no husband."

"You are right in saying, 'I have no husband'; for you have had five husbands, and the one you now have is not your husband. What you have said is true."

"Sir, I perceive that you are a prophet" (John 4:16–19 ESV).

Ultimately this story is not about marriage or divorce, but about Living Water and the hope that is available in Christ (we don't know for sure if this woman was divorced once, five times, or not at all, but the context strongly implies that divorce is very much a part of her story). Jesus knew this woman was intensely thirsty—she had been looking for love in all the wrong places—but He didn't call attention to her marital circumstances in order to shame her; He did so to get her attention so He could talk to her about what would ultimately satisfy her thirst. The result? A woman who drank deeply from the well of Christ's acceptance and restoration. At the beginning of the story this woman who was so heaped in shame that she avoided others by coming to the well in the heat of the day alone, runs back to town with a redeemed version of her story that brought people to Christ. "He told me all that I ever did," she said (John 4:39 ESV), and many came to Jesus and believed. In the end, the first "evangelist" to the Samaritan people in all likelihood was a cohabiting, five-time divorcee.

Bill Heth has written an insightful summary of the teachings of Scripture regarding divorce and remarriage. Understanding God's truth about this subject is vital; we should continue to study the matter with great care so we can point to God's ideal for relationships. And we must be ready to offer a cup of redemptive water to those who have not lived (or in the case of the innocent party to divorce, cannot live) up to God's design.

Ministry to the divorced and/or remarried walks the delicate line of truth and grace and is often theologically challenging and pastorally messy. But walk the line we must. I suggest our efforts include the following basic elements.

Theology should dictate practice

What the Bible teaches about marriage, divorce, and remarriage is not merely academic; it should be the foundation of our ministry efforts.

A good example of this relates to premarital counseling. Heth suggests that ultimately Christ's teaching about divorce calls his people to marital faithfulness and reconciliation. After an invalid divorce, then, the high calling of Scripture (see 1 Cor. 7:11) is to repair the relationship if at all possible. Certainly this admonition has multiple layers that will need to be carefully unpacked, but a respect for Scripture demands that we ask the hard questions.

A very different response is appropriate when ministering to those already remarried after an invalid divorce. Given that they have entered into a new covenant offering marital enrichment does not sanction prior behavior or mean that we are pro-divorce any more than believing in hospitals makes one pro-illness, or believing in grace makes us pro-sin. Remarriage ministry is not about condoning someone's past or lowering God's standard for marriage. It is about offering them living water and calling them to walk in faithfulness to their current marriage and not repeat the sin of the past.

Offer practical support to remarried couples and stepfamilies

When a new marriage does follow divorce, Chuck Hannaford insightfully asks what the church can do to "help the married-again succeed and even flourish." Thankfully in the last two decades a new body of literature on blended family ministry has helped the church understand that remarriage relationships have unique challenges, especially when they involve children and form stepfamilies.[1] Ironically, a step-couple union is often undermined by the dynamics of the very stepfamily it formed. Helping couples anticipate and know how to manage these stressors is one key to helping remarriages succeed and stepfamilies flourish.[2]

Help the entire church "sit by wells"

Prior to the Samaritan woman's conversation with Jesus you can imagine how the people of Sychar chided and condemned her for a sordid past (which makes her courage to testify to the Messiah's grace even more remarkable). I often warn remarried couples that God will not treat them differently because of their past, but that fellow Christians will. Pastoral ministry to divorced and remarried couples includes helping the church as a whole set aside harsh words and shaming judgment. For example, learning to be cautious with terms like "broken family," which may be used meaning "fractured" but often conveys "less than," would help make the church a safe, hope-filled place for those impacted by divorce.

Likewise, pastors should take great care crafting public and private messages. I've long discouraged pastoral leaders from repeating the refrain "God hates divorce" in their teaching. As Heth points out, most translations incorrectly interpret Malachi 2:16 ascribing the word "hate" to God instead of to a man who deals treacherously with his faithful wife. Pastors who repeat this phrase in order to express God's disapproval of invalid divorce are misrepresenting the text, but more importantly, are often leading divorced people, as I have witnessed numerous times, to wonder if God hates them; leading children of remarried parents to doubt if they are part of a legitimate family; and are inadvertently encouraging church members to look down on the divorced. This fractures the church and marginalizes those who need community most. Rather, we should use language that helps the church to "sit by the well" so it can redeem the remarried; to do so, pastors must teach and model grace at every turn.

A redemptive perspective

We should hold high God's design for lifelong marriage between one man and one woman. At the same time, we should hold high a message of grace for those who—whether by their sin or another's—are not living the ideal.

For many adults, a healthy remarriage that brings godly companionship, economic provision, and sexual intimacy is God's redemptive work in their lives. We also now know that a healthy stepfamily (following either divorce or the death of a parent) can be redemptive in the lives of children.[3] The love and sacrifice of a stepparent, the stability of a home living under God's precepts, and a healthy marriage model help to combat the negative repercussions of family dissolution. Indeed, when God is at the center of a second chance on life, the generational pattern of divorce is broken and redemption of the family trajectory, shifting it back toward God's original design, occurs.

To be a part of that process is a great honor the church should pursue without hesitation and with great joy.

SECTION 4

MISSION

CHAPTER 13

MARRIAGE AND COMMUNITY IN THE BODY OF CHRIST

by Donna Thoennes

God has revealed Himself to us as three in one. The concept of the Trinity challenges our intellect and delights us with God's majesty. Regardless of the depth of our understanding of the Trinity, clearly we conclude that God is relational. He has existed harmoniously as three persons throughout eternity, and His inner life and purposes are carried out relationally. In His generous goodness, He made us relational as well. To image God is to be made in His likeness and live communally because we've been invited into the community that is the Trinity. We were made to connect. But unlike the Father, Son, and Holy Spirit, in human relationships we connect with persons whose wills and intentions don't always align with ours, creating unique relationships that challenge and serve and sanctify us in distinct ways. Marriage is one of those.

MADE FOR LOVING FRIENDSHIP IN COMMUNITY

God's overarching purpose is to glorify Himself. One of the ways He does so is by creating a people for Himself and establishing a covenant relationship with them. Within the new covenant, God made a way through Christ to invite His mere creatures into loving familial relationship with Him.

Love for brothers and sisters

When we are adopted into His family, we become God's child among all His others. We are one of countless siblings! As Father, He not only brings us into relationship with Himself, but with His body, meeting our relational needs in fellowship with the body of Christ. He made us to exist and thrive within His established community, unified by the gospel through the death and resurrection of Christ. Because it pleased Him and because we need it, God established His church and instructed us to gather regularly to proclaim, worship, love, serve, and thereby spur one another on to love and good deeds. His people respond to His love by worshiping Him and serving one another. In turn, that proclamation, love, worship, and service spills over to those who are outside the church, and they are drawn into the fellowship with God and His children. In this way, God's kingdom spreads and His church grows.

In *The Compelling Community*, Mark Dever and Jamie Dunlop call the church a "gospel-revealing community" that is characterized by the breadth and depth described in Ephesians 2:18–19. "For through him we both have access in one Spirit to the Father. So then you are no longer strangers and aliens, but you are fellow citizens with the saints and members of the household of God."[1] This community "doesn't merely bring people together to tolerate each other, but to be so tightly committed that Paul can call them a 'new man' (2:15) and a new 'household' (2:19). . . . Supernatural depth and breadth of community make the glory of an invisible God to be visible. This is the ultimate purpose statement for community in churches today."[2] Our relationships with one another not only meet our deep needs to know and be known, but are also an apologetic to a watching world. In John 13:34–35 Jesus gave His disciples a new commandment: "Love one another: just as I have loved you, you also are to love one another. By this all people will know that you are my disciples, if you have love for one another."

What or who we love divulges who we are. Our love for one another is proof of our identity. In 1 John 4, John stuns us by irrevocably binding love for God and love for brother and sister. "If we love one another, God abides in us and his love is perfected in us. . . . Whoever loves God must also love his brother. . . . If anyone says 'I love God' and hates his brother, he is a liar" (vv. 12, 21, 20). Love for God and love for one another seamlessly coexist or we are liars. We might say we love God, but if we don't love our brother, it betrays the fact that we don't really love God!

Again, in Dever's language, we might make the glory of an invisible God to be visible by loving people who seem to be randomly thrown together with only their faith in common. Our spiritual bond, our common love for God, becomes especially evident when typical commonalities, like neighborhood or hobbies, are absent. The supernatural element is undeniable and our identity as disciples is known.

Priorities of love in a believer's life

In *The Four Loves*, C. S. Lewis distinguishes different loves that God provides to season our lives. Three can be experienced by all believers and the fourth by those who are married. He warns that to love demands a willingness to be vulnerable, as "your heart will certainly be wrung and possibly be broken." But the only protection against love is to lock your heart away in a casket where "safe, dark, motionless, airless—it will change. It will not be broken; it will become unbreakable, impenetrable, irredeemable."[3] What choice to do we have, Lewis asks? Love or die.

He starts his treatment with the first love, "Affection," which he identifies as the modest, unique love based on familiarity. It finds "something to appreciate in the cross-section of humanity . . . teaching us first to notice, then to endure, then to smile at, then to enjoy, and finally to appreciate, the people who 'happen to be there.'"[4] Church relationships often comprise this form of love, as over time we grow to appreciate those who have become familiar, even when they are "odder than you could have believed and worth far more than we guessed."[5] We can grow affection for the woman sitting nearby who sings off key or the gentleman who criticizes the drums each week. We will even miss them when they are gone.

C. S. Lewis said his second love, "Friendship," is not necessary to life but arises when companions discover they have a common interest or value the same beauty. Friends ask, "Do you see the same truth?" and delight in their shared appreciation. Lewis continues, "Pathetic people who simply want friends can never make any. The very condition of having friends is that we should want something else besides friends . . . friendship must be about something, even if it were only an enthusiasm for dominoes or white mice. Those who have nothing can share nothing; those who are going nowhere can have no fellow-travellers."[6] Friendship is a great gift for every member of the body of Christ, and the shared commonality is being in Christ and living for His glory.

Lewis's "Eros" is the state of being in love. Eros wants the Beloved, not an experience, but a particular person. It is theologically, naturally, morally, and emotionally serious. Yet, Lewis warns his readers, it's also playful. "Banish play and laughter from the bed of love and you may let in a false goddess."[7] Eros is unique among the other loves because it is exclusive for marriage. Keller points out that Jesus is a friend and lover to us and serves as a model for spouses.[8]

"Charity" is Lewis's highest and most demanding love. After receiving God's Divine Gift-love, God gives grace to believers to offer Gift-love back to God and even to those not naturally lovable. Through grace God also bestows the gifts of Need-love of Himself and Need-love of others. We become "jolly-beggars" experiencing a "delighted acceptance of our Need, a joy in total dependence."[9]

It may be easy to see how Affection, Friendship, and Charity fit comfortably within the church family experience. Perhaps the relationship between Eros and the church is less obvious. Does passionate love within marriage compete with the spiritual love of charity among brothers and sisters, or perhaps the friendship between tennis partners? How can we be committed both to our marriages and other church relationships?

Family priorities

New Testament scholar and pastor Joseph Hellerman helps us understand the role of church in our lives in *When the Church Was a Family* and *Why We Need the Church to Become More Like Jesus*. In the first he highlights a shift away from "church as family" that has occurred among contemporary believers. In the second he emphasizes the impact that shift has had on the spiritual formation that God intended to foster within the church family. Putting the two theses together would look something like this: God's people will not become more like Jesus unless they recapture Jesus' vision for authentic Christian community. God's people throughout the Bible were called to prioritize the community of faith. Hellerman succinctly states, "biblical salvation is a community-creating event."[10] In the first century, Paul encouraged new converts who were often rejected by their non-believing family members, with the good news that God adopted them into *His* family. With salvation, God calls us "His own," and we get to claim the church as our own.

As important as marriage and friendship are in the life of the believer, the New Testament orients the church as the central community in which the follower of Christ enjoys a rich web of relationships and from which sanctification flourishes. John Piper elevates supernatural relations over natural ones. "God's family, that comes into being by new birth and faith in Christ . . . is more central and more lasting than families that come into being by marriage and procreation and adoption."[11] Hellerman suggests that the priority of church in the life of the believer was not just a cultural phenomenon in the first century; rather, "Jesus unequivocally affirmed such an approach to interpersonal relationships when He chose 'family' as the defining metaphor to describe His followers . . . He intentionally adopted 'family' as the key relational image for the social organization of the group He was gathering around Himself."[12]

Hellerman culls through both the New Testament and contemporary church life looking for relational priorities and finds a discrepancy between the two. He concluded that Jesus prioritizes relationships with God and those who are, by faith, part of His family even over relationships within one's immediate family. Jesus' relational priorities could be listed this way: God and His family, my family, others. Yet, as an observant pastor, Hellerman concludes that contemporary Christians appear to prioritize their natural families over the family of God.[13] Contemporary priorities would stack up this way: God, my family, God's family, others. Thus, God is separated from His spiritual family, the head from the body.

Hellerman's work highlights a significant distinction in relational priorities between the New Testament believers and contemporary Christians. He offers the reader a helpful corrective to our tendency to focus on our natural family to the neglect of our church family. Rather, we are to think of our "natural family as my first relational priority under the overarching rubric of the family of God . . . as being organically embedded in the family of God."[14] Perhaps married congregants would find it easier to welcome single adults, who comprise 44 percent of the population, if we retrained our minds to think along the lines of New Testament relational priorities. On the flip side, singles would be doing their part to fellowship with and support their married brothers and sisters. The great divide would not exist! All church members would be part of priority number one rather than number three. "When we allow the family of God to occupy first place in our hierarchy of relational loyalties, marriage ceases to be the crucible for spiritual formation and becomes one of any number of church family relationships that provide a context for growth in Christ."[15] The tendency to exclude singles from extensive marriage and family programing would be replaced by organic, life-giving, growth-inducing relationships.

Singles in the church

Barry Danylak's work *Redeeming Singleness* draws a similar conclusion to Hellerman's while affirming the important role of single adults in the church.[16] In his essay "A Biblical Theology of Singleness," Danylak helps us understand the shift we see in the Bible from a focus on the biological family to the church family. "Jesus does not seek to undermine or destroy traditional family values of house and home; he still affirms the fifth commandment (Mark 7:10; 10:19). But He does announce that something greater now has come—kingdom values. Kingdom values require a greater allegiance to Jesus than even to one's traditional family members (see Matt. 15:4–6). Kingdom values also mean that there is now a new bond of the spiritual family of God that runs deeper than even the traditional family unit. Our bond of mutuality to the family of God through Christ ultimately proves to be a greater bond than even the bond we have with our physical blood relatives."[17] This reorientation was radical within the first century and it still appears radical today, if we judge based on the typical evangelical church experience. How do we rightly focus on our families, taking responsibility for nurturing our children and investing in our marriages, but not become so insular and exclusive that we ignore our affection, friendship, and charity within the body of Christ?

In her article "Choose Love in the Deep," Carrie Stockton, dean of Student Success at Biola University, adjures blog readers to live deeply connected to the body of Christ. She speaks about her life as a professional single woman, deeply connected to her church.

> These individuals (and many more) form a constellation of relationships that God has used to place love and belonging in my life and remind me that I am not alone. What if we believed that this amount of human love is enough? What if married couples similarly depended upon this more holistic vision of human love? What if we then grounded that human love in deep contentment found in Christ alone?
>
> Jesus Christ is my first love. This statement is often made in blogs on singleness, and I don't know how to make it sound less trite. It is a weighty, profound truth, and should be true for all of us as Christians, married or single. Perhaps in my singleness I can demonstrate the sufficiency of Christ differently than a married person, but I'm less and less convinced that's the case. I think, perhaps, I can demonstrate the sufficiency of the family of God and human relationships differently than a married person. I have had married friends tell me that there is no greater loneliness than the loneliness that they have experienced in marriage. Maybe I can help remind married people of their deep need for human relationships beyond their spouse. After all, "people will neither marry nor be given in marriage" (Matt. 22:30) at the resurrection.[18]

Stockton's point is well-taken. Married folk need to foster relationships beyond their spouses, and singles need to invest in friendships with those who aren't also single.

Stockton's experience of deep and meaningful fellowship is a solution to the loneliness that many singles feel within churches filled with married people. Christopher Ash challenges the commonly held idea that Eve was created to fill Adam's loneliness, and by doing so he elevates fellowship within the body of Christ. In addition to being made to fellowship with God, "we are made also for warm fellowship with our brothers and sisters in the family of God. This is what the gospel of Jesus Christ offers to everyone. Now marriage ought also to be a place of friendship and joyful fellowship. For those who are married, their marriages ought indeed to be places of fellowship that are remedies for loneliness. But marriage is not the remedy for loneliness. Wherever there is fellowship there is God's remedy for loneliness. Not all human beings are able to marry, but all human beings are invited into fellowship with God and with one another in Jesus Christ."[19] Ash offers a useful corrective to the idea that marriage fixes loneliness. Some married folk can testify that marriage can be the loneliest place of all. Expecting marriage to remedy loneliness also sets the spouse up for failure when he or she cannot completely deliver. God intends for His family to be a very present reality in the believer's life, whether they are married or not.

Marriage and friendship

Often when we want to communicate the closeness and loyalty of a friend, we say, "He's like family." On the flip side, when we want to communicate ease and enjoyment in relationship with a family member, we say, "My sister is my best friend." Different relationships provide uniquely for us, and we feel especially blessed when one person provides both familial loyalty and friendly enjoyment. A healthy marriage provides both of these in a spouse. Marriage is a lifelong, intensely committed friendship between a man and a woman reflecting the Godhead. Psychologist John Gottman has done extensive scientific analysis of marriage stability and concludes that friendship is foundational to a happy marriage. Friendship, according to Gottman, leads to commitment, intimacy, and trust.[20] Friendship serves as a relational glue to increase the desire to keep one's commitment and also make the commitment-keeping more enjoyable.

Within the larger community of friendship, marriage is a unique friendship with its own exclusive pressures and delights. In *The Meaning of*

Marriage, Timothy and Kathy Keller state that marriage is for friendship, and describes the special kind of friendship. "Friendship is a deep oneness that develops when two people, speaking the truth in love to one another, journey together to the same horizon."[21] The shared journey is one of knowing God more and loving Him better. It's a spiritual friendship, where each one "is eagerly helping one another know, serve, love, and resemble God in deeper and deeper ways." The Kellers advise that true marital friendship requires constancy, transparency, and common passion.[22] A true friend will be there, be honest, and share a desire to honor God with their marriage.

Nearly all marriages, even happy ones, are mistakes: in the sense that almost certainly (in a more perfect world, or even with a little more care in this very imperfect one) both partners might have found more suitable mates. But the real soul-mate is the one you are actually married to.[23] **—J. R. R. Tolkien**

Although marriage is one of many significant friendships within the church, marriages often form a spine from which many other relationships hinge or find strength and stability. The majority of adults in the church marry, and because of its prevalence and challenges, marriage often becomes a focus of ministry efforts. Some, like Wesley Hill,[24] provide a constructive reminder to congregations that other committed friendships with unmarried adults need to factor in to our ministry commitments more than they currently do in some churches. We must be mindful of the relational needs of single adults and provide for them with the same energy that we apply to building strong marriages. Hellerman's injunction helps us here. If we relationally prioritize God and His family over our natural family, we will be less likely to ignore our single brothers and sisters.

FRIENDSHIP AS LOVING SERVICE IN COMMUNITY

Dever and Dunlop's charge to local church bodies to make the glory of God visible by increasing the depth and breadth of community means a lifelong responsibility of intentional service. We make God's glory visible by going deeper and broader in our relationships with our brothers and sisters in

Christ, and that takes work. Whether married or single, this is one of our life purposes. If we are married, we serve the body of Christ alongside our spouse. We also serve our spouse as a means of, and in addition to, serving the greater church family. If we are single, we also serve to glorify God. Either way, we bless the church through loving service; we are married to bless the church or single to bless the church. God decides from which "status" we minister; our job is to keep our focus on faithful and loving service to the family of God.

While all followers of Jesus share in the service to the body of Christ, married and single alike serve uniquely from our maleness and femaleness. Writing about God's purpose for marriage, Christopher Ash in *Married for God* seeks to answer the question why God created us male and female. He goes back to Genesis 1 and 2 (as Jesus and Paul did when they talked about marriage and sex). He concludes that God's purpose for marriage is service to God and His people. He coined the term "sex in the service of God"[25] to summarize his exegetical conclusions. Ash begins with the creation account for clarity on God's intention for male and female. Genesis 1:26–31 reads,

> Then God said, "Let us make man in our image, after our likeness. And let them have dominion over the fish of the sea and over the birds of the heavens and over the livestock and over all the earth and over every creeping thing that creeps on the earth."
>
> So God created man in his own image,
>   in the image of God he created him;
>   male and female he created them.
>
> And God blessed them. And God said to them, "Be fruitful and multiply and fill the earth and subdue it, and have dominion over the fish of the sea and over the birds of the heavens and over every living thing that moves on the earth." And God said, "Behold, I have given you every plant yielding seed that is on the face of all the earth, and every tree with seed in its fruit. You shall have them for food. And to every beast of the earth and to every bird of the heavens and to everything that creeps on the earth, everything that has the breath of life, I have given every green plant for food." And it was so. And God saw everything that he had made, and behold, it was very good. And there was evening and there was morning, the sixth day.

The creation of men and women culminates a series of created things. There is a sense of completion to God's creation that He proclaims to be "very good."

Ash states, "This climax to creation is the making of men and women. The reason this is so very good is that men and women are going to govern and care for God's world and keep it an ordered place, full of life."[26] He draws four conclusions about human beings from this passage. (1) We are made in the image and likeness of God and have a unique dignity not shared by animals or plants. (2) We are entrusted with a unique privilege to fill the earth with men and women who will care for it. (3) We are created male and female and are to use our maleness and femaleness to care for God's world. (4) We are to rejoice in our Creator (implied in Genesis and spelled out in Psalm 8) and live in thankful dependence on God and cheerful obedience to His commands.[27]

Ash then explains Genesis 2:15–25. God put Adam in the garden of Eden to work it and keep it, yet it was too much work for one man, and Adam needed a helper but there was none fit for him. So God provided. "Then the LORD God said, 'It is not good that the man should be alone; I will make him a helper fit for him.'" Verse 25 tells us this is the reason the two will become one flesh and have intimacy with one another, because God gave them to each other to keep the garden! They will fulfill the task of caring for His world side by side. Even among the delights of companionship, sexual intimacy, and child-bearing, there is a higher purpose. "For this is delight with a shared purpose, intimacy with a common goal, and companionship in a task that stretches beyond the boundaries of the couple themselves. As we rejoice with the lovers in the garden, we must not forget that there is work to be done. The garden needs gardening. God's world needs watchful care and careful work. Those who are single will serve in many fruitful ways possible only for the unattached. But for those who are married, this work will be done together as a couple."[28]

This is important because it beckons us to be outward in our marriages. These sacred relationships exist to bless the rest of God's creation, starting within and radiating out from our local churches. Couples are wise to ask themselves, "Are we serving and caring for God's world? Is service central to our marriage? Do we serve in unique ways because of our covenant relationship with each other?" Further, engaged couples would be wise to ask themselves, "Will we be able to uniquely serve God as a married couple?" Not only is service within the church body not the singles' responsibility, but married and single adults partnering together in ministry is a great way to bridge the great divide between the two. Unfortunately, some singles have been left to think that they should joyfully serve at church while married couples go on dates to work on their marriages.

The people of God not only have the privilege of serving one another uniquely depending on their marital status, but according to their gender.

Sam Andreades, author of *enGendered*, highlights that gender is not only a fundamental element of bearing the image of God, but also a means by which we serve one another. According to Andreades, gender cannot be simplified to biological differences alone, but essential differences that demonstrate God's creativity, wisdom, and beauty. Just as God is only understood in relationship, so gender is understood in relationship.

From the New Testament use of Genesis 2, Andreades highlights three grand asymmetries that summarize God's purposeful design: the asymmetry of origin, order, and intent. These asymmetries are different specialties in our posture toward one another and our behavior with one another—the unique ways we serve one another in close relationships. "The logic of asymmetry operates and the relationship is profoundly advanced, when partners differentiate: namely, the man by responsibility-assuming and secure-making and mission-defining, and the woman by promoting and strong-helping and rest-giving."[29] Leaning into these asymmetries results in emotional intimacy within marriage, but also ensures that needs within the local church are met as all men and women serve within their relationships.

MARRIAGE AS A MEANS OF GRACE TO THE CHURCH

Hellerman's conclusion that the biblical pattern for relationships places God and His family at the top of our interpersonal concerns helps us consider how marriage and church commitments coexist happily rather than compete. If Danylak is right that believers' supernatural bond is superior to that of blood or marriage, then we can rightly conceptualize marriage under the umbrella of the church. While marriages benefit from the protective umbrella of the church, the local church also benefits from God-oriented marriages in many ways.

Christopher Ash's premise in *Married for God* is that God intends for marriage to serve God and His people, primarily within the church. How does marriage serve the church? First, by providing a type of covenant-keeping relationship throughout life's storms. It testifies to the long-suffering love of God to keep those who belong to Him. In marriage, we stay committed to the one we promised to have and hold until death parts us. The church desperately needs the example of commitment. The temptation to run to a new body of believers is very real when we disagree with a decision or are held accountable for sin. We are inclined to run and hide rather than walk into conflict. To find a lifer in any church is a rare thing! Oh, but the beauty of commitment over the long haul is undeniable. From the depths of a committed marriage, we can honestly entreat a congregant to hang in there when he doesn't appreciate the music style, or the children's ministry curriculum is not her favorite, or someone hurt her feelings. Your voice has weight from within the bonds of commitment.

Strong marriages are evidence of the truth and power of the gospel. They are a type of relationship that Dever and Dunlop call "gospel-revealing," which point to "the very biblical idea of a sovereign God working in space and time to do what confounds the natural laws of our world."[30] A marriage that lasts sixty years in a culture that allows for no-fault divorce and likens a wife to a ball and chain certainly "confounds the natural laws of our world." Long haul, joy-filled, dying to self, grace-displaying marriages would be nearly nonexistent were it not for the power of the gospel. But when that kind of life-giving marriage does exist, it highlights God's power to transform and sustain. And that is a blessing not only to those within the church, but outside the church as well. Love through suffering, disappointment, and even monotony is inexplicable to those without faith. Our love in these adverse circumstances points to the love of the Father, and is our apologetic in a doubting world: "By this all people will know that you are my disciples, if you have love for one another" (John 13:35).

Marriages also provide stability within the church. Our church is necessarily a sending church as we enjoy university undergraduates and seminary students for a few years before they set out for the ends of the earth. The marriages in our church provide the stability and consistency within a church that rightfully has a revolving door. Those students need (and thankfully desire) the stability of these marriages, and the example of lifelong commitment fortifies them throughout their university years and gives them hope for a Christ-oriented marriage themselves. We regularly hear from young adults that they came to college hopeless about the possibility of a marriage that lasts (or is enjoyable). But worshiping, serving, and enjoying meals with married folk is life-giving to them. It turns their existing paradigm on its head, and they begin to entertain hope and take risks toward relationships. This is one of the great blessings of our ministry commitment to incorporate college students into home groups, rather than allowing them to splinter off from older adults and huddle up with other college students (as they do the other six days of the week!) They need us and we need them.

I have been blessed to watch some single men and women beautifully committed to hospitality within our body. More often, hospitality is exercised within the homes of married couples. It is hard to imagine a healthy church body without home-based hospitality radiating from loving marriages. Warm hospitality is often the rich environment for fellowship, discipleship, premarital counseling, Bible study, informal parent coaching, cooking lessons, prayer, etc. The list is endless. The church is strengthened as a result and hospitality is the starting point.

Marriage is also the context of sanctification and serves as the crucible in which two very different sinners are refined, propelling them toward Christlikeness. Gary Thomas's point in *Sacred Marriage* relates here—marriage is for the purpose of mutual holiness, perhaps even in the dreadful absence of happiness.[31] Discipleship results from a Godward marriage in which children are nurtured to grow in Christlikeness and discern what is pleasing to the Lord. A peaceful home dedicated to ministry is a blessing to the entire congregation, as discipleship happens around the dinner table and on the front porch.

Honest husbands and wives who wisely and cautiously share the struggles of marriage and the important place of forgiveness bless the whole church. Because a spouse may have daily opportunities to forgive a slight, this repetitive dying of self and asking/offering forgiveness is strengthening for believers as they navigate their own relationships.

As families surrender their lives to Christ—jointly in their husband/wife and parent/child relationships toward each other and in their choices as individuals within the family unit—they can operate under divine authority, bringing honor to God.[32] **—Tony Evans**

Last year we celebrated with friends honoring their fiftieth anniversary. They have raised a family, invested their most healthy decades to Africa, weathered disease and loss, and continue to serve and teach at church. They bless us all by their presence! Recently, they shared their life stories with our children over frozen yogurt. Our kids were riveted because these friends light up when they talk about God's faithfulness in bringing them together and using them to bring the gospel to those who hadn't heard. My kids need them. Our whole church needs them. When it just feels hard to keep our vows, we need to look to those who have doubted, or suffered, or felt alone in marriage. Walking through life with other couples reminds us of the beauty of promises kept. There is no quick road to the kind of comfort and depth of years. It's a long and bumpy road to be loved by one who knows all of you, and it's an immeasurable gift.

As Americans, we often hear criticism of the church, especially with regard to diversity. Marriage is instructive for us on this issue. Working on a university campus, I often hear dating couples declare, "We're so much alike!" After being married a short while, the declaration becomes, "We're so different!" Yet, in our reflective moments we also affirm, "It's so worth it!" The differences between a man and woman make the unity within the marriage profoundly beautiful. The unity and diversity displayed in marriage should strengthen and equip us to embrace the other, whether the difference be gender, marital status, race, political party, or schooling choices. Andreades[33] highlights the distinct differences in men and women. From his study on Genesis 1, he concludes that God made us different to increase intimacy as we each fulfill our unique callings within our relationships. As we embrace our differences, our intimacy deepens and our ministries to one another and within the church are enhanced. This is no easy task, though, as any effort toward intimacy requires a side-lining of self and promotion of the other. The challenge to achieve intimacy increases as the intensity in a relationship increases; marriage is a good example. When intimacy grows within a marriage, the relationship is strong and secure and the whole congregation benefits.

While loving, committed marriages benefit the greater church body, so also the church itself offers beautiful benefits to marriage.

CHURCH AS THE GRACE-FILLED CONTEXT FOR MARRIAGE

Even if we agree that our marriage might bring blessing to the church body, we may hesitate to intentionally plant our family within that context. Doing so brings accountability and responsibility that can mean death to our individuality and perceived freedom. It appears this hesitation to commit to a local body of believers is a reality for many American Christians. According to a 2016 Barna report on the state of the church, though 73 percent of Americans identify as Christians, only 31 percent make church a part of their lives. "The Christian church has been a cornerstone of American life for centuries, but much has changed in the last thirty years. Americans are attending church less, and more people are experiencing and practicing their faith outside of its four walls. Millennials in particular are coming of age at a time of great skepticism and cynicism toward institutions—particularly the church."[34]

Barna's conclusion is sobering. After spending twenty-five years interacting with Christian college students, my experience is consistent with Barna's findings. I have witnessed cynicism toward, not only church, but marriage as well.

It is rampant and can lead to bitterness and despair. For those of us married and firmly planted within a local church body, we have the great privilege of joyfully displaying God's divine intention for both institutions. Perhaps fear of marriage would dissipate if the model set before young adults was marriage under the protection and within the warm embrace of the church.

In God's wise plan, there is mutual benefit between the two divinely inaugurated institutions. The church is not only an umbrella institution, but the context in which a marriage flourishes, the fellowship in which it matures. Just by being a part of something bigger and longer lasting than itself, a marriage is kept in its place! Just by sitting side by side each Sunday, a couple who may be in the midst of disagreement is reminded that God's grand plan to glorify Himself and establish a kingdom of faithful followers includes marriage—their marriage. Their marriage is part of His grand plan to restore and redeem. Worshiping together brings perspective and lifts our eyes from mundane routines and stale relationships. In worship, husbands and wives together testify to God's beauty, holiness, and power and it orders their relationship, potentially bringing a forgiving heart, motivation for reconciliation, and a desire to serve the other. And when fractures do occur in marriage, there are couples who have weathered the same storm and can prayerfully walk alongside to help bring hope and healing.

Dever and Dunlop point out that the lasting and vitally important work of the church is relational. They offer strategies for building a culture of spiritually intentional relationships, where God's people are edified in their interactions. Even in the midst of forces that pull us away from church, the authors state, "For most of our people, a wise life will be one centered on the local church."[35] They tell pastors, "You will serve your people well if you help them center their lives around the focal point of God's plan: the local church."[36] Married lives centered on the local church—where church family factors into one's work, recreational, and relational decisions—fortifies the whole. There are positive ramifications not only for married individuals themselves, but for single adults. Even the youth will find that marriage provides an orienting force in a swirl of disorienting voices. Getting the marriage/church relationship right benefits the whole body.

Family life that revolves around the local church gives couples the weekly reminder that a growing relationship with God is not only their first priority, but the centerpiece of their marriage. In his book, Dever warns against building your church on anything but supernatural bonds. So much of his wisdom applies to marriage as well. A marriage that is built on hobbies or shared experience or even shared ministry is on shaky ground. All those commonalities are temporary. It's the gravitational pull of Christ as that center that can keep the constellations, the husband and wife, rightly related to Him and to one another. Christ-centered and, therefore, church-based marriage keeps this reality before our eyes.

The church, as our larger family, also helps us raise our children. With two teen girls in the house, I am keenly aware of the blessing of youth workers! When we adopted our four children, the church came around us in profound ways, by encouraging us to adopt, praying us through the process, sensitively caring for us when we returned home, helping to identify learning challenges and suggesting curriculum, and (perhaps most importantly) preparing their school-aged kids to welcome and love a new child trying to navigate life in a new culture. I am still indebted to those parents and wonder, "How could a couple raise children without the wise, experienced, sensitive, involved people of God on their team?"

Life within the church body shapes so many aspects of our married lives. Every day we have opportunities to choose what kind of life we want to share together. Because of the teaching we hear and the people we rub shoulders with, even our habits and how we spend our money and time are influenced. With our vacation time, do we dig ditches in Mexico or bask in the sun on the French Riviera? When we first married, we realized we had different ideas of proper spending and the priority of recreation. Somehow we missed that conversation during premarital counseling! In my family, weekends were for skiing or camping, definitely not for church workday. Our commitment to our local body, where we sat under the authoritative teaching of the Word helped us to come to agreement on our unique purpose as a family. Learning together helped us craft a common vision and answer the question, "What is our family going to be about?"

Recently a friend sent a group text and in passing mentioned that it had been five months since being on a date with her husband. Another friend responded, "We need to fix this—I'll have your kids so you can go out!" In our church, we are dependent on one another's help, meals, childcare, prayer, advice, and marriage accountability, sometimes all in the same week! We need each other, often for things much more serious than babysitting. Yet, helping one another with everyday things like date nights heightens our awareness of our interdependence and prepares us for the times when greater suffering requires cooperation and service. God knew this when He instructed us in Hebrews 10:24–25 to "Consider how to stir up one another to love and good works, not neglecting to meet together, as is the habit of some, but encouraging one another, and all the more as you see the Day drawing near." We live between the two comings of Christ. Until the Lord returns, we wait, encouraging each other on the happy and hard days. Our church family not only helps us manage during the wait, but reminds us that He will indeed come again.

Coming to the Communion table has always been emotional for me. I'm thankful for the opportunity to look into the eyes of the servers and hear them remind me, by name, that the body of Christ was broken for me and the blood of Christ was shed for me. I never feel more grateful for my salvation than at that monthly meeting. It feels profoundly communal as well. As I watch my brothers and sisters soberly ponder their forgiveness and redemption because of the body and blood of Christ, I am not only encouraged by their faithfulness and God's redemptive work in their lives, but I grow in love and affection for them as well. This sacred event is a profound opportunity for married couples to examine their hearts and seek harmony with each other before taking the Lord's Supper together. We are reminded that our inclusion in the family of God is dependent on the body and blood of Christ, and we are equally in need of the forgiveness and redemption that is ours in Christ. From that equal plane we can move to humbly seek forgiveness from one another.

Coming to the Lord's Supper with your spouse and your church family is fortifying for the soul; there is no substitution for the communal experience with the people of God.

Serving together in church ministry is an opportunity to be reminded that you are on the same team! When working together to corral fifteen toddlers or deliver a third-grade Bible lesson, we are affirmed in our corporate identity and purpose. It's refreshing to regularly see your spouse in ministry roles different from everyday life at home. Seeing a husband humbly serving the poor when his normal work is with executives only increases his respectability in his wife's eyes. More importantly, serving together keeps us from self-centeredness that hinders a church, harms an individual, and withers a marriage.

In an age when many relationships are digitally mediated and alternative selves are commonplace, we are tempted to prove we are Adam and Eve's sons and daughters by hiding from God and running from one another, especially when we have sinned. Our church family was stunned and sad to learn that a beloved couple was suffering from the ravages of broken promises. Infidelity threatened to destroy what God had built: a long-term marriage, beautiful family, and ministry involvement. Because of their commitment to the local church, we had the rare and profound experience of walking with them through the devastation, loss, and beautiful restoration. Here is the wife's testimony of the experience:

After 16 years and 316 days of marriage, it all came crashing down. All of a sudden the pronoun of "we" was full of pain and I found myself using the pronoun "I" in ways that were terrifying. However, I was quickly reminded by the body of Christ that it was not "I." The body of Christ wrapped around me and wrapped around my husband. They confronted my husband's sin and walked with him patiently on his path of repentance. They cried with me, they pointed me to truth when I could not see it, they took care of our children, they fed us, they prayed fervently. There are many battles in a tragedy like this. The battles are physically and emotionally exhausting. There were many times that it felt like it would be easier to leave and to escape, but I could see that any relief from the pain was only an illusion and would be short-lived. The temptation to isolate was intense, but I knew I needed people pointing me to Christ as I did not have the strength to keep my eyes fixed on Him. We (my husband and I) both realized that while our humanness was telling us to "go and escape the oppression," the Holy Spirit was showing us that we needed the church more than ever. The church was our Aaron and Hur holding us up when we had no strength. They joined us in the pit without condescension. They linked arms knowing their marriages were vulnerable. That is attractive. That is beautiful.

The Lord has done amazing work in our marriage, and we both believe that the major conduit of this grace is the church. Certainly, the process has had some bumps, but we both shudder to think where we would be today if we had run either separately or as a family. There are even moments that I think to myself what a privilege it has been to see personally how the Lord through His church transformed our marriage. That is a very strange thing to say when infidelity has devastated a marriage but I truly believe it. The painful path has redemption on the horizon as He is creating beauty from our ashes.

This restored marriage has brought blessing after blessing to our congregation. Leaders are encouraged, couples are inspired to maintain emotional intimacy, singles are encouraged to live honestly, men are recognizing their susceptibility and seeking accountability, women are pointed to God's Word, children have seen a man humbly apologize and a wife graciously forgive. Recently, a song came on the car radio about a marriage that disintegrated when a husband and wife lost one another in the craziness of parenting. In response, my teenage daughter turned off the radio (and fully aware of the situation mentioned above) said, "Mom, this can never happen to you and Daddy. I will babysit whenever you want so you can have fun together." We are already seeing beauty from ashes, and our church will never be the same.

And finally, church reminds us that marriage isn't intended to last forever. It foreshadows heavenly realities. We will live, not as married couples, but brothers and sisters, and we are preparing for that now. This is great motivation for us to enjoy and invest in the body of Christ, those with whom we will feast at the banquet table.

CONCLUSION

God in His great wisdom meets the needs of His people through supernatural fellowship, a deep friendship within the body of Christ. Marriage is one of the relationships within the church body, all of which exist to glorify God and bless His people. Marriage can devolve into an inward and isolated relational island. The church serves as a safeguard against that type of self-serving relationship. Even the marriage that provides the most satisfying friendship is designed to exist within a greater web of relationships as we all link arms and look outward for opportunities to love through serving.

We are to appreciate and devote ourselves to both marriage and our local church body, whether we personally are married or not. The church should help us love our spouse better, and our marriages should help us love and serve our churches better. In either pursuit, we are motivated and empowered by the truth of 1 John 4:19, that "we love because he first loved us." God the Father's amazing and holy love, Jesus the Son's sacrificial and perfect love, and the Holy Spirit's guiding and empowering love leads us to humble gratitude and a desire to love others for the sake of His glory.

THE CHURCH'S MISSION TO ENRICH AND RESTORE MARRIAGES

by John McGee

If you care about the church, you should care about marriage. Why? Churches have an enormous responsibility to reach the lost, disciple believers, and love their cities. One of the most effective ways to accomplish these responsibilities is to prepare, enrich, and restore marriages in their churches and surrounding community.

OPPORTUNITY FOR EVANGELISM

Churches that are successful in reaching nonbelievers understand that people enter through one of two doors. The first is the "front door," which is the Sunday morning service. The second is the "side door," which provides a way into the church through events and programs designed to help people with their different needs or stages in life.

Today many people may not be open to coming through the front door to church and attending a Sunday morning service. However, many will come to a church through the side door if it offered help with something they're looking for. One of the greatest needs most people would like to have met is a good marriage. Opportunities such as classes, retreats, and ministries for marriages can be an effective strategy to attract people to the church. As these couples come to the church for help or encouragement in their marriage, the church has an easy opportunity to share about the love of Christ and His offer of salvation. Churches historically have thought about evangelism in terms of preaching or crusades. Today, thinking in terms of meeting felt needs may be one of the most effective evangelism strategies for the church.

OPPORTUNITY FOR DISCIPLESHIP

Metaphorically, when a couple comes to a church for help with their marriage they should see a sign above the door saying, "Welcome to our marriage ministry." As they walk out, the sign above the door should read, "Thanks for coming to our discipleship ministry."

When a couple comes to the church looking for answers to the question, "How do I have a great relationship with my spouse?" they should leave knowing the answer is to have a great relationship with Jesus. The very things that characterize a good marriage, such as denial of self, forgiveness, commitment, and being others-focused, are also the characteristics of a disciple. Couples often come to the church looking for advice, thinking it will come in the form of tips and tricks. The church has a unique opportunity to leverage this openness to show people how full obedience to Christ is the best marriage "advice" they could ever receive.

OPPORTUNITY TO LOVE OUR CITIES

It has been well documented that kids who grow up in a home with a married mom and dad do better in school, commit fewer crimes, and have more upward mobility.[1] Increasing rates of all of these lead to "peace and prosperity" of a city (Jer. 29:7 NIV). To be sure, the issues of food, shelter, and jobs are important in any community and should be addressed by the people of God. However, one of the most effective ways to ensure the well-being of a community is to ensure the well-being of its children, its future leaders. One of the best ways to ensure the well-being of children is to ensure that the marriages in their city are thriving.

For churches, the idea of seeking the peace and prosperity of their cities has generally been focused on the physical needs of the community through things like food distribution and sometimes locating low-income housing. Increasingly, though, churches are also seeing a great opportunity in meeting the relational needs of their community. There are few issues that Christians should be more qualified to speak into than love and relationships. There are few issues a church could address that would have more of an impact on a community than to improve the marriages in it.

When churches raise the value of preparing, equipping, and restoring marriages, they have an opportunity to be a truly distinct group of people in their community.

The New Testament presents a call to live lives that are distinct from the rest of the world. In previous times Christians answered this call by caring for those that others were not caring for like the poor, sick, or orphans. Today Christians can be distinct by holding firm to and living out a high view of marriage. The common cultural view is that marriage should be personally beneficial and reciprocal. Conversely, a Christian view of marriage is one of self-sacrifice and unconditional commitment. This kind of love was modeled by Christ and is completely different than the pattern commonly found in society.

In John 13:34–35 shortly before the crucifixion, Jesus told His disciples that they were to follow His example and love each other the same way He had loved them. This command was so central to His teaching that when they loved each other this way, it would be the distinctive characteristic of His followers. In effect, Christ taught that someone could spot His followers by the way they loved one another. By implication, watching followers of Christ love each other would help observers understand the way Jesus loves the world.

What if one of the only ways our communities understood the love of God was by observing the marriages in your congregation? The reality is that they *are* observing. The question church leaders need to wrestle with is, "What are our communities seeing when they observe the marriages in our church?"

A PHILOSOPHICAL AFFIRMATION OF MARRIAGE FROM NATURAL LAW

by Sean McDowell

Not too long ago I was invited to speak at a prestigious Christian high school in southern California. Instead of giving a lecture, I decided to engage the students in conversation to see how well they could articulate a biblical view of sex and marriage. I began by offering a counterview of marriage and inviting the students to respond. After merely three minutes of near silence, one twelfth grade girl, who looked both frustrated and anxious, blurted out, "Dr. McDowell, I really want to be able to affirm a biblical view of marriage, but I have no idea how. Where do I start?"

In my experience and research, this young girl summed up how many Christians feel today—they want to affirm in both their words and actions the biblical view of marriage that has been held by the church for two thousand years, but simply do not know how. Despite the narrative that Christians are bigoted and hateful, I am convinced that most Christians, like this student, earnestly want to affirm natural marriage with kindness, love, and charity toward those who see the world differently. And yet many lack the training and confidence to do so.

This is the task before us. The goal of this chapter is to present a case for how we can affirm natural marriage without utilizing Scripture. This is not to downplay the importance of Scripture. Along with the rest of the contributors in this volume, I embrace biblical inerrancy. Nevertheless, our goal is not to reason from Scripture, but to reason *to* Scripture. The Bible teaches that marriage is an exclusive and lifelong commitment between one man and one woman (Gen. 2:24, Matt. 19:1–6). And yet, as we will see, a powerful case can also be made for affirming this view through cultural and philosophical analysis. Our goal is to show how Christians can do so in a reasonable manner without relying on a sacred text.

The reality is that many people have not heard good reasons to affirm natural marriage. Sure, marriage has been a huge topic of discussion over the past few decades. Unfortunately, ad hominem attacks, red herrings, appeals to emotion, sound bites, and personal pleading have characterized much of the cultural conversation. There has been little substantive discussion over the nature and extent of marriage. Here's the bottom line: It's not that the case for natural marriage has been made but found wanting—the case simply has not been made.[1] Few Christians have been trained to understand, articulate, and make the case for affirming natural marriage. And few non-Christians have really been challenged to consider this case either. This needs to change.

Yet, a reformation in the church and culture on issues of sex and marriage will require much more than simply advancing good arguments. Father Stephen Freeman, a priest in the Orthodox Church in America, offers an important qualification:

> Those manning the barricades describe themselves as "defending marriage." That is a deep inaccuracy: marriage, as an institution, was surrendered quite some time ago. Today's battles are not about marriage but simply about dividing the spoils of its destruction. It is too late to defend marriage. Rather than being defended, marriage needs to be taught and lived. The Church needs to be willing to become the place where that teaching occurs as well as the place that can sustain couples in the struggle required to live it. Fortunately, the spiritual inheritance of the Church has gifted it with all of the tools necessary for that task. It lacks only people who are willing to take up the struggle.[2]

Father Freeman is unquestionably correct that marriage needs to be foremost taught and lived. The church must be willing to take up the struggle to help people mend shattered marriages and to lovingly deal with the brokenness that naturally results.

And yet we must not surrender the biblical command to be "prepared to make a defense (*apologia*)" for what we believe and to do it with "gentleness and respect" (1 Peter 3:15 ESV). A holistic response to the sexual revolution will involve living and teaching a biblical view of sex and marriage, as Father Freeman notes, and offering an apologetic for the hope within. Being able to reasonably affirm natural marriage provides confidence for Christians and equips them with answers to lovingly engage their neighbors.

THE ROOT OF THE PROBLEM

Before examining the case for natural marriage, it will be helpful to briefly consider some of the deeper philosophical and cultural changes that have paved the way for its dissolution.[3] The *Obergefell v. Hodges* (2015) Supreme Court ruling, which legalized same-sex marriage in all fifty states, did not happen in a vacuum. In fact, as we will see, same-sex marriage flows naturally for a society that adopts the underlying assumptions of the sexual revolution. Simply put, same-sex marriage is a fruit of cultural change, not the root of it.[4] And same-sex marriage is only one of the more recent "fruits" that has emerged. There are many other examples of cultural "fruit" that result from these societal shifts, such as the widespread acceptance of divorce, cohabitation, abortion, pornography, the transgender debate, and more. Let's begin with the church.

THE FAILURE OF THE CHURCH

The purpose of this section is not to bash the church. I love the church, believe in the church, and have no interest in contributing to the negative view many seem to hold of the church.[5] But before we consider other factors for the demise of a biblical view of sex and marriage, we must have the fortitude to honestly address failures within our own community.

If our response to the continued growth of the sexual revolution is to critique our progressively secular culture without first addressing failures in our own community, then we will have failed our task as the church. It's time to take a long, hard look inward, admit our shortcomings, and ask forgiveness from God, from one another and, where appropriate, from those outside the church.

For instance, pornography use is a significant problem within the church. Yes, the practice of viewing pornography is higher outside the church, but it is still a serious issue within the church laity and leadership. For instance, one in five youth pastors and one in seven pastors use porn, which equals roughly

50,000 church leaders.[6] In my experience, few churches are willing to address the pornography epidemic with honesty, integrity, and consistency.

A similar inconsistency exists with divorce. While divorce for conservative Christians is not statistically as high as for the wider culture—and it is certainly not 50 percent—it is still a significant matter within the church.[7] Jesus spoke strongly against divorce (Matt. 19:1–6). So did Paul (1 Cor. 7). Explicitly, Jesus and Paul only permitted divorce and remarriage in cases of adultery and the death of a spouse. While there is theological debate within the church about whether there are further permissible circumstances for divorce,[8] the biblical record is clear—God hates divorce and intends marriage to last for a lifetime. And yet many Christians get divorced and pastors willingly remarry them with questionable biblical justification.

My point is not to needlessly condemn Christians who wrestle with pornography or who experience broken marriages. God's grace is there to restore all of us for our failures (1 John 1:9). But given the biblical view of sex and marriage we claim to embrace, and our pattern of speaking out publicly against various kinds of sexual immorality prevalent in our society, our inconsistency on these issues is not lost on the wider culture.

I once heard a Christian with same-sex attraction assert that the church's inconsistency on divorce and remarriage made him feel as though the church uniquely singles out gays. As he noted, the Bible condemns both divorce and same-sex sexual relationships. Yet many conservative churches allow divorced people to get remarried without adequate justification, but gays are never allowed to marry someone they love. Does our inconsistency send a mixed message and undermine our moral authority?

According to Matthew Lee Anderson, the question is not whether Christians will adopt "the spirit of the age." Rather, he says,

> It is a decision that has been already made. A "secular spirit" manifests every time an evangelical pastor remarries someone who was divorced without cause. It comes to the surface every time an evangelical couple pursues *in vitro fertilization*, and so undoes the "God-ordained link" between the reproductive organs and the union of the couple's love. Every time an evangelical couple "feels the Lord calling" them to surrogacy, there the "spirit of our age" appears.[9]

In other words, Christians are quick to condemn homosexual acts and transgender surgery, and yet often participate in procreative practices that deny the goodness of our bodily and sexual lives. They get a pass, says Anderson, because we want what they have to offer. He concludes with these sobering words:

> Caitlyn Jenner could *only* become a phenomenon in a world formed from countless choices by ordinary, faithful, well-intentioned people who failed to see that the body has for them the same malleability and plasticity in *other* areas that Caitlyn Jenner expressed about it in the realm of sex and gender. . . . We cannot authentically or authoritatively name and resist the "spirit of our age" until we recognize that before the world made Caitlyn Jenner, we made it.

In fairness, I do recognize (and so does Anderson) that there is debate within evangelical Christianity about the merits of IVF and surrogacy. Not all of these technologies involve donor eggs or sperm; sometimes they are used to help the husband and wife conceive or carry their own child. These issues are complex, and thoughtful Christians have written extensively on how to think biblically about reproductive technologies.[10] Yet we must be willing to ask ourselves the difficult questions about our own consistency (or lack thereof) and the degree to which we have contributed to the cultural demise of the biblical view of sex and marriage.

SECULARISM

Secularism has been the driving force behind much of the sexual revolution.[11] Although it is often presented as a natural evolutionary progression, the Western paradigm shift toward secularism was an intentional effort aimed at implementing secular ideals and overthrowing certain religious standards. In language reminiscent of the Star Wars franchise, sociologist Christian Smith explains:

> The rebel insurgency consisted of waves of networks of activists who were largely skeptical, freethinking, agnostic, atheist, or theologically liberal; who were well educated and socially located mainly in knowledge-production occupations; and who generally espoused materialism, naturalism, positivism, and the privatization or extinction of religion.[12]

The secularization theory is not that atheism, agnosticism, and other belief systems that do not affiliate with any religion will necessarily grow numerically. In fact, according to Pew Research, although increasing in the US and France, these groups will make up a declining percentage of the world's population by 2050.[13] Religion does not appear to be fading away.

Rather, the secularization thesis is that religion has lost its wider cultural influence in terms of the law, politics, entertainment, morality, the economy, and education. In essence, secularism relegates religion to the private realm of feeling and experience, and science to the public realm of knowledge.[14] According to philosopher Charles Taylor, in our secular age, belief in God is merely one option among many, and thus contestable.[15] Hence, there is no collective belief in a personal, authoritative God.

The implications of the secular shift are vast. In a secular age, moral authority shifts from an external source—namely God and His design for reality —to the society or individual. And it results in a radically different view of freedom. R. R. Reno explains:

> Moral relativism, closely related to multiculturalism, is promoted as a cognitive therapy that enhances freedom. Young people are taught to be nonjudgmental, to let others live as they please rather than according to an established moral or social script. Educators who adopt this approach don't see themselves as nihilists. On the contrary, they're proud of the moral purpose of their work, which is to ensure that the next generation has the freedom to define morality for itself. This moral purpose—serving the American dream of freedom—explains why moral relativists can be so judgmental, ferociously denouncing the view that marriage is the union of a man and a woman, for example, or that certain sexual acts are immoral. The moral relativist is defending freedom, the freedom to define moral truth for oneself.[16]

Rather than understanding freedom as serving the higher good (which involves aligning one's life with God and nature), moral relativists recognize freedom as having no moral constraints. The individual is the source of morality, which is subjective and situational. This truth is known through personal belief and through personal experience.[17] Supreme Court Justice Anthony Kennedy famously expressed this individualistic view in *Planned Parenthood v. Casey*: "At the heart of liberty is the right to define one's own concept of existence, of meaning, of the universe, and of the mystery of human life." As a result, students are encouraged to accept all lifestyles as equal and not to judge others. The only "sin" is to consider one's lifestyle superior to another.

If the individual is the source of moral truth, and God or nature does not bind us, then why oppose same-sex marriage? In fact, why oppose any sexual behavior that seemingly doesn't harm anyone? Why stay married if you're seemingly happier divorced? Why not cohabit before marriage? Why resist looking at pornography? Why choose life when an unexpected pregnancy occurs? If the self is the ultimate authority for moral values, and there is no deeper commitment to the communal good, then what objective basis is there for condemning any behavior? The answer is simple—there's none.

Throughout the history of the world, most cultures have not seen the world through such a radically individualistic framework. Rather, people had a familial and communal understanding of themselves. Core questions were not, "What makes me happy?" or "What feels right?" but "What is best for my community?" and "How do I bring honor to my family?" This shift is not insignificant, and is one core factor behind the demise of the biblical view of sex and marriage.

THE SHIFT IN WHAT IT MEANS TO BE HUMAN

Historically, the Western understanding of the human person was that we are fundamentally metaphysical creatures. This doesn't mean everyone in the history of Western civilization shared the same philosophical and religious convictions, but it was commonly held that the most important thing about humans is the metaphysical search for the meaning and purpose of life. For many, this was considered more fundamental to human identity than physical survival or sexual pleasure. In other words, what made human beings human was the struggle with the great, fundamental questions of life—Where did everything come from? Why is there something rather than nothing? Does God exist? What is right and wrong? What is knowledge?

People have wrestled with these questions to different degrees and in different ways. Greek philosophers, Christian theologians, and skeptical philosophers had their own ways of answering these questions, and yet they agreed that the proper orientation of life and society begins with this kind of central reflection on the meaning of reality itself. On this classic Western view of the human person, humans were viewed primarily as metaphysical beings.

Now Western civilization has undergone a complete reversal. Today, people are seen as fundamentally sexual beings, not religious or metaphysical ones. In fairness, every view of sexuality is rooted in metaphysical assumptions about the meaning of life and human identity. But the quest to wrestle with and answer the ultimate questions has been preempted by the conclusion now demanded of everyone upfront: our sexuality is who we are. This new anthropology is proclaimed with an evangelical fervor. Loyalty to sexual autonomy is demanded of everyone, easily as much as the loyalty once demanded by historic church teaching to restricting sexual behavior. In this new way of seeing things, religious belief is relegated to the realm of the personal and private, but sexual choices are enshrined and considered self-defining.

This shift, from seeing people as essentially metaphysical beings to seeing them as essentially sexual creatures, is the fertile ground in which the sexual revolution has flourished. In this brave new world, sexual choice takes precedence over any presumed purpose of sex and marriage.

The details of the story behind this cosmological shift go far beyond the scope of this chapter.[18] But mention of a few of the key figures, and their ideas, is necessary to understand how we have come to where we are today. Let's begin with naturalistic evolution, as propounded by Charles Darwin (1809–1882).

When Charles Darwin published *On the Origin of Species* (1859), religion was in decline in Western culture and science was booming. In the minds of many, Darwin's mechanism of natural selection secured the ultimate triumph of science over religion. According to Darwin's theory, it is nature that selects, not God. By promoting the unguided, blind, and material process of naturalistic evolution, Darwin challenged the idea that man is made in the image of God.[19] Thus, man is merely a complex animal, differing from other animals merely in degree, not kind. Sex, then, loses its transcendent meaning and serves merely to help propagate the species. Even though it took time to unfold, the implication is clear: sex, marriage, and gender have no fixed essences, but have evolved blindly through natural forces, and they may continue to evolve in the future. Sex is merely a physical, biological act.

Sigmund Freud (1856–1939) was also a key player in this cosmological shift. Fundamentally, he argued that sexual repression could account for nearly every psychological disorder, including belief in traditional religion. Sexual ethics grounded in Christianity were, Freud claimed, oppressive and should be abandoned for ethics based in reason and science. While his psychoanalysis has been largely discredited, his basic take on sexuality remains.

Margaret Sanger (1879–1966), founder of Planned Parenthood, went further. Not only should Christian sexual ethics be abandoned, she thought Christianity itself should be replaced with sexual alternatives to heaven and salvation. "Through sex," Sanger wrote, "mankind may attain the great spiritual illumination that will transform the world, which will light up the only path to earthly paradise."[20] For Sanger, birth control was the means of this new salvation, enabling sexual liberation without worry of pregnancy while ridding the world of those she considered to be the "unfit."

Perhaps most influential in this narrative was Alfred Kinsey (1984–1956). His book *Sexual Behavior in the Human Male* (also known as the Kinsey Report) convinced a culture already eager to rid itself of sexual norms that no such norms actually exist. Unencumbered from antiquated ideas about sexual morality, Kinsey thought we should instead look at how humans actually behaved sexually. If any person anywhere does something, it's normal and therefore acceptable. In other words, we can come up with prescriptive notions of how humans ought to behave from simply describing how they do behave.

There are many more figures we can cite who have contributed to this cosmological shift, as well as trends and events, but the point is clear. The traditional view of the human person as a metaphysical being has been replaced with the definition of a human as a sexual being.

And yet there is still much more to this story. Technological advances and legal changes have also fueled the demise of the biblical view of sex and marriage.

TECHNOLOGICAL AND LEGAL CHANGES

Marriage has traditionally been understood as a lifelong union involving a man and a woman that is oriented toward procreation. This is known as the conjugal view of marriage, and is based in the unique bodily and sexual complementarity couples can form.[21] In other words, marriage is: (1) procreative, (2) permanent, and (3) gendered. Through changes in technology and the law, however, each of these elements has been undercut.

Let's consider the first element, procreation. No technological advance has done more to separate sex from babies than the Pill.[22] Marriage used to be the natural outlet for sex and the nurturing of children that resulted from such activity. But the Pill changed this. Albert Mohler Jr. explains:

> So long as sex was predictably related to the potential of pregnancy, a huge biological check on sex outside of marriage functioned as a barrier to sexual immorality. Once that barrier was removed, sex and children became effectively separated and sex became redefined as an activity that did not have any necessary relation to the gift of children. It is impossible to exaggerate the importance of the separation of sex and babies from the moral equation.[23]

The second element of marriage, permanency, was undermined through the introduction of no-fault divorce, in which divorce is allowed for any reason. No-fault divorce was first enacted in Russia right after the Bolshevik Revolution of 1917, in order to completely revolutionize society at every level. And it existed in ancient Rome. Yet the first state in America to enact no-fault divorce was California. In 1969, then California Governor Ronald Reagan signed the first no-fault divorce law, and within fifteen years, nearly every state had followed suit. Marriage became a legal arrangement that someone could opt in and out of for whatever reason they wished.[24] Marriage became about being "in love," not fulfilling a lifelong commitment to one's spouse and children. As sociologist Brad Wilcox writes:

> In this new psychological approach to married life, one's primary obligation was not to one's family but to one's self; hence, marital success was defined not by successfully meeting obligations to one's spouse and children but by a strong sense of subjective happiness in marriage—usually to be found in and through an intense, emotional relationship with one's spouse.[25]

No-fault divorce enshrined a new model of marriage, what Wilcox calls "the soul-mate model," into law. By 1970, the divorce rate had skyrocketed. As Plato observed, the law is a moral teacher, shaping the boundaries of the cultural imagination. Since 1970, faith in the permanence of marriage has plummeted while the cohabitation rate has dramatically increased. This is particularly true of the nation's underclass.[26]

And finally, the Supreme Court ruling *Obergefell v. Hodges* (2015) officially undermined the gender requirement for marriage. After *Obergefell*, marriage essentially became a genderless institution. Marriage is no longer viewed as a

The church is subject to Christ to this extent. She is always to be known by these circumstances; that as her legislator, she receives laws from Christ; as her Lord, she receives commands from Him; as her guide, she follows Him. That religious society, therefore, which renounces the authority of Christ, and sets up for its own directness in matters of faith and morals, is not the church.[27] —**James Bean**

permanent, gendered institution focused on nurturing children. The structure of marriage is now negotiable. And the defining characteristic is no longer an objective bond between man and woman, but emotional intensity between two people.[28] This new view of marriage is known as the revisionist view.

WHAT IS MARRIAGE?

This brings us to the key question about marriage—What is it? Is marriage a human invention, or does marriage have an objective nature? In other words, is marriage like the board game Monopoly, or is it like gravity? These are the only options. Either marriage has a fixed, natural purpose (a "teleology," such as gravity) or it does not. If it does, then we re-describe it at our own peril. If not, then like the game of Monopoly, marriage is merely an invention that can be changed to suit our modern sensibilities, just as the board game has changed over time.[29] There are three reasons to believe marriage is more like gravity than Monopoly.

Reason #1: Marriage is a pre-political institution

First, marriage and family are pre-political institutions that logically precede the state. According to Greg Koukl, marriage is something we describe, not something we define:

> I don't think marriage has been defined by cultures. Rather, I think it has been described by them. The difference in terms is significant. If marriage is defined by culture, then it is merely a construction that culture is free to change when it desires. The definition may have been stable for millennia, yet it is still a convention and therefore subject to alteration. This is, in fact, the argument of those in favor of same-sex marriage.
>
> The truth is, it is not culture that constructs marriages or the families that marriages begin. Rather, it is the other way around: Marriage and family construct culture. As the building blocks of civilization, families are logically prior to society as the parts are prior to the whole. Bricks aren't the result of building because the building is made up of bricks. You must have the first before you can get the second.[30]

His point is that society consists of large groups of families. The family precedes society as its smaller parts, and so society does not define the family, but merely describes a reality that is already there. Laws are created to protect individual families (which naturally consist of one man and one woman and the children that result from their union), which are essential to the whole of society. Koukl concludes, "Marriage begins a family. Families are the building blocks of cultures. Families—and therefore marriages—are logically prior to culture."[31]

In summary, marriage is not an invention of the state. It is a pre-political institution that begins a family. And then multiple families provide the basis and motivation for the creation of the state. Families—as well as marriages—are logically prior to the state and thus are not an invention of the state.

This explains why we see marriage, understood as the public union of at least one man and woman, existing in nearly every culture throughout world history. Marriage is consistently found in societies because it addresses three universal human realities: (1) sex makes babies, (2) society needs babies, and (3) children ought to have a mother and a father.[32] Marriage is not an invention of the state, but an institution that has consistently emerged throughout history to meet the human need for child-rearing and societal stability.

But hasn't marriage changed over time? In his majority opinion for *Obergefell v. Hodges* (2015), Supreme Court Justice Anthony Kennedy points to examples such as the change in voluntary nature of marriage as well as laws against interracial marriage.[33] Others have noted that various cultures have embraced polygamy, supported arranged marriage, formalized marriages differently, and permitted concubines.

Yet as Justice Roberts observes, marriage as the union of a man and a woman has persisted across millennia and that no previous laws changed this "core" definition. Roberts notes, "Removing racial barriers to marriage therefore did not change what a marriage was any more than integrating schools changed what a school was."[34] In other words, even though cultures have varied on the formalities and particulars, there is near universal agreement that marriage involves at least one man and woman. According to Francis Beckwith, "A man may have more than one wife and still be married, but he may not have less than one wife and still be married."[35] With few exceptions, this is the historical norm.

This historical pattern does not prove that marriage is between a man and a woman, but it reveals that marriage is a pre-political institution that naturally arises given certain truths about human nature.

Reason #2: There is no natural right to same-sex marriage

The second reason marriage is more like gravity than Monopoly is the claim that same-sex couples have the right to get married, which is at the heart of the *Obergefell v. Hodges* (2015) Supreme Court ruling. The appeal to the right to marry someone of the same sex only makes sense if marriage is a natural kind of occurrence and same-sex unions qualify as a member of that kind. In other words, there must be an essence to same-sex marriage for people to have a right to it. If same-sex marriage does not exist ontologically, there can be no right to it. Thus, when same-sex marriage advocates claim a right to get married, they are assuming that marriage is a real thing, and that same-sex unions qualify.

Both sides seem to agree that marriage is a naturally existing thing (otherwise, why would same-sex marriage advocates appeal to the "right" to get married?). And so let's focus on the latter question: What justification is there to consider same-sex unions a natural kind?

First, it is critical to clarify what we mean by natural law. According to natural law, certain moral truths, which are commonly built into nature, are understood by human beings. Like gravity, these moral laws are discovered—not created—as part of the fabric of the universe. While Catholics have largely been responsible for articulating and defending natural law, the Lutheran Reformers also appealed to natural law in their understanding of marriage.[36]

So, how then do we recognize natural moral law? According to Aristotle:

> Every craft and every line of inquiry, and likewise every action and decision, seems to seek some good; that is why some people were right to describe the good as what everything seeks. But the ends [that are sought] appear to differ; some are activities, and others are products apart from the activities. Wherever there are ends apart from the actions, the products are by nature better than the activities.[37]

In other words, every object or action has an end for which it is aimed. If we want to understand the natural moral law, we need to uncover the end for which objects and actions are intended. If something is in accordance with its teleology, then it is good; if something deviates from its teleology, then it is bad. Thus, we can evaluate the moral status of certain behavior by considering the larger context of the activity's natural end.

The end of opposite-sex marriage is obvious: the uniting of two people comprehensively and the nurturing of children that naturally result from that union. There is a natural right to opposite-sex marriage because it fulfills the end of male and female gender complementarity. The natural right to marriage is as objective as the law of gravity.

But what about same-sex unions? Is homosexual behavior natural in the same way, and is there a natural right to same-sex marriage?[38] Professor Shannon Holzer is not convinced:

> If homosexuality is unnatural, then suggesting that same-sex couples have the natural right to marry is just as irrational as positing the right to ignore gravity or legislate square circles. According to natural moral law, homosexuality is unnatural. By unnatural, I mean that the acts performed by same-sex partners do not fulfill the purpose for which the body parts are intended. Moreover, not only are the body parts in question not used for their designated purpose, homosexual acts are often injurious to the body.[39]

Homosexual sex cannot perform the same kind of natural function that opposite-sex behavior does. It cannot bring comprehensive unity among partners and it is not procreative in kind. In reality, homosexual behavior violates the natural purpose of sex organs. Here is the bottom line: if homosexual behavior cannot fulfill the natural purpose of sex, then it is not part of natural law. And if it is not part of natural law, there cannot be any natural right to it.

The fact that proponents of same-sex marriage appeal to the right of same-sex couples to get married shows that they understand there is an essence to marriage. But what they have failed to demonstrate is that same-sex relationships are essentially the same as opposite-sex marriages.

Nevertheless, some have tried to identify the "essence" of marriage in criteria such as commitment. For instance, Jonathan Rauch claims, "If marriage has any meaning at all, it is that when you collapse from a stroke, there will be another person whose 'job' is to drop everything and come to your aid."[40] In other words, according to Rauch, marriage is about two people who are totally committed to each other.

Commitment may be a necessary component of marriage, as Rauch suggests. But it is not a sufficient component. After all, I am committed to my job. I am committed to being a good father to my two sons and daughter. I am committed to my friends. And I am personally committed as a follower of Jesus Christ—even more committed than I am as a husband. Commitment is not enough to distinguish marriage from other relationships.

And if commitment is what makes a marriage, why are two people necessary for marriage, as Rauch suggests? What about the trend of sologamy, marriage to oneself?[41] After all, that proves commitment! And what about polyamorous families?[42] Once procreation and the complementarity of genders are discarded as essential characteristics of marriage, there is no logical requirement for marriage to be defined as two people—regardless of how deep the commitment.

Is there any other criterion that captures the essence of marriage that is sufficient to include same-sex unions? What about feeling in love? Jonathan Rauch notes why this fails as a criterion for marriage as well:

> In the West, of course, love is a defining element. The notion of lifelong love is charming, if ambitious, and certainly love is a desirable element of marriage. In society's eyes, however, it cannot be the defining element. You may or may not love your husband, but the two of you are just as married either way. You may love your mistress, but that certainly doesn't make her your spouse. Love helps make sense of marriage emotionally, but it is not terribly important in making sense of marriage from the point of view of social policy.[43]

Reason #3: Males and females form a unique, complementary union

The third reason marriage is like gravity is because of the comprehensive union generated from the unique complementarity of a man and a woman. Every single biological function within the human body—whether respiration, digestion, the muscular system, and so on—can be performed entirely by an individual. But there is one exception in which male and female each has half and becomes united as a whole: procreation. Like a lock and a key that are designed for each other, the male and female collectively accomplish the coordinated end of reproduction. During sexual intercourse, the male and female together perform a biological function neither can perform alone. Reproduction is the only biological function that requires another person. J. Budziszewski explains,

> What this means is that among human beings the male and female sexual powers are radically incomplete and designed for each other. If we were speaking of respiration, it would be as though the man had the diaphragm, the woman the lungs, and they had to come together to take a single breath. If we were speaking of circulation, it would be as though the man had the atria, the woman the ventricles, and they had

to come together to make a single beat. Now it isn't like that with the respiratory or circulatory organs, but that is exactly how it is with the generative organs. The union of opposites is the only possible realization of their procreative potential; unless they come together as a single organism, as one flesh, procreation does not occur.[44]

Marriage commits the couple not only to a single sex act but also to ongoing sexual acts. They will continue to sexually express the cooperation and oneness they agreed to when they married. They are, in an actual sense, one in every way that is possible for them to be one.

In his dissenting opinion to the *Obergefell v. Hodges* (2015) Supreme Court ruling, Chief Justice John Roberts observed,

> This universal definition of marriage as the union of a man and a woman is no historical coincidence. Marriage did not come about as a result of a political movement, discovery, disease, war, religious doctrine, or any other moving force of world history—and certainly not as a result of a prehistoric decision to exclude gays and lesbians. It arose in the nature of things to meet a vital need: ensuring that children are conceived by a mother and father committed to raising them in the stable conditions of a lifelong relationship. The premises supporting this concept of marriage are so fundamental that they rarely require articulation. The human race must procreate to survive. Procreation occurs through sexual relations between a man and a woman. When sexual relations result in the conception of a child, that child's prospects are generally better if the mother and father stay together rather than going their separate ways. Therefore, for the good of children and society, sexual relations that can lead to procreation should occur only between a man and a woman committed to a lasting bond. Society has recognized that bond as marriage.[45]

Marriage connects the bodily union of man and woman with a union of life and purpose. Marriage is not just about having babies but raising them. Marriage orients and commits a married couple to each other and to any child they will produce. It is the only recognized institution that exists to rear children. There is no other human institution recognized as the proper place to form the next generation. Sherif Girgis, Ryan T. Anderson, and Robert P. George observe:

In short, marriage is ordered to family life because the act by which spouses make love also makes new life; one and the same act both seals a marriage and brings forth children. That is why marriage alone is the loving union of mind and body fulfilled by procreation—and rearing—of whole new human beings.[46]

In this vision of marriage, the connection between marriage and procreation is more than just incidental. The connection between marriage and procreation has been historically assumed in both legal and popular thinking about marriage in the United States.[47] In fact, the track record of the courts was "uninterrupted" in affirming the inherent connection between marriage and procreation until recently.[48] And observant Jews, Muslims, Hindus, Buddhists, and even many believers and nonbelievers, including some people who identify as gay, share this understanding of marriage as a conjugal union.[49]

Perhaps the most common objection to this conjugal view of marriage regards infertile couples. According to Jonathan Rauch, "The deeper problem, apparent right away, is the issue of sterile heterosexual couples . . .There are far more sterile heterosexual unions in America than homosexual ones."[50] But this objection is misplaced. Same-sex relationships cannot accurately be described as "sterile," because sterility implies a failure of the reproductive system to function toward its proper end.[51] An opposite sex couple can be sterile if they are unable to conceive, but a same-sex couple cannot be sterile because their bodies are not even oriented toward mutual procreation in the first place.

If the conjugal view of marriage is correct, excluding same-sex couples from marriage isn't an act of animus or hate any more than it would be to exclude college roommates or single sisters from marriage. They should be excluded because their relationship, though sincerely loving and affectionate, just isn't marriage. Marriage has a fixed nature, like gravity, and by definition is an institution that only a man and woman can enter into regardless of what the law proclaims.

CONCLUSION

Along with teaching and living biblical sexuality with integrity, we must be willing and ready to offer reasons for why we affirm natural marriage. While Scripture gives us sufficient reason to embrace natural marriage, we need to be prepared to offer public reasons as well. Regardless of the cultural demise of the biblical view of sex and marriage, Christians must have the kindness and fortitude to both live and appropriately proclaim the truth. Even if you think the politics of the issue are beyond repair, that's not the point. We are not commanded to guarantee a political result—we are commanded to be faithful in our lives and teaching and then to leave the results to God.

CONTINUING INSIGHT:

CHRISTIAN SUFFERING AND THE SAME-SEX ATTRACTED

by L. Eugene Burrus

I was seventeen that unforgettable night I sat in youth group. My youth pastor showed us a video addressing what we then called "homosexuality." My pulse started racing. The room didn't feel real. It was the closest I have ever come to a dissociative experience. I felt terrified. Over the course of an hourlong youth meeting, I was admitting to myself the truth I had refused to accept: I was same-sex attracted.

Secular humanists say that same-sex orientations are natural, morally neutral sexual variations. Some Christians say same-sex attraction (SSA) is a voluntary pursuit. Other Christians say SSA is merely an innocuous temptation. For me, same-sex attraction has been an experience of pain. This is not to say that willfully desiring same-sex intercourse is not an actual sin. Being same-sex attracted does bring about a unique set of temptations. My point, however, is to highlight an often overlooked facet of this experience. The pain of loneliness and the hope of happiness is what empowers same-sex marriage. SSA exacerbates loneliness when the romantic options available to the opposite-sex oriented seem inaccessible. The pain of loneliness and the absence of happiness cause so many same-sex attracted people (and other single people) in our churches to struggle deeply.

Listening to same-sex attracted Christians and being present in their pain is a good starting point. Being same-sex attracted is painful for at least seven reasons.

First, both same-sex intercourse and lusting after (or desiring) same-sex intercourse are sin. In discussing both adultery and "lustful intent" in the Sermon on the Mount, Jesus reminds us to guard against the affections of the heart, not just the body (Matt. 5:28 ESV). Same-sex sexual desires (or lusts) are not morally neutral—they are among the consequences of original sin (Gen. 3; Rom. 5:12). Paul identifies repentance as the primary balm for the sexual lusts of the heart and same-sex intercourse (Rom. 1:24–2:4). Kindly correcting others hardened by sin is a biblical duty (Rom. 2:4; Heb. 3:13). However, it's important we note—even more so, we feel—that sin leads to suffering, as well. Guilt, shame, STDs, and brains permanently changed by fantasy and porn may have long, lingering effects even after repentance. God's grace is good in this suffering, and God's people are at their best when they compassionately relieve the consequences of past and current sin in a believer's life.

Second, same-sex attraction is damage.[1] When I was in sixth grade I jammed my Game Boy in my pocket to stow it away during a baseball game. I was saddened to discover the screen totally damaged when I took it out of my pocket. It sat in my closet for years as I felt incompetent to fix something so sophisticated. I felt similarly about my same-sex attraction. I knew it wasn't what God designed or originally created, and I was desperate to fix it. So, as a teenager, I tried heterosexual porn and fantasy. However, I only found myself feeling guiltier and no less same-sex attracted. Later experiences in ministries addressing SSA brought great relief to the insecurities, fantasies, anxieties, porn use, and social stigma I felt, taking the sting out of the experience. For others, the damage remits with mixed results. Either way, God is glorified. God gets glory when damage heals in dramatic ways (Matt. 9:27–31). God also gets glory when scars and damage remain on this side of eternity and His extraordinary power shines in "jars of clay" (2 Cor. 4:7).

Third, same-sex attracted Christians suffer with the compounding impact of both sin and damage.[2] I find it helpful to distinguish between the overlapping yet distinct concepts of sin and damage. In one sense, men and women who describe themselves as "same-sex attracted" communicate their experience with a unique form of brokenness and suffering. We do well to listen to the specific challenges the same-sex attracted face. In another sense, the desires of the Spirit war with fleshly desires in moments of same-sex attraction (Gal. 5:17). As Christians with renewed minds (Rom. 12:2), we learn to distinguish between "same-sex temptation" and "same-sex lusting."[3] The Christian agonizes as she walks the fine line of minimizing her sinful lusting and falsely naming her suffering through temptation as sin. The consternation compounds so that she cries with Paul, "Who will deliver me from this body of death?" (Rom.

7:24 ESV). She groans and waits for both temptations and sinful capitulations to cease (Rom. 8:23).

More suffering arises, fourth, as our culture promises a "good life" contrary to God's good plan for our lives. The domesticated, monogamous version of same-sex marriage is the most potent and alluring. The appeal of a relationship breeds more anguish when loneliness is painful enough. I'm convinced this pursuit of happiness will ultimately disappoint, either in this life or the next when coming to terms with God's judgment.

I'm reminded by Augustine's and Thomas Aquinas's wisdom: our desires only find rest in the person who designed them. God's path to the good life is one of flourishing in righteousness (Ps. 1). His good plan, though, is not without suffering and pain (Rom. 8:17; 1 Peter 2:19–21). It is a path of steady joy, contentment, and goodness in that pain (James 1:2–4; 1 Peter 1:6–7). Some Christians with same-sex attractions can and do get married to members of the opposite sex. With good support from their Christian community, they can flourish. However, some find this path impractical for them or their potential spouses. Others desire a spouse but find themselves still waiting for one. So they pursue a chaste life, one that can also be filled with joy and love in godly community and friendships in the body of Christ. Given that the single life is lauded by Paul (1 Cor. 7:25–40), marriage should not be sought as the final remedy for same-sex attraction.

Importantly, flourishing—even in the eyes of positive psychologists—entails the resilience, meaning, and virtue made possible by suffering.[4] Neither the married nor unmarried are promised lives free of the pain of SSA; however, both have access to joy in its midst and virtue in its aftermath. The more our Christian communities (e.g., churches and institutions) and our brothers and sisters with SSA work together to mitigate the pain of same-sex attraction, the less attractive same-sex marriage will be.

Also, the American culture wars have resulted in friendly fire, a fifth cause of pain. Christians—both leaders and the average church member—in well-intended attempts to dissuade those in their influence from embracing progressive sexual ethics, have shamed those who experience a kind of brokenness they did not choose or pursue. We have internalized attitudes that stigmatize the same-sex attracted as the worst of sinners, somehow more debased than the rest of us. The same-sex attracted suffer as they internalize such attitudes and rhetoric. In the meanwhile, our more "respectable sins" go unnoticed and unaddressed.[5] Before I became more public about my attractions, I always listened carefully to others when they spoke of "those LGBT people." *If they think that about them,* I thought, *what would they think about me?* It's easy to attack people who seem like they are outside our church walls. It's easy to forget that all of our deceptive, sinful hearts require mercy and transforming grace (Jer. 17:9; 1 Tim. 1:14–16). We can reduce the suffering of the same-sex attracted if we speak kindly of them in every conversation.

Sixth, experiencing same-sex attraction is isolating. One large survey of adults aged 18–44, found 1.6 percent of women only or mostly attracted to the same-sex and 2.3 percent of men only or mostly attracted to the same-sex.[6] In addition to the stigma feared and experienced by many SSA Christians, there are so few who experience it and can encourage and guide others in the same boat. Cultivating a church culture where everyone confesses and acknowledges their sins and weaknesses mitigates this isolation and edifies Christ's entire body.[7]

Finally, many same-sex attracted Christians often feel misunderstood. While connotations abound for the term *same-sex attraction,* those who don't experience it may conjure up obscene imaginings when they hear the term. Not all men with SSA like fashion or pop culture. Not all women with SSA dress like men. Not all same-sex attracted men are promiscuous. If you know someone who experiences SSA, don't be afraid to ask them about their struggle. The same-sex attracted will feel most loved by the church when they are accepted and understood in their weaknesses.

CONCLUSION

My journey through the pain of same-sex attraction has been a roller coaster, but like most roller coaster rides, the worst drop is at the beginning. Some seasons have been particularly painful, but my life has still been the good life. The good life includes joy in suffering. The good life is becoming good in God's way. Moreover, I have realized that it will not be enough for the church to change to reduce my suffering. By God's grace, I too must change. My attitudes, prejudices, assumptions, and tolerances are not above correction from others and realignment with Scripture. Even more so, I have been preserved by Christ's embodied love, affection, and acceptance through fellow brothers and sisters—both in my local church and the universal church. In this and in many other ways, Jesus has kept me buoyant when I was sinking most deeply in sin and suffering.

WHY MARRIAGE: CELEBRATING THE CHRISTIAN VIEW

by Chris Brooks

"If a man and a woman marry in order to be companions on the journey to heaven, then their union will bring them great joy." —St. John Chrysostom

For over two millennia, Christians have argued for the beauty of marriage. The basic worldview of Christians has been that marriage is a gift from God that exists for the good of mankind and for the glory of God Himself. For much of that time, Western society has agreed with the church that marriage is a blessing with immeasurable benefits. The legal systems of Western nations reflect this agreement, featuring laws that were designed to protect both the beauty and benefits of marriage.

The Marriage Act of 1753 was the first statutory legislation in England and Wales to require a formal ceremony of marriage. Also known as Lord Hardwicke's Marriage Act, it stands as an example of the partnership between the state and the church to preserve the splendor and sacredness of marriage. Its intent was to guarantee that those who desired to marry would have the support of the church and the protections of the state in order to ensure that they had optimal opportunity for a successful life together. The act established, among other things, that twenty-one would be the legal age for marriage without parental consent. It also encouraged that all weddings take place within a local church before a clergyman. Its effect was positive and broad-reaching; by establishing strict guidelines that would end clandestine and forced marriages, the law virtually put a stop to these notorious abuses of marriage that were common throughout England. This is just one example of how the church's influence helped make marriage better for society.

The last five decades have seen a steady and dramatic reversal in the way our culture views the involvement of Christians in matters of matrimony. Sadly, Christians are no longer seen as value-adding in terms of our vision of "the good life"; rather we have been condemned as bad actors who espouse bigoted and harmful views on sexuality and marriage. Even worse, we have been denounced as hypocrites who condemn others for abusing an institution that we ourselves have mishandled and manipulated.

Intellectual honesty requires that we admit the hard fact that some of the criticisms levied our way are valid. Christians have often, even consistently, failed to live up to the virtues from Scripture that we champion. At times we have been culpable of driving a wedge between the church and society by a tone and disposition of condescension and even vitriol toward those who do not share our perspective.

If we are going to regain our influence and credibility within the culture surrounding the subject of marriage, we must reframe our argument on why we believe that marriage is good when done in a way that reflects God's wisdom and will. We have majored on proclaiming loudly what we are against. By creating countless theological statements and posting strident social media rants about what we're against, some Christians have left many people, both within and outside the church, confused about what we are for and why we believe that a biblical view of marriage is beautiful and beneficial for society.

The Bible encourages what many have called traditional marriage, and there are a number of positive reasons for this view. As we move beyond simplistic rhetoric, we will be able to shift our attention to the larger question of what is best for humanity to flourish. By recapturing both our passion for marriage and our ability to articulate its virtues with humility and respect, we will gain a hearing and opportunity to win the hearts and minds of those who have been deeply persuaded by a post-Christian narrative.

There are four prevailing benefits for marriage as God envisions it: companionship, children, covenant, and conversion. Each of these values satisfy the intimate longings of our hearts as well as the deepest questions of our minds. The more we embrace God's beautiful vision for marriage, the more we will experience the fulfillment of our emotional, physical, and spiritual needs. Let's take a moment to examine why each of these qualities help make the biblical view of marriage the most compatible with flourishing and the good life.

The first reason Scripture gives for why God blessed Adam and Eve with the gift of marriage is found in Genesis 2:18: "The LORD God said, 'it is not good for the man to be alone . . .'" (NIV). Marriage was designed by God to satisfy the need we each have for companionship. Simply put, we have been wired for relationship. In contradiction to this longing of the soul, our society is moving further and deeper toward isolationism. Loneliness and our sexual desires are not best fulfilled through a hookup culture. Our hearts crave for something more. This profound yearning for companionship is satisfied in an honest and truly intimate relationship with a husband or wife.

The second advantage Scripture gives for why God's view of marriage is right and wise is that it provides a purpose for our sexuality beyond simple self-gratification. The sexual revolution in America, through the hyper promotion of contraception and abortion, has successfully decoupled sex from marriage and procreation, leaving many broken lives in its wake. However, what this movement ignores, to its own peril, is the biological and societal need for children. Communities cannot thrive socially when birthrates are low and do not keep pace with the necessary replacement rate.

Even more significant, the sexual revolutionaries and their followers have created a culture that devalues children and is unwilling to acknowledge the tremendous worth they add to the lives of their parents and to society as a whole. The Christian view of marriage affirms the intrinsic value of all children and places them as a one of the central reasons for marriage itself. Consider the words of Malachi 2:15: "Did he not make them one, with a portion of the Spirit in their union? And what was the one God seeking? Godly offspring. So guard yourselves in your spirit, and let none of you be faithless to the wife of your youth" (ESV).

Further, the Christian view of marriage comes with the understanding that the union between a man and a woman is nothing less than a covenant and should be treated with the utmost respect and obligation. Marriage as God intended was not to be taken lightly; it was a way of ensuring the protection of women in a world that offered very few legal assurances. Baseless divorce was seen in Scripture as an offense against God as well as detrimental to the community because of the harm it inflicted on children and the spouse who was left.

God expresses His displeasure with the concept of divorce on demand and marital unfaithfulness in the fourth chapter of Malachi. He brings a charge against Israel and declares that He is unwilling to bless them. Israel then questions God's decision not to grant them His favor. The Lord's response to their questioning was, *You're asking why?* "Because the LORD was witness between you and the wife of your youth, to whom you have been faithless, though she is your companion and your wife by covenant" (Mal. 2:14 ESV). A society that refuses to embrace marriage as a sacred covenant will hardly honor any other agreement or relational obligations. Conversely, if we desire a more virtuous society, we should promote the Christian view of the covenant of marriage!

The fourth benefit of the Christian view of marriage is far more spiritual in nature and therefore may not be esteemed among those who hold to a secular view of the world. However, it is no less important and should not be minimized. Paul explains in Ephesians 5 that marriage—comprising one man and one woman—was given by God as symbolic of the union between Christ and His church. This is the splendor of marriage. As we celebrate our marriages and love each other with a covenant commitment, our strong marriages become attractive to a watching world, a world that is longing for companionship and for children to enjoy the blessing of being raised in a stable family. Ultimately, our marriages have evangelistic value and, if done right, will lead to the conversion of the souls of men and women. Humanity yearns for intimacy and is crying out for the redemption of broken relationships. We are desperately in need of true love and a covenant relationship that protects and heals. Our marriages provide the world with the clearest example of the unfailing love God has for those who accept Christ's offer of salvation.

It is time for Christians to recapture our voice in today's society! It is our joy to remind those in our culture that Christ came to give us life more abundantly and that marriage is one of the blessings He has given for us to experience the good life He has intended.

CHAPTER 15

MARRIAGE AND
THE MISSION OF GOD

by Mark S. Young and Priscilla R. Young

"Mission is what the Bible is all about."[1] Therefore, to the degree that the Bible says anything about marriage—and, indeed, it has much to say—it does so within the overarching story of God's mission in the world. Put another way, whatever the Bible might say about marriage, its teaching on the matter must be understood as somehow contributing to the accomplishment of God's mission in the world. Marriage is not an end in itself and must not be understood as such in order for it to be fully experienced in the way that God intended. Rather, marriage serves a greater purpose and contributes to the accomplishment of a greater end than just the union of a husband and a wife. In this chapter we will explore marriage and its purpose within the framework of the mission of God.

Perhaps a bit of personal context will help set the stage for this chapter. This writing project has given us the opportunity to summarize what we believe about marriage, how we've attempted to live out those beliefs, and what we've tried to communicate to young couples through the years. That summary includes the following key ideas:

- Our marriage is an entity that is greater than the sum of two individuals. God brings a couple together in marriage to accomplish something different than they could as individuals. Marriage isn't about just our own happiness and satisfaction, or even our own personal holiness, but about participating in the mission of God for the sake of others—those who don't yet know Christ and those who need models of how to follow Him wholeheartedly.

- Our marriage is to be grounded inwardly but focused outwardly. The strength of our marriage and integrity of our family life determine the strength and integrity of our ministry. How we relate to God, to each other, and to our children provides a foundation for how we relate to others.

- Partnership in marriage is the organizing principle of how we do life and participate in the mission of God together.

- As parents we want to create for our children a loving, thriving, and nurturing family environment as an integral part of participating in the mission of God.

- Every Christian marriage is part of God's mission, not just those in which one or both persons are engaged in so-called vocational ministry. Therefore, every believing couple should discuss and define their calling as an expression of their commitment to the mission of God.

These basic commitments have been shaped by our understanding of Scripture, family histories, life experiences, meaningful relationships, and intellectual pursuits. They are the fruit of a long obedience to Christ and a commitment to our marriage, a marriage that has gone through the struggles and successes, griefs and joys, moments of clarity and times of confusion that all couples experience as they strive to make their relationship work for the long haul.

The "mission of God" gives us language, theologically and hermeneutically, for the values, beliefs and desires we share as a married couple. It causes us to focus on the "why" question of marriage more than the "what" and the "how" questions that seem to dominate most Christian literature and teaching on the subject.

WHY THE "WHY" QUESTION MATTERS

The "what" question addresses the definition of marriage. What constitutes a legitimate marriage in God's eyes?[2] The "how" question looks at the roles and behaviors of husbands and wives. How should husbands and wives live together so that their marriage endures? Both the "what" and the "how" questions are important, and the believing community in much of the Western world has no shortage of resources addressing this question. However, without a clear answer to the "why" question, answers to the "what" and "how" questions lack a theological framework that might keep them from becoming little more than common wisdom, pop psychology, or simply "sanctified" norms of a particular culture's view of marriage. Christopher Ash illuminates the need to answer the "why" question.

> Before we delineate what marriage is, let alone address how we may be (and remain) well married or help others to do so, we must ask why the Creator instituted marriage at all, what we may call purpose with a capital "P." The definition of marriage follows theologically and logically from the purpose of marriage.[3]

Focusing on the mission of God turns our understanding of marriage inside out, finding its ultimate meaning and significance outside of itself. Although such a perspective sounds almost foolish in a culture that entices us to seek our own good at almost any cost, developing a sense of purpose in marriage that is focused on something bigger than one's own needs and desires is critical to nurture and sustain a healthy, satisfying marriage. Again, Ash's observations are particularly poignant.

> The couple working at the project of coupledom for its own sake face the problem that introspection is stifling and self-destructive. . . . Couple-centred marriage dissolves into self-centred marriage; and self-centred marriage is like a leech. Or, to put it another way, it is like a pair of parasites trying to feed off one another.[4]

If answering the "why" question is the best starting point in developing our understanding and practice of marriage, Christians must turn to Scripture to find that answer. Biblically and theologically the purpose of marriage is subsumed under the broader rubric of the purpose of God. Purpose is the language of mission; pursuing a mission means sustained effort to accomplish an established purpose. Therefore, we believe that a theology of marriage should be grounded in a consideration of its purpose in the broader mission of God.

Before we explore the importance of marriage in the outworking of God's mission, a brief overview of the meaning and significance of the phrase "the mission of God" is in order.

THE MISSION OF GOD

"The mission of God" (Latin: *missio Dei*) has become relatively common in academic, professional, and sermonic language. Even more common is the adjective "missional," which one can find attached to any number of things associated with the life and ministry of the believing community. Although widely used, "the mission of God," "*missio Dei*," and "missional" aren't often explored deeply enough to do justice to their scope and significance biblically, theologically, and missiologically. The casual way that these terms are popularly used isn't due to a lack of serious research and consideration in the academic arena.[5] Indeed, the mission of God has become an increasingly important theme in the fields of biblical hermeneutics, biblical theology, and systematic theology.

Seeing the Bible as a coherent story that unfolds from Genesis through Revelation is the starting point for developing the mission of God as a framework for biblical hermeneutics and, therefore, a theological framework for understanding marriage. But one quickly has to add that the Bible doesn't see itself as just *a* story. Rather, in a world of competing stories, it makes the audacious claim to be *the* story of God's engagement with all of human history and human destiny.

Standing back from the details of particular texts of the Bible and considering its overarching storyline, it becomes clear that out of His eternal love, God desires to be known and worshiped by all.[6] This desire isn't caused by any lack or need on God's part. Rather, God desires to be known and worshiped by all because only in Him can the fullness of life be found. The Bible narrates the story of how God makes His desire a reality. It describes how God's eternal desire becomes God's mission. From Genesis to Revelation the Bible describes how God acts in human history so that all may know and worship Him.[7]

The language of mission implies that God acts in human history with an end in mind. That end is revealed in the book of Revelation as "the new heaven and the new earth."[8] The Lord Himself describes the accomplishment of His mission with these words: "Behold, I am making all things new" (Rev. 21:5 ESV). John's vision of the new heaven and the new earth is remarkably similar to the original creation as described in Genesis. In both scenarios, God, the source of all life, is known and worshiped. He dwells on the earth in an unencumbered relationship with humanity, who lacks nothing. Evil, death, mourning, and pain are not present (Gen. 1–2 and Rev. 21:1–22:5; see also Isa. 65:17–25).

The accomplishment of God's mission is described as a restoration or re-creation. Noting the similarities between the beginning and the end of the biblical story, we must ask, "Why did God have to create a new heaven and a new earth?" What happened that deprived humanity of the good earth and the life that God had created for them in the beginning? The biblical story gives us an unambiguous answer to that question. Human rebellion against God separated humanity from the life that He created for them. Their rebellion introduced sin and death into the world. But not only did humanity suffer the consequences of their own rebellion, creation itself was degraded and became less than God intended it to be. The Bible paints no romantic picture of humanity after their rebellion against their Creator. Rather, it describes in sometimes cringe-inducing detail the tragic consequences of it.

And so God intervened to rescue humanity from the full penalty of their sin and begin the process of restoring creation. In order for God to accomplish His desire to be known and worshiped by all, He took the initiative to step toward humanity with justice, mercy, and grace. God's desire became God's mission of redemption. The rest of the story of the Bible narrates God's redemptive engagement in human history. John's vision of the new heavens and the new earth reveals that when God's mission is accomplished everything that's now wrong in the world will be made right, everything that's broken in the world will be made whole, and everything that's ugly in the world will be made beautiful.

The centerpiece of God's redemptive mission is the life, death, and resurrection of Jesus Christ. Through Him the penalty of sin is paid, death is defeated, and life is made new. Only when He returns will the mission of God be fully accomplished. The Cape Town Commitment, crafted for the Third Lausanne Congress on World Evangelization in Cape Town, South Africa, captures well the centrality of Christ in God's mission.

> The whole Bible reveals the mission of God to bring all things in heaven and earth into unity under Christ, reconciling them through the blood of the cross. In fulfilling his mission, God will transform the creation broken by sin and evil into the new creation in which there is no more sin or curse. God will fulfill his promise to Abraham to bless all nations on the earth, through the gospel of Jesus, the Messiah, the seed of Abraham. God will transform the fractured world of nations that are scattered under the judgment of God into the new humanity that will be redeemed by the blood of Christ from every tribe, nation, people and language,

and will be gathered to worship our God and Saviour. God will destroy the reign of death, corruption and violence when Christ returns to establish his eternal reign of life, justice and peace. Then God, Immanuel, will dwell with us, and the kingdom of the world will become the kingdom of our Lord and of his Christ and he shall reign forever and ever.[9]

One more critical dimension of the story of God's mission needs to be explored in order to build a theology of marriage grounded in the *missio Dei*. For reasons never fully explained in Scripture, God has chosen humans as the agents through whom He will execute His mission. Jesus Christ, fully divine and fully human, is the centerpiece of God's redemptive engagement with humanity. Ultimately, He is the one who accomplishes the mission. Yet humans throughout Scripture are given the privilege of participating in God's redemptive mission. Even in the beginning of the story (Gen.1:27; 2:15–25), we note that God created humans, male and female, as His agents through whom He would make himself known and exercise dominion over all creation. Later, when God creates for Himself a special people through Abram, His promise is that all peoples would be blessed through them (Gen. 12:1–3).

In the New Testament, Jesus commissions His disciples, and the Spirit empowers them to testify to the risen Christ to all nations, even to the ends of the earth (Matt. 28:18–20; Acts 1:8). And so it is only fitting that John's final vision of God's completed mission includes people from all nations coming to worship the one true God (Rev. 21:24–26). God's mission is universal because it is grounded in God's desire that all people know Him, experience life in its fullest in relationship with Him, and worship Him alone. God's people are the people of God's mission, the agents through whom all people may come to know him and experience His redemptive work.

Most of the Bible describes how God shapes His people for His mission. His involvement in their history, His redeeming acts, His protection, His instruction, His judgment, His blessing, His provision, His care and ultimately, the sending of His Son and the Holy Spirit—all this should be understood within the framework of how God shapes His people for mission. Throughout this chapter we will note how marriage plays a central role in our engagement in God's mission. Whatever the Bible has to say about marriage, it does so in order to shape God's people for participation in God's mission. That's where marriage finds its ultimate purpose, meaning, and significance.

But we're getting ahead of ourselves at this point. To sum up, we are arguing that the mission of God is a powerful paradigm that shapes the way we read the Bible, frames the way we think about God, and directs the way we live as His people. It provides an answer to the "why" question as we read the Bible and attempt to understand particular texts in relation to the whole story. The mission of God gives us a sense of the whole so that we can make sense of the parts, including those parts that speak about marriage.

In order to build a theological understanding of marriage in the framework of the mission of God, we will explore its relationship to three key themes in Scripture: the image of God, the people of God, and the mystery of God.

Love is a lifting no less than a swelling of the heart. What changes, what metamorphoses, transformations, purifications, glorification, this or that love must undergo ere it take its eternal place in the kingdom of heaven, through all its changes yet remaining, in its one essential root, the same, let the coming redemption reveal. The hope of all honest lovers will lead them to the vision. Only let them remember that love must dwell in the will as well as in the heart.[10] **—George MacDonald**

MARRIAGE AND THE IMAGE OF GOD

God establishes marriage as the union of male and female image bearers. Understanding the role marriage plays in the mission of God requires that we explore God's purpose in creating humans as His image. Once again, we return to the "why" question. Why did God create humans, male and female, as His image and bring them together as one flesh?

The biblical record never wonders *if* God created the heavens and the earth. Its first affirmation is simply, "In the beginning God created the heavens and the earth" (Gen. 1:1). From that point forward until the very end of the Bible, God is assumed to be, and worshiped as, the Creator.

Although every detail of the creation narrative demands our careful consideration, in this essay we focus on the question of God's purpose in creation. Why did God create humans, male and female, as His image and bring them together as one flesh?[11] The answer to that question guides us to a biblically grounded answer to the "why" question regarding marriage.

The creation of humans on the last day of God's creative activity indicates that the previous five days were designed to establish an environment within which humans could thrive. It is clear from the structure and content of the narrative that humans are given a unique place in the created order. Only they are created "as the image of God" and only they are given the mandate to fulfill what it means to be the image of God (Gen. 1:28; 2:15). In addition, although humans are identified alongside animals as a "living being" (*nefesh*), only humans are animated by the "breath of life" (*nešāmâ*) from the Creator (Gen. 2:7). This "breath of life" gives humans the capacity to enter into a unique spiritual relationship with God and to bear moral responsibility before him.[12]

Although the phrase "image of God" as used in Genesis 1:27–28 is sparsely attested elsewhere in Scripture,[13] it is the foundational concept for a theological understanding of humanity. Theologians and biblical scholars have interpreted the phrase and explored its meaning in several different directions.[14] Historically, systematic theologians have focused on trying to discern what makes humans different from the rest of the created order.[15] In recent years, however, biblical scholars have led the way in looking at the image of God from a more functional perspective. Comparing the widespread use of physical images in ancient Near Eastern cultures to represent the presence and rule of earthly kings or the gods those rulers served, Richard Middleton concludes,

> When the clues within the Genesis text are taken together with comparative studies of the Ancient Near East, they lead to what we call a functional—*or even missional*—interpretation of the image of God in Genesis 1:26–27. On this reading, the imago Dei designates *the royal office or calling of human beings as God's representatives and agents in the world*, granted authorized power to share in God's rule or administration of the earth's resources and creatures.[16] (emphases added)

In further support for the functional understanding of the phrase, Eugene Merrill believes that the Hebrew word *bᵉselem* frequently translated "in the image of God" ought to be translated "as the image of God." He notes,

> Man is not in the image of God, he is the image of God. The text speaks not of what man is like but of what man is to be and do. It is a *functional statement* and not one of essence. Just as images and statues

represented deities and kings in the Ancient Near East, so much so that they were virtually interchangeable, so man as the image of God was created *to represent God Himself* as the sovereign over all creation.[17] (emphases added)

As the image of God, humans are established on the earth to represent the divine person and act as agents of His sovereign rule. Thus, being the image of God gives humanity a mission. Humans are created to make God and His rule known throughout all creation. By our very nature and mandate we are an expression of God's desire to be known and worshiped by all. We are privileged to bring God's desire into reality. We are created for His mission.

The scope of humanity's mandate is universal. In Genesis 1:28 (NIV), God commissions His image bearers to "be fruitful and increase in number; fill the earth and subdue it." Humans, created male and female, are to reproduce after their kind and fill the earth with generations of image bearers. The phrase "fill the earth," brings to mind the stirring prophecies of Isaiah and Habukkuk that when God's mission is complete "the earth will be filled with the knowledge of the Lord."[18]

Now an answer to the "why" question begins to emerge. The very essence of being human is representing God so that He can be known and worshiped throughout all the earth. But not only are God's image bearers mandated to represent God's person, they are also commissioned to act as agents of God's rule. God's image bearers reveal His person and character as they act as agents of His sovereign rule.[19]

Men and woman are equal, we may say, in having been created by God. Both male and female are created in His image. They bear the divine stamp. They are equally called to obedience and responsibilities. Both Adam and Eve sinned and are equally guilty. Therefore both are equally the objects of God's grace.[20] **—Elisabeth Elliot**

Genesis 1:28 and 2:15 provide four verbs that describe how image bearers are to exercise their role as agents of God's rule over creation. Only humans, as the image of God, are given this privilege. The four verbs can be translated "subdue" and "rule" (Gen 1:28 NIV), "work" and "keep" (Gen. 2:15 ESV). "Subdue" and "rule" stress authority; "work" and "keep" emphasize nurture. Although biblical scholars have demonstrated that there are various ways of translating and interpreting these verbs, whatever general picture emerges must be consistent with the way the Bible describes God's sovereign rule. Humans fulfill their mandate as God's image at His pleasure. Therefore, the way they subdue, rule, serve, and keep must reveal His character, His manner of exercising dominion, and His purpose in doing so.

The sovereign rule of God over creation is often described with the language of kingship. Psalm 47:7 states, "For God is the King of all the earth," and Psalm 95:3 (ESV) adds, "For the LORD is a great God, and a great King above all gods." The New Testament uses kingdom language frequently in relationship to Jesus' life, death, resurrection, and ascension. Jesus speaks of "my kingdom" when questioned by Pilate. And when Pilate infers that Jesus has made a claim to kingship, Jesus does not disabuse him of that understanding (John 18:36–37).

God's rule as revealed throughout Scripture is constant, consistent with His character, grounded in His love and seeking the benefit of those He rules. God rules as a servant not a tyrant. He does not abuse or take advantage of those He rules. He does not greedily consume or callously waste the resources over which He rules. He protects the most vulnerable and ensures that all enjoy the benefits of His reign. God's rule creates good for those under His care, perpetuates the goodness of creation from generation to generation, and maximizes that goodness for the benefit of all.[21]

The language of the mandate to reign as God's representatives in the garden of Eden (2:15) reinforces the idea of dominion as service. Subjugation and authority (1:28) are clarified by the language of service and protection. The NIV translates the two verbs of the mandate in 2:15 as "work it" and "take care of it." Other translation options include "to care for it and to maintain it" (NET) and "to tend and watch over it" (NLT).

Interestingly, marriage, as the union of male and female image bearers, emerges in the creation narrative after God gives Adam the mandate to serve and take care of the garden (2:15) and to obey Him in all things (vv. 16–17).[22] What follows in the text is God's assessment that Adam cannot fulfill this mandate on his own (v. 18). Rather than simply a sentimental statement about the human need for companionship, God's assessment, "It is not good that the man should be alone" (ESV), makes it clear that in order for Adam to represent God's person and exercise God's rule throughout all creation someone else is needed. As God parades before Adam the animals and birds of His good creation, no suitable solution is found (vv. 19–20). So God creates a blessed alliance[23] of woman and man to fulfill the privilege and mandate of being God's image bearers (vv. 21–22). Man's delight in the woman is unmistakable (v. 23). The language of the text clearly indicates that the two image bearers will bring joy and satisfaction to each other that could not be found with any other creature.

Although the temptation is strong to interpret this passage through the lens of the centuries of romantic poetry, song, drama, and literature based on it, that temptation must be held in check. Furthermore, as North Americans we must resist the instinct to read this passage from a highly individualistic and psychologized perspective. This passage isn't just about the joy and satisfaction of two individuals and it is not to be read as simply God's solution for human loneliness.[24] It must be read within the broader, transcendent purpose of God's creation of humans, male and female, as the image of God. Commenting on this passage, Christopher Ash notes,

> Yet we must not conclude that the final goal of this delightful and intimate companionship is to be found in the delight, the intimacy or the companionship. This is delight with a shared purpose, intimacy with a common goal, and companionship in a task beyond the boundaries of the couple themselves. As we rejoice with the lovers in the garden, we must not forget that there is work to be done. The garden still needs tilling and watching. The purpose of the man-woman match is not their mutual delight, wonderful though that is. It is that the woman should be just the helper the man needs, so that together they may serve and watch.[25]

As the male and female image bearers come together in marital union, the possibility of an earth full of image bearers becomes a reality. This union is established as the context of procreation and the establishment of families. Procreation is not the sole purpose of sexual union in marriage, but we must never underestimate its importance. Sexual union in marriage provides relational intimacy unavailable in any other human relationship, and it strengthens the bonds of commitment between husband and wife. In order for humans to fill the earth with the image of God and to exercise His beneficent care over all creation, they must thrive and multiply.

Marriage as the union of image bearers is established by God to make Himself known and to exercise His rule throughout all the earth. Through marriage humans can fill the earth with image bearers who will bring order and nurture creation. As families bring order and nurture the earth, God will cause it to bring forth more of the goodness of creation so that His image bearers will thrive. Through their faithful and beneficent care of the earth families can be fruitful, multiplying and filling the earth with God's image bearers so that He may be known and worshiped. This vision of marriage answers the "why" question in the framework of the mission of God.

Some may argue that the first couple's rebellion eradicated the image of God in humans and nullified the mandate given to them. Although the consequences of human rebellion are tragic and severe, including damage done to the way image bearers experience their marriage union, the biblical record affirms that being the image of God and fulfilling their mandate remains their privilege (Gen. 5:1–3) after the fall. When Eve bears Adam's son and declares, "I have created a man just as the LORD did!" (Gen. 4:1b NET),[26] she demonstrates that the privilege of living out the mandate to fill the earth with image bearers remains possible. Additionally, as the descendants of Adam develop essential features of human civilization and culture—farming, animal husbandry, city building, making of tools and music—they demonstrate how it will be possible to fulfill the mandate to live as God's agents of rule in creation even while suffering the tragic consequences of human depravity (4:19–22). They cause the earth to bring forth good and allow the image bearers to continue to multiply. The conclusion of this description of the lives of Adam and Eve's children is the stunning affirmation, "At that time people began to call upon the name of the LORD" (4:26b ESV).

Expressing His will to be known and worshiped by all, again and again in the biblical record God responds to human rebellion with judgment, mercy, and grace. He judges sin, demonstrates mercy to those who have sinned, and extends grace to rescue and restore them to a semblance of the life experienced in the garden. In the early chapters of Genesis this pattern is evident in God's dealings with Adam, Eve, Cain, and Noah. It establishes the pattern of redemption that will characterize God's engagement with humanity in the fulfillment of His mission. God takes the initiative and humanity is given the opportunity to respond.

MARRIAGE AND THE PEOPLE OF GOD

God's promise to make Abram into an expansive, blessed, and honored nation (Gen. 12:1–3) is the next key theme in the biblical record for developing a theology of marriage framed by the mission of God. It is tempting to think that

God's selection of Abram and His promise to bless his descendants is an act of exclusion. However, God did not create one people at the expense of all others. The election of one man and his descendants as God's special people was for the purpose of realizing His desire to be known and worshiped by all peoples.[27]

God's promise to Abram that the number of his descendants will be as vast as the stars of the sky (Gen. 15:5) is reminiscent of the mandate given to the first humans to "fill the earth" with His image. God's chosen people will be the vehicle through whom He will make Himself known to all people. God's chosen people are the people of God's mission.

The bulk of the biblical record describes how God shapes His people to be the people of His mission. Everything God does to, with, and for His people enables them to fulfill God's desire to be known and worshiped by all. God's promises to make Abraham's descendants a great nation, to bless them and to make their name great means that they will be a prosperous and powerful nation whose way of life and God will be the envy of the nations. The contribution of stable marriages and families in fulfilling the mission of God through His chosen people cannot be underestimated. The equation seems relatively simple. God will bless His people as they remain faithful to worship Him alone and obey His instruction. As families thrive on the land allotted to them, the nation will be strengthened and prosper. Israel will become the envy of the nations around it. More importantly, Israel's God will be known and feared among the nations. Thus, the mission of God through His people will be realized.

In the Law, God gives Abraham's descendants a charter to guide the founding of the nation and instruct them how they are to demonstrate the character and power of their God in every area of life.[28] Much of that instruction involves marriage and the family. Although some of the marriage and family practices in the customs and laws of the Old Testament seem culturally distant, even bizarre when compared to our own, when taken as a whole and interpreted in their cultural setting, we can discern that they were given to build strong family units that would perpetuate faithfulness to God, create social stability, generate prosperity and, ultimately, make Him known among the nations.[29]

Obedience to the laws related to marriage and the family was more than just a matter of one's own blessing, it was a matter of national importance. The establishment and nurture of stable families played a critical role in Israel's national stability and security. Just as marriage in the garden of Eden served a greater purpose than the satisfaction of a single couple, so sustaining stable marriages and families served a much greater purpose in Israel than just the blessing of any one single family unit. Israel could not thrive and prosper if the fabric of the nation unraveled because of unstable marriages and families.

Faithful, stable, and thriving families played a key role in Israel's ability to fulfill God's mission as His chosen people. Their role included the following responsibilities:

- worship the One True God and obey His law
- perpetuate the knowledge and worship of God generationally through the instruction of children in the ways of the LORD
- preserve possession of the land through the provision of heirs
- regulate sexual behavior in order to maintain social stability
- provide for, protect, and honor women and children
- generate wealth for the benefit of all, especially the weak and vulnerable
- defend the land and support the king to sustain the nation against her enemies

As families fulfilled these obligations they lived out their mandate as image bearers to reveal the character of God and exercise His rule over creation. The prosperity and stability of the nation would provoke the nations to marvel at the character and strength of Israel's God and His reputation would spread throughout the world (Deut. 4:5–8). In this way, marriage played a key role in the execution of God's mission.

Behaviors that threatened the integrity of the family were deemed to put the stability of the entire nation at risk. Therefore, penalties for breaking laws intended to protect the family were severe. Idolatry, adultery, and rebellion against parental authority each warranted the death penalty because each threatened the family, the social unit upon which the stability of the nation was built.[30] The dissolution of a marriage and the breakdown of a family weren't just personal matters; they mattered to the nation as a whole.

> Adultery was a crime against God inasmuch as it was a crime against the relationship between God and his people, Israel; and it was a crime against that relationship inasmuch as it was an attack upon the social basis on which it rested. We have argued that any attack on the stability of the household unit was a potential threat to the nation's relationship with God.[31]

Marriage provides a powerful metaphor of the relationship between God and His people. God takes the initiative to establish and bless the nation and His people are called upon to respond to Him with obedience and worship. When the people of God do not respond to God's presence and blessing in their lives, they abandon their responsibility and threaten their privilege to live as the people of His mission. The abandonment of one's God, idolatry, is described with the language of adultery by God's prophets. Using the language of adultery to describe the sin of idolatry validates the vital importance of marriage in the life of God's people. A faithful marriage poignantly communicates the nature of God's relationship with His people.

All other relational claims must yield to the primacy of marital union. It requires an exclusive, lifelong bonding of one man with one woman in one life fully shared. It erects barriers around the man and woman, and it destroys all barriers between the man and the woman. God so joins them together that they belong fully to one another, and to one another only. This is the vision of human marriage which provides the coherent network of meanings necessary for an understanding of the covenanted nation's relationship with Yahweh, as the story unfolds in the rest of Scripture.[32]

Sadly, Israel's struggle with idolatry permeates their history. With unflinching honesty, the biblical authors portray the tragedy of their unfaithfulness. Israel's disobedience destroyed their enjoyment of the blessing God had promised and put the nation at risk. But that wasn't the only tragic outcome of their unfaithfulness. When Israel refused to worship YHWH as the One True God, they hid Him from the nations. How could all the peoples of the earth know God if God's people failed to worship Him alone? Israel suffered the awful consequences of their unfaithfulness but they were not the only ones who experienced loss. The same is true with unfaithfulness in marriage. The damaging consequences of the unfaithfulness of a spouse and the dissolution of a marriage extend far beyond the experience of the couple.

In spite of their betrayal, God's unfailing love for His people is steadfast. He judges them harshly because He loves them. In the midst of their rebellion He continues to take the initiative to draw them back to Himself. Ultimately He superintends the shameful defeat of the nation, the destruction of the temple, and the exile of His people at the hands of brutal rulers. These severe actions create an opportunity for Israel to respond and return to Him. And in the midst of their defeat and expulsion from the land, He promises them a future relationship with Himself that will surpass anything they have known before.

It is not surprising, therefore, that God uses the marriage of the prophet

Hosea and his unfaithful wife, Gomer, to mirror the relationship between God and His people. Gomer chased after other lovers and was judged harshly for her sin. In like manner Israel chased after false gods and was expelled from the land in shame. Yet God commanded Hosea to take Gomer back and restore his relationship with her (Hosea 3:1).[33] So it was with Israel and her God. God restored His people to the land from their exile in Babylon. Even though God's mission was compromised by Israel's rebellion, it was not annulled. The prophetic vision is certain. God will ultimately restore His people and reestablish His relationship with them so that they will be a light to the nations (Isa. 9:2; 41:2–6).

The central role that marriage played in the life of God's people in the Old Testament is instructive for a theology of marriage framed by the mission of God. First, just as the purpose for which God established and shaped His people was to bless all peoples, so the purpose of marriage must be located beyond the couple themselves in the lives of others. Second, stable marriages and families were the foundation of Israel's prosperity and stability as a nation. As marriages and families prospered, the nation prospered. As the nation prospered, the surrounding nations could see the character and power of Israel's God. Thus, stable and thriving marriages played a central role in making God known among the nations. Third, a faithful and loving marriage is the dominant metaphor in the Old Testament for God's relationship with Israel. This relational pattern—God's loving initiative and Israel's response—forms the centerpiece of the metaphor. The power of marriage to communicate the nature of God's relationship with His people continues into the New Testament.

MARRIAGE AND THE MYSTERY OF GOD

The final foundational theme for building a theology of marriage in the framework of God's mission is the central role that marriage plays in revealing the mystery of Christ and the church.[34] Although the marriage metaphor is found in the Gospels, primarily in parables that reveal the coming of Messiah to establish His kingdom (see Matt. 22:1–14), the plainest use of the image for this purpose is found in Revelation 21:2–3 (NIV), the apostle John's vision of the completion of God's mission in the new heaven and the new earth.

I saw the Holy City, the new Jerusalem, coming down out of heaven from God, prepared as a bride beautifully dressed for her husband. And I heard a loud voice from the throne saying, "Look! God's dwelling place is now among the people, and he will dwell with them. They will be his people, and God himself will be with them and be their God."

The apostle Paul uses marriage as a metaphor for the relationship between Christ and the church in one of his most extensive passages on the topic, Ephesians 5:22–32. His instruction about marriage ends with a quotation of Genesis 2:24, the establishment of marriage as the one flesh union of image bearers as the primary human relationship. Although commentary on the interpretation and application of Ephesians 5:22–30 has generated enough print to fill thousands of pages and enough heat to cause far too many controversies and church splits, the flow of the passage indicates that Paul's insight into the purpose of marriage in verses 31 and 32 should be considered his primary point.

"For this reason a man will leave his father and mother and be united to his wife, and the two will become one flesh." This is a profound mystery—but I am talking about Christ and the church. (NIV)

The particular behaviors and attitudes to be adopted by husbands and wives in verses 22–30 serve a far greater purpose than simply creating a satisfying marriage. A marriage characterized by these behaviors creates something glorious and mysterious—a compelling picture of the relationship between a loving Christ and a responding church. Throughout Scripture God takes the initiative to make Himself known and gives humanity an opportunity to respond to Him in worship. This pattern of initiative and response is clearly seen in the instructions Paul gives both the husband and wife in verses 22–30. In making verses 31–32 the climax of his teaching on marriage Paul stays true to his calling and mission as an apostle, the proclamation of the gospel of Jesus Christ. We dare not interpret any of Paul's writing apart from that call. Ortlund notes,

Paul's foremost interest does not lie in human marriage as such, for its own sake. He is not a family therapist; he is a steward of the mysteries of God (1 Cor. 4:1). Human marriage claims his personal attention primarily because it speaks of Christ and the church, and he longs for married people reading his letter to honour Christ in their marriages. Christ did not send Paul to baptize, or to teach "marriage skills," but to preach the gospel.[35]

And what is this mystery that marriage so poignantly reveals? Nothing other than the gospel, the good news of how God's desire to be known and worshiped leads ultimately to the sacrificial love of Christ on the cross redeeming humanity from the curse of sin, the power of evil, and the grip of death. Just as God, in the creation of image bearers and in the establishment of His chosen people, took the initiative to make Himself known so that humanity could respond to Him in worship, so in Christ God has taken the initiative to reveal Himself in a way never before seen (Heb.1:1) so that humanity can believe and worship. Again, Ortlund sums it up beautifully.

> The net message of the text [Eph. 5:32], then, is that a Christian marriage faithful to its "one flesh" meaning incarnates the ultimate reality of sacrificial divine love in Christ wedded to the joyful human devotion in the church. Paul's theological vision of the overtures of divine love finding a response in human hearts instructs believers as to how the Christian home reproduces in miniature form the beauty shared between the Bridegroom and his Bride. A Christian husband loves his wife by offering a lifetime of daily sacrifices, so that she might become ever more radiant as a woman of God. She, for her part, affirms and responds to her husband's Christlike initiatives. Through it all, the mystery of the gospel is unveiled.[36]

And so, marriage finds its "why," its sense of purpose, as a microcosm of the purpose of God's image bearers and the purpose of God's people—to participate in the mission of God by making Him known so that He may be worshiped by all.

> From the beginning, the institution of human marriage embodied a message of divine romance pursuing a human response. As God called Hosea to the tragedy of a broken marriage to symbolize Yahweh's love for wayward Israel, so the gospel calls a Christian husband and wife to "one flesh" authenticity to symbolize Christ's love for his devoted church. And Paul is showing that these correspondences are not coincidental or whimsical but intrinsic to reality. Human marriage has always been only penultimate. No marriage is or can be a final experience. *And every human marriage is truest to itself when it points beyond itself, representing something of Christ and the church in their perfect union.*[37] (emphasis ours)

Indeed, marriage must never be viewed as an end in itself. Its purpose is found in the pursuit of God's transcendent mission. A couple finds their greatest satisfaction and joy as they pursue God's mission together as husband and wife. Marital intimacy provides a depth of delight that can be found in no other relationship. But the pursuit of that intimacy as an end in itself undermines the very purpose of the marriage union.

> The love of a husband for his wife is to be a visible image of the love of the Lord for his people, and this relationship is so central to reality that the project of imaging it is seen as the primary purpose of marriage. The paradox is that when we begin to think of the marriage relationship as an end in itself, or even as an end that serves the public signification of the love of God, we slip very easily into a privatisation of love that contradicts the open, outward-looking and gracious character of God's covenant love. By this I mean that the covenant love of the Creator for his people is a love that has the world, the whole created order, as its proper object; in loving his people with a jealous love he has in mind that people should be a light to the nations and that through them blessing should spread more and more widely. But the moment we begin unquestioningly to treat marital intimacy as the primary goal of marriage we contradict this outward-looking focus and the project becomes self-defeating.[38]

CONCLUSION

We began this chapter with the startling statement, "Mission is what the Bible is all about," arguing that the story of the Bible is the story of God's mission, the story of how God fulfills His desire to be known and worshiped by all. Perhaps we should conclude this essay with an equally startling affirmation: "Mission is what marriage is to be all about." For marriage finds its ultimate purpose outside of itself in the central role it plays in the mission of God. No other human relationship reveals the pattern of God's relationship with humanity and with His people as well as a loving and stable marriage. What a privilege and responsibility is given to every believing married couple. The intimacy of their union, the life-giving vitality of their relationship, and constancy of their faithfulness to one another in marriage reveals the very gospel of Jesus Christ.

CONTINUING INSIGHT:

GOD'S ORDAINED VEHICLE

by James Spencer

The pairing of the first human couple early on in the story of God's creation, which instituted marriage, certainly points to the importance of marriage both as the context for appropriate, intimate sexual expression and for the fulfillment of the divine commission to "be fruitful and multiply and fill the earth and subdue it" (Gen. 1:28 ESV). It would seem that the original purpose of marriage was, at least in part, to form a bond between these female and male image bearers that would allow the human couple to participate with God in achieving the commission set for humankind. Marriage was the God-ordained vehicle for fruitfulness and multiplication.

Understanding marriage, however, strictly in terms of multiplication minimizes the significance of the institution. The female and male image bearers are not joined together simply to produce offspring, but to raise offspring prepared to carry the mantle of image bearer faithfully into the next generation. While this is not made explicit in the leaving and cleaving principle of of Genesis 2:24, it becomes far clearer throughout the rest of the Pentateuch. The significance of passing on the mantle of the covenant to the next generation is certainly clear in the struggles of Abraham, Isaac, and Jacob.

Abraham's preoccupation with an heir begins with Lot, leads to Hagar and Ishmael, is tested in the near sacrifice of Isaac, and underscored when he requires Isaac to swear to take a wife from Abraham's family and not from the Canaanites, which Isaac fulfills in marrying Rebekah. Whereas Abraham's tension for an heir was largely related to the supposed barrenness of his wife, Sarah, Isaac has a slightly different problem . . . twins. Despite the Lord's pronouncement to Rebekah that "the older [Esau] shall serve the younger [Jacob]" (Gen. 25:23), Isaac loved Esau. Despite Esau's selling of his birthright to Jacob for a bowl of soup, Isaac is still prepared to give the patriarchal blessing, which would establish his heir, to Esau. Rebekah, who favors Jacob, assists Jacob in deceiving his father and stealing Esau's blessing. Jacob is then sent away so that he can find a wife from among Rebekah's family.

Family dysfunctions aside, what we see in these narratives is the working out of God's covenant with His people. God promises Abraham an heir through Sarah. He stays the hand of Abraham when he is about to sacrifice Isaac and provides a substitute offering of the ram. God leads Isaac's servants to Rebekah making it clear that she is Isaac's bride-to-be. The pronouncement that "the older shall serve the younger" combined with God's ongoing protection and interaction with Jacob underscores God's commitment to installing Jacob the next in the line of Israelite patriarchs.

In addition to the preservation of the chosen line of succession from one patriarch to the next, there are also clear instructions related to the importance of an active, ongoing instruction of the next generation. Deuteronomy urges parents to teach their children the Law, to cultivate the remembrance of the exodus from Egypt, and to instill in the next generation a fear of the Lord. Sheer volume was not the goal. Rather, the goal was the raising up of successive generations of God-fearers who would carry on the unique witness of Israel to the Lord. The family structure was crucial to achieving this goal.

Marriage and the family structure surely retain a similar discipleship function within the context of the church's broader mission in the New Testament and today. Marriage continues to be an important vehicle through which children are raised to fear and love God. At the same time, the New Testament does not exhibit the same preoccupation with biological reproduction as the Old Testament. Being single or barren does not hold the same threat to one's legacy as was the case in the Old Testament. Rather, marriage is to demonstrate the love that Christ has for His church. Raising children in the faith would certainly be a central function for married couples who have children, but having children in order to perpetuate the faith becomes a subset of the church's broader call to evangelism and discipleship.

While it may be tempting to suggest that the family unit was more significant in the Old Testament and is diminished in the New Testament, it seems more fitting to suggest that the family has always served the purpose and mission of larger community. In Israel, the family served the purposes of the nation, which revolved around the preservation of land, seed, and blessing through ongoing covenant faithfulness. This service included having and raising children who could carry on the faith of Israel across generations. Today, the family serves the purposes of the church. Married couples are witnesses of Christ's love for His bride, the church, by loving and serving one another, faithfully honoring the marriage covenant. When married couples have children, they also take on the responsibility of raising their children to fear and love God as part of a local congregation of believers and within the context of the global community of faith.

While marriage and childbearing are not givens in the Christian life, they do play an important role in the general functioning of the church. When a man and a woman choose to become husband and wife, they do so as members of the body of Christ who commit to a marital relationship, peculiar, as it is distinct from the world, subject to the Scriptures, and focused on fulfilling God's mission. Paul speaks of this focus in 1 Corinthians 7. Though a married man is "anxious about worldly things, how to please his wife" (v. 33 ESV), Paul calls husbands, as well as the single, to live focused on the things of the Lord. Paul's point is not that husbands or wives should ignore or neglect their spouse. Instead, Paul is calling those who are married not to be distracted from the mission God has given to all of the members of the church, whether married or not. He is calling those who are married to focus on eternity and to live a life of distinction as a married couple dedicated to glorifying God, intent on service in His kingdom.

He is calling on married couples to serve together, mutually supportive, in the mission to which God has called them.

CHAPTER 16

FOR A TIME WE CANNOT SEE

by Crawford W. Loritts Jr.

Sammy Davis Jr. was a legendary, remarkably gifted entertainer. Show business was his life. He was virtually born performing. His trailblazing career took him from performing as a young child in vaudeville to small nightclubs, Las Vegas, television, and movies. He used his influence and platform to encourage and provide opportunities for other promising entertainers.

Davis had a profound impact on the life and career of the late entertainer Gregory Hines. In fact, shortly before Davis died of throat cancer, Hines went to visit him and for one final time pay tribute to his mentor and friend. The disease had taken its toll. Davis could no longer talk and could barely walk. It was a tearful reunion. Hines thanked him for all he had done for him and once again told Davis how much he loved and deeply appreciated him. Then something wonderfully strange happened.

As Hines began walking toward the door he heard the faint sound of shuffling feet. He turned around and to his amazement Davis was slowly moving toward him. Then Davis stood still, pretending he had a basketball in his hands. In one moving gesture he passed the imaginary ball to his protégé. Shortly after that visit Sammy Davis Jr. died.

That story is a picture of the mission of marriage and the family. Marriage and family are not just about the here and now. What we do today is shaping and influencing a time that we cannot see. So the question is, what's in our hands, what are we intentionally placing in the hands of this and future generations? God instituted marriage, and thus the family as the missional means by and through which He would pass on His purposes and plan for each generation. That indeed must be our intentional passion.

But how do we do this? What do we deliberately focus on?

Psalm 78:5–7 shows us the way forward. Psalm 78, picturing Israel as a family, is the celebration of God's faithfulness and also a sobering warning concerning what happens when we wander off mission. God's heart for the mission for the family is highlighted in verses 5–7.

These verses outline the passion, process and, by God's grace, what will be produced in future generations because we have been faithful to the mission.

Something has been given to us, placed in our hands. Verse 5 says, "He established a testimony in Jacob and appointed a law in Israel" (ESV). "Testimony" is a reference to the proven character of God, the ways in which He has made Himself known in each generation. The point is that God has been near and personal. He has answered prayer. He has intervened in difficult and impossible circumstances. He has honored our faith and obedience as well as disciplined us when we veered off course. He has shown us His ways and revealed His heart. His love and mercy is woven into the tapestry of our lives.

"Law" is a reference to the Word of God. He has given us His Word to guide, encourage, and protect us. His Word has brought clarity and provided direction as we have wrestled with what to believe and what to do. It has been both the wall that has protected us and the source and force that has driven us to know, discover, and do the will of God.

The character ("testimony") of God and the content of Scripture ("law") have been placed in our hands. This is the treasure that we have drawn from time and again to fuel our marriages and to give strength and stability to our families.

The character of God and the content of Scripture were not meant to be some inspirational memory to make future generations feel good about their heritage. No, it is our passionate mission to not only place it in the hands of the next generation but to do it in such a way that they are compelled to do the same.

That's why verses 5 and 6 point us to a passionate process: "which he commanded our fathers to teach to their children, that the next generation might know them, the children yet unborn, and arise and tell them to their children."

A few years ago our oldest son, Bryan, and I visited the cemetery in Conover, North Carolina, where several generations of Lorittses are buried. The last time we had been there Bryan was a small boy. As we looked at the grave markers and read the inscriptions, I was suddenly overcome with emotion. I thought about Peter, the former slave and the patriarch of our family. I remembered the stories my dad told me about Peter's love for the Lord and for His Word. This former slave's commitment to the character of God and the content of Scripture has shaped our family, including a time he could not see. I turned to Bryan and said, "Son, these people paid our tuition." We are stewards of the treasure that's been placed in our hands.

We are passionate about placing in the hands of the next generation the character of God and the content of Scripture not only because it is right to do so but also because of what God will produce in them. Verse 7 says, "so that they should set their hope in God and not forget the works of God, but keep his commandments." It is our prayer and passion that every generation in our family will have an unshakable confidence in God ("set their hope in God"); a conscious awareness of God's faithfulness ("not forget the works of God"); a will to obey ("keep his commandments").

Some years ago I spoke on the campus of the college where Bryan was attending. After I spoke we were hanging out together and he told me a story about how God had met a financial need he had. I asked him why he didn't call me to let me know what he was facing. He told me that he started to call but then he remembered our family devotional times when we would read God's Word around the table and his mom would write our prayer requests in a notebook. He remembered how God met our needs and answered prayer as we trusted Him. He said, "I didn't call you, Dad, because I figured it was my turn to trust Him."

Marriage and family is not just about our lifetime but about a time that we cannot see. Let's make sure that we build our marriage and family on the character of God and the content of Scripture and do all we can to encourage future generations to be faithful stewards of what has been placed in their hands.

THE IMPORTANCE OF CONTINUING THE CONVERSATION

by Curt Hamner and John Trent

We began this book with a reference to a royal wedding, which from earthly standards was nothing short of spectacular. Yet as we close this book, we do so looking toward an even greater marriage feast—the wedding supper of the Lamb (Rev. 19:6–9 esv).

There we read,

> "Hallelujah!
> For the Lord our God
>   the Almighty reigns.
> Let us rejoice and exult
>   and give him the glory,
> for the marriage of the Lamb has come,
>   and his Bride has made herself ready;
> it was granted her to clothe herself
>   with fine linen, bright and pure"—

for the fine linen is the righteous deeds of the saints.
    And the angel said to me, "Write this: Blessed are those who are invited to the marriage supper of the Lamb." And he said to me, "These are the true words of God."

This great feast, complete with a beautiful bride, is the picture God Himself chose to describe His love and purpose for His people. Marriage then, not only reflects a couple's love for each other, but is the completion of a metaphor of Christ's love for His church. Yet that time without sin and suffering and full of joy and completed promise is still to come.

Even now, after this comprehensive study on marriage's foundation, theology, and mission, each of us will put down this book and pick up a life lived "between two trees." That's the metaphor, my (Curt's) wife, Rhonda, and I chose for our ministry. We chose this term because of the two references to the Tree of Life in Scripture. The first is found in Genesis 2, at the beginning of time, when Adam and Eve flourished in a perfect creation. Imagine the incredible unspoiled freedom, love, and beauty in the garden around that tree! No anger. No fear. No hiding or hurting. Yet all that would come after the fall. And all of us, from that sad day forward, have indeed felt the effects of sin and loss, of fear and shame.

Yet every couple has been given the hope of a wonderful future as well—a future in a new heaven and earth, made possible by the Lamb of God who came and gave up His life to cover our sin. It is Jesus' love, accepted as a free gift into our lives, that grants to us that "invitation" mentioned above—to be a part of that wedding feast.

But for now, we do live "between two trees," meaning we do life during a time *after* the Tree in the garden and *before* the second time the Tree of Life appears. That second appearance of the Tree of Life comes in Revelation 22, after the great marriage feast. At the very end of time as we know it, all things once again will be spotless and unmarked by sin. But until that time, as we read in Romans (8:20–23), the whole world groans because of our lost and fallen state. Yet we may live in light of the sure hope in a Savior who will one day set all things right.

So until that great wedding feast and the Tree's second appearance, we need to continue the conversations that have begun with this book. As we close, here are several ways in which we'd encourage you to do just that.

- *Visit www.ContinuingConversations.com.*

Technology provides a wonderful platform to do a number of things to stimulate you to continue the conversation. For example, on the website specifically built around this book, you'll find short contributor videos. Some writers will share their passion for the topic they chose to write about in this volume. Writers will also expound on specific points or discuss extra material on their subject that isn't in the book.

You'll find additional material from other theologians and experts in these fields, as there are many exceptional writers, commentators, teachers, and counselors we simply couldn't include. Look for a number of other outstanding voices on marriage to be added on this website. The ministries Between Two Trees and StrongFamilies.com will be hosting and helping promote and proctor these discussions from the time this book launches for as long as we can see into the future.

• *On the website, you'll find a list of Continuing Conversations questions and suggestions based on each chapter.*

Each chapter of this book forms a key teaching point on marriage. It is also the basis for a continuing, and often crucial, conversation on the importance of that particular aspect of marriage. Again, as long as these ministries continue, we'll keep adding insights and highlighting conversations that people like you are having in your place of ministry! We'll ask you to contact us through the website and let us know how you're using this book. We'd love to receive and post pictures and ideas you have in getting the word out in your part of the world regarding marriage. While we can't promise to post everything that comes in, we'll post as much as we can. Be watching for ideas and thoughts that will come from you and other readers on what you're doing in a group, class, or in your own marriage as well.

• *Visit the website often for information on conferences or other special events that may be a part of our keeping the conversation going.*

May the Lord bless, guide, and keep you as you unleash and promote marriage in your own home first, and then, we pray, all across your part of the world. Picture us and a heavenly host lining the street, waving and cheering you on as you drive by in your carriage to walk into all the joys and challenges that are a part of marriage.

ACKNOWLEDGMENTS

We are incredibly grateful for the partnership of Moody Bible Institute and Moody Publishers in the creation of this book. In particular, our deepest thanks go out to John Hinkley, Randall Payleitner, and Pam Pugh who, from the beginning, have carefully listened and at the end, put the final edits on the book you hold in your hand. From the beginning, this team has believed that these conversations are needed today and are of critical importance for future generations as well.

It was also obvious that a book of this scope and magnitude would need a team of theologians and practitioners to join with us to become the editors of this book. Joining us from the beginning of this project are three outstanding scholars, Dr. Eric L. Johnson, Rebekah Byrd, and Dr. Erik Thoennes. Together, the five of us, along with John Hinkley from Moody Publishers, met to hammer out the key issues and topics that a book like this should address. Over the course of the past three years, we have spent countless hours debating, storyboarding, praying, editing—and reviewing topics, chapters, and additional insights—seeking to make this a true "conversation starter" for some of the most important discussions of our day. A special note of thanks to Rebekah Byrd who, in addition to all her other duties, became the key collection and communication point for each of the writers who contributed to this work, a significant and much appreciated task. Each of these team members is also deeply indebted to their families for the sacrifice required in all the meetings, writing, review, and conversation.

Special thanks to the scholars at the Marian E. Wade Center and Special Collections on the campus of Wheaton College. Also personal thanks to the faculty of the following schools—Moody Bible Institute, Wheaton Graduate School, Trinity Evangelical Divinity School, Talbot School of Theology, Dallas Theological Seminary, Denver Seminary—with whom we consulted and gained insightful feedback from the beginning to the completion of the contents of this book.

Finally, there is "a contributor" whose name doesn't show up in a chapter or insight section, but whose writing and teaching on marriage echoes throughout this book. He is Dr. Howard Hendricks who, along with his wife, Jeanne, taught and demonstrated the truths of this work in their almost sixty years' tenure at Dallas Theological Seminary. The initial idea of this book began in "Prof's" Christian Home Class. As he did at the start of each class, he gave the assignment to exegete Genesis 2:24, which for us (Curt and John) was in the 1970s.

To all who have contributed, we thank you and ask God's blessing on you.

Curt Hamner and John Trent

NOTES

Chapter 1: The Trinity, the Incarnation, and the Meaning of Marriage and Sex

1. Michael Reeves, *Delighting in the Trinity: An Introduction to the Christian Faith* (Downers Grove, IL: IVP Academic, 2012), 62.

2. John Zizioulas writes: "The only way for a true person to exist is for being and communion to coincide. The triune God offers in Himself the only possibility for such an identification of being with communion; He is the revelation of true personhood." *Being as Communion* (Crestwood, NY: St. Vladimir's Seminary Press, 1985), 107.

3. James B. Torrance, *Worship, Community, and the Triune God of Grace* (Downers Grove, IL: IVP Academic, 1996), 38. A Christian anthropology that begins with the solitary Adam as the image of God is not very Christian at all, implying as it does a unitarian understanding of God.

4. For a skillful summary of prominent interpretations, see Anthony Hoekema, *Created in God's Image* (Grand Rapids: Eerdmans, 1986), 33–65.

5. We hasten to note that the emphasis on male and female is reiterated in a striking way in Genesis 5:1–2: "When God created man, he made him in the likeness of God. Male and female he created them, and he blessed them and named *them* Man [*adam*] when they were created."

6. On the nature of the plural "us" in God's address, see Bruce Waltke, *An Old Testament Theology* (Grand Rapids: Zondervan, 2007), 212–13. Waltke affirms that "several strong arguments" favor the view that the plural is a reference to God's plurality as Father, Son, and Spirit, only to finally challenge that view on what he calls the "accredited grammatico-historical rules of interpretation." Accredited by whom? Historical and grammatical technicians? Or the collective pastoral wisdom of the church through the ages?

7. "Lecture on Genesis 1:2," in *LW*, 1:9; cf. 1:58–59. John Calvin concurs: "Christians, therefore, properly contend, from this testimony, that there exists a plurality of Persons in the Godhead." Calvin on Gen. 1:26, *Comm.*, 1/1:92.

8. Dorothy Sayers, *The Mind of the Maker* (San Francisco: HarperCollins, 1987), 38, quoting from *The Zeal of Thy House*.

9. Karl Barth writes, "Is it not astonishing that again and again expositors have ignored the definitive explanation given by the text itself, and instead of reflecting on it pursued all kinds of arbitrarily invented interpretations of the *imago Dei*?" *Church Dogmatics*, 3/1, ed. G. W. Bromiley and T. F. Torrance, trans. G. W. Bromiley (Peabody, MA: Hendrickson, 2010), 195. Henri Blocher adds, "If we cannot find exegetical grounds for explaining 'the image of God' by the phrase 'male and female', our thoughts should turn to the undoubted analogy between the non-solitude of God and the communal structure of humanity." *In the Beginning: The Opening Chapters of Genesis* (Downers Grove, IL: IVP, 1984), 97. Blocher goes on to argue that this is more than a mere analogy.

10. Colin E. Gunton, *Christ and Creation* (Grand Rapids: Eerdmans, 1992), 101.

11. Blocher, *In the Beginning*, 96.

12. We cannot help but wonder if a reticence to see Eve's existence as necessary to the image of God has had a sometimes deleterious effect on the church's view of women. If the solitary Adam was complete as that image, it is difficult to see how Eve could be much more than a creational addendum, necessary for the *continuation* of human life but not for its basic constitution.

13. Ray S. Anderson writes: "Adam has no fundamental 'encounter of being with being' in his relationship with the other creatures such as occurs when the woman is presented to him as a 'being from and for him.' Quite clearly the *imago* is not totally present in the form of individual humanity but more completely as co-humanity." *On Being Human: Essays in Theological Anthropology* (Grand Rapids: Eerdmans, 1982), 73.

14. Barth, *Church Dogmatics*, 3/1, 290. Helmut Thielicke observes, "The solitary Adam is not yet 'man'; he is still not the fulfillment of the creation of man." *The Ethics of Sex*, trans. John W. Doberstein (New York: Harper & Row, 1964), 4.

15. Had Adam remained alone, Calvin avers, he would have been but "incomplete." Calvin on Gen. 1:27, *Comm.*, 1/1:97. Calvin reflects further: "[Adam] lost, therefore, one of his ribs; but, instead of it, a far richer reward was granted him, since he obtained a faithful associate of life; for he now saw himself, who had before been imperfect, rendered complete in his wife. And in this we see a true resemblance of our union with the Son of God; for he became weak that he might have members of his body endued with strength." Calvin on Gen. 2:21, *Comm.*, 1/1:33. Apparently it was not even good for Christ, the second Adam, to be alone.

16. Precisely here we are reminded that gender distinction is both *created* and a *reflection*, not an exact replication. Gender distinction is not to be projected back onto God, whose personal distinctions are reflected in ours but nevertheless transcend them.

17. The male-female relation, T. F. Torrance asserts, "extends beyond its specific form in marriage: it has to do with the interpersonal structure of human being to which all men and women belong, whether they are married or not. Those who are not married do not exist outside the inter-personal structure of human being as it came from the creative will and love of God." *The Christian Doctrine of Marriage* (Edinburgh: Scottish Academic Press, 1989), n.p.

18. Christopher A. Hall and Steven D. Boyer write: "Do we not find here a fascinating convergence? Ultimate reality consists in divine persons perfectly united in ecstatic love— and every human person discovers an intrinsic longing for just this kind of interpersonal intimacy." *The Mystery of God: Theology for Knowing the Unknowable* (Grand Rapids: Baker, 2012), 112. Cf., Stanley J. Grenz, *The Social God and the Relational Self: A Trinitarian Theology of the* Imago Dei (Louisville, KY: Westminster John Knox Press, 2001).

19. Cornelius Plantinga Jr., *Not the Way It's Supposed to Be: A Breviary of Sin* (Grand Rapids: Eerdmans, 1995), 29.

20. This is a point on which Calvin insisted. See his notes on Col. 1:15 and 2 Cor. 4:4, *Comm.*, 21/2:149–150 and 20/2:192–197.

21. Calvin on Eph. 1:23, *Comm.*, 20/1:218.

22. Given that Genesis 2:24 is ultimately fulfilled in Jesus Christ, we are reminded of Jesus' insistence that he is the subject of the teaching of Moses and the Prophets (John 5:39–40, 46; Luke 24:27).

23. Jonathan Edwards, *Miscellanies* (No. 702), in *The Works of Jonathan Edwards*, ed. Ava Chamberlain (New Haven, CT: Yale University Press, 1994), 18:298.

24. C. S. Lewis, *Mere Christianity* (New York: HarperCollins, 1952), 175.

25. Edwards, *Miscellanies* (No. 571), in *Works*, 18:110.

26. This is a good time to be reminded that we tend to express ourselves—maritally, sexually, and otherwise—in accordance with who we believe God really is. Marital and sexual unholiness in the church, of the types we shall describe below, strongly suggests that we view God as unitarian rather than Trinitarian. False views of God invariably lead to false views of ourselves and others. See Reeves, *Delighting in the Trinity*, 116.

27. It is certainly worth pointing out that when Jesus was himself questioned about divorce, he referred his interlocutors to Genesis 2, setting marriage in the context of creation (Matt. 19:4–6).

28. Torrance, *The Christian Doctrine of Marriage*, n.p.

29. Blocher, *In the Beginning*, 103.

30. The contradiction of pornography is one that it shares with "casual sex" more generally. Lewis Smedes is right: "Casual sex is a contradiction in terms." *Sex for Christians* (Grand Rapids: Eerdmans, 1994), 67.

31. But the order is not unimportant, notes Alexander Schmemann: "One does not love *in order* to have children. Love needs no justification; it is not because it gives life that love is good: it is because it is good that it gives life." *For the Life of the World: Sacraments and Orthodoxy* (Crestwood, NY: St. Vladimir's Seminary Press, 1973), 87.

32. The denial of life that characterizes abortion is a kind of sexual idolatry shared by the adulterer and fornicator. R. R. Reno writes: "The future-oriented fertility of the sexual act threatens rather than fulfills the adulterer's or fornicator's desires. Fear of the children that naturally come from sexual intercourse . . . is why sexual desire misdirected and twisted into service of present pleasures becomes the Old Testament's favored image of idolatry. The idolater is like the man who visits prostitutes. He wants to discharge his need for worship while reserving power to live as he pleases. The silence of idols is no disappointment . . . idols are charming in their convenient emptiness." *Genesis*. Brazos Theological Commentary on the Bible (Grand Rapids: Brazos Press, 2010), 57.

33. Christopher West, *Theology of the Body for Beginners* (West Chester, PA: Ascension Press, 2004), 13.

34. This personal and relational devastation constitutes an urgent matter of ministry for the church. Her Savior, whose body was torn apart and whose life was terminated, can alone bring peace and healing to those who suffer the ravages, heartbreak, and loneliness that abortion inevitably brings.

35. Post-Communion Prayer for Marriage, *Lutheran Book of Worship*, Minister's Desk Edition (Minneapolis, MN: Augsburg Fortress, 1978), 192.

Chapter 2: The Revelation of God's Commitment

1. Alison Doyle, "How Often Do People Change Jobs?" *The Balance Careers*, January 24, 2018.

2. Peter Beinart, "Breaking Faith," *The Atlantic*, April 2017.

3. Mark Regnerus, "Cheap Sex and the Decline of Marriage," the *Wall Street Journal*, September 29, 2017, https://www.wsj.com/articles/cheap-sex-and-the-decline-of-marriage-1506690454.

4. Bethany M. Wood, *Healthy Attachment and Commitment Levels in Early Marriage*, Brigham Young University, Provo Utah (2005), http://scholarsarchive.byu.edu/cgi/viewcontent.cgi?article=1264&context=fhssconference_studentpub.

5. All Scripture in this chapter, unless otherwise noted, is from the English Standard Version.

6. For an insightful and humorous examination of the troubling terms we use to describe being in love, see the excellent TED Talk, by Mandy Len Catron, https://www.ted.com/talks/mandy_len_catron_a_better_way_to_talk_about_love. She shows that these ways of describing love as a negative and out-of-control state can be found in sources from Shakespeare, "Love is merely madness," to Nietzsche, "There is always some madness in love," to Beyoncé, "You got me looking so crazy in love." The metaphor Catron recommends we use for being in love is joining a "collaborative work of art."

7. A recent study by University of Virginia sociologist Bradford Wilcox shows the detrimental effects of cohabitation across the globe: http://worldfamilymap.ifstudies.org/2017/files/WFM-2017-FullReport.pdf. See also Scott Stanley's work on the effect that cohabitation has on the increase of divorce and marital distress, http://onlinelibrary.wiley.com/doi/10.1111/j.1741-3729.2006.00418.x/abstract.

8. https://priceonomics.com/at-what-age-do-people-get-married-around-the-world/.

9. The full explanation of this summary can be found in Robert J. Sternberg, "Triangulating Love" in Thomas Jay Oord, ed., *The Altruism Reader: Selections from Writings on Love, Religion, and Science* (West Conshohocken, PA: Templeton Foundation, 2007).

10. Ibid., 258.

11. For a full treatment of the jealousy of God from a biblical perspective, see Erik Thoennes, *Godly Jealousy: A Theology of Intolerant Love* (Geanies House, Fearn, Ross-Shire, Scotland: Christian Focus, 2005).

12. E.g., Ex. 20:5, 34:14; Num. 25:11; Deut. 4:24, 5:9, 6:15, 29:20, 31:16–18, 32:16, 21; Josh 24:19; 1 Kings 14:22; 2 Kings 19:31; Pss. 78:58, 79:5; Isa. 9:7, 26:11, 37:32, 42:13, 59:17, 63:15; Ezek. 5:13, 8:3–5, 16:38, 42, 23:25, 36:5–6, 39:25; Joel 2:18; Nah. 1:2; Zeph. 1:18, 3:8; Zech. 1:14–15, 8:2; John 2:17; 1 Cor. 10:22; 2 Cor. 11:2; James 4:5.

13. This relational distinction is explained in Daniel M. Farrell, "Jealousy," *The Philosophical Review* 89, no. 4 (October, 1980): 527–59. Also helpful in defining jealousy is Farrell's "Jealousy and Desire" in *Love Analyzed*, ed. Roger E. Lamb (Boulder, CO: Westview Press, 1997) and D. H. Semdahl, "God and the Concept of Jealousy" (ThM thesis, Dallas Theological Seminary, 1983).

14. E.g., Num. 5:11–31, 11:29, 25:11, 13; Deut. 32:21; 1 Kings 19:10, 14; 2 Kings 10:16; Pss. 69:9, 119:139; Prov. 6:34, 23:17; Song 8:6; John 2:17; 2 Cor. 11:2.

15. The rituals for determining the justification of the jealousy of a husband detailed in Numbers 5 assume that there were times that the husband's jealousy was unjustified. Joshua's jealousy on behalf of Moses was also unwarranted in Numbers 11:29.

16. In 2 Kings 10:16, Jehu to seems to have had an appropriate godly jealousy that was taken too far in the massacre at Jezreel, as Hosea 1:4 indicates.

17. One notable exception is the *Anchor Bible Dictionary*, which has no entry for jealousy. It does have an extensive entry for "Zealots," in which it deals with the concept of zeal. It defines zeal as "behavior motivated by the desire to protect one's self, group, space, or time against violations." David Rhoads, "Zealots," in *The Anchor Bible Dictionary*, ed., David Noel Freedman (Garden City, NJ: Doubleday, 1992) 6:1044.

18. Walter C. Kaiser, *Exodus,* EBC, ed. Frank E. Gaebelein, vol. 2 (Grand Rapids: Zondervan, 1990), 423.

19. H. Gispen, *Exodus*, trans., Ed van der Mass, *Bible Students Commentary* (Grand Rapids: Zondervan, 1982), 191.

20. Ibid.

21. Augustine, *Confessions*, I, 5.

22. It is worth noting that other central attributes of God that are more commonly associated with God are never given this kind of name recognition. God never says His name is "love," or "grace," or "patience," but He does say His name is "jealous." Not that these other attributes are any less important to who God is. Indeed, the unity of God demands that we consider His attributes interdependently. None of them is incidental or unessential. However, that God's jealousy is given name status demands that we recognize this emotion as a vital aspect of God's nature and His relational demands.

23. Before this use of "harlot" it had only been used in reference to Diana in Gen. 34:31 and Tamar in Gen. 38:15, 24. After this occurrence it becomes a common description of unfaithful Israel, occurring in fifty verses used in this way. Cf. Lev. 17:7, 20:5, 6; Num. 15:39, 25:1; Deut. 31:16; Judg. 2:17, 8:27, 33; 1 Chron. 5:25; 2 Chron. 21:11, 13; Ps. 106:39; Isa. 1:21, 23:15, 16, 17; Jer. 2:20, 3:1, 6, 8; Ezek. 6:9, 16:15, 16, 17, 26, 28, 30, 31, 34, 35, 41, 20:30, 23:3, 5, 30, 44; Hos. 2:5, 3:3, 4:10, 12, 13, 14, 15, 18, 5:3, 9:1; Amos 7:17; Mic. 1:7; Nah. 3:4.

24. Of the 224 OT passages where God is clearly jealous for the faithfulness of His people, twenty-four have explicit sexual/marriage imagery. These passages are: Ex. 34:12–17; Lev. 20:1–8; Deut. 31:16–18; Judg. 8:27, 33; 1 Chron. 5:24–25; 2 Chron. 21:10–13; Isa. 54:5–10, 57:3–13; Jer. 2:1–25, 4:30, 5:7–11, 31:31–32; Ezek. 6:1–63, 20:30–33, 22:9, 23:1–31, 36–49, 24:13, 43:7–9; Hos. 1:1–11, 2:1–23, 3:1–5.

25. John Piper, *The Lord Whose Name Is Jealous (Exodus 34:10–16)*, 1998, available from http:// www.soundofgrace.com/piper84/102884m.htm.

26. Dan Allender and Tremper Longman III, *The Cry of the Soul: How Our Emotions Reveal Our Deepest Questions about God* (Colorado Springs: NavPress, 1994), 132.

27. Daniel I. Block, *The Book of Ezekiel*, NICOT, ed. R.K. Harrison and Robert L. Hubbard, vol. 1–2 (Grand Rapids: Eerdmans, 1997), 13.

28. Ibid., 14.

29. Victor P. Furnish, *II Corinthians*, Anchor Bible, ed., William Foxwell Albright and David Noel Freedman, vol. 32A (Garden City, NJ: Doubleday, 1984), 487.

30. Murray J. Harris, *2 Corinthians*, EBC, ed., Frank E. Gaebelein (Grand Rapids: Zondervan, 1976), 385.

31. R. A. Batey, "Paul's Bride Image: A Symbol of Realistic Eschatology," *Interpretation* 17 (1963): 176–82.

32. Furnish, *II Corinthians*, 499.

33. Richard P. Hanson, *The Second Epistle to the Corinthians*, Torch Bible Commentaries, ed., John Marsh, vol. 47 (London: SCM, 1954), 79.

34. R. A. Batey, *New Testament Nuptial Imagery* (Leiden, Netherlands: Brill, 1971), 68.

35. Colin G. Kruse, *The Second Epistle of Paul to the Corinthians: An Introduction and Commentary*, TNTC, ed. Leon Morris, vol. 8 (Grand Rapids: Eerdmans, 1987), 183.

36. Raymond Ortlund, *Whoredom: God's Unfaithful Wife in Biblical Theology* (Grand Rapids: Eerdmans, 1996), 149.

37. Fredrick F. Bruce, *1 & 2 Corinthians*, NCBC, ed. Matthew Black (Grand Rapids: Eerdmans, 1971), 234.

38. Ortlund, *Whoredom*, 152.

39. Ralph P. Martin, *2 Corinthians*, WBC, ed. David A. Hubbard, vol. 40 (Waco, TX: Word, 1986), 333.

40. John Chrysostom, *Nicene and Post-Nicene Fathers, Series I, Vol. XIII*, Homilies on First Corinthians, available from www.ceel.org/fathers2/NPFN1-12/npfn1-09.

41. *The Quotable Oswald Chambers,* compiled and edited by David McCasland (Grand Rapids: Discovery House, 2008), 155.

42. Robertson McQuilkin, *A Promise Kept* (Carol Stream, IL: Tyndale House, 1998). For a moving clip of portion of McQuilkin's resignation speech see https://vimeo.com/85110047.

Continuing Insight: Loving Like Jesus in Our Marriage

1. Rev. William Pringle, trans. *Calvin's Commentaries, vol. 22, The Epistle of Paul: Galatians and Ephesians by John Calvin* (Grand Rapids: Baker, 1979), 322.

2. George MacDonald and Marianne Wright, ed., *The Gospel in George MacDonald: Selections from His Novels, Fairy Tales, and Spiritual Writings* (Elsmore, Australia: Plough Publishing House, 2016), 218. From the novel *Sir Gibbie*.

Chapter 3: The Foundational Language of Marriage in Scripture

1. M. L. Rosenzweig, "A Helper Equal to Him," *Judaism* 139 (1986): 277–80.

2. Elizabeth Clark, *Women in the Early Church* (Collegeville, MN: 1983), quoting St. Augustine, "On the Good Side of Marriage."

3. Ludwig Koehler and Walter Baumgartner, eds., *Hebrew and Aramaic Lexicon of the Old Testament* (Leiden, Netherlands: Koninklijke Brill, 2000), 666.

4. For a helpful treatment of these themes, see Michelle Lee-Barnewall, *Neither Complementarian nor Egalitarian* (Grand Rapids: Baker, 2016), 136–45.

5. Edith Schaeffer, *A Celebration of Marriage: Hopes and Realities* (Grand Rapids, Baker: 1994).

6. Jesus also comments on divorce in Matthew 5:31–32 and Luke 16:18. These remarks on divorce grow out the perspective of what Jesus says about marriage in Matthew 19 and Mark 10.

7. This text makes it clear the husband could not dictate who the released woman could marry and have it still be a valid certificate of divorce.

8. Adela Yarbro Collins, *Mark: A Commentary: Hermeneia: A Critical and Historical Commentary on the Bible* (Minneapolis: Fortress, 2007), 465.

9. Walter Bauer, W. F. Arndt, F. W. Gingrich, F. W. Danker, *A Greek-English Lexicon of the New Testament and Other Early Christian Literature*, 3rd ed. BDAG (Chicago: University of Chicago Press, 2001), 555.

10. Ibid., 954.

11. For a consideration of the complex issues tied to this topic, see Christopher Yuan and Angela Yuan, *Out of a Far Country: A Gay Son's Journey to God. A Broken Mother's Search for Hope* (Colorado Springs: WaterBrook, 2011).

12. Cohabitation has become so common that one news outlet called it the "new normal." JoNel Aleccia, "'The new normal': Cohabitation on the rise, study finds," *NBC News Health*, April 4, 2013, http://vitals.nbcnews.com/_news/2013/04/04/17588704-the-new-normal-cohabitation-on-the-rise-study-finds?lite. Cohabitation has increased by a stunning 900 percent in the last fifty years. In 2012, 7.8 million couples lived together as compared to 2.9 million in 1996. A 2007 poll showed only 27 percent of Americans disapproved, showing that society's attitude toward cohabitation has changed. Statistics from Lauren Fox, "The Science of Cohabitation: A Step Toward Marriage, Not a Rebellion," *The Atlantic*, March 20, 2014, http://www.theatlantic.com/health/archive/2014/03/the-science-of-cohabitation-a-step-toward-marriage-not-a-rebellion/284512.

13. Dietrich Bonhoeffer, *Sanctorum Communio, A Theological Study of the Sociology of the Church* (Minneapolis: Fortress Press, 2009), 80.

14. Elizabeth Thomson and Sara S. McLanahan, "Reflections on 'Family Structure and Child Well-Being: Economic Resources vs. Parental Socialization,'" *Social Forces* 91, no. 1 (2012): 45–53. The authors are at Princeton and the University of Wisconsin-Madison. A concluding statement in their study reads, "The fact that single-, step-, and cohabiting-parent families continue to grow and the fact that they are associated with poorer outcomes for parents and children means that the implications of today's and tomorrow's research on these topics are enormous for both individuals and the societies in which they live." Yet another article making the same point is W. Bradford Wilcox and Anna Sutherland, "Less Marriage, More Inequality," *National Review Online*, April 15, 2016, http://www.nationalreview.com/article/434124/income-inequality-marriage-closes-gap.

Continuing Insight: Cohabitation in Biblical and Theological Perspective

1. Although the details of the situation are sketchy, it is likely that the man's father remarried a younger woman and, after the death or departure of the father, the man and his stepmother became romantically involved and continued to live together in an ongoing sexual relationship. This reconstruction is encoded in several modern translations: "someone is cohabiting with his father's wife" (NET), and "a man is sleeping with his father's wife" (NIV).

2. For a discussion on the nature of the prostitution that existed in ancient Corinth and its connection to the temple, see Roy Ciampa and Brian Rosner, *The First Letter to the Corinthians*, PNTC (Grand Rapids: Eerdmans, 2010), 245–49.

3. Judy Klemesrud, "An Arrangement: Living Together for Convenience, Security, Sex," *New York Times*, March 4, 1968.

4. William McWhirter, "'The Arrangement' at College," *Life*, May 31, 1968, 56.

5. Arielle Kuperberg, "50 Years since the LeClair Affair, Is Living Together Outside of Marriage a Problem?" The Society Pages, Council on Contemporary Families, March 27, 2018, https://thesocietypages.org/ccf/2018/03/27/50-years-since-the-leclair-affair-is-living-together-outside-of-marriage-a-problem/.

6. Barna Group, "Majority of Americans Now Believe in Cohabitation," June 24, 2016, https://www.barna.com/research/majority-of-americans-now-believe-in-cohabitation/.

7. This is especially important when cohabiting couples want to be married in the church. For practical help in this area, see Jeff VanGoethem, *Living Together: A Guide to Counseling Unmarried Couples* (Grand Rapids: Kregel, 2005).

8. Glenn Stanton, *The Ring Makes All the Difference: The Hidden Consequences of Cohabitation and the Strong Benefits of Marriage* (Chicago: Moody, 2011); 39–53 and 62–65 focuses on the sociological dangers of cohabitation based on secular studies.

9. A good case can be made for an additional Corinthians slogan in 1 Corinthians 6:18b. Translating the passage as "Every sin—whatever a person does—is outside the body" (author's translation, cf. HCSB) communicates the Corinthian thinking that what is done with the body is not sin. This translation takes the following Greek conjunction as adversative rather than introducing an exception ("every sin . . . *except* sexual sin" or "every *other* sin", but this is a rare or perhaps nonexistent use of the conjunction). For support of this view see Jay Smith, "A Slogan in 1 Corinthians 6:18b: Pressing the Case," in *Studies in the Pauline Epistles: Essays in Honor of Douglas J. Moo* (Grand Rapids: Zondervan, 2014), 74–98.

10. For a discussion on the ethics of this passage, see Denny Burk, *What Is the Meaning of Sex?* (Wheaton, IL: Crossway, 2013), 43–59.

11. David Gudgel, *Before You Live Together* (Ventura, CA: Regal Books, 2003), 29–36.

Chapter 4: The Choice and High Calling of Marriage and Singleness

1. See http://www.apa.org/about/index.aspx.

2. See http://www.apa.org/topics/divorce/.

3. Ronald J. Sider, *The Scandal of the Evangelical Conscience: Why Are Christians Living Just Like the Rest of the World?* (Grand Rapids: Baker, 2005), 121–30.

4. See, e.g., Robert P. George, "After Same-Sex Marriage, Is Polyamory Next?" *American Interest*, August 25, 2015, http://www.the-american-interest.com/2015/08/25/is-polyamory-next/.

5. See Matthew 5:17–20. This is true wherever a person falls on the spectrum of dispensationalism to covenant theology. All views acknowledge *some* discontinuity between the testaments and all views acknowledge *some* continuity. See esp. John S. Feinberg, ed., *Continuity and Discontinuity: Perspectives on the Relationship between the Old and New Testaments* (Wheaton, IL: Crossway, 1988).

6. William W. Klein, Craig L. Blomberg, and Robert L. Hubbard, Jr., *Introduction to Biblical Interpretation,* 2nd ed. (Nashville: Nelson, 2004), 482–503.

7. See, e.g., the 1789 U.S. Book of Common Prayer, http://justus.anglican.org/resources/bcp/1789/Marriage_1789.htm.

8. See Pat E. Harrell, *Divorce and Remarriage in the Early Church* (Austin, TX: Sweet, 1967).

9. David W. Chapman, "Marriage and Family in Second Temple Judaism," in *Marriage and Family in the Biblical World,* ed. Ken M. Campbell (Downers Grove, IL: IVP, 2003), 204–5.

10. Jelmut T. Lehmann, "A Sermon on the Estate of Marriage" in *Luther Works: American Edition, vol. 44: The Christian in Society I* by Martin Luther, James Atkinson, gen. ed. (Philadelphia: Fortress Press, 1966).

11. All biblical quotations come from the 2011 New International Version unless otherwise specified. The parallel texts in Matt. 19:29 and Mark 10:29 lack "or wife," perhaps wishing to avoid the misunderstanding that Jesus was promoting permanent separation or divorce. This may also suggest that some of the disciples might have renounced or postponed the right to marry for this period of time. Cf. Robert H. Stein, *Luke* (Nashville: B&H Publishing Group, 1992), 459.

12. Stein, Ibid., 397.

13. Cf. Ben Witherington III, *Women in the Ministry of Jesus* (Cambridge: Cambridge University Press, 1984), 116–18.

14. Ibid., 101.

15. See esp. Randy Alcorn, *Heaven* (Carol Stream, IL: Tyndale House, 2004), 336–40.

16. So most translations. The New English Translation and the Christian Standard Bible have her living as a widow for eighty-four years but this is linguistically and historically less likely.

17. Alice Mathews, *A Woman Jesus Can Teach* (Grand Rapids: Discovery House, 1991), 24–26.

18. E.g., J. David Hester, "Eunuchs and the Postgender Jesus: Matthew 19.12 and Transgressive Sexualities," *Journal for the Study of the New Testament* 28 (2005): 13–40.

19. Much better, therefore, are A. E. Harvey, "Eunuchs for the Sake of the Kingdom," *Heythrop Journal* 48 (2007): 1–17; and Stephen R. Llewelyn, Gareth J. Wearne, and Bianca L. Sanderson, "Guarding Entry to the Kingdom: The Place of Eunuchs in Mt. 19.12," *Journal for the Study of the Historical Jesus* 10 (2012): 228–46.

20. David L. Turner, *Matthew* (Grand Rapids: Baker, 2008), 464.

21. The Voice™. Copyright © 2012 by Ecclesia Bible Society. Used by permission. All rights reserved.

22. Origen, *1 Cor. Fragment* 33, cited in Anthony C. Thiselton, *The First Epistle to the Corinthians* (Grand Rapids: Eerdmans, 2000), 494.

23. David E. Garland, *1 Corinthians* (Grand Rapids: Baker, 2003), 254.

24. John C. Hurd, Jr., *The Origin of 1 Corinthians* (New York: Seabury, 1965), esp. 213–39.

25. Cf. Gordon D. Fee, *The First Epistle to the Corinthians*, rev. ed. (Grand Rapids: Eerdmans, 2014), 309–10.

26. Roy E. Ciampa and Brian S. Rosner, *The First Letter to the Corinthians* (Grand Rapids: Eerdmans, 2010), 284.

27. Madeleine L'Engle, *Two-Part Invention: The Story of a Marriage* (New York: Farra, Straus & Giroux, 1988), 62.

28. Fee, *The First Epistle to the Corinthians*, 319.

29. Cf. ibid., 319–20, n93.

30. There is thus no contradiction with 1 Corinthians 7. See further I. Howard Marshall with Philip H. Towner, *A Critical and Exegetical Commentary on the Pastoral Epistles* (Edinburgh: T & T Clark, 1999), 604.

31. The verb for "bind" here is not the same as in v. 39, but they are synonyms. Since the latter appears in a context that allows for remarriage after being widowed, presumably legitimate divorce (the context here) also allows for it.

32. The one exception being if slaves can gain their freedom, they are encouraged to do so (v. 21) in virtually all major translations except the New Jerusalem Bible and the New Revised Standard Version.

33. In an age when, at least in Jewish circles (Paul's background), the two could normally be equated!

34. So esp. Bruce W. Winter, *After Paul Left Corinth: The Influence of Secular Ethics and Social Change* (Grand Rapids: Eerdmans, 2001), 215–68.

35. Thiselton, *The First Epistle to the Corinthians*, 572–76.

36. It is less likely, though just possible, that these verses should be translated so that they refer to a father giving his daughter in marriage instead. See the alternative translation in the NIV footnote.

37. E.g., R. Albert Mohler, "The Case for (Early) Marriage," *Albert Mohler*, August 3, 2009, http://www.albertmohler.com/2009/08/03/the-case-for-early-marriage/.

38. Marshall with Towner (*Pastoral Epistles*, 538) think a distinction is made between the people who go astray and those whose influence leads them astray. In other words, the latter are worse than the former.

39. At the very least, Paul believes the whole package of false teaching being promoted will lead its followers into full-fledged apostasy. See, e.g., Jerome D. Quinn and William C. Wacker, *The First and Second Letters to Timothy* (Grand Rapids: Eerdmans, 2000), 354–55.

40. My understanding of this difficult verse combines elements of two studies: M. D. Roberts, "'Women Shall Be Saved': A Closer Look at 1 Timothy 2:15," *TSF Bulletin* 5.2 (1981): 4–7; and Andreas J. Köstenberger, "Ascertaining Women's God-Ordained Roles: An Interpretation of 1 Timothy 2:15," *Bulletin for Biblical Research* 7 (1997): 107–44.

41. See, e.g., Carl Owen, *Celibacy and Religious Traditions* (Oxford: Oxford University Press, 2008).

42. The pastor was Lee Eclov, who has had a wonderful career in ministry, nicely encapsulated in his *Pastoral Graces: Reflections on the Care of Souls* (Chicago: Moody, 2012).

43. The best definition of Christian love I have ever encountered outside of the Bible itself comes from Richard Walker, founder of AMOR Ministries, a Baptist ministry to the indigenous people of the upper Amazon basin in Brazil. The organization's motto is that love is "the unsolicited giving or the very best you have on behalf of another regardless of response."

44. "What Do Arranged Marriage Statistics Tell Us?" Everything Engagement, n.d., http://www.everythingengagement.com/definition-of-marriage/arranged-marriage-statistics.html.

45. For the relevant Jewish backgrounds, showing that all marriages were viewed as God-ordained and at least *intended* to be permanent, see David Instone-Brewer, *Divorce and Remarriage in the Bible: The Social and Literary Context* (Grand Rapids: Eerdmans, 2002), 136–41.

46. Joseph F. Jensen, "Does *Porneia* Mean Fornication? A Critique of Bruce Malina," *Novum Testamentum* 20 (1978):161–84.

47. The main point of the miracle is actually to show "the replacement of the old purifications by the wine of the kingdom of God."—D. A. Carson, *The Gospel according to John* (Grand Rapids: Eerdmans, 1991), 166.

48. Instone-Brewer, *Divorce and Remarriage in the Bible*, 132.

49. Ibid., 110–14.

50. In fact, the Gospels "abrogate all Mosaic grounds for divorce," since *porneia* was not mentioned in the Law per se.—Andrew Cornes, *Divorce and Remarriage: Biblical Principles and Pastoral Practice* (Grand Rapids: Eerdmans, 1993), 213.

51. Craig S. Keener, "Adultery, Divorce," in *Dictionary of New Testament Background*, eds. Craig A. Evans and Stanley E. Porter Jr. (Downers Grove, IL: IVP, 2000), esp. 6–7.

52. David Atkinson, *To Have and to Hold: The Marriage Covenant and the Discipline of Divorce* (Grand Rapids: Eerdmans, 1981), 83.

53. See further Craig L. Blomberg, "Marriage, Divorce, Remarriage and Celibacy: An Exegesis of Matthew 19:3–12," *Trinity Journal* 11 (1990): esp. 161–85.

54. Cf. esp. Ciampa and Rosner, *The First Letter to the Corinthians*, 296–302.

55. Blomberg, "Marriage, Divorce, Remarriage and Celibacy," esp. 186–96.

56. See, e.g., Larry Richards, "Divorce and Remarriage under a Variety of Circumstances," in *Divorce and Remarriage: Four Christian Views*, ed. H. Wayne House (Downers Grove, IL: IVP, 1990), 215–48.

57. E. Randolph Richards and Brandon J. O'Brien, *Paul Behaving Badly: Was the Apostle Paul a Racist, Chauvinist Jerk?* (Downers Grove, IL: IVP, 2016).

58. Paul may well be applying the principle of loving your neighbor as yourself. See Peter T. O'Brien, *The Letter to the Ephesians* (Grand Rapids: Eerdmans, 1999), 426–27.

59. Which translation one uses makes a huge difference here, since several try to smooth out the English by rendering "not *only* to your own interest." The Greek has no "only"!

60. Cf. further Craig L. Blomberg, "Dream Job," *Journal for Case Teaching* 5 (1993): 67–70.

61. "Sapphira is evidently a capable woman, able to operate independently of her husband—she arrives three hours later, apparently on her own," but "She misses the opportunity to change their story and tell the truth."—Eckhard J. Schnabel, *Acts* (Grand Rapids: Zondervan, 2012), 286.

62. That a wife made this decision, flaunting the social convention that she accept the religious commitments of her husband, was itself a most non-submissive action.—J. Ramsey Michaels, *1 Peter* (Waco: Word, 1988), 157.

63. It is also possible that Peter is combining a reference to this passage with Sarah's controversial obedience to Abraham in posing as his sister in Genesis 12:20, given the way God providentially used it.

64. Cf. Peter H. Davids, *The First Epistle of Peter* (Grand Rapids: Eerdmans, 1990), 121.

65. Cf. esp. Steven R. Tracy, "Domestic Violence in the Church and Redemptive Suffering in 1 Peter," *Calvin Theological Journal* 41 (2006): 279–96.

66. John H. Elliott (*1 Peter* [New York: Doubleday, 2000], 575) takes it as understanding both that she is the weaker vessel and that she is a co-heir of the gift of life—i.e., what the rest of the verse goes on to delineate about her.

67. Davids, *First Epistle of Peter*, 123.

Continuing Insight: Keys to Premarital Training

1. S. M. Stanley, "Making a Case for Premarital Education, *Family Relations*, 50, 272–80.

2. David H. Olson and Amy K. Olson, *Empowering Couples: Building on Your Strengths* (Minneapolis: Life Innovations, 2000).

3. Lois M. Collins, "U. S. Marriage Rate Hits New Low and May Continue to Decline," *Deseret News*, May 20, 2015, https://www.deseretnews.com/article/865629093/US-marriage-rate-hits-new-low-and-may-continue-to-decline.html.

4. Marriage and Divorce," CDC, https://www.cdc.gov/nchs/fastats/marriage-divorce.htm.

5. For example, Focus on the Family has an excellent assessment: https://www.focusonthe family.com/marriage/couple-checkup.

Chapter 5: The Language of "Embodied" Differences in Marriage

1. Gregg R. Allison, *The Baker Compact Dictionary of Theological Terms* (Grand Rapids: Baker, 2016), 92.

2. C. S. Lewis, *The Four Loves* (New York: Harcourt Brace, 1960), 101.

3. All Scripture references in this chapter are taken from the English Standard Bible.

4. "Though Christian interpreters of Scripture have traditionally understood 'the breath of life' to refer to the spirit (Hebrew *ruach*) or immaterial aspect of human beings (with others understanding the last phrase 'and the man became a living soul' [Hebrew *nephesh*] to refer to the soul, another element of the immaterial aspect), this is not my position. First, 'the breath of life' is a property that is shared by all living creatures (Gen. 1:30), and it is this energizing principle that is given at conception and withdrawn at death (Gen. 7:22; Eccl. 12:7). Second, the last phrase of Gen. 2:7 explains 'the man became a living being' and does not indicate that to his immaterial spirit was added an immaterial soul. Rather, the material entity formed by God, the lifeless 'lump of clay' (Luther), was enlivened by the vitalizing principle, and it thus became a living person. If a complaint is registered that this interpretation demeans man's existence by relegating him to the same level as all other living creatures, it should be noted that the text specifies that God himself breathed this breath of life into the man's nostrils, something that is not said of any of the other creatures. This personal impartation of the energizing principle to the man distinguishes him from, and elevates him above, all other creatures." Gregg R. Allison, "Toward a Theology of Human Embodiment," *Southern Baptist Journal of Theology* 13, no. 10 (Summer 2009): 14n3.

5. This interpretation coheres with Paul's understanding of Genesis 2:24 in his argument against fornication: the physical act of sexual intercourse between a Christian brother and a prostitute effects a one-flesh union (1 Cor. 6:12–20).

6. A. W. Tozer, *The Knowledge of the Holy* (New York: HarperOne, 1961) in *A. W. Tozer: Three Spiritual Classics in One Volume* (Chicago: Moody, 2018), 56.

7. Lynn B. Jorde, "Genetic Variation and Human Evolution," https://www.ashg.org/education/pdf/geneticvariation.pdf.

8. For additional information about prenatal development, consider reviewing the *Merck Manual*, http://www.merckmanuals.com/home/women-s-health-issues/normal-pregnancy/stages-of-development-of-the-fetus.

9. Janet S. Hyde and John D. LaLamater, *Understanding Human Sexuality, 9th edition* (New York: McGraw-Hill Education, 2005), 100.

10. Ibid., 100.

11. Scott F. Gilbert, "Chromosomal Sex Determination in Mammals" in *Developmental Biology, 6th edition* (Sunderland, MA: Sinauer Associates, 2000).

12. R. Bukowski et al., "Human Sexual Size Dimorphism in Early Pregnancy," *American Journal of Epidemiology* 165, no. 10: 1216–18.

13. Adel K. Afifi and Ronald A. Bergman, *Functional Neuroanatomy* (New York: McGraw Hill, 1998), 495–96.

14. Marco Iacoboni and John C. Mazziotta, "Mirror neuron system: basic findings and clinical applications," *Annals of Neurology* 62 (2009): 213–18.

15. John M. Allman et al., "The Von Economo Neurons in Frontoinsular and Anterior Cingulate Cortex in Great Apes and Humans," *Brain Structure and Function* 214 (2010): 495–517.

16. Daniel J. Siegel, *Pocket Guide to Interpersonal Neurobiology* (New York: Norton, 2012).

17. World Health Organization, "Health Impact Assessment," http://www.who.int/hia/evidence/doh/en/.

18. Siegel, *Pocket Guide*, 20–23.

19. Frederica Mathewes-Green, "The Subject Was Noses," *Books & Culture*, January/February 1997. Her reference is to Dave Barry, *Babies and Other Hazards of Sex: How to Make a Tiny Person in Only Nine Months, with Tools You Probably Have around the Home* (New York: Rodale Books, 2000).

20. James R. Roney, Stephen V. Mahler, and Dario Maestripieri, "Behavioral and hormonal responses of men to brief interactions with women," *Evolution and Human Behavior* 24 (2003): 365–75.

21. Saul L. Miller and Jon K. Maner, "Scent of a woman: men's testosterone responses to olfactory ovulation cues," *Psychological Science,* 21 (2009): 276–83.

22. Donatella Marazziti and Domenico Canale, "Hormonal changes when falling in love," *Psychoneuroendocrinology* 29 (2004): 931–36.

23. Calvin Miller, *A Covenant for All Season: The Marriage Journey* (Wheaton, IL: Harold Shaw Publishers, 1005), ix.

24. Sandra J. Berg and Katherine E. Wynne-Edwards, "Changes in testosterone, cortisol, and estradiol in men becoming fathers," *Mayo Clinic Proceedings* 76 (2001): 582–92.

25. Dirk Scheele, Nadine Striepens, Onur Güntürkün, Sandra Deutschländer, Wolfgang Maier, Keith M. Kendrick, and René Hurlemann, "Oxytocin modulates social distance between males and females," *The Journal of Neuroscience* 32 (2012): 16074–9.

26. Marie S. Carmichael, Valerie L. Warburton, Jean Dixen, and Julian M. Davidson, "Relationships among cardiovascular, muscular, and oxytocin responses during human sexual activity," *Archives of Sexual Behavior* 23 (1994): 59–79.

27. For further discussion, see Marva J. Dawn, *Keeping the Sabbath Wholly: Ceasing, Resting, Embracing, Feasting* (Grand Rapids: Eerdmans, 1989); Dorothy C. Bass, "Keeping Sabbath: Reviving a Christian Practice," *Christian Century* (January 1997), 12–16.

28. Mathias Basner, Hengyi Rao, Namni Goel, and David F. Dinges, "Sleep deprivation and neurobehavioral dynamics," *Current Opinion in Neurobiology*, 23 (2013): 854–63.

29. Toni Moi-Prince and Ted Abel, "The impact of sleep loss on hippocampal function," *Learning and Memory* 20 (2013): 558–69.

30. There is a well-established literature on the psychology of stress that has looked at a wide variety of psychological and physiological effects. For a beneficial review, see Neil Schneiderman, Gail Ironson, and Scott D. Siegel, "Stress and Health: Psychological, behavioral, and biological determinants," *Annual Review of Clinical Psychology* 1 (2005): 607–28.

31. For further discussion, see Craig G. Bartholomew, *Where Mortals Dwell: A Christian View of Place for Today* (Grand Rapids: Baker Academic, 2011).

32. Neil Young, "The Needle and the Damage Done," *Harvest* (Reprise Records, 1972).

33. Alan Booth and James M. Dabbs Jr., "Testosterone and Men's Marriages," *Social Forces* 72 (1993): 463–77.

34. Karl M. Pirke, Götz Kockott, and Franz Dittmar, "Psychosexual stimulation and plasma testosterone in man," *Archives of Sexual Behavior,* 3 (1974): 577–84.

35. Daniel J. Siegel, *Mindsight: The New Science of Personal Transformation* (New York: Bantam, 2012).

36. Ibid., 176.

37. Patricia Ribeiro Porto, Leticia Oliveira, Jair Mari, Eliane Volchan, Ivan Figueira, and Paula Ventura, "Does cognitive behavior therapy change the brain? A systematic review of neuroimaging in anxiety disorders," *Journal of Neuropsychiatry and Clinical Neurosciences* 21 (2009): 114–25.

Chapter 6: The Beauty and Design of Marriage: An Image for the Church and Its Gospel

1. This and all Scripture references in this chapter are from the New American Standard Version of the Bible.

2. We want to qualify that we are not speaking globally about marriage, since culture and societal norms can bring distinction in statements that we don't feel qualified or experienced to address or comment. We are compelled by the transformative work of the gospel and the Holy Spirit to be the agent by which change comes in cultures that do not function as or accept similar language as that based in Western culture.

3. Catherine P. Roth and David Anderson, trans., Saint John Chrysostom, "Marriage Sermon" in *On Marriage and Family Life: Popular Patristic Series* (Crestwood, NY: St. Vladimir's Seminary Press, 1986), 86ff.

4. Belinda Luscombe, "How to Stay Married," in special *Time* edition "The Science of Marriage: All About About Attraction, What Keeps Love Strong, Making the Union Last," April 28, 2017, 6.

5. Marc Cortez, *Theological Anthropology: A Guide for the Perplexed* (New York: T&T Clark International, 2010), 60.

6. "At the same time they were created for a relationship characterized by unity. The larger question then revolves around the significance of these differences and their intended union," in Michelle-Lee Barnewall, *Neither Complementarian nor Egalitarian* (Grand Rapids: Baker Academic, 2016), 122.

7. St. John Chrysostom, *On Marriage and Family Life*, 46.

8. John H. Walton, *The Lost World of Genesis One* (Downers Grove, IL: InterVarsity Press, 2009), 69. Another explanation of his use of archetype can be found in John H. Walton, *The Lost World of Adam and Eve* (Downers Grove, IL: InterVarsity Academic, 2015), 74ff.

9. Louann Brizendine, *The Female Brain* (New York: Broadway Books, 2006), 1.

10. Dan Allender and Tremper Longman III, *Intimate Allies: Rediscovering God's Design for Marriage and Becoming Soul Mates for Life* (Forest, VA: American Association of Christian Counselors, 1995), 144.

11. George E. Ladd, *A Theology of the New Testament*, rev. ed. (Grand Rapids: Eerdmans, 1993), 592.

12. Brad Harper and Paul Louis Metzger, *Exploring Ecclesiology: An Evangelical and Ecumenical Introduction* (Grand Rapids: Brazos, 2009), 203.

13. St. John Chrysostom, *On Marriage and Family Life*, 46–47.

14. Wayne Grudem, *Bible Doctrine: Essential Teachings of the Christian Faith* (Grand Rapids: Zondervan, 1999), 367.

15. Dietrich Bonhoeffer, *Sanctorum Communio: A Theological Study of the Sociology of the Church* (Minneapolis: Fortress Press, 2009), 171.

16. Wesley Hill, *Spiritual Friendship: Finding Love in the Church as a Celibate Gay Christian* (Grand Rapids: Brazos, 2015), 100–101.

Chapter 7: The Dance of Gender in New Covenant Marriage

1. I especially want to thank my wife, Rebekah, for conversations on these issues throughout our marriage that God used to help me see my own patriarchy and its sin, though I'm still learning (see chapter 11). Thanks also to Shari and Bob Stewart for countless conversations on these issues and detailed responses to previous versions of the chapter. I also want to thank my friend Tom Schreiner for his thoughts on this chapter.

2. For a discussion on the difference between sex and gender see Laurie A. Rudman and Peter Glick, *The Social Psychology of Gender* (New York: Guilford, 2008), 6.

3. J. Budziszewski, *Written on the Heart: The Case for Natural Law* (Downers Grove, IL: InterVarsity, 1997).

4. Simon LeVay and Sharon M. Valente, *Human Sexuality* (Sunderland, MA: Sinauer Associates, 2003).

5. Eric L. Johnson, *God and Soul Care: The Therapeutic Resources of the Christian Faith* (Downers Grove, IL: InterVarsity, 2017). Mark A. Yarhouse, *Understanding Gender Dysphoria* (Downers Grove, IL: InterVarsity), 2015.

6. Andrew T. Walker, *God and the Transgender Debate* (Epsom, UK: The Good Book Co., 2017).

7. Janet T. Spence, "Gender-Related Traits and Gender Ideology: Evidence for a Multifactorial Theory," *Journal of Personality and Social Psychology* 64, no. 4 (1993): 624–35.

8. Dietrich Bonhoeffer, *Letters and Papers from Prison* (Minneapolis: Fortress Press, 2015), 54. "A wedding sermon for his friend Eberhard Bethge and cousin Renate" while in prison, May 15, 1943.

9. W. Robert Godfrey, "Headship and the Bible," in *Does Christianity Teach Male Headship?* D. Blankenhorn, D. Browning, and M. S. Van Leeuwen, eds. (Grand Rapids: Eerdmans, 2004), 82–91.

10. Janet Shibley Hyde, "The Gender Similarities Hypothesis," *American Psychologist* 60, no. 6 (2005): 581–92. DOI: 10.1037/0003-066X.60.6.581.

11. Eleanor E. Maccoby and Carol N. Jacklin, *The Psychology of Sex Differences* (Stanford, CA: Stanford University Press, 1975).

12. Ibid.

13. Janet S. Hyde, Elizabeth Fennema, and Susan J. Lamon, "Gender Differences in Mathematics Performance: a Meta-analysis," *Psychological Bulletin* 107, no. 2 (1990): 139–55. DOI: 10.1034/0033-2909.107.2.139.

14. Andrea Norton, Ellen Winner, Karl Cronin, Katie Overy, Dennis J. Lee, and Gottfried Schlaug, "Are There Pre-existing Neural, Cognitive, or Motoric Markers for Musical Ability?" *Brain and Cognition* 59 (2005): 124–34. DOI:10.1016/j.bandc.2005.05.009.

15. Paul T. Costa Jr., Antonio Terracciano, and Robert R. McCrae, "Gender Differences in Personality Traits Across Cultures," *Journal of Personality and Social Psychology* 81, no. 2 (2001): 322–31. DOI: 10.1037//0022-3514.81.2.322.

16. Alice H. Eagly, Steven J. Karau, and Mona G. Makhijani, "Gender and the Effectiveness of Leaders: A Meta-Analysis," *Psychological Bulletin* 117 (1995): 125–45.

17. Hyde et al. "Gender Differences in Mathematics Performance."

18. Michelle Lee-Barnewall, *Neither Complementarian nor Egalitarian: A Kingdom Corrective to the Evangelical Gender Debate* (Grand Rapids: Baker, 2016).

19. LeVay and Valente, *Human Sexuality,* ch. 5.

20. Jerry R. Thomas and Karen E. French "Gender Differences Across Age in Motor Performance: A Meta-Analysis," *Psychological Bulletin* 98, no. 2 (1985): 260–82.

21. Darren W. Campbell and Warren O. Eaton, "Sex Differences in the Activity Level of Infants," *Infant and Child Development* 8 (1999): 1–17; Stewart G. Trost, Russell R. Pate, James F. Sallis, Patty S. Freedson, Wendell C. Taylor, Marsha Dowda, and John Sirard, "Age and Gender Differences in Objectively Measured Physical Activity in Youth," *Medicine & Science in Sports & Exercise* 34, no. 2 (2002): 350–55.

22. John Archer, "Sex Differences in Aggression in Real-World Settings: A Meta-Analytic Review," *Review of General Psychology* 8, no. 4 (2004): 291–322.

23. Eleanor E. Maccoby, *Social Development* (New York: Harcourt Brace Jovanovich, 1980).

24. Maccoby and Jacklin, *The Psychology of Sex Differences.*

25. Ibid.

26. J. G. Richardson and C. H. Simpson, "Children, Gender, and Social Structure: An Analysis of the Contents of Letters to Santa Claus," *Child Development,* 53 (1982): 429–36. Gerianne M. Alexander, Teresa Wilcox, and Rebecca Woods, "Sex Differences in Infants' Visual Interest in Toys," *Archives of Sexual Behavior* 38 (2009): 427–33. DOI: 10.1007/s10508-008-9430-1.

27. L. A. Serbin, I. J. Tonick, and S. Sternglanz, "Shaping Cooperative Cross-sex Play," *Child Development* 48 (1977): 924–29.

28. Kathrin Koch, Katharina Pauly, Thilo Kellermann, Nina Y. Seiferth, Martina Reske, Volker Backes, Tony Stocker, N. Jon Shah, Katrin Amunts, Tilo Kircher, Frank Schneider, Ute Habel, "Gender Differences in the Cognitive Control of Emotion: An fMRI Study," *Neuropsychologia* 45 (2007): 2744–54.

29. Roy Baumeister, *Is There Anything Good About Men?* (New York: Oxford University Press, 2010). M. Van Vugt, D. De Cremer and D. P. Janssen, "Gender Differences in Cooperation and Competition: The Male-Warrior Hypothesis," *Psychological Science* 18, no. 1 (2007): 19–23.

30. James P. Byrnes, David C. Miller, and William D. Schafer, "Gender Differences in Risk Taking: A Meta-Analysis," *Psychological Bulletin* 125, no. 3 (1999): 367–83.

31. Mary Beth Oliver and Janet Shibley Hyde, "Gender Differences in Sexuality: A Meta-Analysis," *Psychological Bulletin* 114, no.1 (1993): 29–51. Jennifer L. Petersen and Janet Shibley Hyde, "A Meta-Analytic Review of Research on Gender Differences in Sexuality, 1993–2007," *Psychological Bulletin* 136, no. 1 (2010): 21–38. DOI: 10.1037/a0017504.

32. Sara Jafee and Janet Shibley Hyde, "Gender Differences in Moral Orientation: A Meta-Analysis," *Psychological Bulletin* 126, no. 5 (2000): 703–26. DOI: 10.1037//0033-2909.125.4.703.

33. Maccoby, *Social Development.*

34. Gerianne M. Alexander, Teresa Wilcox, and Rebecca Woods, "Sex Differences in Infants' Visual Interest in Toys," *Archives of Sexual Behavior* 38 (2009): 10.1007/s10508-008-9430-1.

35. Baumeister, *Is There Anything Good About Men?*

36. Judith A. Hill and David Matsumoto, "Gender Differences in Judgments of Multiple Emotions from Facial Expressions," *Emotion* 4, no. 2 (2004): 201–206.

37. Tor Wager, Luan Phan, Israel Liberzon, and Stephan Taylor, "Valence, Gender, and Lateralization of Function Brain Anatomy in Emotion: A Meta-analysis of Findings from Neuro-Imaging," *NeuroImage* 19 (2003): 513–31. doi:10.1016/S1053-8119(03)00078-8.

38. Kathryn Dindia and Mike Allen, "Sex Differences in Self-Disclosure: A Meta-Analysis," *Psychological Bulletin* 112, no. 1, 106–124.

39. K. V. Petrides and Adrian Furnham, "Gender Differences in Measured and Self-Estimated Trait Emotional Intelligence," *Sex Roles* 42, no. 5/6 (2000): 449–61.

40. Kathleen A. Eldridge and Andrew Christensen, "Demand-withdraw Communication During Couple Conflict: A Review and Analysis," in P. Noller and J. A. Feeney (eds), *Advances in Personal Relationships. Understanding Marriage: Developments in the Study of Couple Interaction* (New York: Cambridge University Press: 2002), 289–322.

41. Emily A. Impett and Letitia Anne Peplau, "'His' and 'Her' Relationships? A Review of the Empirical Evidence," in *The Cambridge Handbook of Personal Relationships*, A. L. Vangelisti and D. Perlman, eds. (New York: Cambridge University Press, 2006), 273–92.

42. Julia T. Wood, "Gender and Personal Relationships," in *Close Relationships: A Sourcebook*, C. Hendrick and S. S. Hendrick, eds. (Thousand Oaks, CA: Save, 2000), 301–13.

43. Deborah Belle, "Gender Differences in the Social Moderators of Stress," in *Stress and Coping: An Anthology*, A. Monat and R. S. Lazarus, eds. (New York: Columbia University Press: 1991), 258–74.

44. Lisa A. Neff and Benjamin R. Karney, "Gender Differences in Social Support: A Question of Skill or Responsiveness," *Journal of Personality and Social Psychology*, 88, no. 1 (2005): 79–90.

45. Jaffe and Hyde, "Gender Differences in Moral Orientation: A Meta-Analysis."

46. Timothy Grall, "Custodial Mothers and Fathers and Their Child Support: 2013," United States Census Bureau (January 2016).

47. Most of the research cited used meta-analysis, which pools the results from dozens to hundreds of studies and reports an "effect size," which is a measure of the mean difference of interest across all the studies, scaled in terms of standard deviation from the overall mean.

48. David Bakan, *The Duality of Human Existence* (Chicago: Rand McNally & Co., 1966) was the first to suggest this as a way of contrasting the genders; see also Alan Feingold, "Gender Differences in Personality: A Meta-Analysis," *Psychological Bulletin* 116, no. 3 (1994): 429–56; Janet T. Spence and Robert L. Helmreich, *Masculinity & Femininity: Their Psychological Dimensions, Correlates & Antecedents* (Austin: University of Texas Press, 1978).

49. In *God and Soul Care* (Downers Grove, IL: InterVarsity, 2017), I argue that the Trinity ought to be viewed as "personal agents-in-communion," and the Trinity therefore serves as the archetype for humans made in His image.

50. Dietrich von Hildebrand, *Man and Woman: Love and the Meaning of Intimacy* (Manchester, NH: Sophia Institute Press, 1966), 37.

51. Lea Pulkkinen, Taru Feldt, and Katja Kokko, "Personality in Young Adulthood and Functioning in Middle Age, in S. L. Willis and M. Martin, eds., *Middle Adulthood: A Lifespan Perspective* (Thousand Oaks, CA: Sage, 2005), 99–141.

52. Ted L. Huston, "The Social Ecology of Marriage and Other Intimate Unions," *Journal of Marriage Family* 62, 298–319.

53. Robert Davidson, *Genesis 1–11* (Cambridge: Cambridge University Press, 1973), 45.

54. Some have assumed that the desire here refers *only* to a desire for control, but that conclusion is underdetermined by the text. The interpretation advanced here originates in a corruption of a feminine strength, corollary to the curse on the male in the previous phrase, while allowing for multiple fallen female expressions.

55. Bonhoeffer, *Letters and Papers from Prison,* 52.

56. Again, these are symbolic generalizations. Fallen humans have individual differences, so there are certainly husbands more passive than their wives and wives less loving than their husbands. But even significant minorities of these kinds do not falsify generalizations about masculine and feminine tendencies, assuming their validity. Regarding pride and sloth as archetypal masculine and feminine sins, see Alistair McFadyen, *Bound to Sin: Abuse, Holocaust and the Christian Doctrine of Sin* (Cambridge: Cambridge University Press, 2000).

57. Though, to provide a fuller picture on this score, research on gender differences in aggression has found that men and women are just as likely to be aggressive toward others; but men are more likely to do so with strangers (and get arrested), whereas women are more aggressive with those they know, though expressed with fewer physical consequences. See Archer, "Sex Differences in Aggression in Real-World Settings: A Meta-Analytic Review."

58. Shari Stewart (personal communication, May 28, 2018).

59. Ronald F. Levant, Rosalie J. Hall, Christine M. Williams, and Nadia T. Hasan, "Gender Differences in Alexithymia," *Psychology of Men & Masculinity* 10, no. 3 (2009): 190–203.

60. Mark D. Kramer, Robert F. Krueger, and Brian M. Hicks, "The Role of Internalizing and Externalizing Liability Factors in Accounting for Gender Differences in the Prevalence of Common Psychopathological Syndromes," *Psychological Medicine* 38 (2008): 51–61.

61. Eric Rassin and Peter Muris, "To Be or Not To Be . . . Indecisive: Gender Differences, Correlations with Obsessive-Compulsive-complaints, and Behavioral Manifestation," *Personality and Individual Differences* 38, no. 5 (2005): 1175–81, https://doi.org/10.1016/j.paid.2004.07.014

62. Richard J. Foster, *Celebration of Discipline: The Path to Spiritual Growth*, 4th ed. (New York: Harper Collins, 2018), 21.

63. Of course, I am aware that most Christian marriages, my own included (see chapter 11), fall short of such ideals, and, for a variety of reasons, some fail.

64. Michael J. Gorman, *Cruciformity: Paul's Narrative Spirituality of the Cross* (Grand Rapids: Eerdmans, 2001).

65. This is what Michelle Lee-Barnewall calls the ironic "reversal" that is at the heart of this passage, in *Neither Complementarian nor Egalitarian: A Kingdom Corrective to the Evangelical Gender Debate* (Grand Rapids: Baker, 2016), 162.

66. Jonathan Edwards, *Charity and Its Fruits* (Edinburgh: Banner of Trust, 1969), Lecture XVI.

67. John Miller suggests as much in *Biblical Faith and Fathering* (New York: Paulist, 1989).

Continuing Insight: Uncomfortable Love

1. Unless otherwise noted, Scripture in this article is from the English Standard Version.

2. Scot McKnight, *Fellowship of Differents* (Grand Rapids: Zondervan, 2015), 58.

3. Richard Hays, *The Moral Vision of the New Testament* (New York: HarperOne, 1996), 348.

4. Jim Hinch, "Evangelicals Are Losing the Battle for the Bible. And They're Just Fine with That," *Los Angeles Review of Books*, Feb. 15, 2016, https://lareviewofbooks.org/essay/evangelicals-are-losing-the-battle-for-the-bible-and-theyre-just-fine-with-that/.

5. C. S. Lewis, *The Four Loves* (London: Collins, 1960), 111.

6. David Wells, *God in the Whirlwind* (Wheaton, IL: Crossway, 2014), 95–96.

7. David Platt, *Counter Culture* (Carol Stream, IL: Tyndale, 2015), 138.

8. All quotes in this paragraph are James K. A. Smith, "Marriage for the Common Good," *Comment*, July 17, 2014, https://www.cardus.ca/comment/article/4247/marriage-for-the-common-good/.

9. Josef Pieper, *Faith, Hope, Love* (San Francisco: Ignatius Press, 1997), 187.

10. David Wells, *God in the Whirlwind*, 85.

11. Ibid., 86–87.

12. See Barry Corey, *Love Kindness: Discover the Power of a Forgotten Christian Virtue* (Carol Stream, IL: Tyndale, 2016).

13. Joshua Ryan Butler, *The Skeletons in God's Closet* (Nashville: Thomas Nelson, 2014), 189.

Chapter 8: Reclaiming Holy Sexuality

1. Found at "Don Shrader," Quotery, http://www.quotery.com/authors/don-schrader/.

2. David Platt, *Counter Culture* (Carol Stream, IL: Tyndale, 2015), 138.

3. Billy Graham, "Sermon Notes on Marriage," collection 265 records of the BGEA: Montreat Office: Billy Graham—papers; part III: File Cabinet Sermons 1951, 1953–2006, Box 25 folder 38, Marriage, Gn. 24:67, sermon #636.

4. Russell Moore, *Onward: Engaging the Culture without Losing the Gospel* (Nashville: B&H, 2015), 167, 184.

5. Pope John Paul II has done extensive writing and teaching on this concept. Christopher West has translated and adapted his teaching, "Theology of the Body," for the modern church.

6. All quotations from Scripture are from the New International Version of the Bible.

7. John Piper, ed., *Sex and the Supremacy of Christ* (Wheaton, IL: Crossway, 2012), 26.

8. Timothy Keller, "Love and Lust" (sermon, Redeemer Presbyterian Church, New York, May 6, 2002).

9. Juli Slattery, *Rethinking Sexuality: God's Design and Why It Matters* (Colorado Springs, Multnomah, 2018), 60.

10. Christopher West, *Theology of the Body for Beginners* (West Chester, PA: Ascension Press, 2004), 12.

11. John Piper, *Desiring God*, rev. ed. (Colorado Springs: Multnomah, 2011), 80.

Chapter 9: From Shame to Wholeness

1. This and all other biblical quotes are taken from the New International Version of the Bible.

2. Quoted from *The Nicene Creed* (Grand Rapids: CRC Publications, 1987).

3. Pope John Paul II, Theology of the Body, 19:4.

4. Christopher West, *Theology of the Body for Beginners: A Basic Introduction to Pope John Paul II's Sexual Revolution* (West Chester, PA: Ascension Press, 2004), 24.

5. All this probably explains why human beings are so naturally interested in sex. The editors of *Time* magazine put it like this: "Why in the world are we so consumed by [sex]? The impulse to procreate may lie at the heart of sex, but . . . bursting from our sexual center is a whole spangle of other things—art, song, romance, obsession, rapture, sorrow, companionship, love, even violence and criminality. . . . Why should this be so? Did nature simply overload us in the mating department . . . ? Or is there something smarter and subtler at work, some larger interplay among sexuality, life and what it means to be human?" (*Time*, Jan. 19, 2004, 64). If the Judeo-Christian view is correct—that our sexuality is grounded in our very nature as human beings created in the image of a triune God—then all this makes perfect sense. Indeed, sex is not just about a biological urge to reproduce. There really is "something smarter and subtler at work."

6. Roman Catholicism and the Orthodox tradition regard marriage as a sacrament, but most Protestants do not. Given these truths about human sexuality and its grounding in the Trinity, perhaps more Protestants should reconsider this!

7. Compiled from John Witte Jr., *From Sacrament to Contract: Marriage, Religion, and Law in the Western Tradition*, 2nd edition (Louisville, KY: Westminster John Knox Press, 2012); Walter A. Elwell, *Evangelical Dictionary of Theology*, 2nd edition (Grand Rapids: Baker Academic, 2001); Alexander Schmemann, *For the Life of the World* (Crestwood, NY: St. Vladimir's Seminary Press, 1973); John Anthony McGunckin, ed., *The Encyclopedia of Eastern Orthodox Christianity, Vol 1, A–M* (West Sussex, UK: Wiley-Blackwell, 2011); Ken Parry, ed., *The Blackwell Companion to Eastern Christianity* (West Sussex, UK: Wiley-Blackwell, 2010).

8. Jonathan Edwards, "Original Sin" in *The Works of Jonathan Edwards* (Edinburgh: Banner of Truth Trust, 1974), 153.

9. John Calvin, *Institutes of the Christian Religion*, trans. Ford Lewis Battles (Philadelphia: The Westminster Press, 1960), 242–43.

10. John Wesley, "On Sin in Believers," *The Works of John Wesley, vol. 1* (Nashville: Abingdon, 1984), 323.

11. John Piper, "If I Fail to Forgive Others, Will God Not Forgive Me?" *Desiring God*, August 24, 2015, http://www.desiringgod.org/interviews/if-i-fail-to-forgive-others-will-god-not-forgive-me.

12. This metaphor for the church appears in such passages as 1 Corinthians 12:27, Colossians 1:24, Colossians 3:15, and Ephesians 4:12.

13. Brené Brown, *Daring Greatly: How the Courage to Be Vulnerable Transforms the Way We Live, Love, Parent, and Lead* (New York: Gotham Books, 2012), 41–42.

14. Mike Mason, *The Mystery of Marriage: As Iron Sharpens Iron* (Portland, OR: Multnomah, 1985), 139.

Chapter 10: Reclaiming Beauty Amidst Brokenness

1. Unless otherwise noted, Scripture references are taken from the English Standard Version of the Bible.

2. Anthony C. Thiselton, *Systematic Theology* (Grand Rapids: Eerdmans, 2015), 102; emphasis added.

3. Ellen J. Van Wolde, "Rhetorical, Linguistic and Literary Features of Genesis 1," in *Literary Structure and Rhetorical Strategies in the Hebrew Bible*, L. J. de Regt, Jan de Waard, and J. P. Fokkelman, eds. (Winona Lake, IN: Eisenbrauns, 1996), 149.

4. Walter Brueggemann, "Listening," in *Reverberations of Faith: A Theological Handbook of Old Testament Themes* (Louisville, KY: Westminster John Knox, 2002), 125.

5. Patrick D. Miller, "Man and Woman: Toward a Theological Anthropology," in *The Way of the Lord: Essays in Old Testament Theology* (Grand Rapids: Eerdmans, 2007), 311–12.

6. Ibid., 311.

7. Miroslav Volf, *Exclusion and Embrace: A Theological Exploration of Identity, Otherness, and Reconciliation* (Nashville, TN: Abingdon Press, 1996), 187.

8. John Goldingay, *Old Testament Theology: Israel's Gospel* (Downers Grove, IL: InterVarsity, 2003), 1:102.

9. Volf, *Exclusion and Embrace*, 186.

10. Robin Stockitt, *Restoring the Shamed: Towards a Theology of Shame* (Eugene, OR: Cascade Books, 2012), 71.

11. Volf, *Exclusion and Embrace*, 174.

12. See the helpful essay by Clark Barshinger, "The Spouses of Adult Survivors: How to Respond Christianly," in *The Long Journey Home: Understanding and Ministering to the Sexually Abused*, ed. Andrew J. Schmutzer (Eugene, OR: Wipf and Stock, 2011), 325–37; also the excellent book by Bessel van der Kolk, *The Body Keeps the Score: Brain, Mind, and Body in the Healing of Trauma* (New York: Penguin Books, 2015), esp. "Trapped in Relationships: The Cost of Abuse and Neglect" (125–37), and "Developmental Trauma: The Hidden Epidemic" (151–72).

13. Volf, *Exclusion and Embrace*, 184.

14. Jürgen Moltmann, *God in Creation: An Ecological Doctrine of Creation* (London: SCM Press, 1985), 279.

15. Miller, "Man and Woman," 312.

16. Richard M. Davidson, *Flame of Yahweh: Sexuality in the Old Testament* (Peabody, MA: Hendrickson, 2007), 31.

17. Bruce K. Waltke, *Genesis: A Commentary* (Grand Rapids: Zondervan, 2001), 89n39.

18. Davidson, *Flame of Yahweh*, 34.

19. A. S. Van der Woude, "*panim*," *Theological Lexicon of the Old Testament*, Ernst Jenni and Claus Westermann, eds. (Peabody, MA: Hendrickson, 1997), 2:1001.

20. Roger Scruton, *The Face of God* (London: Bloomsbury, 2012), 93.

21. Jesus' teaching on divorce in Matthew 19:4–8 reflects what the Jews called: *dabar halamed me 'inyano* (literally, "word of instruction from the context"). Moses may have allowed divorce, but it is also true that the Creator never intended the marriage union to be broken (cf. Rom. 4:10–11; Heb. 11:1–13, 35–40).

22. John Milton, *Paradise Lost*, Book IV, 310–43.

23. Craig C. Broyles, "Traditions, Intertextuality, and Canon," in *Interpreting the Old Testament: A Guide for Exegesis*, ed. Craig C. Broyles (Grand Rapids: Baker Academic, 2001), 172–73.

24. Nahum Sarna, *Genesis: The JPS Torah Commentary* (Philadelphia, PA: JPS, 1989), 23.

25. Jerome H. Neyrey, "Nudity," in *Handbook of Biblical Social Values*, John J. Pilch and Bruce J. Malina, eds. (Peabody, MA: Hendrickson, 2009), 140.

26. Robert A. Di Vito, "Old Testament Anthropology and the Construction of Personal Identity," *Catholic Biblical Quarterly* 61 (1999): 217–38. A good illustration of this corporate solidarity is Genesis 28:14, where God says to Jacob: "Your descendants [plural] will be like the dust of the earth, and you [singular] will spread out."

27. Iain Provan, *Discovering Genesis: Content, Interpretation, Reception* (Grand Rapids: Eerdmans, 2016), 66.

28. I owe the steps in this scheme of the temptation (Gen. 3:1–13) to my *Doktorvater*, Dr. Dick Averbeck (Trinity Evangelical Divinity School).

29. Sarna, *Genesis*, 27.

30. John Goldingay, *Biblical Theology: The God of the Christian Scriptures* (Downers Grove, IL: IVP Academic, 2016), 182.

31. Provan, *Discovering Genesis*, 89.

32. Stockitt, *Restoring the Shamed*, 11.

33. William P. Brown, "Creation," in *Eerdmans Dictionary of the Bible* (Grand Rapids: Eerdmans, 2000), 293.

34. Stockitt, *Restoring the Shamed*, 56.

35. Ibid., 71.

36. Ronald Potter-Efron and Patricia Potter-Efron, *Letting Go of Shame* (New York: Hazeldon Foundation, 1989), 45.

37. Stockitt, *Restoring the Shamed*, 71.

38. For further discussion of how abuse fractures the paradigm of intended marriage, see my "A Theology of Sexual Abuse: A Reflection on Creation and Devastation," in *Journal of the Evangelical Theological Society* 54 (2008): 785–812.

39. Walter Brueggemann, "Death," in *Reverberations of Faith*, 48.

40. Herbert W. Helm Jr., Jonathan R. Cook, and John M. Berecz, "The Implications of Conjunctive and Disjunctive Forgiveness for Sexual Abuse," *Pastoral Psychology* 54 (2005), 25.

41. Miroslav Volf, *The End of Memory: Remembering Rightly in a Violent World* (Grand Rapids: Eerdmans, 2006), 83–84.

42. Scruton, *The Face of God*, 158.

43. Ibid., 105; quoting *The Four Loves* (London: Harvest Books, 1960).

44. Ibid., 155.

45. Ibid., 157.

46. Stockitt, *Restoring the Shamed*, 44, 63.

47. Kenneth A. Mathews, *Genesis; New American Commentary*, 1A (Nashville, TN: Broadman & Holman, 1996), 1:225.

48. Stockitt, *Restoring the Shamed*, 49.

49. Ibid., 119.

50. Ibid., 9.

51. Jewish Publication Society of America version; jps.org.

52. Donald A. Hagner, *Matthew 14–28*; Word Biblical Commentary 33B (Dallas, TX: Word, 1995), 550.

53. Stockitt, *Restoring the Shamed*, 27.

54. Walter Brueggemann, "The Crisis and the Promise of Presence in Israel," in *Old Testament Theology: Essays on Structure, Theme, and Text*; ed. Patrick D. Miller (Minneapolis, MN: Fortress, 1992), 174.

55. Stockitt, *Restoring the Shamed*, 143, 151.

56. Ibid., 140.

Continuing Insight: Shame: Creating/Finding a Healing Marriage

1. Dan B. Allender, *Healing the Wounded Heart* (Grand Rapids: Baker, 2016), 199.

2. Ibid., 200.

Chapter 11: When Marriage Falls Short of the Christian Ideal

1. Madeleine L'Engle, *Two-Part Invention: The Story of a Marriage* (New York: Farrar, Straus & Giroux, 1988), 73.

2. This grace has been called "common" to distinguish it from special or saving grace, because it is distributed commonly across the human race, irrespective of one's relationship with God. Following Barth and König, we will use the adjective *creation* for this type of grace to underscore its dependence on God's creational and providential activity, to highlight its sphere of operation: humans as creatures; and to make clear its continuity with God's

activity throughout the rest of the created order. See Karl Barth, *Church Dogmatics: 4.1* (G. W. Bromiley, trans.) (Edinburgh: T. & T. Clark, 1956), 8–9; Adrio König, *The Eclipse of Christ in Eschatology: Toward a Christ-Centered Approach* (Grand Rapids: Eerdmans, 1989), 54. One problem with the distinction is it might be supposed to imply their mutual independence. Christians writing on the subject, however, have generally concluded that God's purposes in creation grace are subordinate to His redemptive purposes in the saving of His people and His desire to save everyone (Eph. 1:3–11; 1 Tim. 2:4; Rom. 2:4). At the same time, redemptive grace builds upon the operation of creation grace, or there are no humans, no culture, and no creation within which redemptive grace can operate. Abraham Kuyper, "Common Grace," in *Abraham Kuyper: A Centennial Reader*, ed. James D. Bratt (Grand Rapids: Eerdmans, 1998).

3. "Psychopathology" comes from Greek, *psyche*, the soul, and *pathos*, disorder. Psychopathology is the study of mental disorders.

4. Biopsychosocial: "Pertaining to the complex of biological, psychological, and social aspects of life; from the Greek, *bio* (life), *psyche* (mind), and Latin, *socius* (companion)," https://medical-dictionary.thefreedictionary.com/biopsychosocial.

5. A much elaborated discussion of the following framework can be found in Eric L. Johnson, *Foundations for Soul Care: A Christian Psychology Proposal* (Downers Grove, IL: InterVarsity, 2007; ch. 10, 11, 15); and Eric L. Johnson, *God and Soul Care: The Therapeutic Resources of the Christian Faith* (Downers Grove, IL: InterVarsity, 2017, ch. 8–11).

6. All quoted Scripture in this chapter, unless otherwise noted, is taken from the English Standard Version of the Bible.

7. Alistair McFadyen, *Bound to Sin: Abuse, Holocaust and the Christian Doctrine of Sin* (New York: Cambridge University Press, 2000).

8. See Alexander Pruss, *One Body: An Essay in Christian Sexual Ethics* (South Bend, IN: Notre Dame University, 2013); Eleonore Stump, *Wandering in Darkness: Narrative and the Problem of Suffering* (New York: Oxford University Press, 2010).

9. Jude Cassidy and Phillip R. Shaver, eds., *Handbook of Attachment, 3rd ed. Theory, Research, and Clinical Applications* (New York: Guilford, 2016); Christopher Clulow, ed., *Adult Attachment and Couple Psychotherapy* (Philadelphia: Taylor & Francis, 2001); Daniel Siegel, *The Developing Mind*, 2nd ed. (New York: Guilford, 2012).

10. Tim Clinton and Gary Sibcy, *Attachments: Why You Love, Feel, and Act the Way You Do* (Nashville: Thomas Nelson, 2009); Richard Plass and James Cofield, *The Relational Soul: Moving from False Self to Deep Connection* (Downers Grove, IL: IVP, 2014); Curt Thompson, *Anatomy of the Soul: Surprising Connections between Neuroscience and Spiritual Practices That Can Transform Your Life and Relationships* (Wheaton, IL: Tyndale, 2010).

11. Daniel J. Siegel, *The Developing Mind*, 2nd ed. (New York: Guilford, 2012); Erik Hesse, "The Adult Attachment Interview: Protocol, Method of Analysis, and Empirical Studies: 1985–2015," in Jude Cassidy and Philip R. Shaver, eds., *Handbook of Attachment*, 3rd ed. (New York: Guilford, 2016), 553–97.

12. "Dissociation is a mental process that causes a lack of connection in a person's thoughts, memory, and sense of identity," quoted in "Dissociation and Dissociative Disorders," Mental Health America, http://www.mentalhealthamerica.net/conditions/dissociation-and-dissociative-disorders.

13. Siegel, *The Developing Mind*, 109.

14. John Bowlby, *Attachment and Loss Volume One: Attachment* (New York: Basic Books, 1969); *Attachment and Loss Volume Two: Separation: Anxiety and Anger* (New York: Basic Books, 1973); *Attachment and Loss Volume Three: Loss: Sadness and Depression* (New York: Basic Books, 1980).

15. Judi Mesman, Marinus H. Van Ijzendoorn, and Abraham Sagi-Schwartz, "Cross-Cultural Patterns of Attachment," in *Handbook of Attachment: Theory, Research, and Clinical Applications*, 3rd ed., Jude Cassidy and Phillip R. Shaver, eds. (New York: Guilford, 2016), 852–77. The actual cross-cultural percentages of securely attached infants range from 56–80 percent and of insecurely attached infants from 20–44 percent.

16. Ross A. Thompson, "Early Attachment and Later Development: Familiar Questions, New Answers," in *Handbook of Attachment: Theory, Research, and Clinical Applications*, Jude Cassidy and Phillip R. Shaver, eds. (New York: Guilford, 2008), 348–65. See also Hesse, "The Adult Attachment Interview," cited above, n11.

17. James Fisher and Lisa Crandell, "Patterns of Relating in the Couple," in *Adult Attachment and Couple Psychotherapy*, ed. Christopher Clulow (London: Brunner-Routledge, 2001), 62–82.

18. "Attachment Security in Adult Partnerships," in Christopher Clulow, ibid., 28–42.

19. Lee E. Kirkpatrick and K. E. Davis, "Attachment style, gender, and relationships stability: A longitudinal analysis, *Journal of Personality and Social Psychology* 66 (1994): 502–12. Also, Fisher and Crandell, in *Adult Attachment and Couple Psychotherapy*.

20. Judith A. Feeney, "Adult Romantic Attachment: Developments in the Study of Couple Relationships," in Cassidy and Shaver, *Handbook of Attachment*, 456–81.

21. Susan Johnson and Ann Sims, "Attachment theory: A Map for Couples Therapy," in *Handbook of Attachment Interventions*, ed. Terry M. Levy (Boston: Academic Press, 2000), 169–92, quote on 171.

22. Kay Warren, *Christianity Today*, June 12, 2017, https://www.christianitytoday.com/women/2017/june/sacred-privilege-kay-rick-warren-we-were-in-marital-hell.html.

23. Johnson and Sims, "Attachment theory."

24. Guidelines for such interpretation can be found in Eric L. Johnson, *Foundations for Soul Care*, ch. 7.

25. Søren Kierkegaard, *For Self-Examination* (Princeton, NJ: Princeton University Press, 1990).

26. It is, of course, possible that the percentages are slightly more positive in Christian churches, assuming that a majority of churchgoers have grown up in Christian homes where, although not free from pathology and brokenness, parents strove to pursue healthier relationships with their children than they experienced with their own parents and had greater social resources in the church to help them do so. But research is needed to know whether or not this is happening.

27. Humphrey Carpenter, ed., *Letters of J. R. R. Tolkien* (New York: Houghton Mifflin, 2000), Letter to Christopher Tolkien, July 11, 1972.

28. Good works "arise from the principle of true faith" and "are done for [God's] glory. They are therefore distinct from the virtues of the pagans and the virtues of all who do not have such saving faith. The Reformed have always fully acknowledged the existence and moral

value of such virtues. Since after the fall people have remained human and continue to share in the blessings of God's common grace, they can inwardly possess many virtues and outwardly do many good deeds that, viewed through human eyes and measured by human standards, are greatly to be appreciated and of great value for human life." Herman Bavinck, *Reformed Dogmatics: Vol. 4.* (Grand Rapids: Baker, 2008), 256–7.

29. But such questions should not be despised; seeking to answer them is one of the many distinctives of a Christian science of psychology.

30. Johnson, *God and Soul Care*, ch. 8–11.

31. For a fuller exploration of this idea see Jonathan T. Pennington, *The Sermon on the Mount and Human Flourishing: A Theological Commentary* (Grand Rapids: Baker Academic, 2017).

32. For further discussion see Jason B. Hood, *Imitating God in Christ: Recapturing a Biblical Pattern* (Downers Grove, IL: IVP Academic, 2013).

33. J. Todd Billings, *Union with Christ: Reframing Theology and Ministry for the Church* (Grand Rapids: Baker Academic, 2011), 1. For a couple of recent, more exegetical and technical treatments, see Constantine R. Campbell, *Paul and Union with Christ: An Exegetical and Theological Study* (Grand Rapids: Zondervan, 2012), and Grant Macaskill, *Union with Christ in the New Testament* (Oxford: Oxford University Press, 2014).

34. "We urge you, brothers, admonish the idle, encourage the fainthearted, help the weak, be patient with them all" (1 Thess. 5:14). See also St. Gregory the Great, *Pastoral Care* (New York: Newman Press, 1950); Martin Bucer, *Concerning the True Care of Souls*, trans. Peter Beale. (Edinburgh: The Banner of Truth Trust, 2010) (though the tone of Bucer is much more "law-dominant," than that of Gregory the Great!).

35. Both of us have been helped in our journeys through personality inventories like the Enneagram and Myers-Briggs. My marriage (Jonathan), in particular, has been impacted and improved as my wife and I have come to appreciate how our relational dynamics are a function of personality types that differentially perceive the world and are motivated.

Continuing Insight: A Social Sacrament

1. American Association of Christian Counselors, Dr. Tim Clinton and Dr. Jared Pingleton, eds., *The Struggle Is Real: How to Care for Mental and Relational Needs in the Church* (Bloomington, IN: WestBow, 2017), aacc.net/resources/.

2. For a discussion of differences between a covenant and contract see Jared Pingleton, *Making Magnificent Marriages* (Springfield, MO: Marriage Improvement Tools, 2013), ch. 2, 39–60.

Chapter 12: Divorce and Remarriage

1. Unless otherwise noted, Scripture in this chapter is taken from the English Standard Version.

2. William A. Heth, "Another Look at the Erasmian View of Divorce and Remarriage," *Journal of the Evangelical Theological Society* 25 (1982), 263–72; "The Meaning of Divorce in Matthew 19:3–9," *Churchman* 98 (1984), 136–52; "Divorce and Remarriage" in *Applying the Scriptures: Papers From ICBI Summit III* (ed. K. S. Kantzer; Grand Rapids: Zondervan, 1987), 219–39; "Unmarried 'for the Sake of the Kingdom' (Matthew 19:12) in the Early Church," *Grace Theological Journal* 8 (Spring 1987): 55–88; "Divorce, but

No Remarriage" in *Divorce and Remarriage: Four Christian Views* (ed. H. Wayne House; Downers Grove, IL: InterVarsity, 1990), 73–129; "The Changing Basis for Permitting Remarriage after Divorce for Adultery: The Influence of R. H. Charles," *Trinity Journal* 11NS (1990), 143–59; "Divorce and Remarriage: The Search for an Evangelical Hermeneutic," *Trinity Journal* NS 16:1 (Spring 1995): 63–100. With Gordon J. Wenham, *Jesus and Divorce: Towards an Evangelical Understanding of New Testament Teaching* (London: Hodder & Stoughton, 1984; Nashville: Thomas Nelson, 1985). In the updated edition of *Jesus and Divorce* (Paternoster, 1997) we added a 34-page appendix and over 350 additional bibliographical entries, most of them appearing since 1984.

3. Craig L. Blomberg, *Matthew: New American Commentary* (Nashville: Broadman, 1992), 111. Cf. C. D. Osburn, "The Present Indicative of Matthew 19:9," *Restoration Quarterly* 24 (1981): 193–203.

4. Joseph Fitzmyer, "The Matthean Divorce Texts and Some New Palestinian Evidence," *Theological Studies* 37 (June 1976): 197–226. Charles C. Ryrie also defended this view in "Biblical Teaching on Divorce and Remarriage," *Grace Theological Journal* 3 (1982): 177–92. This, too, is the view of J. Carl Laney, *The Divorce Myth* (Minneapolis: Bethany, 1981) and his "No Divorce and No Remarriage" in *Divorce and Remarriage: Four Christian Views*, ed. H. Wayne House (Downers Grove, IL: InterVarsity, 1990), 15–54. So also Ben Witherington III, "Matthew 5.32 and 19.9—Exception or Exceptional Situation?" *New Testament Studies* 31 (1985): 571–76 ("except in the case of incest").

5. The best defense of the betrothal view is Abel Isaksson, *Marriage and Ministry in the New Temple. A Study with Special Reference to Mt. 19. 13 [sic]–12 and 1. Cor. 11. 3–16* (translated by Neil Tomkinson with the assistance of Jean Gray; Acta Seminarii Neotestamentici Upsaliensis 24; Lund: Gleerup; Copenhagen: Munksgaard), 1965. It has been revived by David W. Jones, "The Betrothal View of Divorce and Remarriage," *Bibliotheca Sacra* 165 (2008), 68–85. See the extensive interaction with the betrothal view in Andreas J. Köstenberger with David W. Jones, *God, Marriage, and Family: Rebuilding the Biblical Foundation* (Wheaton, IL: Crossway, 2004), 239–44.

6. We have collected and commented on many of these texts in Heth and Wenham, *Jesus and Divorce*, 23–38. Gordon J. Wenham defends the early church fathers' view in *Remarriage after Divorce in Today's Church: 3 Views*, ed. Mark L. Strauss (Grand Rapids: Zondervan, 2006), 19–42.

7. Cf. C. S. Keener, "Marriage, Divorce and Adultery" in *Dictionary of the Later New Testament & Its Developments*, Ralph P. Martin and Peter H. Davids, eds. (Downers Grove, IL: InterVarsity, 1997), 712–17.

8. For more details on why I changed my view, see William A. Heth, "Jesus on Divorce: How My Mind Has Changed," *Southern Baptist Journal of Theology* 6:1 (Spring 2002): 4–29; "Remarriage for Adultery or Desertion" in *Remarriage after Divorce in Today's Church: 3 Views*, ed. Mark Strauss (Grand Rapids, MI: Zondervan, 2006), 59–83.

9. Craig S. Keener, . . . *And Marries Another: Divorce and Remarriage in the Teaching of the New Testament* (Peabody, MA: Hendrickson, 1991). Even more definitive now than Keener is David Instone-Brewer, *Divorce and Remarriage in the Bible: The Social and Literary Context* (Grand Rapids: Eerdmans, 2002) and his more practical and pastoral book, *Divorce and Remarriage in the Church: Biblical Solutions for Pastoral Realities* (London: Paternoster; Downers Grove, IL: InterVarsity, 2003). Building on the work of Instone-Brewer most

recently is Colin Hamer, *Marital Imagery in the Bible: An Exploration of Genesis 2:24 and Its Significance for the Understanding of New Testament Divorce and Remarriage Teaching* (Foreword by William A. Heth; Apostolos Old Testament Studies; London: Apostolos, 2015).

10. Gordon P. Hugenberger, *Marriage as a Covenant: Biblical Law and Ethics as Developed from Malachi* (Supplements to Vetus Testamentum 52; Leiden: Brill, 1994; Grand Rapids: Baker Books, 1998), 3n25. Cf. also Instone-Brewer, *Divorce and Remarriage in the Bible*, 1–19.

11. Cf. Dennis J. McCarthy, *Treaty and Covenant: A Study in Form in the Ancient Oriental Documents and in the Old Testament* (Analectca Biblica 21a; Rome: Biblical Institute, 1981 [1st ed. 1963]), 175.

12. Hugenberger, *Marriage as a Covenant*, 174.

13. Instone-Brewer, *Divorce and Remarriage in the Church*, 7. Cf. Craig L. Blomberg, "Marriage, Divorce, Remarriage, and Celibacy: An Exegesis of Matthew 19:3–12," *Trinity Journal* 11 NS (1990): 169–70; Bruce Kaye, "'One Flesh' and Marriage," *Colloquium* 22 (1990): 51.

14. For further details see Heth, "Remarriage for Adultery or Desertion," 63–66; Raymond Westbrook, "The Prohibition on Restoration of Marriage in Deuteronomy 24:1–4," in *Studies in the Bible 1986* (Scripta Hierosolymitana 31; Jerusalem, Magnes, 1986): 387–405. John H. Walton ("The Place of the *Hutqattēl* within the D-Stem Group and Its Implications in Deuteronomy 24:4," *Hebrew Studies* 32 [1991], 7–17) makes a slight correction to Westbrook.

15. "Jesus' position is not far from that of his near-contemporary Shammai, and from Deuteronomy 24:1–4 as well" (D. J. Moo, "Law," in *Dictionary of Jesus and the Gospels* [J. B. Green and S. McKnight, eds.; Downers Grove, IL: IVP Academic, 1992], 455). Cf. Heth and Wenham, *Jesus and Divorce*, 168.

16. Instone-Brewer, *Divorce and Remarriage in the Bible*, 134–36, 154.

17. Cf. Hugenberger, *Marriage as a Covenant*, 67–76. So also Instone-Brewer, *Divorce and Remarriage in the Bible*, 7n30; Richard A. Taylor and E. Ray Clendenen, *Haggai, Malachi NAC* (Nashville: Broadman, 2004), 359–68.

18. Actually, Robert H. Stein made a similar case in "Is It Lawful for a Man to Divorce His Wife?" *Journal of the Evangelical Theological Society* 22 (1979), 115–21. He first alluded to the rhetorical overstatement approach to Jesus' teaching in *The Method and Message of Jesus' Teachings* (Philadelphia: Fortress, 1978), 11: "Certainly the 'exception clause' in Matt 5:32 and 19:9 reveals that Mark 10:11 is an overstatement in the eyes of Matthew." See also his *The Synoptic Problem: An Introduction* (Grand Rapids: Baker, 1987), 151–53.

19. I am using Instone-Brewer's translation (*Divorce and Remarriage in the Bible*, 111), one that is much more clear than Blackman's edition (vol. 3: *Nashim*, 444).

20. Ibid., 94–97.

21. Martin Luther, "A Sermon on the Estate of Marriage," in *Luther Works: American Edition, vol. 44: The Christian in Society I,* James Atkinson, gen. ed., Jelmut T. Lehmann, ed. (Philadelphia: Fortress Press, 1966), 8–9.

22. Craig S. Keener provides five observations for why Jesus' saying should be read hyperbolically ("Remarriage for Circumstances beyond Adultery or Desertion" in *Remarriage after Divorce in Today's Church: 3 Views*, ed. Mark Strauss [Grand Rapids: Zondervan, 2006], 106–9).

23. Cf. Instone-Brewer, *Divorce and Remarriage in the Bible*, 147–52; Hamer, *Marital Imagery in the Bible*, 230–31.

24. John Murray, *Divorce* (Phillipsburg, NJ: Presbyterian & Reformed, 1953), 99.

25. Ibid., 100

26. Instone-Brewer, *Divorce and Remarriage in the Church*, 104.

27. Blomberg, *Matthew*, 293.

28. Cf. Rubel Shelly, *Divorce and Remarriage: A Redemptive Theology* (Abilene, TX: Leafwood, 2007, 2012), 106–8.

29. Instone-Brewer, *Divorce and Remarriage in the Bible*, 275. "No new grounds for *initiating* a divorce are given in 1 Corinthians 7. . . . Paul was merely articulating the logic of the Scriptural position [in Ex. 21:10–11]" (Hamer, *Marital Imagery in the Bible*, 245).

30. Keener, "Remarriage for Circumstances beyond Adultery or Desertion," 135n38.

Continuing Insight: Pastoral Considerations

1. David Instone-Brewer, *Divorce and Remarriage in the Church: Biblical Solutions for Pastoral Realities* (London: Paternoster; Downers Grove, IL: InterVarsity, 2003), 173–91; Rubel Shelly, *Divorce and Remarriage: A Redemptive Theology* (Abilene, TX: Leafwood, 2007, 2012), 141–68.

2. Timothy Keller and Kathy Keller, *The Meaning of Marriage: Facing the Complexities of Commitment with the Wisdom of God* (New York: Riverhead Books, 2011), 91.

3. Ibid.

4. For a practical exploration of this topic, see *Anger: Taming a Powerful Emotion* by Gary Chapman.

Continuing Insight: Ministry, Remarriage, and God's Redeeming Power for the Next Generation

1. Today over 113 million Americans have a step-relationship of some kind (a stepparent, stepsibling, or stepchild) and it is predicted that one of two Americans will have a step-relationship at some point in their lifetime. In addition, 40 percent of married couples with children are stepfamilies. See stepfamily statistics at http://smartstepfamilies.com/view/statistics.

2. Understanding healthy stepfamily dynamics is the focus of *The Smart Stepfamily: Seven Steps to a Healthy Family* by Ron L. Deal (Bloomington, MN: Bethany, 2014).

3. Ibid., 44–46.

Chapter 13: Marriage and Community in the Body of Christ

1. This and all following biblical quotes are taken from the English Standard Version.

2. Mark Dever and Jamie Dunlop, *The Compelling Community: Where God's Power Makes a Church Attractive* (Wheaton, IL: Crossway, 2015), 25–26.

3. C. S. Lewis, *The Four Loves* (Boston, MA: Mariner Books, 1960), 121.

4. Ibid., 37.

5. Ibid.

6. Ibid., 66.

7. Ibid., 99.

8. Timothy Keller and Kathy Keller, *The Meaning of Marriage: Facing the Complexities of Commitment with the Wisdom of God* (New York: Riverhead Books, 2011), 130.

9. Lewis, *The Four Loves*, 131.

10. Joseph H. Hellerman, *When the Church Was a Family: Recapturing Jesus' Vision for Authentic Christian Community* (Nashville, TN: B&H Academic, 2009), 221.

11. http://www.desiringgod.org/messages/marriage-singleness-and-the-christian-virtue-of-hospitality.

12. Hellerman, *When the Church Was a Family*, 31.

13. Ibid.

14. Joseph H. Hellerman, *Why We Need the Church to Become More Like Jesus* (Eugene, OR: Wipf & Stock, 2017), 33.

15. Ibid. 36.

16. Barry Danylak, *Redeeming Singleness* (Wheaton, IL: Crossway, 2010).

17. Barry Danylak, *A Biblical Theology of Singleness* (Cambridge, UK: Grove Books Limited, 2006), 20.

18. http://cmr.biola.edu/blog/author/carrie-stockton/.

19. Christopher Ash, *Married for God: Making Your Marriage the Best It Can Be* (Wheaton, IL: Crossway, 2016), 21–22.

20. The Gottman Institute, https://www.gottman.com/.

21. Keller and Keller, *The Meaning of Marriage*, 127.

22. Ibid., 122.

23. Humphrey Carpenter, ed., *The Letters of J. R. R. Tolkien* (New York: Houghton Mifflin, 2000), 51.

24. https://spiritualfriendship.org/author/wahill/.

25. Christopher Ash, *Married for God*, 21–22.

26. Ibid. 19.

27. Ibid.

28. Ibid., 22.

29. Sam A. Andreades, *enGendered: God's Gift of Gender Difference in Relationship* (Wooster, OH: Weaver Book Company, 2015), 226.

30. Dever and Dunlop, *The Compelling Community*, 22.

31. Gary Thomas, *Sacred Marriage: What if God Designed Marriage to Make Us Holy More Than to Make Us Happy?* (Grand Rapids: Zondervan, 2015).

32. Tony Evans, *Kingdom Disciples* (Chicago: Moody, 2017), 180.

33. Andreades, *enGendered*, 226.

34. https://www.barna.com/research/state-church-2016/.

35. Dever and Dunlop, *The Compelling Community*, 124.

36. Ibid., 125.

Continuing Insight: The Church's Mission to Enrich and Restore Marriages

1. W. Bradford Wilcox, *Why Marriage Matters, Third Edition: Thirty Conclusions from the Social Sciences* (New York: Broadway Publications, 2011).

Chapter 14: A Philosophical Affirmation of Marriage from Natural Law

1. I am not meaning to downplay the excellent books written in defense of marriage, many of which I cite in this chapter. Rather, I am speaking on a wider cultural level both within and without the church. And I certainly don't pretend to be making new arguments here. I rely heavily on those who have come before me and simply hope to help advance these arguments more widely.

2. Fr. Stephen Freeman, "Marriage as a Lifetime of Suffering," May 5, 2015, https://blogs.ancientfaith.com/glory2godforallthings/2015/05/05/marriage-as-a-lifetime-of-suffering/.

3. There are many other factors beyond the cultural and legal challenges mentioned here. For instance, some have argued that Western culture's embrace of nominalism as the primary view of human nature as opposed to teleological and essentialist views have resulted in the acceptance of a liberationist view of human sexuality, which fosters acceptance of homosexual behavior and openness toward same-sex marriage. See David A. J. Richards, *Toleration and the Constitution* (New York: Oxford University Press, 1989). Jake Meador has argued that the roots of the cultural change toward accepting same-sex marriage trace back to how the industrial economy changed the understanding of home life in America. See Jake Meador, "The Inevitability of Same-Sex Marriage," https://mereorthodoxy.com/the-inevitability-of-same-sex-marriage/. Stephanie Coontz lists a number of contributing factors to the transformation of marriage including the development of nutrition and medicine, the growth of urbanization, and the legal and economic independence of women from men. See Stephanie Coontz, *Marriage, a History* (New York: Penguin Books, 2006).

4. See Sean McDowell and John Stonestreet, *Same-Sex Marriage: A Thoughtful Approach to God's Design for Marriage* (Grand Rapids: Baker, 2014), 86.

5. For instance, see the following book, which is based upon an in-depth analysis of how outsiders view Christians today: David Kinnaman and Gabe Lyons, *unChristian: What a New Generation Really Thinks about Christianity . . . and Why It Matters* (Grand Rapids: Baker, 2007).

6. *The Porn Phenomenon: The Impact of Pornography in the Digital Age* (Ventura, CA: The Barna Group, 2016), 80.

7. See Bradley R.E. Wright, *Christians Are Hate-Filled Hypocrites . . . and Other Lies You've Been Told* (Bloomington, MN: Bethany, 2010).

8. For instance, see Gordon J. Wenham, William A. Heth, and Craig S. Keener, *Remarriage*

after Divorce in Today's Church: 3 Views, ed. Mark L. Strauss (Grand Rapids: Zondervan, 2006).

9. Matthew Lee Anderson, "Why I Won't Sign the Nashville Statement," August 30, 2017, https://mereorthodoxy.com/nashville-statement/.

10. For example, *Outside the Womb: Moral Guidance for Assisted Reproduction* by Scott B. Rae and D. Joy Riley (Chicago: Moody, 2011) offers a compassionate and comprehensive discussion of these issues.

11. To be fair, it could also be argued that the sexual revolution is the driving force behind secularism. Many atheists have admitted that their problem with God is not a lack of evidence, but a desire to live without accountability. In many cases, their desire for sexual "freedom" is why they reject God. As Aldous Huxley conceded in his book *Ends and Means*, many people embrace secularism because they desire to live without sexual restraints.

12. Christian Smith, "Introduction," *The Secular Revolution: Power, Interests, and Conflict in the Secularization of American Public Life*, ed. Christian Smith (Los Angeles: University of California Press, 2003), 1.

13. Pew Research Poll, "The Future of World Religions: Population Growth Projections, 2010–2050" (April 2, 2015), http://www.pewforum.org/2015/04/02/religious-projections-2010-2050/.

14. See Nancy Pearcey, *Total Truth: Liberating Christianity from Its Cultural Captivity* (Wheaton, IL: Crossway, 2004).

15. James K. A. Smith, *How (Not) to Be Secular: Reading Charles Taylor* (Grand Rapids: 2014), 21.

16. R. R. Reno, *Resurrecting the Idea of a Christian Society* (Washington, DC: Regnery Faith, 2016), 23.

17. See Josh McDowell and Sean McDowell, *The Beauty of Intolerance* (Uhrichsville, OH: Shiloh Run Press, 2016), 19.

18. Interested readers might check out chapter 6, "The 'Cosmological' Shift: How Same-Sex Marriage Got Here" in my book with John Stonestreet, *Same-Sex Marriage: A Thoughtful Approach to God's Design for Marriage* (Grand Rapids: Baker, 2014).

19. I am not assuming that all theories of evolution are necessarily materialistic/atheistic. There is a lively debate among evangelicals about the evidence for evolution and what it would mean for the Christian faith. For instance, see *Old Earth or Evolutionary Creation: Discussing Origins with Reasons to Believe and BioLogos*, ed. Kenneth Keathley, J. B. Stump, and Joe Aguirre (Downers Grove, IL: InterVarsity Press, 2017), and *Four Views on Creation, Evolution, and Intelligent Design*, ed. J. B. Stump (Grand Rapids: Zondervan), 2017.

20. Margaret Sanger, *The Pivot of Civilization* (Lenox, MA: Hard Press, 2006), 104. Cited in Benjamin Wiker, *10 Books That Screwed Up the World: And 5 Others That Didn't Help* (Washington, DC: Regnery Publishing, Inc., 2008), 138.

21. Sherif Girgis, Ryan T. Anderson, and Robert P. George, *What Is Marriage? Man and Woman: A Defense* (New York: Encounter Books, 2012), 3.

22. See Mary Eberstadt, *Adam and Eve after the Pill* (San Francisco, CA: Ignatius, 2012).

23. R. Albert Mohler Jr., *We Cannot Be Silent: Speaking Truth to a Culture Redefining Sex, Marriage, and the Very Meaning of Right and Wrong* (Nashville: Thomas Nelson, 2015), 20.

24. As law professor David Pimentel has observed, no-fault divorce also "undermined the power of marriage to ensure material support for children, as a pattern emerged in which divorcing mothers negotiated for custody, and gave up claims to spousal and child support in return." David Pimentel, "The Impact of Obergefell: Traditional Marriage's New Lease on Life," *BYU Journal of Public Law* 30 (2016): 262.

25. W. Bradford Wilcox, "The Evolution of Divorce," *National Affairs* (Fall 2009).

26. Ibid.

27. James Bean, *The Christian Minister's Affectionate Advice to a Married Couple, 1860* (New York: The American Tract Society, n.d., from Special Collections at the Billy Graham Archives at Wheaton College), 45.

28. Patrick Lee and Robert P. George, *Conjugal Union: What Marriage Is and Why It Matters* (New York: Cambridge University Press, 2014), 7.

29. See http://www.worldofmonopoly.com/history/.

30. Greg Koukl, "Is Marriage a Social Construction?" March 31, 2013, https://www.str.org/articles/marriage-is-a-social-construction#.

31. Ibid.

32. Maggie Gallagher, "The Case Against Same-Sex Marriage," in *Debating Same-Sex Marriage*, John Corvino and Maggie Gallagher (New York: Oxford, 2012), 108–9.

33. The majority ruling of the Supreme Court case: *Obergefell v. Hodges* (2015), Justice Anthony Kennedy, 6, 13, https://www.supremecourt.gov/opinions/14pdf/14-556_3204.pdf.

34. The dissent by Justice John Roberts (2015), 17, https://www.supremecourt.gov/opinions/14pdf/14-556_3204.pdf.

35. Francis J. Beckwith, "Marriage, Sex, and the Jurisprudence of Skepticism: A Response to Ronald E. Long," *Philosophia Christi*, 7, no. 1 (2005): 42.

36. See John Witte Jr., *From Sacrament to Contract, Second Edition: Marriage, Religion, and Law in the Western Tradition* (Louisville, KY: Westminster John Knox Press, 2012), 121–23. Also see Scott Stiegemeyer, "Robert George's Natural Law Argument against Same-Sex Marriage," *Concordia Theological Quarterly* 78 (2014): 129–153.

37. Aristotle, *Nichomachean Ethics*, Book 1, 1094a, trans. Terence Irwin, 2nd edition (Indianapolis: Hackett, 1999), 1.

38. Advocates of same-sex marriage often claim that since animals perform homosexual acts, then same-sex unions are natural. Frank Turek responds: "This 'animals-do-it' argument is seriously put forth by homosexual activists. Yes, some animals engage in homosexual behavior on occasion, but some animals eat their young too. Should we do that as well? When homosexual activists extol animals as their moral examples, what does that say about their own behavior? They are looking down when they should be looking up." Frank Turek, *Correct, Not Politically Correct* (Charlotte, NC: CrossExamined.org., 2008, updated and expanded in 2016), 83.

39. Shannon Holzer, "Natural Law, Natural Rights, and Same-Sex Civil Marriage: Do Same-Sex Couples Have a Natural Right to Be Married?" *Texas Review of Law & Politics* 19, no. 1 (June 18, 2014): 19.

40. Jonathan Rauch, *Gay Marriage: Why It Is Good for Gays, Good for Straights, and Good for America* (New York: Holt, 2004), 22.

41. Timothy George, "Same-Self Marriage," Nov. 17, 2014, https://firstthings.com/web-exclusive/2014/11/same-self-marriage.

42. Abbie Boudreau, "Two Moms, One Dad, Two Babies Make One Big Happy Polyamorous Family," July 23, 2015, http://abcnews.go.com/Lifestyle/moms-dad-babies-make-big-happy-polyamorous-family/story?id=31184051.

43. Jonathan Rauch, "For Better or Worse?" *The New Republic* (May 1996), as cited in *Same-Sex Marriage Pro & Con: A Reader*, ed. Andrew Sullivan (New York: Vintage Books, 2004), 171.

44. J. Budziszewski, "The Illusion of Gay Marriage," *Philosophia Christi* 7, no. 1 (2005): 48.

45. The dissent by Justice John Roberts (2015), 5, https://www.supremecourt.gov/opinions/14pdf/14-556_3204.pdf.

46. Girgis, Anderson, and George, *What Is Marriage?*, 30.

47. For a thorough discussion of marriage and procreation, see Patrick Lee, Robert P. George, and Gerard V. Bradley, "Marriage and Procreation: The Intrinsic Connection," *Public Discourse* (March 28, 2011): http://www.thepublicdiscourse.com/2011/03/2638/.

48. See Maggie Gallagher, "(How) Will Gay Marriage Weaken Marriage as a Social Institution: A Reply to Andrew Koppelman," *University of St. Thomas Law Journal*, 2, no. 1 (Fall 2004), http://ir.stthomas.edu/cgi/viewcontent.cgi?article=1047&context=ustlj.

49. See Patrick Lee and Robert P. George, *Conjugal Union: What Marriage Is and Why It Matters* (New York: Cambridge University Press, 2014); Robert P. George and Jean Bethke Elshtain, *The Meaning of Marriage* (Dallas, TX: Spence Publishing Company, 2006); Alexander R. Pruss, *One Body: An Essay in Christian Sexual Ethics* (Notre Dame, IN: Notre Dame Press, 2012).

50. Jonathan Rauch, "For Better or Worse?" *The New Republic* (May 1996), as cited in *Same-Sex Marriage Pro & Con: A Reader*, ed. Andrew Sullivan (New York: Vintage Books, 2004), 176.

51. See S. Gurunath, Z. Pandian, Richard A. Anderson, and Siladitya Bhattacharya, "Defining infertility—a systematic review of prevalence studies," in *Human Reproductive Update* 17, no. 5 (April 2011): 575–88.

Continuing Insight: Christian Suffering and the Same-Sex Attracted

1. For more on the relationship between sin and biopsychosocial damage, see Eric L. Johnson, "Biopsychosocial Damage and Psychopathology," in *God and Soul Care: The Therapeutic Resources of the Christian Faith* (Downers Grove, IL: InterVarsity, 2017).

2. Ibid., 293–95. In this case, Johnson names the compounding impact of both sin and damage "fault."

3. Christopher Yuan, *Giving a Voice to the Voiceless: A Qualitative Study of Reducing Marginalization of Lesbian, Gay, Bisexual and Same-Sex Attracted Students at Christian Colleges and Universities* (Eugene, OR: Wipf and Stock, 2016), 28. Yuan says "same-sex temptation is not sin *per se*" while carefully reminding us that it is a result of original sin and is not morally neutral.

4. Paul T. P. Wong, "Positive Psychology 2.0: Towards a Balanced Interactive Model of the Good Life," *Canadian Psychology* 52, no. 2 (2011): 69–81, https://doi.org/10.1037/a0022511.

5. For more on this topic, see Jerry Bridges, *Respectable Sins* (Colorado Springs, CO: NavPress, 2007).

6. Casey E. Copen, Anjani Chandra, and Isaedmarie Febo-Vazquez, "Sexual Behavior, Sexual Attraction, and Sexual Orientation Among Adults Aged 18–44 in the United States: Data From the 2011–2013 National Survey of Family Growth," *National Health Statistics Reports*, no. 88 (January 7, 2016), https://www.cdc.gov/nchs/data/nhsr/nhsr088.pdf. These percentages are the sum of respondents reporting "mostly same sex" and "only same sex" attractions for both men and women. I omitted statistics for those attracted to both sexes equally. This study was created and conducted by secular researchers.

7. I am thankful for Andrew Comiskey and Desert Stream Ministry's Living Waters for cultivating my thinking in this direction.

Chapter 15: Marriage and the Mission of God

1. Christopher J. H. Wright, *The Mission of God: Unlocking the Bible's Grand Narrative* (Downers Grove, IL: InterVarsity Press, 2006), 29.

2. Certainly this question has been brought into sharper focus by recent changes in the cultural and legal perspectives on same-sex marriage. This chapter is not the place to explore that topic but suffice it to say that it seems unlikely that the authors of Scripture had any concept of covenanted, committed same-sex marriage relationships.

3. Christopher Ash, "The Purpose of Marriage," *Churchman* 115 (2001): 7, http://archive.churchsociety.org/churchman/documents/Cman_115_1_Ash.pdf.

4. Ibid., 23–24.

5. Three seminal works were: Darrell L. Guder and George R. Hunsberger, *Missional Church: A Vision for the Sending of the Church in North America* (Grand Rapids: Eerdmans, 1998); David J. Bosch, *Transforming Mission: Paradigm Shifts in Theology of Mission* (Maryknoll, NY: Orbis Books, 1992); and the above referenced work by Christopher Wright, *The Mission of God: Unlocking the Bible's Grand Narrative*. See also Michael W. Goheen, *Light to the Nations: The Missional Church and the Biblical Story* (Grand Rapids: Baker Academic, 2011).

6. For an excellent extended discussion of this critical theme see Wright, *The Mission of God*, 75–135.

7. Wright affirms ". . . that the whole Bible renders to us the story of God's mission through God's people in their engagement with God's world for the sake of the whole of God's creation" (*The Mission of God*, 51).

8. John's apocalyptic vision of the new heavens and the new earth recorded in Revelation 21:1–4 contains images and language that parallel Isaiah's prophetic vision of God's restoration of His people from exile recorded in Isaiah 65:17–25.

9. The Cape Town Commitment, Part 1, Section 10, © 2011 by the Lausanne Movement.

10. George MacDonald and Marianne Wright, eds., *The Gospel in George MacDonald, Selections from His Novels, Fairy Tales, and Spiritual Writings* (Elsmore, Australia: Plough Publishing House, 2016), 216. From the novel *The Marquis of Lossie.*

11. We recognize that considerations of the creation narrative have already been presented in preceding chapters. However, the hermeneutical framework of the mission of God provides some distinct understandings that other hermeneutical approaches may not identify or emphasize.

12. See Job 32:8 and Proverbs 20:27. The NET note on Proverbs 20:27 describes *neshemat* as "the inner spiritual part of human life that was breathed in at creation (Gen 2:7) and that constitutes humans as spiritual beings with moral, intellectual, and spiritual capacities." Victor Hamilton, in his commentary of Genesis 2:7, writes, "Instead of using *rûah* for 'breath' (a word appearing nearly 400 times in the OT), Gen. 2:7 uses *nešāmâ*, is applied only to Yahweh and to man." (Victor Hamilton, *The Book of Genesis: Chapters 1–17*, New International Commentary on the Old Testament series [Grand Rapids: Eerdmans, 1990], 159).

13. The phrase is only found in Genesis 1:27–28; 5:1; 9:6 in the Old Testament and with reference to humanity in 1 Corinthians 11:7 and James 3:9 in the New Testament. Paul identifies Christ as "the image of God" in 2 Corinthians 4:4, a designation also found in Colossians 1:15. See also Colossians 3:10 where "the image of its Creator" is used to describe the new self in Christ.

14. For an excellent historical and interdisciplinary survey of approaches to interpreting *imago Dei* in see Kenneth A. Matthews, *Genesis 1–11:26. New American Commentary. 1A* (Nashville: Broadman & Holman, 1996), 164–72. See also Gerald Bray, "The Significance of God's Image in Man," *Tyndale Bulletin* 42 (1991): 195–225.

15. Stanley J. Grenz, whose masterful book *The Social God and the Relational Self: A Trinitarian Theology of Imago Dei* (Louisville: Westminster John Knox Press, 2001) provided one of the best considerations of the various approaches used by systematic theologians in understanding what it means that humans are created in the image of God. Grenz identified three major streams of thought on the image of God: substantialistic, ethical-relational, and developmental.

16. J. Richard Middleton, *The Liberating Image: The Imago Dei in Genesis 1* (Grand Rapids: Brazos Press, 2005), 27.

17. Eugene Merrill, "A Theology of the Pentateuch" in *Biblical Theology of the Old Testament* (Chicago: Moody, 1991), 14–15. See also Eugene H. Merrill, *Everlasting Dominion: A Theology of the Old Testament* (Nashville: Broadman & Holman, 2006), 170.

18. Isaiah 11:9 and Habakkuk 2:14.

19. Eugene Merrill adds, "What is lacking apparently after the whole cosmos has been spoken into existence is its management, a caretaker as it were who will govern it all according to the will of the Creator. He could have done it himself without mediation, but for reasons never revealed in the sacred record, God elected to reign through a subordinate, a surrogate king responsible to him . . . the purpose of God in creation was channeled largely to man's faithfulness in bringing it to pass" (*Everlasting Dominion,* 136).

20. Elisabeth Elliot, *Let Me Be a Woman* (Wheaton, IL: Living Books, 1987), 139.

21. Chris Wright provides an excellent summary of the sort of kingship the Old Testament raises as a model for image bearers to emulate as the act of agents of his rule. He writes, "Possibly the most succinct statement of the ideal comes from the older and wiser advisors of the young King Rehoboam, when his northern subjects sought relief from the oppressive policies of his father Solomon. This is how they told him to be King: 'If today you will be a servant to these people and serve them . . . they will always be your servants' (1 Kings 12:7). Mutual servanthood was the ideal. Yes, it was the duty of the people to serve and obey the king, but his primary duty of kingship was to serve them, to care for their needs, provide justice and protection, and avoid oppression, violence and exploitation. A king exists for the benefit of his people, not vice versa." Christopher J. H. Wright, *Old Testament Ethics for the People of God* (Downers Grove, IL: InterVarsity Press, 2004), 122.

22. G. K. Beale notes that the commands related to Adam's responsibilities in the garden are consistent with the mandate given to Adam in 1:26–27. Further they are semantically related to language that is later used to describe the care of the temple. G. K. Beale, *The Temple and the Church's Mission: A Biblical Theology of the Dwelling Place of God* (Downers Grove, IL: IVP Academic, 2004), 66–70 and 83–84.

23. Carolyn Custis James introduced us to the phrase "blessed alliance." See *Half the Church: Recapturing God's Global Vision for Women* (Grand Rapids: Zondervan, 2015).

24. Marriage is not presented in Scripture as the only solution to human loneliness. Companionship, friendship, family relationships, and camaraderie in discipleship and in mission are also seen as potential human solutions to loneliness.

25. Christopher Ash, "The Purpose of Marriage."

26. Compare the NIV: "With the help of the Lord I have brought forth a man" and the ESV: "I have gotten a man with the help of the Lord."

27. We must never underestimate the importance of Genesis 12:1–3. Although one might be tempted to read this passage as an exchange between an individual and his God, the last line of the promise makes that understanding unlikely. The Hebrew syntax employed in verses 1–3 points to verse 3 as the result or intended purpose of the promised blessings described in the lines before (See Wright, *The Mission of God: Unlocking the Bible's Grand Narrative,* 201). The significance of the last line of verse 3, "*so that all peoples on earth will be blessed in you,*" is reaffirmed in Galatians 3:8 where Paul refers to it as "the gospel in advance."

28. Moses reminded Israel of this great responsibility and privilege in Deuteronomy 4:5–8. "See I have taught you decrees and laws as the Lord my God commanded me, so that you may follow them in the land you are entering to take possession of it. Observe them carefully, for this will show your wisdom and understanding to the nations, who will

hear about all these decrees and say, 'Surely this great nation is a wise and understanding people.' What other nation is so great as to have their gods near them the way the Lord our God is near us whenever we pray to him? And what other nation is so great as to have such righteous decrees and laws as this body of laws I am setting before you today?"

29. Some of the specific commands in the Bible related to marriage are so culturally distant from contemporary practices that their relevance for us today may be questioned. A good example would be levirate marriage. See Deuteronomy 25:5–6 (among other passages).

30. Deuteronomy 13:6–11; Leviticus 20:9–16.

31. Christopher Wright, "The Israelite Household and the Decalogue: The Social Background and Significance of Some Commandments," *Tyndale Bulletin* 30 (1979): 123.

32. Raymond C. Ortlund Jr., *Whoredom: God's Unfaithful Wife in Biblical Theology* (Leicester, England: Apollos, 1996), 23.

33. There is not consensus among Old Testament scholars regarding the identity of the woman Hosea married in 3:1. Some believe that he took Gomer back as his wife after their separation; others believe that chapter 3 introduces a different woman. For the view that Hosea took Gomer back as his wife, see J. Andrew Dearman, *The Book of Hosea,* New International Commentary on the Old Testament (Grand Rapids: Eerdmans, 2010). For an opposing view, see Douglas Stuart, *Hosea-Jonah,* volume 31, Word Biblical Commentary (Grand Rapids: Zondervan, 1988).

34. For a helpful discussion of Paul's use of the word "mystery" in Ephesians, see Peter T. O'Brien, *The Letter to the Ephesians* (Grand Rapids: Eerdmans, 1999), 10–11 and 430–35.

35. Ortlund, *Whoredom,* 157.

36. Ibid., 158.

37. Ibid.

38. Christopher Ash, *Marriage: Sex in the Service of God* (Vancouver, BC: Regent College Publishing: 2003), Kindle edition.

SCRIPTURE INDEX

SUBJECT INDEX

G
Galatian church, 146
Gelder, Grace, 341
gender (male/female)
biopsychosocial differences, 159–61
complementarity of, 28–29, 142–45,
341–43
created for service, 313–15
in dancing, 155
defined, 156
differences, 142–45, 157–61, 170–71,
172, 318, 386n16, 403n56–57
double standards based on, 101
equality of, 157–58, 165, 386n12
God's glory manifested in, 172
in heaven, 228
in *imago Dei*, 26–29, 227–28, 385n5
impact of Christ's redemption on,
165–66
impact of the fall on, 156, 158–59,
161–64, 403n54
individual variations, 172, 403n56
and marriage, 336–37
in the new covenant, 164–71
in the procreation mandate, 37–38
relational differences, 170–71, 318
relation to biological sex, 156–57
and sexual compatibility, 187
society's views of, 142–43
See also sex (biological)
genetic code (DNA), 120–21, 143
George, Robert P., 342–43
Girgis, Sherif, 342–43
gnostic dualism, 136
gnosticism, 117
God (triune). See triune God (Trinity)
Gomer, 174, 368, 423n33
gospel
and God's moral law, 256
grace in, 214–16
Kenosis principle in, 216–19
marriage revealing, 35, 316, 369, 370
sanctification through, 56
"union with Christ" doctrine, 262–63
Gottman, John, 311
grace
creation grace, 247, 254, 257–58,
409n2, 411n28
forgiveness through, 214–16

in pastoral ministry, 301
redemptive grace, 257–58, 409n2
and same-sex attraction, 345
works of, 219–21
Graham, Billy, 183
Grudem, Wayne, 147
Gunton, Colin, 27–28

H
Habukkuk, 361
Hagar, 73, 372
hagiazo, 64
Hagner, Donald A., 241
Hall, Christopher A., 386n18
Hannaford, Chuck, 300
Harper, Brad, 146
Harry (prince of England), 18–19
Hays, Richard, 175
Hellerman, Joseph, 308–9, 312, 315
Hendricks, Howard, 197
Herod, 75
Herodias, 75
Hill, Wesley, 148–49, 312
Hillel (rabbinic school), 75, 100, 280, 285,
287
Hines, Gregory, 375
Hodges, Obergefell v., 329, 336–37, 338,
339, 342
Holzer, Shannon, 340
homosexuality
current Christian attitudes toward, 79,
90, 346–47
and idolatry, 38
and the *imago Dei*, 37–38
inconsistent responses to, 175, 330,
346–47
natural/unnatural debate, 340, 419n38
pain associated with, 344–47
and teachings on celibacy, 94
See also same-sex marriage
hormones, 121, 125–26, 131, 185
Hosea, 174, 189, 368, 370, 423n33
human genetic code (DNA), 120–21, 143
humanity
anatomical differences, 125
emplacement of, 123
flourishing through suffering, 259–60, 346
hormonal differences, 125–26
impact of the fall on, 130–32